PRIMITIVE TECHNOLOGY II

PRIMITIVE TECHNOLOGY II
Ancestral Skills

From the Society of Primitive Technology
Edited by David Wescott

SALT LAKE CITY

05 04   5432

Published by
Gibbs Smith, Publisher
P.O. Box 667
Layton, Utah 84041
Web site: www.gibbs-smith.com

Design by David Wescott

The articles in this book are reprinted from issues 1-10 of the *Bulletin of Primitive Technology*. The publisher bears no responsibility for their accuracy or content. Neither the publisher or editor bear responsibility for the results of any project described herein or for the reader's safety during participation. Caution and common sense are recommended for every activity. For additional information, refer to *Primitive Technology I: A Book of Earthskills*.

Library of Congress Cataloging-in-Publication Data

Primitive technology II: ancestral skills / edited by David Wescott.
        p. cm.
Articles reprinted from issues 1-10 0f The Bulletin of Primitive Technology,
     ISBN 1-58685-098-9
1. Industries, Prehistoric, 2. Archaeology-Experiments. 3. Handicraft. I. Title: Primitive technology 2. II. Wescott. David, 1948- . III. Society of Primitive Technology. IV. Bulletin of primitive technology

Contents

(more)

Mike Peters

The 2000 Society of Primitive Technology Board of Directors who approved the publication of Primitive Technology II: Ancestral Skills - (clockwisw from left rear) Scooter Cheatham (TX), Alice Tulloch (CA), Jack Cresson (NJ), Maria-Louise Sidoroff (NJ), SPT President - Steve Watts (NC), Norm Kidder (CA), Managing Editor - David Wescott (ID), Scott Jones (GA). Not present for photo: Margaret Mathewson (OR) and Advisory Board Members Errett Callahan (VA) and Jim Riggs (OR). We also wish to express our appreciation to the wonderful SPT authors who's contributions have made the Bulletin and this volume possible.

Section 1

INTRODUCTION
Searching The Past

WHEN THE PEOPLE GATHER

Family reunions, powwows, karaboris, heritage festivals ... all cultures maintain some sort of vehicle for staying in touch with the past. Without this grounding humans seem to wander rather than progress. When the crew of Apollo 13 struggled for survival on their ill-fated flight to the moon, it was the ever-present view of the earth that gave them hope and direction, and ultimately a target with which to direct their efforts.

Primitive Technology II: Ancestral Skills is a compilation of technologies that have been either handed down, rediscovered, or replicated from extinct traditions. Their compilation is timely in as much as we moderns have elected to use the word "progress" for every new development we experience...whether it takes us on a trajectory that will lead us in healthy directions or not.

Taking a look back, and reexamining our beginnings gives us a chance to reestablish the foundations we need to help us to plan our route to the future - based on where we have come from, and taking us to whatever destination we intentionally choose.

From a less self-important standpoint, **Primitive Technology II** is a collection of neat tricks that are fun to do. Whether your goal is to learn to perfect a craft, improve/expand yourself through mastery of new skills, or simply spend leisure time in the act of learning something unique, **PT II** provides a continuing plan established by the "first skills" you've already experienced in **Primitive Technology: A Book of Earthskills** or through membership in the Society of Primitive Technology.

Both books are landmark publications providing foundations, rationale, and the tools for anyone interested in the skills - skills that are your shared inheritance - needed to start you on your own journey to the past...a journey that should ultimately lead you back to a better future.

David Wescott, Editor

tradition - 1. Passing down the elements of a culture from generation to generation, especially by oral communication. 2. a, A mode of behavior or thought followed by people continuously from generation to generation; a cultural custom or usage. b. A set of customs and usages viewed as a coherent body of precedents influencing the present. 3. Any time-honored practice or a set of such practices.

ancestor - 1. a person from whom others are descended. 2. The form or stock from which an organism has developed or descended. 3. An object, idea, style, or occurrence (phenomenon) serving as a prototype, forerunner, or inspiration to a later one. 4. A person from whom mental, artistic, or spiritual descent is claimed.

skill - 1. proficiency, ability, or dexterity: expertness. 2. An art, trade, or technique particularly one requiring the use of the hands and body.

The learning and practice of ancestral skills can help us all get in touch with our own roots - no matter what our particular heritage may be (American Indian, European, African, Asian, etc.). Here in North America, we look to Native Americans and the ancestors of these people to teach us the skills that are "native" to this place. Yet, if we go back far enough into our own pasts, we discover that we are all aboriginal peoples at some time, in some place. The "stone age" is the great common denominator of humanness. "Primitive"("first") skills are our shared inheritance. It is my hope that the Society of Primitive Technology can lead the way in helping individuals rediscover these old skills anew.
Steve Watts, President of the SPT

We cannot recreate the past. Nor is it our goal. Instead, we simply seek to open new windows of insight into the past - ancient lifestyles, ongoing histories, and the continuing relationship between human beings and their environment. Our research efforts are akin to the process of hunting and gathering - tracking down information here, picking up data there, and returning to share our bounty with others. [We have] sought to collect the works of archaeologists, historians, ethnologists, folklorists, and linguists...
The practice of primitive technologies give us new insights into ancient lifeways. By replicating and using material culture items, we begin to move past the high points of history to explore everyday solutions to everyday problems. This practice also connects us directly to the natural environment and the resources it provides.
Steve Watts, Practicing Primitive

A PAUSE FOR THOUGHT

COLLECTIVE VISION AND OUR EVOLVING CULTURE
By Catherine St. John, PhD.

Man is the only picture making and picture appreciating animal in the world. It is an element so distinctive and universal as is evidenced by childhood delight in pictures. Children discover that a few dots and a curved line will do for a face, which smiles back at them.

Art is a language. This extraordinary function enables us to convey our human nature. In all languages, one of our earliest expressions is "Let me see." (Wm. White, Jr.) The artist says "Look! I'll make it worth your while. I'll reconfigure your sense of time and place. I'll show you something you think you already know and invite you to see it again as if for the first time."

Art rules out no subject. From nothing, something can be generated. The pose of a moment can be set down forever. The artist builds a bridge between the world of habitual seeing to genuine insight. Artists vary the landscape or give us a new place from which to view it. They can change the proportions and texture of our experiences of life.

Human expression helps us to understand the complexities of life.

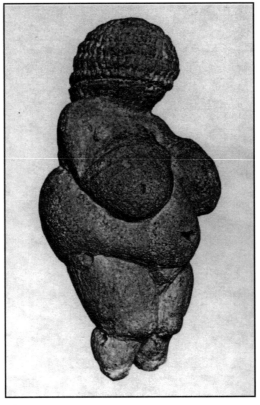

"Through art we can outlive our times, and foreshadow later times." A Venus figurine from the caves of France.

By the light of oil lamps prehistoric artists used charcoal to trace the outlines of animals on the cave walls. For paint the Neanderthals, who ultimately evolved into us, ground lumps of earth, ochre and red-iron rich ore, into colored powder which was blown through hollow bones or reeds. Paint, mixed with water or animal fat was spread with leaves, moss, or wads of fur.

In France in 1940, four teenagers discovered a cave called Lascaux where there are two thousand paintings and engravings of bulls, horses, and reindeer which are believed to be 14,000 years old. In a grotto, La Grotte Cosquer, near Marseilles (featured in *BPT #7*) entered from 120 feet below the sea, there are over 100 incredibly beautiful paintings of horses, deer, bison, wildcat, seals, penguins, and chamois which are small goat-like antelope. In the Pyrenees in the deepest cave known, elegant paintings and reliefs of horses, deer, mountain goat, boar, bison, antelope, even a fish can be viewed, over one mile from the entrance. 260 miles south of Paris, discovered in December 1994 in La

Creating is a form of seeing and knowing. "Art just like any other form of life is an identity that contains an idea." (Jannis Kounellis, contemporary artist in *Art Since 1940: Strategies of Being*, p. 331, by Jonathan Fineberg, published in 1995 by Harry N. Abrams, Inc., New York)

Art connects us with an enterprise that is 30,000 years old. "What do we have from the past?," asks Susan Sontag. "Art and thought. That's what lasts." (Susan Sontag, *New York Times Magazine*, August 2, 1992, p. 43.) Art saves people and events from being consigned to oblivion. Through art we can outlive our times, and foreshadow later times.

What is it exactly that makes us human? When did we first recognize human beings as we are today? Some say the sudden change took place when, for the first time, examples of symbolic expression in the form of Venus figurines and cave paintings were created. (Brenda Fowler, *The New York Times Book Review,* December 17, 1995, p. 21.)

Grotte Chauvet a Vallon Pont-d'Arc are paintings of mammoths, bison, reindeer, boar, horses, large cats, as well as a

Artist and educator, Dr. Catherine St. John received her doctorate in art from New York University. Her paintings have been exhibited in New York and metropolitan area galleries and at the National Academy of Design, the Whitney Museum in Stamford, and the Heckscher Museum.

As a teacher at Berkeley College, Professor St. John teaches studio courses in color, design, sketching, contemporary art criticism and theory, as well as special topics in the humanities.

"It's very nice, Gronk, but I want them facing the other way.

half-human, half-bison (sorcerer) figure cut into the rock by Stone Age artists.

There are more than 200 known caves in which Neolithic paintings by creative people have been explored and while they may be independent of each other, the impulses to create images in these societies "...arose spontaneously wherever there were people." (Arthur C. Danto, "Art for Our Sake," in Op-Ed, *The New York Times*, August 27, 1995) It is at least thinkable that many more images were affixed to surfaces—bark, skin, bone— that did not have the lasting power of the cave walls. (Danto)

The implication is that art had significance in prehistoric culture whether or not Neolithic culture had a concept of art or not. "The production of those vital images...had to have had a profound meaning for that society as a whole..." (Arthur C. Danto) To note that man is a recorder of his own experience is to say that man is an artist. (Eric Newton, "Introduction, *The Arts of Man*, p.11. Published by New York Graphic Society, Greenwich, CT, 1969) "Art making, however conceptualized, seems to have sprung spontaneously from human beings whose genetic endowment was in every respect the same as our own..." (Danto) Art is connected with very deep human beliefs and attitudes and "...must lie very close to whatever is distinctively human.. (Danto) Art allows us to reflect deeply on ourselves and our futures on earth as sensitive thinking human beings.

"To be human," then, "is to have a natural, unalienable interest in art." (Danto) Man is an im-

age maker and our memory banks are flooded with thousands of forms created by the imagination. Visual art effects our collective vision and our evolving culture which consists of the ideas, people, things, and events that are memorable. "Art is the signature of man." (Sister Mary Madeleva, American poet, from a *NY Times* advertisement for Praemium Imperiale, international prizes in the arts)

It takes an artist to invent or remember the details by which we know the world. To have any real meaning for us, art must ultimately help us to focus on our own experiences and our values. What is the relationship between the artist and the viewer? How does the artist interpret and transform his or her experiences and insights into visual symbols? Art is a tool, a medium of communication. This symbol making function is one of mankind's primary activities.

Making art is a form of thinking that can be accessed through empathy. We see the world through the artist's eyes and in so doing, we begin to know the artist. The artist speaks to us through our empathetic responses to his or her account of experience.

The artist humanizes what is going on in the world and in ourselves by speaking of it. In the course of this communication, we learn what it is to be human. Watch the artist. The artist shows us "... the world...to which we are always, sooner or later, saying good-bye." (Robert Kelley, *The New York Times Book Review*, October 3, 1993, p. 11)

It takes an artist to invent or remember the details by which we know the world.

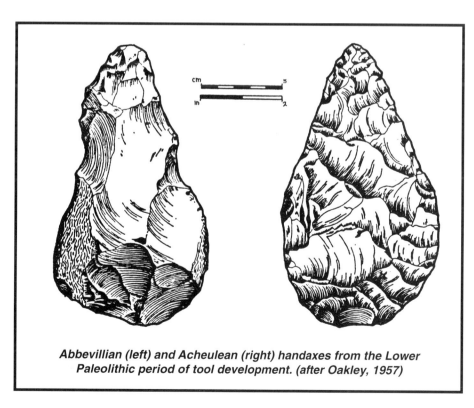

Abbevillian (left) and Acheulean (right) handaxes from the Lower Paleolithic period of tool development. (after Oakley, 1957)

Metaphors for Living
Questing For Insights
By Thomas J. Elpel

A metaphor is a story about life which is simplified into characters and settings of stereotypes and symbols. We learn simple lessons about life from fanciful stories about princes and princesses or Old Man Coyote. We may not be able to describe exactly what those lessons are or how they affect us, but the stories do nonetheless make change in our lives. In today's complex world, primitive living is like a metaphor, but it is better. Primitive living is a metaphor we participate in and act out. Life is simplified down to the bare essentials such as physical and mental well-being, shelter, warmth, clothing, water, and food. We go on an expedition to meet those needs with little more than our bare hands. As we quest to meet those needs we learn to observe, to think, to reach inside ourselves for new resources for dealing with challenging and unfamiliar situations. We build up our personal

Trekking and living in the hunter-gatherer mode.

strengths, and at the same time we interact with and learn about the world around us. In a story we can only join a quest in our imaginations. But in primitive living, we physically leave the contemporary world. We journey into the world of primitive stone-age skills, and we return with knowledge, wisdom, and strength to enrich our lives in contemporary society.

I experienced the power of this "participatory metaphor" when I was sixteen. I went on a twenty-six day expedition with a survival school, where we hiked 250 miles, ate little, and generally endured a lot. The personal strengths, the wisdom, and the ability to persevere that I brought back from that "quest" have helped me to be successful in contemporary life more than any other single thing I have done.

In a similar way, my wife Renee and myself went on a "quest" together, an adventure where we started in Pony and walked five hundred miles across Montana to Fort Union on the North Dakota border. That was a year before we were married. At the time we could not give a definitive answer as to why we were doing it. But looking back, I would say we were testing and building our relationship and our abilities to work together towards common goals, before formally committing ourselves to a long-term relationship.

Thus, primitive living is a metaphor that brings out our inner resources. At the same time, it is also a metaphor that teaches us about the resources of the earth as well. You see, the person who carries in a lot of gear, from tents, to propane stoves, with the intent of living "no-impact", is, metaphorically speaking, living a lie. Such a person may claim to practice no-impact camping, but the truth is, the resources they pack in had to come from somewhere.

Our contemporary lives have become so removed from hand-to-mouth survival, that we sometimes delude ourselves into thinking our items of survival come from the store, rather than from nature. We think of ourselves as being somehow separate from nature. We think we can draw lines on the map and separate "wilderness" from "non-wilderness", but really, there is only one wilderness and only one ecosystem, and we are part of it. Like the deer eating grass, or the robin bringing materials back to build a nest, we all must use the resources of the earth to maintain our own survival. This is true whether we live in an apartment building in the city, or in a wickiup in the woods.

Primitive living allows us to practice living on a model scale. By "living" I means that process of procuring our needs for physical and mental well-being, including such things as shelter, fire or energy, water, and vegetable or animal resources. In primitive living we are faced with these needs as realities we must meet. We are faced with the realization that in order for our lives to go onward, we must take from the world around us; like the coyote stalking a mouse, we must kill and use to survive. It is too easy to forget that in the contemporary world. We think resources come from the store, and we forget that there are impacts and consequences, throughout the ecosystem, from our every purchase, our every decision. In primitive living we face those consequences directly. We can see the effect of our needing to eat causing the loss of life of a plant or an animal. We can sense that by picking the berries from the bushes we may be taking someone else's meal. Primitive living is a metaphor that gives us an awareness of the true costs of living, no matter where we are.

The metaphor of primitive living can also teach us that it may be okay to take from the earth; that perhaps we do not need to feel guilty about our actions, only aware of them. The deer takes from the ecosystem and causes surprising impacts; it's presence causes successional shifts throughout plant and animal communities, destroying habitat for some and creating it for others. Similarly, the presence of humankind living primitive, today or yesterday, creates all kinds of havoc in the ecosystem. Groups of primitive peoples rewrote the ecosystem daily as they hunted and gathered for their needs, or torched the brush to drive the game out. Even an individual person displaces habitat, competes for food, and forces the animals to take new trails, all influencing successional communities. Perhaps our contemporary cities are not so different. They are still wilderness; only different successional plant and animal communities are favored there. Primitive living, as a metaphor, can teach us that, like a blue-

bird eating a fly, perhaps it is okay to take from and alter the ecosystem. It is neither good nor bad, it is simply reality.

Of course, primitive living also reminds us that our link to the ecosystem goes both ways. We are participants in the ecosystem and therefore we have no choice but to take from it, and we will inevitably alter it, but also, for our own survival, we must <u>maintain</u> it. Our actions affect successional communities of plants and animals in the ecosystem, and we are included in those communities. Succession will forever be in a state of flux, for as long as life exists. Nature will continue on, ever changing, destroying habitats, and creating them. In the face of global climate change and ozone depletion, it is important that we consider what successional changes may mean for our own species.

Primitive living is a metaphor for living. It brings us face to face with our own survival. It brings out our inner resources for dealing with challenging situations, and it reminds us, that no matter what technologies we have, we are still in integral component of the ecosystem. Primitive living is a model for living that gives us the basic foundations, the very laws of nature, upon which all of our solutions, in primitive *and* contemporary living, must be built.

Thomas and Renee Elpel own and operate Hollowtop Outdoor Primitive School (HOPS) in Pony, Montana. For more information write to HOPS, Box 691, Pony, MT 59747, or call (406) 685-3222. Go to - hollowtop.com

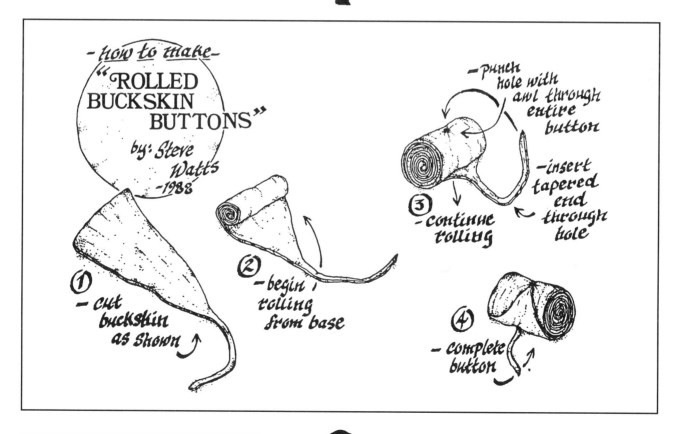

- how to make -
"ROLLED BUCKSKIN BUTTONS"
by: Steve Watts -1988

① - cut buckskin as shown ↑

② - begin rolling from base

③ - continue rolling

- punch hole with awl through entire button
- insert tapered end through hole

④ - complete button ↙

Primitive Technology
And The "New" Archaeology
By Maria Sideroff

The primitive technologist adds a whole new dimension to an archaeological project.

We all know that the term primitive technology hardly means "primitive" in the sense of crude, rough and untrained. We realize that the term refers to skillful methods of producing objects from natural materials using procedures as similar as possible to those of a particular prehistoric culture. We are also aware that about 30 years ago archaeology evolved into an interdisciplinary science which involves a team of many specialists who interpret the data retrieved through stratigraphic excavation. We appreciate this new approach to archaeology in spite of the popularity of films like *"Raiders of the Lost Ark"*, and its sequels. These films encourage us to believe that this field of science is the domain of charismatic adventurers, representing colonist powers, who command legions of poor natives in the desecration of their patrimony. In the fantasy scenario these workers are paid a meager wage to remove objects from their native soil for delivery to some foreign museum.

In today's reality the excavation director is the "native", usually a professor at a university in the host country who coordinates the careful scientific procedures. Rather than concentrate on one precious object ripped from the earth by a worker, who may receive a little extra *baksheesh* to reward a sharp eye, every excavated item is considered a potential source of valuable information. Even dirt itself is important to members of the team who conduct soil analysis for data on environmental conditions during an ancient era. Workers today are both native and foreign (usually students or lovers of archaeology) who pay with their own time and money for privilege of participation. Thus the *"new"* archaeology is a communal effort which brings together the archaeologist, artist, biologist, botanist, climatologist, geologist, photographer, physical anthropologist, restorer, student, surveyor, and volunteer (among others). The common goal of the team is to scientifically retrieve, document and interpret the material remains of the society under excavation.

The primitive technologist is a recent addition to the team in the field. As a participant in the excavation of a site yielding for example, stone tools or pottery, the primitive technologist can make informed observations about the methods of manufacture, material procurement and artifact interpretation based upon technological experience with those materials. Through demonstration of ancient techniques or by directing workshops, the specialist can offer an immediate contribution, in the field, to understanding the culture under excavation.

Before working at Tel Hadar I conducted a ceramic replication workshop for Professor Herbert Kraft, Seton Hall University, in association with his excavation at the Bell-Philhower site on the New Jersey side of the Upper Delaware River. During another summer Professor Tony Ranere, Temple University, invited me to demonstrate prehistoric pottery making techniques at his site in New Jersey.

For two summers I attended classses in conservation, restoration, artifact drawing and ceramic technology at the Institute of Archaeology, University of London, England. When I became aware of the extended plans for the excavation at Tel Hadar in 1988 I felt that I was ready to develop a long term relationship with an excavation team as a primitive technologist. I had studied the basics and honed my skills to a level that prepared me for the task.

ARE YOU INTERESTED IN WORKING AT AN EXCAVATION?

To expand your concept of sharing knowledge, why not offer to join an archaeological expedition? For information about local sites contact your state museum, State Archaeological Society, or the Anthropology Department of the State University. Another good source of information is Archaeology magazine where summer excavation opportunities in the Old World (Europe and the Middle East) are listed in the March/April issue and the New World excavations (North and South America) are listed in the May/June issue.

A typical day at Tel Hadar begins at 4:30am. We leave the Kibbutz at 5:00am to dig all morning at the site and return at noon, after a swim in the Galilee to clean off some of the grime of the excavation. After lunch in the air conditioned dining room on the Kibbutz everyone takes a two hour midday rest. We either loll around the Olympic size pool or take a nap in our cottages. After 4 o'clock tea we wash the artifacts excavated that day, then attend "pottery reading" sessions where the Israeli and American staff interpret the artifacts which were washed the day before and have by now dried in the brilliant sun. After dinner there is often a lecture on some topic relating to the site or I hold workshops in ceramic replication focusing on a different clay artifact each season.

During previous seasons we replicated a beer strainer, an oil lamp and a female figurine. The ceramic object chosen for the replication project must be small enough to dry and fire quickly for we have only two weeks for the workshops. The artifact must not be too difficult to copy since many of the participants have no experi-

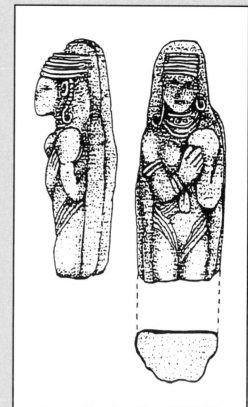

Female Figurine. Circa 800 B.C.E. Tel Hadar, Isreal. Reduced 50%

ence working with clay. The first step is to analyze the paste composition and hardness of the fired clay artifact and then photographs and drawings are made. The photographs will be developed later but the drawings serve as a guide to workshop participants for proportions and details, since the original is usually stored away in the laboratory for safe keeping.

After designing a production sequence and fire plan I begin instruction in pottery making techniques. We form the replication by hand, since no wheel is available, dry them in the sun for a few days, and then conduct an above ground firing of all replications. (Due to the many restraints that exist at the Kibbutz our work falls into the category of Level II in the guide for Experimental Archaeology as outlined by Errett Callahan - see page --- BPT#2).

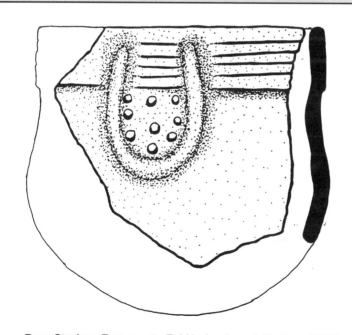

Beer Strainer Fragment - Tel Hadar, Isreal. Reduced 50%

How The Ceramic Technologist Can Work With A Team

It is a unique experience to be on hand at the moment an artifact is uncovered for the first time in thousands of years. As a primitive technologist in ceramics I have been rewarded for the past few summers at the Tel Hadar Excavation in Israel. Tel Hadar is one of five sites in The Land Of Geshur Project. The site is being excavated by the New Jersey Archaeological Consortium which, in addition, provides an experiential opportunity for elementary and secondary educators through a three-week Teacher's Seminar.

I can now appreciate the significance of each piece of pottery in relation to the whole picture of this royal distribution center (1100 B.C.E.) on the northeast shore of the Sea of Galilee, and value the opportunity each summer to learn from other members of the Israeli/American team directed by Professor Moshe Kochavi, University of Tel Aviv, and Professors Ira Spar, Ramapo College and Timothy Renner, Montclair College.

The goal of the Tel Hadar project in ceramic replication is to provide a Level II experience for individuals participating in the excavation. "By reproducing his actions, the archaeologist can better understand the technical abilities of ancient man. This is the kind of information all archaeologists need, the meaning behind the surviving relics." *(John Coles, Experimental Archaeology, Academic Press, 1979, pg.3)*

There are three levels of investment in experimental archaeology projects" according to American Experimental Archaeologist Errett Callahan. He regards Level I as simulation, non-authentic, and non-scientific. Level II replications, according to Callahan, are successful functional units undertaken with correct period tools, materials and procedures. This level is an experience rather than an experiment. To qualify as a Level III experiment, a project requires record keeping and long term monitoring to provide data for analysis and formulation of conclusions.

To The Lithics Technologist:
"Wish you were here, flintknapper!"

Last summer, after the dig in Israel, I spent a month in France working at La Grotte du Lazaret, the site of a Homo Erectus encampment (150,000 B.C.) on the out skirts of the city of Nice. Although no pottery exists at a site of this great antiquity we daily excavated examples of lithic technology. Many times during the month of August I wished for a primitive technologist, an expert on lithics, to conduct a workshop as I had done in ceramics at Tel Hadar. At Lazaret there were many experts in geology to describe the rocks, specialists who could analyze and measure the stone tools but there was no one who could set up a few sessions to show us precisely how those particular rocks were bashed. When a cache of bifaces was uncovered near the entrance to the cave I longed to hear the rap-rap-rap sounds I had come to recognize as knappers music to bring alive the techniques of this ancient tribe.

As our technological society rushes headlong to its dubious future, a new interest in primitive peoples has sprung to life.....There have been thousands of societies on this planet and some of them hold secrets that we could well learn from. It is those secrets we are looking for.
The Challenge Of The Primitives
R. Clark & G. Hindley, 1975

Field Archaeology: It Begs To Be Taught

Archaeology, the subdiscipline of anthropology that deals with the scientific reconstruction of past lifeways through the systematic study of the artifacts and cultural evidence left behind, is seldom taught, in any meaningful form, outside of the university setting.

But field archaeology is a discipline that begs to be taught-especially to the young. It contains too much that is valuable...."Archaeology is the opera of the social sciences." It entails the marshalling of a multitude of skills and wraps them up in a setting of fresh air, sunshine, and hard work.

While we may concede that field archaeology is a valuable learning tool, we must also remember that teaching it means teaching it correctly. The proper instruction of archaeological techniques involves at least three primary considerations:

1. The instruction of students in the proper and recognized manner of excavating prehistoric and historic remains - development of the required motor skills and the rationale attendant to them.

2. Instillment of the appreciation of what is being done, as well as the general recognition of the fact that archaeological sites are non-renewable resources.

3. The post-instructional analysis and publication of the findings. It is a strict rule among professionals that a site dug but left unpublished is worse than one left undug. It is generally agreed upon by professional archaeologists that instruction alone is not sufficient reason for carrying out the excavation of a real site.

Adherence to the above considerations rules out pothunting and dilettantism as being valid practice or instruction. The first is, of course, the drawing card. The actual fieldwork and the retrieving of the data provides great satisfaction to the student.

The appreciation and respect for archaeological sites as irreplaceable cultural resources is a lesson that once learned benefits all of us and insures perpetuation of our cultural heritage for generations to come.

The field instructor should be a professional archaeologist. Adherence to this requirement insures that the archaeologist will at least do right by his instruction, for he will want the data recovered accurately for his own good.

Archaeology: An old discipline, popularized by a new movie, provides an excellent teaching tool for campers.
By John R. White, from *Camping Magazine*, April 1983.

THE FIRE WATCHERS

The following letter is an interesting lead-in to the articles selected for this column. We all need to be aware of what brought us to this field, where we learned our craft, and what we can do with it as we pursue new knowledge and experience. It's hard to make a call for a back-to-basics movement in a field such as ours, but a solid foundation in the basic principles of what makes a technology work is essential to mastery of the art. Something about houses built on sand....? The Editor

Dick attended a recent knap-in and had a wonderful, educational experience. But alas, he questioned how much pride one can have in a primitive arrow that is notched with a coping saw? His arrowhead constructed with a deer antler was labeled as "crude" and he was ashamed to display it alongside those chipped with metal tools, which seemed necessary to make "show" points (it appears, sadly, that many abos are relying on Black and Decker to make primitive tools and weapons).

Nevertheless, Richard marveled at the lithics expertise he saw there, which gave me cause to think about the last Rabbit Stick we attended...in 1990. We were thrilled to meet craftsmen and women with such marvelous skills. It was very intimidating. In planning to attend in 1991 I wondered what little skills I could teach that someone else could not address far better than I. Larry Olsen made the same comment, that he was overwhelmed by the craftsmanship he saw.

[My point in writing this is]..... can the new "experts" actually live the primitive lifestyle? As you know, there are only a scant few "experts" who have ever actually been on the trail....On the trail you learn to do a lot of different things that are necessary for basic survival. One seldom has the time to advance any specific skill to perfection, you must balance all of the lifeskills in such a way as to secure shelter and enough food and water to sustain life until the next day....Trail life develops a philosophy about the earth and life in general, in a way that some "experts" only read about, and you keep going back because it empowers (and overpowers) you.

As a result of your perseverance, you get a feel for the primitive people that once inhabited the places you make your temporary home, and feel their presence as you imitate their lifeways; you learn to appreciate the resources that sustain your very life and take more care to preserve them; and you learn the value of cooperation and human caring as you form hunting groups and determine who will lead and who will follow. You literally "touch time".

You learn to improvise.....a universally valuable skill that can be a benefit in any walk of life. You learn these things by personally experiencing them, and you can learn by sitting at the knee of someone else who has experienced them. Sadly, I think, the "new" abos are missing what was an integral part of primitive life, one that is grossly absent from modern life...respect for the older, wiser members of the clan. ...we'd love to be involved and contribute in any way we can.

D & L Jamison, Salt Lake City, UT

Random Thoughts On Tradition vs. Technology
By Norm Kidder

Objects, possessions (pride in having), materialism, Western culture vs. process (pride in doing), relationships, results, indigenous cultures. Primitive technology used whatever was available to get the result, but the result wasn't in making something to have and put on display, it was to provide food, water, shelter, family, fun and/or the future. Pride in workmanship often went beyond making things that were pleasing to look at, but also that would impress the spirits who controlled the world. Doing your best and following traditions were a way of showing respect both to your elders (teachers) and to the materials you depended on for the object.

Our Society has both kinds, those that collect artifacts and/or make them for show and sale; and those who learn to make things to use. Both have value and can help broaden the inquiry, but the pursuit of primitive technology implies also the pursuit of the values and purposes behind the technologies. Often this means doing the job at hand with the simplest tools, often unmodified objects, as most hunter gatherers didn't have pickups to haul around all their stuff. An exhibit in the California Academy of Science in San Francisco

(more)

tradition - *the handing down of statements, beliefs, legends, customs, etc., from generation to generation especially by word of mouth (Random House).*

explained the apparent lack of artifacts in an exhibit on the Australian Aborigines with the idea that the apparent simplicity of the tool kit belied the knowledge of materials that allowed the hunter to use what he found to accomplish the task. The tool kit is in the head, not the hand.

Maybe we need a labeling system which classifies "replicas" as High, Medium, or Low Tech, with Low Tech reserved for objects made with all stone age materials and tools; Medium would allow metal hand tools like adzes and knives, copper knappers, etc.; High Tech would allow power tools, cut slabs, or anything else. Personally I'd like to know how to do things at all three levels. There is something almost mystical about making and using a tool completely with things you've made yourself from 'the wild'. It helps you put yourself in perspective, as part of the place you inhabit, and builds your relationship with the earth. It also gives you greater respect for our ancestors who functioned at this level normally. At the same time there is something strange about not using the best or easiest tool to do a job.

A group of people, including local Indians while rebuilding a dance house, commented they were glad no archaeologists were involved or they couldn't have used chain saws to cut the timbers. To them traditional meant the task and the group effort and feelings, not the specific tools. Everything depends on the intent and feelings of the practitioner.

From my observations, we each go through our own evolution. We begin wherever we get inspired. Someone turns us on, and they may be functioning at any technological level. At first we are inspired to produce something, which then becomes an object of pride. Once the skill is mastered just doing it isn't enough, and the process must be shared in some way, by giving away the product or teaching the skill. Eventually we need to explore the edges of the envelope, in at least one direction (high or low tech), or maybe both. The need is to make the technology relevant to 20th (and soon 21st) century life. Some of us attempt to "go bush" and live the skills. This is personally gratifying but not a practical choice for large numbers of Folk. Possibly we commercialize the pursuit and produce for sale, or teach for money, treating the skills as a commodity. A few of us even make our living this way. Most of us would probably consider our endeavors as a hobby, with no purpose but satisfying our curiosity. Many folk I've talked with have at least a mild fear that these skills may again be he dominant survival strategy in a few years.

The challenge I feel while sitting at my computer is to use what I lean from the 'old ways' and apply it to my 'now ways.' The most obvious for me is in being a maker of useful things. I get a deep sense of reality when I produce my own food, build my own structure, or make my own everyday tools. Recycling and composting contribute to a sense of being part of the cycle. This gets extended whenever I buy handmade things to use, when possible from the maker, to encourage this kind of direct involvement in the world. When shopping I may look to buy the least processed foods, so I have the maximum involvement with food I don't grow.

One of the most important aspects of old ways was the sense of community, and cooperation. Where I live these are hard to find. Sharing tools and time with a few neighbors is all that's left. The sharing that goes on in the **SPT** takes on aspects of a community, Primitive technology by its nature tends to be communal. As population grows we spend less time dealing with people and more with stuff. The flickering light and story telling of the campfire has given way to the flickering light and storytelling of the television. No more gathering of women to wash their clothes at the well, now each sits alone with a work saving machine.

technology - *the sum of ways in which a social group provide themselves with the material objects of their civilization (Random House).*

ANOTHER THOUGHT

At the Texas Board Meeting (Nov. 1992) it was decided to adopt a Statement of Ethics for the Society. This statement was drafted to identify the guidelines for implementing one of our purposes - to set standards for authenticity, ethics, and quality. It is the intent of this statement to clarify the position of the Society on issues regarding ethics and to provide members a framework for identifying with the Society. The purpose for adopting this standard is not to exclude or condemn, but to educate about the importance of ethically dealing with ancient and contemporary artifacts.

ARTIFACTS AND ETHICS: History Belongs to Everyone
By Thomas J. Elpel

The artifact was slender and long, perhaps one and a half inches in diameter and fourteen inches long, tapering at both ends. Apparently a uniquely shaped stone for grinding grain on a metate, it had been shaped from a piece of hard sandstone through many hours of careful pecking with another rock. It may have lain in the sand below that overhang in the canyonlands of southern Utah for a hundred years, or perhaps a thousand. Either way, it was in mint condition as if its creator had just finished it and reached through a window of time to place it on my lap.

1 inch scale

Whatever its history, it was on my lap, and it was my dilemma. According to the law I should have left it there and I should not have even disturbed it from its original resting place. Archaeologists and anthropologists need to study artifacts in context of their original locations. By examining artifacts where they find them, these professionals can piece together a story of the past and give a voice to these otherwise silent vestibules of time.

The right thing to do was to put the artifact back. However, the moment that I set it down would have been the moment that someone else in the group would have gleefully picked it up and hauled it a thousand miles away to set it on their bookshelf or to hang it on their living room wall, a piece of knowledge forever lost to the public.

I did not want the artifact on my own living room wall anymore than I wanted it on anyone else's wall. I would learn little from it, and humanity would learn nothing. To pack this unique and exotic artifact home for display would have degraded it from a voice of the past to just another testament of materialistic ego.

In context, or out of context, I felt that this unique piece should be kept in the public trust. I did not know what legal consequences I might face, but nonetheless, I decided to take it to the local state-operated museum/archaeological center.

I first looked around the museum to ascertain that it was indeed a unique artifact. The museum displays had nothing like it. I cautiously queried the museum staff with hypothetical questions: "What if a person were in this situation......?" I asked. When I felt certain that I would not be penalized for disturbing a historical site then I brought the unique stone in. I gave it to them and I marked the location of the site on a topographic map. This established a local context for the artifact, even if the immediate context was forever severed. More so, it established the site as a potentially valuable archaeological site in need of study by a team of experts.

The people at the archaeological center never acknowledged that I made the right decision. But they never said that I was wrong either. It is possible that since they worked for the state it would have been inappropriate for them to be informing people that it is alright to disturb historic sites. I decided that from then on I would do something to protect any artifacts I came across that were at risk of being taken or damaged.

STATEMENT OF ETHICS
Through the stated goals of the Society of Primitive Technology as defined by the Society of Primitive Technology mission statement, the Society will not condone, encourage, or sanction any of the following activities as they may be attempted by any individual, group, business or organization:

1. The sale of prehistoric artifacts, and/or any intentional alteration of aboriginal items. This includes the sale of modern replicas as authentic aboriginal artifacts.
2. The sale of any modern replica, in any medium, which does not clearly display a distinctive and permanent "maker's mark" which could be used to distinguish said item as a modern replica.
3. The sale or trade of products which all or in part, contain remains of any endangered animal or plant species, where the maker does not possess a proper permit or license.
4. Any activity which as a primary intent or result, conflicts with the stated goals of The Society of Primitive Technology. Conflicts with the above statement will be considered by The Board of Directors, who may or may not decide to take action.

ETHICS & COLLECTING - A Question
By David Wescott, Editor

"Let's talk about the law...The law seems to have different interpretations in different parts of the country....We feel that there is no harm in digging villages or trash pits on private property with permission of your land owner. There should be more cooperation between professionals and the private collectors....Most everyone we talk to would go along with not disturbing sites with human remains...why not sell a relic hunting license...We believe it is better for a young person to be walking a beach, searching for an arrow, than roaming the streets looking for trouble...."   The Confident Collector, Robert Overstreet, 1993 p.22-25.

How do you feel about the issue of collecting? I know that the thrill of discovery is intoxicating. But I also know that the thrill wears off after a while and personal treasures can soon become junk. I've also come to realize that treasures out of context lose their magic (that flowered shirt and palm-leaf hat looked real good in Hawaii, but not in Montana). Being a packrat by nature, however, it's hard for me to pick up things and then put them back down, leaving that same thrill of discovery for someone else....perhaps someone who knows even less about what they've found and puts it in their pocket to take home. But I do feel strongly that what I find isn't mine to sell or hide in a basement closet for my own access, or to sell tickets to see. And what I make should be marked in some way to eliminate the potential for further confusing an already fragmented record. There is no argument to support those who dig for profit or intentionally introduce counterfeit artifacts into the record, just as there is equally no argument for the exclusive access to prehistory in the name of "science".

I still don't know what my personal position is on the overall issue of "collecting" ... for both "amateurs" and "professionals". My jury is still out...I'm still learning and every resource is an asset to my education. Can I be an ethical person and still listen to people that have opinions that vary from my own? If listening to them means buying their books and magazines am I unethical for "supporting" their existence? Do I have to choose between friends because they refuse to deal with the issue and alienate rather than educate each other?

With the announcement of the Society of Primitive Technology Statement of Ethics first published in **BPT #5** and now included on page 2 of each issue, the Society chose to take a stand on part of the issue of collecting by stating that "the sale of prehistoric artifacts, and/or any intentional alteration of aboriginal items" is contrary to our Statement of Ethics. This policy was adopted to make clear the position of the Board and the guidelines by which the Bulletin is published. It is a benchmark by which others might identify what this particular group stands for.

It is unfortunate, however, that this can be a limiting rather than an empowering process. If we refuse to recognize resources available for our membership...albeit resources with differing opinions and "ethics" are we accomplishing what we

originally set out to do....create a network between practitioner and researcher, layman and professional, collector and manufacturer, teacher and student ? If we bow to the pressure of one group saying "if you include them, then we'll take our sticks and rocks and go home", or if the Editor withholds valuable information from readers because part of the information is tainted by an alternative position are we truly filling our purpose ? Yes and No!

The Society of Primitive Technology Board of Directors has chosen to identify a position in which it believes. The fact that there are ethics involved in what we do and creating guidelines that help us to hold to those ethics is a positive step toward why the SPT was created..."to set standards for authenticity, ethics, and quality". But in the process, the battle lines that have already been drawn and the biases harbored by those who have been in the fray (on both sides...one side is just as guilty as the other) creates real confusion for those of us just looking for as much quality information as possible...regardless of the source. Our other purpose, "to foster communication", seems to take a back seat to a few vocal factions who are unable to deal with an issue that needs immediate attention for the benefit of us all.

The SPT supports the need for an ethical approach to dealing with prehistory. The ethic provides a foundation from which all of us can learn, professional and layman. **The Bulletin of Primitive Technology** reflects this ethic in it's advertising and content, while editorial content allows us to present and explore issues that are of concern to all of those interested in our common heritage.

Section 2

FOOD SOURCES
Eating To Live

SLIM, TRIM, AND PALEO-INDIAN:
WHY OUR DIETS ARE KILLING US

By Vaughn M. Bryant, Jr.

When I visited my first archaeological site I was full of curiosity and awe. It was a hot August day in 1964, and I remember how hot and dry it was when we walked the several miles from the end of the last dirt road to the site. It was my first introduction to the field of archaeology, other than what I had heard in courses taken at the University of Texas or read in books.

The site was a large rock shelter located not far from the small town of Comstock in Val Verde County. Perched on a bluff overlooking a dry tributary canyon that emptied into the Rio Grande, the exposed, powder-dry profiles looked like layers of a chocolate cake. There were thick, dark bands of ash and charcoal and lighter thin zones. Both were filled with lithics, sand and pieces of dried plant remains.

The archaeologist mentioned several points that did not have much of an impact on me at the time. Nevertheless, looking back I can see they were significant because it reflected how little was known about some analytical techniques that have now become routine at most sites. For example, he said he wished he knew what types of foods the prehistoric occupants of that site had eaten, what kinds of animals they may have hunted, what types of seeds they may have ground in the metates found at the site, and whether or not their overall diet was nutritious. He pondered these questions as he sat near the shelter's entrance skipping dry cowpatty shaped human coprolites (prehistoric dried feces) into the updrafts of hot thermal winds that swirled upward from the canyon below.

For him, those dried coprolites were nothing more than a nuisance. At times, he admitted, they were so plentiful in the deposits that they clogged the screens when they sifted for artifacts! Years later I learned how important coprolites can be, and how they often contain the answers to questions about diet, nutrition, food preparation techniques, and even the health of prehistoric peoples.

Coprolites are among the most ideal forms of dietary evidence because their contents represent undigested materials that we know actually traveled through a human digestive system. Other forms of evidence in the soils of archaeological sites, such as seeds, animals hairs, insects,

Savoring the last bits of tasty open-hearth cuisine.

bones, shells, fibers, and leaves, may represent items actually eaten or used by humans. On the other hand, these same items might have been deposited at the site by rodents, birds, carnivores, or even the wind during times when the area was not occupied by humans.

My studies of coprolites from sites in southwest Texas provide a glimpse into the dietary habits of cultures who lived in that region for nearly 9000 years. In summary, these foragers ate a diet consisting of about 66-75% carbohydrates and 25-33% protein and fats. The plant foods they ate were nutritious and many were high in fiber. Their diet included sunflower seeds, ground mesquite and cactus seeds, acorns, walnuts, pecans, persimmons, grapes, berries, the soft basal portion of sotol and agave, and the flowers, fruits, and pads of cactus. These ancient Texas foragers balanced their plant-food diets with meal protein and fats mostly from small animals such as mice, rat-sized rodents, fish, land snails, freshwater clams, small lizards, caterpillars, grasshoppers, small birds, eggs and, when they were lucky, an occasional rabbit or deer.

Vaughn Bryant, Jr. is a professor in the Department of Anthropology at Texas A & M University.

We also know that these ancient Texans were generally healthy. Anthropologist Karl Reinhard, formerly of Texas A&M and now at the University of Nebraska, is an authority on ancient human parasitic infections. His examination of coprolites from southwest Texas sites indicates that those hunting and gathering populations were almost totally free of internal parasitic infections and overall were in good health.

Diet Comparisons

From my studies of human coprolites and human nutrition I have been able to identify important comparisons between the diets and lifestyles of our ancient ancestors and ourselves. First, both men and women of those early Texas cultures were physically fit. They lived a life that was in harmony with our biological design. As a result, they enjoyed longer and healthier lives than their descendants of the southwest who later became our first farmers. Most of these ancient Texans lived what can be considered the "perfect" lifestyle and ate the "perfect" diet for which our bodies were designed. And, when we compare ourselves to them, we notice some stark differences.

As a group, our predecessors were slim and trim because they relied on their physical strength and stamina for survival. They ate less than half the amount of fat eaten by today's Americans and the fat they ate was mostly of the less harmful, polyunsaturated type. These early Texans also ate large amounts of complex carbohydrates and very few simple carbohydrates (sugars). On average, they ate 5, 10, or even 15 times more fiber than most Americans eat today, and their foods were bulky and filling, not the calorie-rich and highly refined types we eat today. They ate foods rich in potassium and low in sodium, and their foods probably contained more than twice the amount of calcium we consume today. However, of all the differences between the diets of these early Texans and ourselves, the most chilling is the amount and types of fats eaten by both groups.

Throughout most of human prehistory, human diets have been low in fat. The diets of the ancient southwest Texans were no exception. Fats are found in some plant foods, such as seeds and nuts, and in the meat of animals. In prehistoric southwest Texas, fats would have been a hard-to-find food resource because most of the animals these groups hunted had lean bodies with less than 4% body fat. By contrast, today 30% or more of the total carcass weight of most American cattle and pigs is fat.

Most fats are composed of long chains of triglyceride molecules, each containing three fatty acids and a glycerol. Cholesterol, often discussed with fats, is needed to produce numerous hormones and bile acids, but it is not really a fat. Instead, cholesterol is a complicated substance composed of molecule rings that reacts more like a wax than a true fat.

There are many types of fatty acids found in nature. Some are called saturated fats, others are unsaturated fats. The unsaturated group is divided into two categories: mono or poly, depending on whether they are linked with one or more double bonds of carbon. The chemistry of fatty acids is complex, and, for most of us, knowing how the human body uses them is more important than the actual chemistry.

Diversity within a species. Examples of biscuit root (Cymopterus). Specimen on the left was dug at 8,000 feet elevation and the one on the right at 5,000 feet. Both specimens were dug on the same day.

Some polyunsaturated fats are called structural fats because our bodies use them to build and repair nearly all cell membranes. We also need these fats to build various types of hormones that regulate our body functions. When digested, our bodies extract nine calories of energy from each gram of fat.

Most saturated fatty acids are called storage or adipose fat because excess amounts can be stored for later use. Some subcutaneous tissues in animals contain storage fat because it provides thermal insulation. However, the majority of saturated fats are stored in other body locations, such as the abdominal cavity and within muscle tissue. Saturated fats are solid at room temperature.

Unsaturated fats come mostly from plant sources and they are liquid at room temperature. Most unsaturated fats are polyunsaturated. However, two important sources of monounsaturated fats are found in the diets many of us eat. These are: olive oil (77% monounsaturated fat—the rest is

(more)

Group efforts often produce a higher yield than working on ones own.

1) *Prime Beef = 46%+ percent fat*
2) *Choice Beef = 40-45% fat*
3) *Good Beef = 34-39% fat*
4) *Standard Beef = 27-33% fat*

It is the amount of saturated fat in our diet that should be cause for alarm. The US Senate's Select committee on Nutrition and Human Needs reports that 42% of the total calories in the typical American diet comes from fats and that the ratio of polyunsaturated to saturated fat is an alarming 7:16. By comparison, it is estimated that our ancient southwest Texans ate meat with a fat ratio no higher than 7:5, and their total calories from fat, including those from plant sources, could not have been higher than 20-25%.

Both the total amount of fat and the high percentage of saturated fats make many modern diets unhealthy. Specifically, Dr. Edward Giovannucci and his research team at the Harvard University School of Medicine report that high fat diets, derived from animal fats rather than plant sources, are considered a contributing factor in the development of advanced forms of prostate cancer. This supports earlier research by others who found correlation between some forms of breast and colon cancer and diets rich in fat, especially saturated fats. And, although we are not able to prove it, we feel these were afflictions rarely seen among ancient southwest Texans.

polyunsaturated) and peanut oil (48% mono and 52% poly). The reason monunsaturated fats may become an important issue in planning future diets is because preliminary tests suggest that eating a diet that includes a higher ratio of monounsaturated types, as compared to other types of fats, may actually help to elevate the body's HDL (high-density lipoproteins) levels. However, I stress that these findings are not yet fully accepted by the medical profession.

The wild animal meat eaten by the early Indians in southwest Texas provided more protein than fat. Wild animals do have small amounts of fat, and it is usually distributed uniformly throughout the body. Also, except for a few species of marine mammals, most fat on wild animals is the unsaturated, structural type. However, the domestic animals we raise for slaughter and many of the animals we overfeed as pets or keep in zoos all have one thing in common—their bodies contain more fat than protein and most of their fat is saturated, storage fat.

Of the foods Americans like most, the majority contain fats. It is unfortunate that we enjoy eating fats and that fats will satisfy our hunger pangs quicker than either protein or carbohydrates. Maybe it's nature's way of encouraging us to eat this essential food item. If so, it may have served our ancient southwest Texans well, but it has become a liability for may of us today. What is worse for many of today's overweight people, our intestines are very efficient at digesting fats, generally allowing no more than 5% to escape before being absorbed. This digestive advantage provided an essential source of calories for our prehistoric Texas predecessors, but it is one of the factors that contributes to making more than 50% of the people in the US overweight.

Comparing the types and amounts of fats eaten by us today to those eaten by our hunting and gathering predecessors in southwest Texas reveals that from 2,000 to 10,000 years ago a pound of meat from wild game contained one-sixth the amount of total fat and one-tenth the amount of saturated fat found in a pound of most supermarket beef today. What's worse, according to the USDA, is that the quality of meat is rated on the amount of saturated fat it contains. From most to least expensive, the grades of meat are:

There's nothing quite like native foods cooked in a clay pot and served with a wooden spoon from a gourd bowl.

I also doubt that any of the ancient southwest Texans ever had to worry about coronary heart disease, one of today's major killers in the world's more developed countries, like the US. High levels of serum cholesterol, diet, age, sex, and genetics are all potential contributors to coronary atherosclerosis; yet, of these, we can potentially control only one, our diet.

Many people mistakenly believe that their serum cholesterol level is directly linked to the amount of cholesterol they eat. Ironically, a high cholesterol diet usually only slightly raises a person's serum cholesterol level. For example, the Masai tribe of east Africa drink large amounts of milk and their daily intake of cholesterol often exceeds 1000-2000 mg. However, tests of Masai warriors reveal they have low serum cholesterol levels of only 115-145 mg/dl.

I suspect that the ancient Texans of southwest Texas also had low serum cholesterol levels even though they may have consumed occasional high levels of cholesterol, depending on their meat and shell fish supply. Recent research confirms that high-fat diets—especially ones high in saturated fat—have a greater influence on raising serum cholesterol levels than does the amount of cholesterol a person eats.

Levels of lipoproteins are another important factor related to one's overall health. The fats and cholesterol we eat cannot be directly transported by our blood. Instead, those molecules have to be attached to special protein carriers called lipoproteins. There are two kinds of lipoproteins utilized by our bodies, low-density lipoproteins (LDL) and high-density proteins (HDL). The LDL type are often called the "bad" lipoproteins because they carry cholesterol to our body tissues, including our blood vessels where some of it becomes deposited as plaque and eventually clogs our arteries. When this happens, a person can experience a stroke or heart attack.

Medical research confirms that the more total fat we eat and the higher the level of saturated fats in our diets, the higher the LDL level in our blood. And, the use of tobacco also raises the LDL level, and being obese—defined as being more than 20% over the ideal weight listed in insurance actuarial tables—also contributes to high LDL levels. However, because our southwest Texas predecessors were slim and trim, and ate diets low in total fats and especially low in saturated fats, we believe they had corresponding healthy, low LDL levels.

The HDLs are the so-called "good" lipoproteins because they carry serum cholesterol away from our tissues, especially away from the lining of our blood vessel walls. Once removed, the cholesterol is carried to the liver where it is burned or excreted. Rigorous exercise, not just walking around the block, will raise HDL levels as will diets that are low in total fats and especially low in saturated fats. Also, as mentioned earlier, diets high in monounsaturated fats may help to elevate HDL levels. As for our predecessors, even though HDL levels are not revealed during coprolite analyses, we believe that the lifestyle of the early southwest Texans would have ensured them a high HDL ratio.

Finally, I believe one piece of evidence shows how far we have diverged from the lifestyles of our ancient southwest Texas predecessors. In 1976 my colleagues and I di-

rected the excavation of a large archaeological site in southwest Texas that was located halfway up the side of a canyon. Of the 21 college-age students who participated, 18 lacked the strength and stamina to make the climb without ropes and ladders. As we later discovered, the site had been occupied for nearly 9000 years by cultures whose men, women, and children probably made the climb from the canyon bottom dozens of times each day unaided by anything more than strength and endurance.

How can we benefit from what we are learning about the lifestyles and diets of these ancient southwest Texans? Our advantage today is that we can make informed choices. We don't have to give up the blessings of civilization, but we do need to live in harmony with our physiology. By selecting a diet approximating the proportions of fats, fiber, protein, and complex carbohydrates eaten by these early Texans, and by reducing our intake of sugar and sodium, we can benefit from eating a near-"perfect" diet. Then, by adding regular exercise and avoiding tobacco and other harmful substances, we should be able to maintain reasonable levels of strength and stamina as we age, and continue to enjoy many aspects of the "perfect" lifestyle for (years to come).

Wild Plants Economics

Text and Photos By Thomas J. Elpel

As a beginner in the primitive skills I had read that "nature was like a banquet", and "all you had to do was eat", so I anticipated that I should be able to set up camp anywhere I wanted, and I would always find a well-balanced meal right there. I was therefore quite discouraged on my camping trips when I ended up going hungry. I learned virtually every plant of any significance across southwestern Montana, and I knew hundreds of edible species, but could never seem to find any to eat on my camping trips. Sure there were lots of salad plants, but it is kind of hard to live on just greens.

I realize that many other practicing primitives have had similar experiences with trying to find wild plant foods to eat, and I would like to share some insights that helped me break through the barriers and find success at nature's banquet.

At first I looked for excuses. For instance, historically the native peoples used my area only seasonally, and no group was known to have lived here full time. Bands of Shoshone from Idaho and Wyoming visited the area in the summer, primarily for hunting. Other native peoples, including the Nez Perce, Blackfeet, and Flathead were seen in the area, but did not occupy southwest Montana on a regular basis. It seemed that my area had too few edibles for even the native peoples! This helped me to justify my failure to find harvestable foods. I grew envious of other parts of the country that had seemingly inexhaustible food supplies, like acorns or wild plums, or big camas bulbs. I told myself that the Indians ate corn and beans and squash and potatoes, and provided over half of our modern food crops, all of which could not survive in the wild any more because of breeding. I further decided that most of our wild plants were forage for the big game animals that dominate this landscape.

Now that has changed. In a moment of analytical insight I realized that I had not fully tried to use edible plants, and that my excuses were true, but irrelevant. I realized that it is true that the plants of my area are primarily forage for big game animals, but that "primarily" does not mean "exclusively". I acknowledged that, sure, many Indians of the New World ate foods like corn, beans, and squash, but that, wild or domestic, those crops never existed in my area anyway. I understood, finally, that primitive peoples used this area only seasonally, because that is the nature of a hunter-gatherer lifestyle—to walk from one meal to the next as each comes into season. I realized nature really is like a banquet, and that the buffet table was only a little longer than I expected. It was, in fact, many miles longer than I expected. I was always at the table, just not at the right parts of the table at the right times!

I already knew every plant of any significance in my entire mountain range, and indeed, across all of southwestern Montana. I was not going to find some new plant with a big

Nature is like a banquet, except that the food is always on different parts of the buffet table.

Thomas J. Elpel is the owner/director of Hollowtop Outdoor Primitive School (HOPS) in Pony, Montana. Tom's Field Guide to Primitive Living Skills and Field Guide to Money are available for $20 each or $32 for both, including postage. Send check or money order to HOPS - Box 691 - Pony, MT 59747, or use your Visa or Mastercard and call HOPS toll-free at 1-800-685-3202.

One hour of picking wild strawberries generally yields about one cup of the fruit.

were unpalatable, because I knew I would not be motivated to harvest something that did not taste good.

I also eliminated those plants which were edible, but too rare to be harvested, and those which were edible, but definitely not worth the expense of energy. In order to survive on a particular food source you have to be able to harvest more calories than you expend. You have to harvest enough calories to replace those spent, and to allow you to build a shelter and meet all your other needs. Many "edible" wild plants require so much work to harvest them that you could starve to death even if you ate all day long every day. Other roots could sustain you very easily, but only if you have a good system for harvesting them.

I kept on my list those plants which were abundant, tasted okay, and had nutritious properties. Mostly that included roots, seeds, and fruits, but also a few greens which are noted for exceptional nutritional properties. I also kept on

starchy root like a potato, or some tree with a nut like an acorn. The native peoples were using this area at least seasonally, and that was far more than I was. I knew every plant they did, plus additional species introduced from Europe. I had not yet found anything to eat, but suddenly understood that I was very close to using the resources of my area as efficiently as any primitive peoples who ever lived here. Good or bad, that got me excited about edible plants again for the first time in years.

I realized I needed to concentrate my efforts on the few key species that could really support a person, and to plan my camping trips to coincide with the harvest times for each of those resources. So I made a list of those key plants that seemed like they might be worthwhile to work with.

To make my list, I eliminated all the non-edible plants, and all the "edible" plants which are useful only as tea. I eliminated all salad greens and potherbs, which are edible, but which could not sustain a person. I eliminated all the "starvation foods" because I was not interested in starving. I eliminated any plants which experience had shown me

(more)

A harvest of bistort roots.

the list some fruits, such as the wild strawberry and the dwarf huckleberry (*Vaccinium scoparium*), which are not particularly economical to harvest (one cup per hour of effort), but which are still worthwhile to collect for their exceptional flavor.

Many of the potentially sustainable wild foods on my list turned out to be species that grew only in the fertile, warm valley bottoms, around the farms and towns. This is really no surprise, since that is also where the native peoples camped. It is only us modern primitives that expect to eke out a living perched on the mountain tops! If you want to be as successful as the natives were at finding food resources, then you have to follow in their footsteps. I used to camp only in the mountains behind my home, but now I frequently venture out along the fringes of the farmlands.

An hour of digging for spring beauties yields a modest, but delicious meal.

My range currently extends in about a thirty mile radius in every direction from our home. That is about as far as I can reasonably go by foot on my regular camping trips, and still walk back home. You can make a pretty good guess as to where I will be camping according to what is in season.

True hunter-gatherer cultures were much more nomadic than I am, and they regularly traveled hundreds of miles from one food source to another. They lived full-time as nomads and had no homes to return to, so they kept walking forward. Today, in my recreational camping, I have both advantages and disadvantages compared to what the native peoples experienced.

One advantage I have is that as an individual I can take advantage of much smaller crops, that would not have sustained a larger group of people. A crop that is big enough to sustain me for two weeks would only feed a band of fourteen people for one day—hardly worth stopping for. Another difference between my experience and theirs is that they had to find food. For them it was a matter of survival. For me it is recreation and education. They had to harvest food no matter what the crops were like, while I can plan my camping trips to coincide with the peak of each crop, and take advantage of the best nature's banquet has to offer.

On the other hand, the native peoples had an advantage in covering so much more ground, because they encountered many excellent crops that do not occur in my territory. Service berries (*Amelanchier spp.*), for instance, are one of my favorite wild foods, but the nearest good patch I have found is in a subdivision 60 miles away, out of my camping range. Hawthorn berries (*Crataegus spp.*) and huckleberries (*Vaccinium spp.*) also grow abundantly near that area. The delicious blue camas (*Camassia quamash*) first appears

about 100 miles in another direction, and sego lilies (*Calochortus spp.*) are also 80 miles away. Wild plums (*Prunus americana*), wild grapes (*Vitis spp.*), and "Indian turnips"(*Psoralea esculenta*) are 200 miles away. It is not practical for me to harvest any of these foods on my camping trips, but I do gather them when modern life happens to bring me in the right area at the right time.

Next, I conducted timed studies of many of the wild foods on my list. I brought a watch along on my camping trips and clocked how much of each resource I could harvest per hour (see table). For the first time I had a procedure for determining whether or not I was wasting my effort with any given food resource, and for the first time I found a relative abundance of wild foods in my area.

One thing I learned during my timed studies is that surprisingly few people have the patience to spend even one hour harvesting a resource, much less the two to three hours per day that was typical of most primitive peoples. Harvesting wild foods can be remarkably tedious for us modern primitives, since we come from such a fast-paced culture. Nevertheless, I recommend the experience for everyone at least once, to find out what it is really like to earn a living as a "hunter-gatherer".

I also discovered that many of the wild foods in my area are genuinely stunted (typically 1/3 the size) compared to the same plants in other regions, especially the root crops like salsify (*Tragopogon spp.*), yampah (*Perideridia gairdneri*), and glacier lilies (*Erythronium grandiflorum*). The smaller roots in my area are apparently an effect of the grainy soils of decomposing granite; the soil dries out as soon as the rain stops. Working with these anemic plants has enabled me to hone both my skills and my patience, so that other areas seem comparatively lush and abundant.

Perhaps the most important lesson I learned, however, is the value of having a quality experience. For instance, I have noticed that wild foods taste much better if I harvest and eat them because I am excited and want the variation in my diet, than when I force myself into a situation where I must find food whether I feel like it or not. Also, I have learned to appreciate gourmet cooking. A sautéed dish of roots, greens, mushrooms, and some kind of meat, for instance, is much more enticing than just a pot of boiled roots. Quality experiences will always bring you eagerly back for more, and therefore I recommend bringing whatever you need to maintain that quality. A few basic foods like rice and flour can make the difference between a good trip and a bad one. I also like to bring a gold pan for stir-frying, sautéing, and for winnowing wild grains. These kinds of adaptations are not technically primitive, but they keep me returning, and that's what it is all about!

Mashing chokecherries on a metate stone.

Harvest Results of One Hour Studies

Common Name	Latin Genus	Edible Part	Final Yield	Process Time	Processing
Yellow Bells	Fritillaria	roots	1 cup	10 min.	washing
Bitterroot	Lewisia	roots	1.5 quarts	8 hrs.	peeling
Spring Beauty	Claytonia	roots	1 cup	10 min.	washing
Glacier Lily	Erythronium	roots	1-2 cups	10 min.	washing
Yampah	Perideridia	roots	1 cup	10 min.	washing
Biscuit Root	Lomatium	roots	1 quart	40 min.	wash & peel
Burdock	Arctium	roots	1 quart	10 min.	washing
Bistort	Polygonum	roots	1 cup.	10 min.	washing
Cattail	Typha	root	4 gallons		(unprocessed)
		roots buds	1 gallon		
Timothy Grass	Phleum	seeds	1 cup +	20 min.	winnowing
Lamb's Quarter's	Chenopodium	seeds	1 gallon		(unprocessed)
Pigweed	Amaranthus	seeds	1 gallon	45 min.	winnowing
Plantain	Plantago	seeds	1.75 cups	20 min.	winnowing
Wild Strawberries	Fragaria	fruits	1 cup		
Strawberry Goosefoot	Chenopodium	fruits	3 quarts		
Wild Raspberries	Rubus	fruits	1 quart		
Gooseberries/Currants	Ribes	fruits	1 quart +		
Dwarf Huckleberry	Vaccinium	fruits	1 cup		
Serviceberry	Amelanchier	fruits	3 quarts		
Chokecherry	Prunus	fruits	1 gallon	40 min.	metate
Wild Rose	Rosa	fruits	3 quarts		
Buffaloberry	Shepherdia	fruits	1 quart +		

"Every plant has a unique name in Latin and the name is always in two parts. For example, "sweet cicely", a local plant with a potent anise-like flavor, is called Osmorhiza occidentalis. The first part is the genus or genera name, and is always capitalized. The second part is the species name, and it is always lower case. As Robyn Klein likes to point out, these two-part Latin names are much like the system of first and last names we use to describe each other".

from Thomas J. Elpel's Herbal Field Guide to Plant Families.
Available from HOPS at hollwotop.com.

ROAST OF THE CENTURY
Mescal and the Mescalero Apache
By Mark Rosacker with Susan Burneson
Illustrations By Regina Watson

For six years now we have conducted an annual mescal roast here at Living Desert State Park, a zoo and botanical garden in Carlsbad, NM. The idea for the roast grew out of our realization that, while the park focused on the plants and animals of the Chihuahuan Desert, it lacked a connection with the native people of the area. When I went to Mescalero, NM to discuss my ideas about conducting a special event at the park, I was directed to the Mescalero Apache Traditional Counselors, a branch of the Apache tribal government, to whom I made a plea for guidance and assistance. I was immediately greeted with a flood of friendship and good will.

Together, we made plans to hold a mescal roast. The Mescalero Apache chose to share their ancient knowledge of mescal, *Agave neomexicana*, with us. Without their support and guidance, the annual event we hold each May would not have been possible. They deserve the credit for its success, which is solely the result of their kindness and generosity.

To the Mescalero Apache *Agave neomexicana* (also called mescal or century plant) is a sacred, living part of their cultural heritage, prepared and eaten annually for special occasions. Each task associated with harvesting and baking the mescal is carried out with the mindful accompaniment of appropriate prayers.

Mescal has been a primary food source for generations of Mescalero Apache people; it has sacred significance to them for that reason. For the Apache mescal is a staff of life, just as the buffalo was for the Plains Indians and corn for the Pueblo tribes. The plant is considered a sacrament, food for the body and

Mark Rosacker is the Wildlife Supervisor at Living Desert State Park in Carlsbad, New Mexico, where he has worked for 16 years. Susan Burneson is a writer with special interests in herbology and meteorology and publications designer in Austin, Texas. Regina Watson is an Austin-based graphic artist and photographer with a longtime interest in the outdoors, nature, hiking, and camping.

Agave neomexicana (Mescal).

the soul; it survives year-round, even in times of severe drought. (The food-source mescal, *Agave neomexicana*, should not be confused with the mescal, *Lophophora williamsii*, which is the source of a hallucinogenic drug or the toxic mescal bean, *Sophora secundiflora*).

The human history of preparing mescal in the New World goes back at least 9000 years. In addition to being used for food, mescal, which is very fibrous, has also been used to make hairbrushes, sandals, ropes, baskets, and fiber netting. The large bulbs have also been used to make canteens and fiddles and the tall, sturdy stalks have been used to make poles for tipis. Mescal is also easily dried and stored for future use. (One story from the 1860s tells of an attack on the Mescalero Apache by people who destroyed as much as 20,000 pounds of dried mescal in storage.)

An important aspect of the mescal roast is the way it bonds human beings living on the land to the land itself. Rooted in the soil, mescal is sustained by natural elements of both earth and sky. The breakdown of the very mountains themselves provides a medium for which the plant can grow; in turn, each plant is supported by the sun, the winds, the clouds, the rain, and the snow.

When we harvest, prepare, and eat mescal, we add a small part of each of these elements to our own lives and beings. We become connected, physically and spiritually to the land on which we live, and to all life forms and elements it holds. We recognize that it is ultimately this earth that provides us with the resources to nourish our own lives. Only through this awareness and a sensitive, respectful approach to living with the land can we ever hope to endure and ultimately thrive in the desert environment.

To prepare for the roast each year, we harvest 18 to 20 mescal plants from the nearby Guadalupe Mountains and other areas, always taking care not to overutilize a particular site. We remove the plants from the ground at about the second leaf layer in the rosette. This eliminates the sometimes laborious task of chopping off the roots, and it also leaves them in the ground where they will send out up to six or eight new shoots. The tool we use for this is a simple oak wedge about 4 feet long and 4 to 5 inches in diameter.

During the harvest, each part of the plant is treated respectfully and blessed. For the Mescalero Apache, part of the mystery of this ritual is that, even though they harvest the plant and prevent it from blooming and producing seed, it nevertheless regenerates itself and produces new plants vegetatively.

Before we can use the pit to bake the mescal, we begin with a thorough cleaning, down to bedrock. When it is completely cleaned out the pit is 4-1/2 to 5 feet deep and extends over an area of about 18 feet across—much larger than its size the first year of the roast.

Then we line the pit with a foot or more of rock. The Apache tend to prefer rounded limestone river cobbles, which range from fist size up to about the size of a football. Three or four rocks of even larger size are spaced evenly among the other rocks, and one especially large rock is reserved for the center of the pit.

When the pit is prepared, we gather up large amounts of dry side-oats gramma grass stems and set them aside. After the mescal have been harvested and the leaves chopped off around the basal stem to remove all visible green portions, we are ready to begin.

We burn oak in our pit, as it tends to be favored by the Apache because it makes the best coals. The fires is started in the pit at about midnight on a Wednesday and burns hard all night until 10 o'clock the next morning. Then, accompanied by appropriate prayers in the native Mescalero (Athapaskan) tongue, the mescal plants are placed directly on the hot coals. The gramma grass, which has been dampened, is quickly added on top of the plants in the pit. The hole is then covered with a layer of dampened burlap sacks as extra insurance against loss of heat and moisture and to prevent any dirt from falling onto the mescal heads.

The pit is completely sealed with as much as three feet of soil and left to bake for four days. During the sealing process particular care is given to ensure that no steam escapes along the edges of the pit. The pit is monitored periodically for the development of any vents or cracks that may form during the first few days, and these are sealed up when ever they are discovered.

After four days the pit is opened and the still-hot mescal is shared with everyone present. The flavor of the mescal varies, from sweeter on the outside to more vegetable-like toward the center of its heart. People have compared its flavor to that of sweet, sticky molasses, fresh pears, sweet potatoes, or even high-quality raisins. (Mescal also can be easily sun dried by removing the waxy cuticle on the outer layers of the leaf and splitting the remaining fibers to about 1/2-inch thickness. It can then be eaten in this dried state or reconstituted by soaking in hot water or boiling for several minutes.) Many regard mescal as they would jerked, sun-dried beef or game meat. Mescal pudding, a favorite Apache recipe, requires mixing fiber-free pulp with pinon, ground shell and all, and sumac berries.

Each year, the Traditional Counselors return up to 10 of the baked mescal heads, which range from 8 to 35 pounds each, to the Mescalero Apache Reservation. These are distributed among the Feast Givers for their own purposes. Among the sacred used of the baked mescal is food served during puberty rites for young Mescalero Apache women, who are initiated into womanhood during an eight-day ceremony.

Mescalero Apache Traditional Counselors, men and women who perform a variety of religious duties, also play a vital role in the roast. This year, dance prayers were done under the direct control and supervision of Nathaniel Chee; prayers for the harvest and during placement of the mescal in the pit were done by Evelyn Martine. We also feature a traditional blessing ceremony by the Mescalero Apache Mountain Spirit Dancers, who add their special prayers to the proceedings. They bless the plants and animals, their own people, the people of the community, and those present at the ceremony.

Other activities include social dances, where everyone dances together in a large circle around a bonfire. Something magical happens during the Apache singing and drum-

(more)

ming that accompanies the dancing, which begins and ends with a special blessing. As they look across the fire to see the faces of many other cultures, people can experience the sense of being, like everyone else, an equal part of the great community of humankind. On the last day, as a final farewell, we sponsor a "giveaway" and share simple gifts of fruit and candy with participants and their families and all other visitors.

Anyone is welcome to attend the mescal roast, which is held in mid-May—an ideal time to harvest and prepare the plant. Typically, up to 2000 people attend the four-day event, but only 200 to 300 are present at any given time. We extend a special invitation to the people of Mescalero and Carlsbad. We also see many family-oriented groups and people who have traveled here for the ceremony. This year's roast helped cement the relationship among the people of the area; for the first time, six of the 10 members of the Mescalero Tribal Governing Body attended the ceremony. Each year, we encourage more of the Mescalero Apache people to become involved.

The mescal roast at Living Desert State Park began as a grassroots effort among individuals rather than bureaucracies to encourage mutual understanding and appreciation among cultures that live side by side in our area. The Living Desert State Park provides the format and site location, the Mescalero Apache people provide the interpretation. The

roast is a living, sacred ritual with ancient roots—not a reenactment of a historic event. The Mescalero Apache people who speak in their own words and native language to convey the power of their beliefs to everyone there.

Many who have attended the roast experience a renewed reverence for life and for others, as well as a greater appreciation for tribal people. People who may never before have interacted with native people get to know them for what they really are, not through any kind of secondhand filter.

Other people are inspired to connect with and acknowledge their heritage, sometimes for the very first time. Often, a visitor will come up and say proudly, "My great-grandmother (or other relation) was a Mescalero Apache."

Truly, nothing we could have planned at the park would have been as meaningful without the cooperation and assistance of the Mescalero Apache people. They have openly shared their knowledge and guided us every step of the way. Their kindness and generosity have made our original idea a powerful reality.

Experiencing the Apaches' reverence for the mescal and for all other beings that co-exist on the planet helps us view the world and participate in it with greater awareness and respect. We no longer see ourselves simply superimposed on the planet. Instead, we are an inherent part of it, just as the mescal, and the earth, and other natural forces that have nurtured it, are now a part of our own bodies.

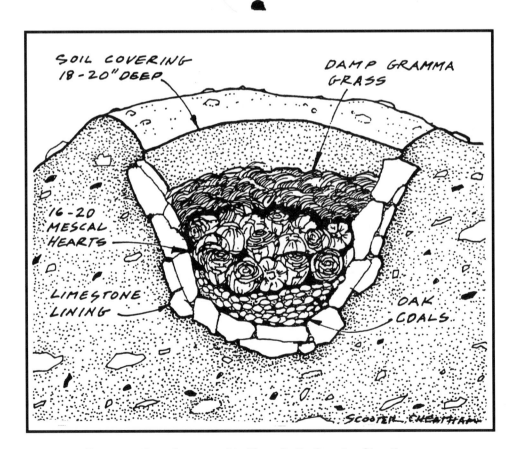

Cross-section of a mescal baking pit. By Scooter Cheatham.

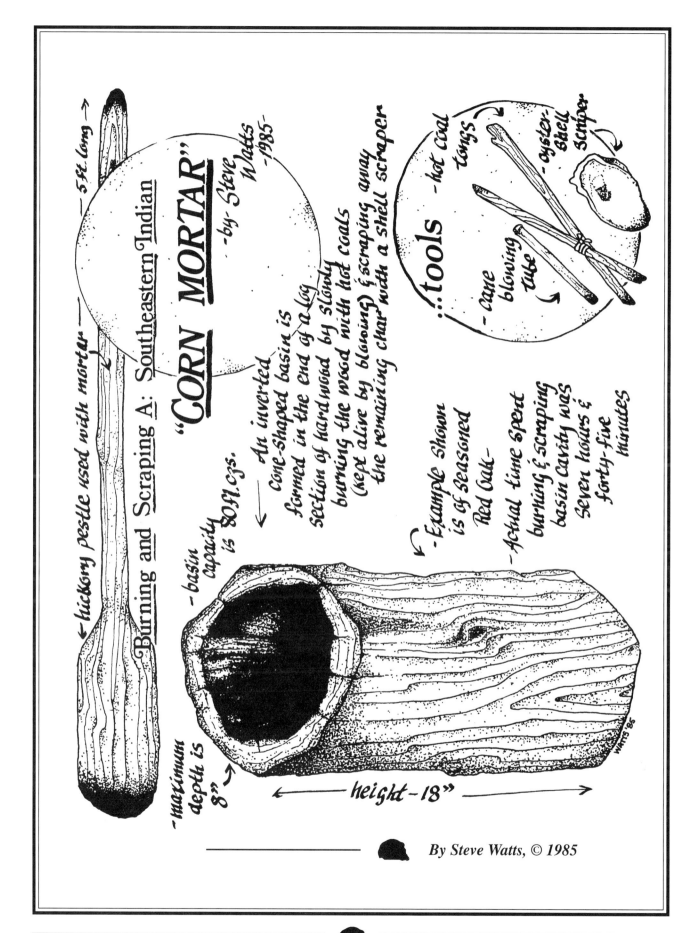

Burning and Scraping A: Southeastern Indian

"CORN MORTAR"

-by- Steve Watts -1985-

← 5 ft. long →

← hickory pestle used with mortar —

— basin capacity is 80 fl. ozs.

— An inverted cone-shaped basin is formed in the end of a log section of hardwood by slowly burning-the wood with hot coals (kept alive by blowing) & scraping away the remaining char with a shell scraper

...tools

— hot coal tongs

— oyster-shell scraper

— cane blowing tube

↳ -Example shown is of seasoned Red Oak-

— Actual time spent burning & scraping basin cavity was seven hours & forty-five minutes

-maximum depth is 8" →

← height - 18" →

WATTS 86

By Steve Watts, © 1985

Aboriginal Cookery

By Alice Ross

From the Complete Drawings of John White, 1585

Introduction

The fire beckons. The utensils are well-crafted and admired; where is the "abo" student who is not hungry to try them out? Not just fine toys, the lovely pots of clay or soapstone, the carved wooden stirrers and polished stone celts demand use. Getting them out into the woods and cooking appropriately in the fire and smoke enhances each piece, placing each into intended roles and testing for functional success. As we approach the hearth, we become aware that there is as much need for authenticity and esthetics in the cookery as there has been in tool-making. How else to assess efficacy or the social environment? And why not edible--even delicious--research!

But as it happens, the re-creation of "abo" cooking is not so straightforward. There is no guidance from excavated pre-contact cookbooks equivalent to stone or pottery artifact-models, and we have only the beginnings of food waste analysis. The oral history record, another area of information, is all too full of post-Columbian adaptations. Nor can we trust out "instincts" with palates attuned to modern high sugar, fat, chemical, and salt diets. Nevertheless, as we turn to elemental fuels and smoke, working down on ground level and making do inventively with wild resources, we are easily persuaded that we are in touch with life as it always was. Food has this way of reaching our inner barriers, for good or bad. At

its worst, it blinds us with fears, preconceptions, and prejudices. At best, it draws on lifetimes of familiarity with social and sensory eating to entice our minds and bodies to the pleasurable experience of another culture.

Unfortunately, while enriching and pleasing, the familiarity can also undermine the quest for authenticity. Foodways are invariably highly charged, cultural, personal, and deeply ingrained, and sometimes this gets in the way. It's hard for the culinary historian to drop the hard-won tricks and triumphs of the modern repertoire, the sure, preferred tastes, even when they are inappropriate. Nor is it very easy to overcome the dietary loves, hates, fears, and axioms of this age, regardless of how much we might wish to. For example, consider our emotional connection to "the best chocolate chip cookie" and its place in an abo dinner; or compare an enthusiastic cook's

Alice Ross conducts hands-on classes in traditional cookery at her Hearth Studios in New York state. She has dedicated 20 years to being a teacher, collector and historian of food and culture. She is a founder of the Culinary Historians of New York, and teaches at Queens College. Contact her at www.li.net/~aross/.

temptation to "improve" an abo stew (with black pepper, wine, or cream?) to the flintknapper's dearth of contaminating modern counterparts. And food fears can be phobic: no matter how often one hears that certain roasted grubs taste like shrimp, trying them remains unthinkable.

Consequently this essay will not try to change anyone's taste buds or to impose a "reconstructed, living cuisine" onto modern eating habits, as if such a thing were possible. Instead, it offers some rules for reconstruction, for evidence and logic of aboriginal regional, historical cookery, and leaves the rest to you. The key parameters are indigenous foods, fuels, technology, a cautious look at the earliest European observations, and the pragmatics of what works.

> *Food has this way of reaching our inner barriers, for good or bad. At its worst, it blinds us with fears, preconceptions, and prejudices. At best, it draws on lifetimes of familiarity with social and sensory eating to entice our minds and bodies to the pleasurable experience of another culture.*

The "Neo-Primitive" Supermarket: What and Where

Lists of flora and fauna existing in pre-contact times are the logical starting place in the study of New World abo food. From the moment of Columbus's landfall, these were of vital interest to prospective colonists and European food producers. The ensuing global food exchange and its effects have taken much attention in the recent Columbian quintcentennial, and one can find numbers of new books on the subject.

Lists in hand, then, all seems easy, but there's a snag. Few of these enumerated foods grew in all latitudes and elevations within the Western Hemisphere. The predominating corn culture was widespread but not universal. Although centuries of maize hybridizing had produced hundreds of varieties well suited to regional conditions and needs, other grain/starch agricultures existed locally, among them amaranth in the South-West or potatoes and quinoa in the Andes. Needless to say, they structured a somewhat different cuisine. Hunting and gathering systems existed in some places: the basic Northwest aboriginal food culture depended on salmon and foraged nuts. Growing zone locations made a difference--Mexican tomatoes and chiles, chocolate and vanilla had not moved into the temperate north.

Just as important as the knowledge of existing foods were the many Eurasian foods unknown by native Americans, an equally impressive list. For example, there were almost no domesticated animals in the new world. Livestock was limited. Andean llamas, Mexican guinea pigs and chihuahuas, and occasional dogs: these were not animals that produced large amounts, if any, of animal meat and fats, eggs, or dairy products. European-derived milk, butter, lard, and eggs that we use so freely today were non-existent before colonization. Moreover, most of the grains so common today were also native to the old world--wheat, rye, rice, millet, oats. Nor were there apples or walnuts. Note that in cooking, the early

> *Note that in cooking, the early western hemisphere wild meats/fish and local grains: maize, amaranth, or quinoa, etc., cook up in entirely different ways, and structure a very different cuisine.*

western hemisphere wild meats/fish and local grains: maize, amaranth, or quinoa, etc., cook up in entirely different ways, and structure a very different cuisine.

Time-Line and Cuisine: When

Change, ever-present, adds a further complication in determining what was eaten. One of the biggest traps is the "olden times" image in which vast periods of the past assume an amorphous, fixed character. In fact, change has been as constant as the clock, the critical difference being that of rate. For example, consider the gradual spread of Central American corn culture (the interdependent planting of corn, beans, and pumpkins together, along with sunflowers, gourds, and tobacco) into the Northeast woodland, where it was well under way at the time of European discovery. Replacing a simpler hunting-gathering society, it was in place in New York's interior and just appearing in coastal areas by 1600. Archaeologists debate whether colonization hastened the change, or whether it was simply part of a pre-existing transition. Such timing can obviously be critical in determining local historical foodways.

From the Complete Drawings of John White, 1585

FOODS TRAVEL
Alice Ross, Hearth Studios, © 1992

Foods Native to New World   Taken To

Corn (hundreds of   -Africa: starch staple in steamed
   varieties orig. in   breads   ITALY: staple polenta
    Mexico)   NORTHERN SPAIN AND PORTUGAL
         MEDITERRANEAN: Europe, N. Africa,
     Near East - EASTERN EUROPE:
           Romanian mamaliga
Beans (over 100 varieties)   -Everywhere
   (kidney, lima etc.)
Winter Squash and pumpkins   -Europe, N. Africa, India
Sunflowers
Tomatoes   -Everywhere, slowly
   (central/south America)
Chili and sweet peppers   -Tropics everywhere: India,
   (capiscums; paprikas)   -Africa, S. Asia, Hungary
Other Grains:
   amaranth (major Aztec crop)
   quinoa (S and Central America)
   wild rice (N. America)
White potatoes (varieties):   Everywhere a wet growing
    season: (Peru and higher Andes) -Europe, Ireland, India
ulluco (Andec tuber)
Sweet Potatoes (Caribbean Africa) -N. Europe, India, China
Peanuts (South America)   -Africa, China, India, SE Asia
Ground Nuts (N. America)
Jerusalem Artichokes (N. America)
Yucca root (Caribbean, S. America)   -Africa
Manioc (cassava, tapioca)   -Africa, Pacific
Plums - sloes, beach plums (N. America)
Strawberries (superior to European - Pan America)
    6 varieties, incl. white
Wild Grapes, Scuppernongs
Persimmons, Tiny Apples
Pineapple (S. America, Tropical area, Pacific)
Raspberries, Blackberries,   -Europe
   Blueberries and Huckleberries
   Cranberries, Black caps, Wineberries
Avocado Mexico
Papaya (C. America, Caribbean Tropics)   -Everywhere
Guava
Black Walnuts, Hickories,   -Europe, India, Asia
Filberts, Pecans, Chestnuts (N. America)
Brazil nuts (S. America)
Domesticated animals:
   llama, vicuna, dog, guinea pig (C. and S. America)
Wild animals:
   opossum, raccoon, turkey, wild, pidgeon, duck, geese,
   moose, elk, etc. - North America
Chocolate (S. and C. America)   -Europe and everywhere
Vanilla (S. and C. America)   -Europe and everywhere
Sassafras (N. America)   -England, Europe
Ginseng (N. America)   -Asia
Sumac, scarlet and staghorn (N. America)
Maple sugar (N. America)   -Not widely spread
Tobacco (N. America)   -Everywhere

Foods Brought to the New World By Europeans   Originated Here

Wheat, Rye, Barley	Near East originally; via Europe
Oats	Northern Europe
Rice, Millet	Thailand, China, Orient, India, Africa
Honey (?)	Middle East, Northern Europe
Apples	Orient, Middle East, Rome
Pears	Ancient Greece
Peaches, Plums, Cherries, Melons, Grapes (some)	Near and Far East via Europe
Citrus	China vs. Arabs to Europe
Almonds	Arabs
Walnuts	England, N. Europe
Bananas	Asia
Figs, Olives	Middle East, Mediterranean
Currants	N. Europe
Broad Beans (Fava Beans)	Egypt
Chick Peas, Lentils	Middle East, India, N. Africa
Soy Beans	China
Garlic, Leek	Near East, Mediterranean, Orient
Cucumber	Near East
Lettuce, Cress, Onion, Cabbage, Turnip, Carrot, Parsnip, Radish	Northern Hemisphere
Spices	Orient, plantations in East Indies
Coffee	Ethiopia: N. Europe/E. Indies, Brazil
Tea	China: E. Indies plantations
Sugar	India: Arabs: N. Europe: Brazil Caribbean and Louisiana plantations
Chickens, Duck, Goose	India: Nr.Europe, N. Africa, China
Beef (milk, butter, cheese)	England, Western Europe
Pork	North Europe, China
Goat (milk and cheese)	Near East, Europe
Sheep	Northern Europe and Asia Middle East: Africa: India
Horse	Middle East, N. Asia
Dog (domesticated)	N. Europe
White Potato, Tomato	Returned by English

Brought to the New World from Africa
- probably by slaves, or via those routes:

Sesame Seed (benne), Okra, Coconut
Breadfruit (esp. Caribbean), Yams, Cowpeas
And assorted beers, wines, whiskey, brandy, ciders

Take another case, that of New World potatoes originally cultivated high in the Andes. Pre-Columbian North Americans did not know them until after the tubers had been brought first to Europe, adapted there to its agriculture and diet, and then returned with emigrating colonists in a second Atlantic Crossing. At that time, they were as new to Northern Native Americans as they had been to earlier Europeans. Another example: Plains Indian culture, originally corn-based, shifted to hunting-gathering after adopting the Spanish horse. There were clear advantages to following the migrating buffalo seasonally, and a basic increase in meat eating.

A time-line of technological advance is also a good guide to identify which of our familiar, modern foods and cooking processes to avoid. Many of our modern-day ingredients were developed after colonization, and a great many more in the 18th- and 19th century technological revolution, among them the chemical leaveners baking powder and baking soda.

suggests that such hearths were both fairly permanent and flexible. In addition to clay pots, the tripods were doubtless used to support a propped stone griddle (for cornmeal flat breads or grilled meats), but left ample space for additional steatite "saucepans" (for fruit and nut sauces?) or "ovens" of clay pots propped on their sides. There were also pit baking (or, more properly, steaming), the smoking or broiling of meats and fish lashed onto split-branch or woven racks or dangling from a gently spinning cord. And finally, there was the commonplace method of cooking something directly in the fire, perhaps wrapped in leaves.

Boiling in non-clay containers made of such materials as wood or animal tissue was enhanced by the use of a succession of preheated stones, which boiled water readily and easily kept it at desired cooking temperatures. This basic technique enabled more flexible cookery, the possibility of more pots than would fit in the hearth, and a greater array of dishes for special or festive occasions, and for travelers, sturdy animal hide pots that worked well with the hot-stone technique had obvious advantages over fragile ceramics.

Considering the many possibilities this arsenal of cooking utensils open to the cook, and in light of the varied conditions of Native American life, there seems to be little in the way of interesting food. Did every tribe know these techniques? It seems likely that they did, but each may have leaned most heavily on the techniques best suited to their terrain, access to fuel and utensil materials, and seasonal ingredients and sites.

Technology: How

Technology is conceived broadly here to encompass materials, design, and cooking processes, and includes both utensils and cookery. This is probably the easiest area to deal with, as the archaeological record has set many limits. While it is probably unnecessary to discuss the inappropriateness of iron, aluminum, glass, or plastic utensils, definition may be found in the particular shapes and cooking properties of round-bottom clay pots, for example.

Principles of prehistoric fuel and cooking utensils seem to be consistent with early methods everywhere. The task of cutting and hauling in dead wood for a culture without iron or the wheel was at the very least a time-consuming chore that limited fires. Raging bonfires had their place but were too hot to cook over, and in any case were not required for daily cookery. Pots were designed for limited fuel and manageable heats. Round-bottom, thin-walled, and reinforced with grit and compression paddling construction, they were still large enough to prepare standard one-dish meals of stews and soups. Like the iron wok of China and European kettles, they transmitted heat evenly, did not collect burned food in corners, and were easier to stir and to wash. But more fragile than iron, they required some sort of stand to hold them upright--often a tripod of 3 long, upright stones anchored in a flat, shallow pit, stone-lined for additional heat-retention and radiation. The pots sat high and far enough apart to allow for coals and small fires underneath, with generous air channels to supply oxygen (see BPT #4, pages 87-89).

Archaeological evidence for this kind of arrangement

The Cuisine: What

With some limits on available indigenous ingredients, utensils and cookery techniques, and with an eye to time and place, we are ready to dig in and cook. Without scientific measurements or detailed instructions which can be so useful (and sometimes crippling) for modern cooks, it helps to understand the food properties and cooking chemistry that are universal and independent of ethnicity. This is the moment when the novice benefits from the experience of the skilled modern cook. In determining the character of the cuisine it also helps to know something about the frequencies of usage and relative proportions of foodstuffs, one to another. Agricultural corn cultures consumed more corn than any other food, according to some estimates at least 65% of the day's calories. Meats and fish were commonly eaten in small

(more)

amounts, about 20% yearly, depending on season, and were often used more as flavorings (especially when dried or smoked) than as main courses. On the special occasions of a good hunt or large amounts of some rare or seasonal delicacy, there was more likelihood for hearty overindulging, although this was not usual. The daily combination of beans and corn (complementing vegetable proteins), was probably a more dependable source of protein, and often the basis of ubiquitous stews and soups. These were apparently served as the one large, mid-day meal, but kept available hot for the snacking that comprised the rest of the day's eating.

Despite the presence of cuisines grounded on potato, salmon, or other central foods, corn remained the most important food for the clear majority of aboriginal people and therefore merits special attention. Consider corn varieties: while the contemporary cook is happy to find stone-ground cornmeal, masa, and perhaps even blue corn meal, we are generally unaware of the may kinds of corn grown, each with specific cooking qualities. Soft corn (field-ripened and dry) is easier to grind, and more likely used in cornbreads, while flint or hard corn is not only harder to grind, but also requires special lye treatments to remove the hulls. Such hard corn was used cracked, not ground, in corn stews sometimes called succotash or samp porridge. Parched corn (roasted and dried green, unripe), ground popped-corn meal cooked into dumplings, and other unusual-to-us corn preparations hinge on characteristics of individual corn varieties. And regarding color: it seems to surprise many to fine that the colored "Indian corn" which we decorate our Thanksgiving tables was grown in all varieties, and is totally edible when cooked appropriately. In addition to corn, a number of indigenous plants can be grown successfully in home gardens. Heirloom beans, tomatoes, and chiles, Jerusalem artichokes, ground nuts and cherries are possible regionally, and add to the total sense of aboriginal culture.

Flavorings are to some degree an area of confusion. Even salt usage is debated. Known and used extensively in Europe, Africa, India, and Asia for both flavoring and preserving, it is not so clearly established in the American aboriginal cuisine. While some early travelers' reports stated that no salt was used, others describe flavors as good as any in Europe, suggesting that other enhancers may have been available. Commonly-used leaf ashes of different plants may have provided some "salting," but were perhaps misinterpreted by Europeans as non-foods and not recorded. And then there is the possibility that the job was done by dried clams and oysters, highly saline and apparently valuable in cross-country trade. Sugar, pepper, kitchen-garden herbs and imported spices, commonly used today are largely of foreign origin.

On the other hand, a number of indigenous flavorings added to the quality of food. The red berries of wild sumac are intensely lemon-like; nut oils and pastes have dramatic flavors; dried fruits and berries add their own kind of sweetness. Wild onions, garlic, sassafras, juniper, black birch, and leaf of spice bush are only a few. [Note the need to discriminate within botanical families, for example between choice red upright sumac vs poisonous low, marshy white-berried sumac.]

Ultimately the matter of taste and flavor are controlled by the tastes of the eater. While there is evidence of genetic differences in perception of flavors, my own experience suggests that food considered good within any culture has the potential of appreciation by someone from another culture, providing that it is approached with a mind free of prejudice.

Seasonality is one more factor in the recreation of early foodways. Eggs were available in the nests of wild birds at very limited times of the year, minimizing their role as an ingredient and limiting them to occasional tasting. No breakfasts of fried eggs! The yearly cycle of spring agriculture, summer fishing and gathering, fall harvest, and winter hunting reflect a basically seasonal cuisine.

Sources

With all these constraints, what does one trust? Where does one begin? For those who enjoy digging through early writings and modern research, there is the historical and archaeological record. Caution here: early accounts of travelers and explorers have recorded usable data mixed with confused and mistaken impressions, not to mention downright lying. The English distortion of John White's 17th-century drawings of Virginia aborigines is just one case in point. The rule of thumb is to back up one source with 2 or 3 others, possibly from other disciplines. The dovetailing of oral history folklore with early reports and some archaeology are more reliable than any one alone. Anthropology itself may help, but with the admonition that it has been operative for only 100 years old; be wary in reading the early works, as they may include fairly recent aboriginal adaptations in cuisine, technology, agriculture, hunting, fishing, and gathering. Forced removes and blending of tribal people and cultures have resulted in major changes in food production and diet.

Cookbooks, read critically, suggest possibilities. Local, tribal recipe collections have the advantage of regional style, but they, like the larger, general works on Indian cookery, can not claim to portray pre-contact cuisine. Some contain historical material, often based on oral tradition that implies change. Deleting inappropriate ingredients and processes sometimes works, provided the basic form of the dish is not Eurasian in style. Pre-contact cornbreads, for example, made in the modern style but without wheat flour, butter, eggs, milk, sugar, salt, and leavening seem to be rather limited. But when rethought as dumplings, or as the griddle-type flat breads (tortillas), when steamed in leaves and flavored with bits of meat, nuts, fruits, or vegetables (tamales) or when baked in ashes and then eaten brushed and hot, the menu takes a less bleak cast.

Finding appropriate ingredients is another key to integrating the cooking and eating experience with abo culture. Foraging with an ethnobotanist transforms the field and forest into a vast supermarket. Gardening makes available a number of early, heirloom varieties of corn, beans, pumpkins, tomatoes, chiles, etc. with surprising taste results. In addition, health food stores and regional mail-order catalogs are sometimes helpful. And as for utensils: well, that's your department.

VARIOUS FOOD GATHERING METHODS

Chas. Spear, © 1994

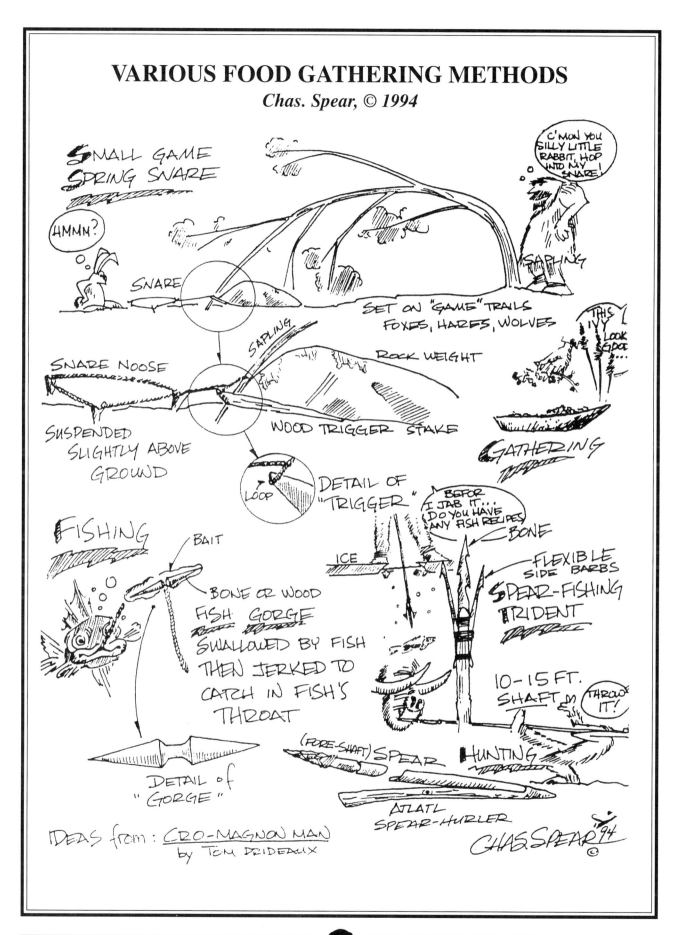

TRAPPING
Take A New/Old Look
By Matt McMahon

Because of Jim's feature on traps of this issue, I felt it necessary to address a few other issues related to this topic. Unfortunately, the word "trapper" conjures up images of a heartless brute using viscous steel claws to kill hundreds of animals for money. Environmental concern and outright disgust have made "trapping" a bad word. Traps and snares are,however, a justifiable means of harvesting game. We [Matt, Molly, and daughters] live a semi-private lifestyle in remote areas in Montana. We look to the forest and rivers to provide us with firewood, drinking water, edible plants and of course meat. Deer and elk provide us with bulk meats and hides, but when they are not available we depend on the trapping of small game. We harvest animals with great respect and as little suffering as possible. Properly constructed snares and deadfalls kill an animal instantly. The critter does not linger for hours, trying to chew off his own foot to escape a steel trap. Snares and deadfalls can be so subtle that often the animal and those of its tribe, will never even know it was killed by a man. In the case of snares for instance, they will think they are tangled up in brush, pull on the snare and then quickly and quietly lose consciousness. No blood, no gaping painful wounds, no damage to meat or hide. Just a quick and painless death. We are personally of the belief that there is no more humane way to harvest an animal.

Also let us consider dwindling wildlife populations and the "fur industry". Here in Montana, we have a vast abundance of small game including rabbits, squirrels, gophers, porcupine and coons. They are legal to trap, even by primitive means, giving us plenty of opportunities to practice aboriginal hunter/gatherer techniques. We are utilizing a practically unlimited source of fresh-organic meat, body parts and hides (that we earn through skill and respect). Aboriginal tribes harvested large quantities of hares, squirrels and yes even mice and cut their hides into long strips to be woven into incredibly warm blankets, and robes. Bones, sinew, feathers and teeth were fashioned into tools. We have found no primitive method that puts meat on our table faster. Check your own local game laws to determine the animals whose tribes can be thinned. Why is this legal?

Our forests are literally teeming with certain small game animals. We are not killing off the last of the valuable "fur-bearers" like lynx, wolf, mink and wolverine, to be sent to the fur markets in France. We are simply utilizing animals that are abundant and give thanks for what we are allowed to harvest from the forest. So if you are a person who connects the word "trapper" with wanton waste and violence, stand back, refocus and take a new look. You may begin to understand how traps and snares can be a very efficient and humane method of harvest.

> *We are utilizing a practically unlimited source of fresh-organic meat, body parts and hides (that we earn through skill and respect). Aboriginal tribes harvested large quantities of hares, squirrels, and yes, even mice and cut their hides into long strips to be woven into incredibly warm blankets, and robes. Bones, sinew, feathers and teeth were fashioned into tools. We have found no primitive method that puts meat on our table faster.*

Trap Placement

So now you've chosen a trap to set, maybe a twitch-up snare, and you made it work out in the front yard. The obvious next question is: "Where to set the trap?" and at this stage of the game we separate the trapper from the occasional trap builder. In the art of trapping there is a golden rule; "The best made trap is worthless if you don't know where to put it!" There is an abundance of information on how to build a particular trap, but little on how, when and where to set it. Likely, there will be 20 year veteran trappers who will disagree with some of the following information. I will only be discussing what I have proven for myself.

Molly and I live a fairly primitive existence in the Northern ecosystem and traps, mostly snares, can provide us with food everyday in otherwise meat-lean times. We frequently snare snowshoe hares and squirrels and save the hides for our rabbit-fur robe. The meat in the pot is greatly welcome to stretch out our regular deer/elk diet. I will speak mostly of snares although most of the knowledge presented applies equally to deadfalls and their ilk. Personally, I find snares to be the most effective primitive device that puts meat on the table. They are deadly but humane. They are lightweight, easily constructed and will kill anything from a mouse to a moose. They are out there hunting for you when its 30 below zero and you're home chopping wood. Snares work in trees, under ice, on snow, in thickets; wherever critters are located. In winter 50-75% of our meat intake is from snares. They are easily constructed from most any fiber at hand. Sinew, rawhide, nettles, dogbane, horsetail hair, your hair, picture wire, bootlaces and clothing strips to name only a few. Stick with strong cord that slides easily through an eye made of itself. (See Fig. 1)

In the case of rabbits and squirrels, no locking device is needed to secure the game. Usually these animals panic when snared. They will "fight the snare" by lunging and choke down all the faster. Wary animals like fox or coyote require much preparation to make the set location "scent-free" and with fewer revealing props. These animals will chew out of any snare (except wire) unless it kills them immediately. We have plenty of hares here and they taste much better than coyotes and are much easier to catch.

The first task when surveying new trapping grounds is determining where the animals feed, eat, drink and sleep, and the paths or trails that connect these areas. TEST BAITING

paths that avoid your snare. PROP STICKS are used to hold open snares allowing them to hang naturally in the trail. Fencing is tolerated by rabbits and squirrels and other "prey" animals. Predators are most often caught with very little fencing or other "construction" at set locations. They simply are wary and may smell your activity at the set. But rabbits, squirrels, grouse, beaver, muskrat and even big game mammals can be "fenced" or squeezed through a given location. Some "squeezers" are naturally occurring, require no set construction and take less time. For instance a trail pinched between a lake and a cliff or a well-worn log crossing a fast creek. These sites actually call out for a snare.

Other "squeezers" include hollow logs, culverts, fencelines, waterslides and den holes. Also check holes

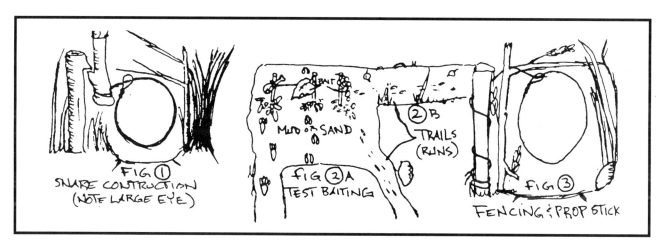

FIG ① SNARE CONSTRUCTION (NOTE LARGE EYE)

FIG ②A TEST BAITING

MUD or SAND

②B TRAILS (RUNS)

FIG ③ FENCING & PROP STICK

is a common tool that identifies target critters in the vicinity. It is accomplished by finding a dusty or muddy clearing where tracks will register and proceeding to leave food offerings of various types in separate piles or on marked stakes. Simply go back in the morning and read who showed up for what. (See Fig.2)

Mammal tracking is one of the most crucial skills in trapping and is not witchcraft! It is simply reading the ground. In our area snow allows us to track animals over great distances and is one of the best (easiest) ways to learn track patterns. Field guides will get you started but get out and start tracking where you plan to trap. Research and observation will tell you what critters eat and no doubt many of their trails (runs) will lead to these feeding grounds. Observe grazed vegetation and scat content at feed areas. Lets say I notice a hare, around dusk after chopping wood and the hare darts into a rose thicket and is on familiar terrain amongst the many trails and runs it has developed over time. If I walk over to the thicket and get down on my knees I can see the rosehips have been eaten 2 feet up off the snow. I even see fresh tracks and scat that tell me when trails are used the most. Here I will hang a snare.

I may even use FENCING to guide/force the critter through a given spot, for instance under a log, to ensure that he walks through my snare. Fencing is the ability to use sticks or branches to create a wall or "fence" which narrows down the

leading into old buildings and barns. If a path or trail does not go where you need it to go you can create your own. Animals commonly use man-made trails and this is to your advantage. Imagine a field with 3 feet of fresh snow on it. If I plow through on snowshoes and create a trail many critters will use it just because it is the path of least resistance. Humans create many natural trails and critters use them too.

So now you've identified a run or a feeding area and you are prepared to set a trap. You should now decide on a "baited" set or a "blind" set. A baited set uses food to distract or draw an animal through your set. A blind set relies only on your ability to read trail sign and to camouflage your traps so the animal hits the trap while on the run and totally by surprise (also called a "running set"). Baited sets are very efficient but in a survival situation bait may not be available. Also, for the beginning trapper, "running" sets teach you more about placement and animal habits by making you go find them instead of drawing them to you. Both sets are equally effective and both have their appropriate locations. In the case of rabbit and squirrels in my area they readily take bait. We have found apple rings dried or fresh to be an irresistible bait. Nuts, grains and salty veggies do well too. Test baiting will answer any questions here. A word of advice on bait. Do not transfer juice or odors from your bait onto your snare or you may find your snare is eaten too! Build a set trap, and bait just before leaving.

(more)

It is often preferred to shelter your trap and bait from the elements (or birds!). A "cubby" lends itself well to this. A cubby is an enclosure with a roof that both protects traps and bait and fences/guides the critter through the door and into your trap. A cubby should be built sturdy enough so that animals will not simply tear it apart to get at the bait. Many trappers build a long series of cubbies and bait them days before actually setting their traps. The animal has gotten accustomed to crawling in and out and will easily be caught when the trap is live.

POWER SNARES employ a bent sapling or liftpole to quickly (humanely) hang the prey. This device can also prevent "chewing out" of a snare as well as suspending it out of reach of predator. Sets for water animals employ a heavy rock or a bag of rocks to accomplish the same thing by quickly drowning the critter. Be sure to set in water deep enough to completely submerge the animal. Although power snares are very efficient they are not always crucial. We have caught small game on simple snares made of straight rawhide lace, with no locking device at all. The animal simply panics, lunges and chokes down.

Regardless of what set you choose to build, you will now have to match the size of the snare opening to the size of the target animals head. Equally crucial is the distance from the bottom of the snare to the ground. I find an opening of one hands width and a hand-width distance to ground to work fine on my local snowshoe hares. Jackrabbits are larger and cottontails are smaller. Likewise we use a 3-finger width snare opening for our red squirrels, 2-3 finger width distance from ground. It is very important that the target animal puts its head only through the loop to ensure that it dies quickly and humanely by hanging, when the loop is too large or too close to the ground, the critter steps into the loop thereby becoming "body-snared" which is a lingering death if it doesn't just chew out altogether.

A myriad of problem solving events will naturally occur when learning to trap. This is to be expected. Successful trapping is not black magic. It is simply applied observation combined with know-how and of course a pinch of luck. I hope I have shed some light on trap placement as it is the most important ingredient in your recipe to success. Make Meat!

More traps by Matt McMahon.

PATHS OF LEAST RESISTANCE

BAITED TWICH-UP

BAITED PEN fig 6

BLIND OR RUNNING SNARE

BAITED CUBBY fig 8

DROWNING SET

"ROCKING ON" WITH THE PAIUTE DEADFALL
ITS PREHISTORY, CONSTRUCTION & USE
Text, Photos & Drawings By Jim Riggs, © 1992

Setting & Prehistory

The major geographical and cultural focus of my studies and experience in archaeology and primitive technology has been the Northern Great Basin, those contiguous high desert portions of southeastern Oregon, central and northern Nevada and western Utah. Physiographically, this region of hot dry summers and cold dry winters is characterized by hundreds of parallel-oriented 4-6,000' flat-to-rolling valley floors separated by predominantly north-south running fault-block mountain ranges occasionally reaching 12,000'. In this vast region of internal drainages run-off water from adjacent higher country is sufficient and constant enough into a few widely scattered valleys to create large resource-rich freshwater lakes, marshes and meadows, but most valleys, plains and intermediate uplands are considerably drier-sinks, playas, dunes, low escarpments, seemingly endless expanses of xerophytic shrubs and grasses with infrequent, intermittent stream courses and springs. I long ago figured if I could sufficiently internalize the natural history, ecology, aboriginal survival strategies, the natural history, ecology, aboriginal survival strategies, material culture and skills necessary to comfortably exist in this "marginal" environment, I could probably get by primitively almost anywhere.

While the overall human carrying capacity of the Great Basin environment is considerably lower than most of North America, the appearance of barrenness is deceptive. For over 10,000 years in this setting the Northern Paiute, Western Shoshone and earlier peoples became masters through necessity at seasonally and successfully exploiting nearly all food resources--grass seeds to grasshoppers, roots to coots--from all habitats within their territories. Vital to this success was knowing "when to be where" at precisely the right time, especially with regard to variables in weather patterns, spatial fluctuations in floral productivity and more predictable faunal population cycles. Lacking a plethora of easily obtainable large game, predominantly elusive pronghorn and bighorn advantageously hunted when appropriate, the more prolific and regularly available rabbits and rodents provided the bulk of animal protein over the annual cycle.

Concerning the evolution of aboriginal human subsistence and adaptation in the Great Basin, Cressman states, "Long before the bow and arrow came into use the archaeo-

(more)

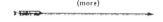

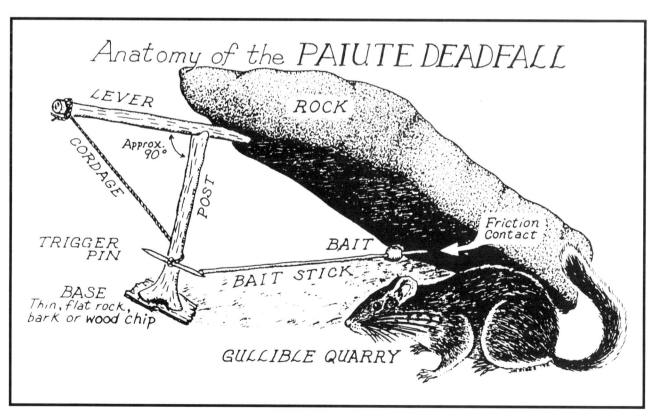

Anatomy of the PAIUTE DEADFALL

LEVER

ROCK

CORDAGE

Approx. 90°

POST

Friction Contact

TRIGGER PIN

BAIT

BAIT STICK

BASE
Thin, flat rock, bark or wood chip

GULLIBLE QUARRY

logical record shows that hunters were using other devices for taking small game. Various kinds of trap-the snare, the deadfall, and others-were in use, together with nets which may have been used in variety of ways. Using traps in the food quest represents a sharp psychological break with the method of killing the quarry with a weapon in that there is no longer direct involvement between the hunter and the hunted. The man with a trapline thus had a device for supplementing his food supply beyond that which his skill and luck as a hunter could possibly provide. The traps set along the game trails, whether those of rodents or large mammals, would work for him while he was engaged in some other activity or doing nothing at all".

particular trap include: **1)** What animals are available and, of these, which seem most lucrative to try for? **2)** Does some sort of trap seem the best means for success, say in contrast to direct hunting? **3)** What tools and/or raw materials are necessary and available? **4)** What projected energy and time are required to construct and set any trap? What seem the most efficient investment for the best return? The more elaborate or complicated--the more parts and materials requiring collecting and modifying--the more time you'll spend on any one set for one animal. If you're seeking larger game, especially with a group of people working collectively while "living out" for an extended period, this might be time well spent. But for smaller critters-some birds, occasional lagomorphs

Paiute Deadfall set for a wood rat in rocky habitat. Note, it is set on another rock, as no open ground is available

Contemporary Considerations

In any primitive living situation where one is depending on the natural environment for sustenance, employing one or more forms of traps or snares is prudent and often quite lucrative. With minimal initial effort (and some practice), one can assess the available small game in the area and set up a number of appropriate traps. Once the trapline is established, it need be checked only once or twice a day for harvesting, rebaiting and resetting. In effect, it becomes a passive potential provider of meat, as Cressman indicated, freeing you to actively pursue hunting, fishing, collecting or processing plant foods, manufacturing tools or even sleeping! You'll also experience a definite anticipatory thrill, mentally and gastronomically, as you check your traps...Wow, Food!

Sounds idyllic, but what traps do you choose to try, especially if you are just learning and have no backlogue of experience? I'm convinced that in the history of humankind there have probably been more traps, snares, trigger mechanisms and various combinations thereof conceived than any one person could ever catalogue, let alone try out. On a global scale, many of these were ingeniously designed for catching some very specific creature indigenous to an equally specific climate and habitat and may not be seriously applicable elsewhere (no need to continue brainstorming your surefire traps for wooly mammoths or California condors!). But others, no matter where their origins, are quite adaptable to a variety of creatures and environments.

Pertinent considerations in selecting and setting any

and especially rodents as mice, chipmunks, woodrats, marmots and multifarious squirrels-I've concluded the simpler a proven-effective trap is, the better. While I've experimented with dozens of primitive-style traps over the last 25 years, the ones I emphasize most in teaching, actually use most frequently and depend on to regularly put animal protein into my stomach, are two: the simple snare (many variations and sets) and the Paiute deadfall. This article will be limited to the construction and use of the Paiute deadfall; I'll offer some of my thoughts and experiences using simple snares in a later article.

The Paiute Deadfall

Several older archaeological and ethnographic reports concerning Great Basin cultures briefly mention, describe and/or illustrate (often incompletely and inaccurately) a variety of deadfalls involving a main rock and one or more sticks, pebbles, lengths of cordage, etc., that all could be labeled "Paiute deadfalls". For contemporary descriptions and illustrations of some of these variations, see Jamison and Olsen. While I believe these to be viable and advantageous to learn and practice as part of one's "deadfall repertory", I personally have found them less effective. For simplicity's sake I choose to label the specific trigger components described and illustrated in this article as THE Paiute deadfall, state of the aboriginal art, if you will! Although a bit more complex than the simpler "two-stick" deadfalls and occasionally trickier to set, the bottom line is - IT WORKS. Although it was born in the

Great Basin, the Paiute deadfall had successfully served me in a wide variety of habitats in the American west. I'd consider it viable in any region that harbors small-to-medium sized, mostly ground-dwelling rodents or other creatures succeptible to a baited trap.

I don't pretend to wholly understand the physics involved, but I believe the deadfall's effectiveness is attributable to two main factors. Primarily, the weight of the rock is efficiently and successively diffused and/or distributed via eight or more contact points amongst the stick and cord components. In setting, when the bait stick is lastly positioned, baited end in friction contact with the underside of the rock and butt end against the trigger pin, only minimal pressure from the initial weight of the rock remains to hold it in place. This in effect creates a hair trigger (with luck, a "hare" trigger!) in that the tip of the bait stick contacting the rock surface is the most easily dislodgeable (weakest) part of the whole apparatus. Secondarily, when the bait stick is tripped, the falling rock neatly flips the lever assembly and post out of its path, leaving only the thinner, unobstructive bait stick under the rock with the quarry.

The subtleties of the "perfect" Paiute deadfall are many, but only a few basics are truly critical to a potentially successful set. Once you've practiced enough to understand how the components must work together, you'll be surprised how quickly and sloppily (visually, at least) you can make and set a line of deadfalls-they don't have to look pretty, they just have to work! Many times I've set lucrative deadfalls employing no tools (steel or stone) and no premade or specifically modified parts other than simply breaking dry sticks to appropriate lengths, quickly twisting an adequate length of cordage from even marginally strong or long plant fibers (sagebrush bark, moistened dry grass, etc.) and baiting with a fortuitously found rose hip, wild onion or grasshopper. In some situations or environments I suppose unavailable natural fibers for cordage could seem a problem; remember, you are almost always wearing something that already is, or could be twisted into, an 8-10" length of string.

I suggest studying the accompanying illustrations to familiarize yourself with the anatomy, relative proportions, positionings and possible variations of the deadfall components. The configuration and angles of lever and post to each other and to the rock that I have come to prefer are closest to those illustrated in Wheat, and differ considerably from Jamison and Olsen. Among the criteria for my perferences here are overall deadfall stability and ease of setting, lower angle of rock to the ground and increased likelihood the rock will flip lever and post out of the way when it falls. The terminology I use here for deadfall components has been adapted from a handout from the School of Urban and Wilderness Survival (SUWS), Hagerman, Idaho. The following descriptions of deadfall components should become increasingly meaningful as you gain some hands-on experience with the deadfall and subsequently discover and incorporate whatever best suits your needs and options in any specific situation.

Deadfall Components

The Rock: Fortuitously, many of the best places to set deadfalls-rimrock outcroppings, bouldered hillsides, bases of talus slides, along streams, etc.--also harbor adequate deadfall rocks. I suggest gearing the size of the rock you select to the size of the largest potentially catchable quarry you believe to live in that habitat. If mice or chipmunks are the only critters you assess to be in your trapping area, smaller flat rocks will suffice, but ideally a rock size large enough to kill a cottontail or marmot, set with a trigger mechanism delicate enough to be tripped by a mouse, will provide you with the most meat. Wiley woodrats for example seem to delight in gleefully "running through" lightweight deadfalls!

The configuration of my ideal "generic" deadfall rock for up to cottontail size would be rectangular in shape, roughly 15" long, 3-5" thick with a flat bottom, gritty surface texture and weight of 30+ lbs.. The back end should be squarish so that when the front is lifted there is no wobble, rocking or sliding, as if it were hinged to the ground. Any side-to side instability can make setting trigger components extremely frustrating. Often you can square-up irregular spots by percussing them off with another rock used as a hammerstone. If reshaping isn't feasible, you can sometimes shim the back to stability with smaller rocks. If the deadfall rock wants to slide backwards, slightly gouge the back end into the ground or butt it against another rock. I cannot emphasize enough taking a few minutes to carefully select or modify the most appropriate rock available.

The underside of the deadfall rock should be as regularly flat as possible to mesh closely with the ground surface to insure a quick clean kill. This is most important toward the back where the bait is and the animal's head should be. An extremely irregular or deeply concave rock surface may only maim the quarry or temporarily confine it until it digs its way out unscathed. Toward the rear area of the underside of the rock where the tip of the bait stick must hold itself in place by friction contact, a grittiness or some other flaw or irregularity of rock surface is necessary. If that surface is too smooth to grip the bait stick, peck it with a hammerstone to roughen it or even create a small concavity. Frequently I've set deadfalls in areas where tabular rocks were perfectly sized and shaped, but too thin and lightweight to be effective. Here the solution is to stack additonal rocks on top of the deadfall rock until it's heavy enough to work. Rock on!

Trigger Parts: Always use dead (not rotten) dry wood if possible for all components. For lever and post I prefer barkless, somewhat weathered straight shoots up to about finger thickness of willow, currant, red osier dogwood, etc. Anything rigid, straight and preferably not smooth-surfaced will work. Green shoots or really wet wood can be too pliable, tend to slowly bend or buckle from the weight of a large rock and can prematurely trip the deadfall. Actual lengths and thicknesses will vary with your rock size and intended quarry, but a handy relativity for sizing trigger components is: Make the lever, the post and the working section of cordage all the same length. For my standard woodrat or squirrel sets this is 6-7" long and approximately 1/2" diameter,. Remember, the initial piece of cordage must be a few inches longer so it can

(more)

PAIUTE DEADFALL
Troubleshooting Comparisons

TYPICAL RIGGS SET

TYPICAL OLSEN 4,10 SET

LOW ROCK ANGLE

+ Quick falling time when tripped. Rock to quarry contact almost immediate, with minimal reactionary escape time.
+ Quarry must be mostly under rock to reach bait, especially with adequate fencing.
+ Potentially broad and stable contact area between lever and rock.
+ shorter fencing materials adequate.
- Bait stick normally must be longer, thus strong spine more critical, though I've not found this to be a problem
- Friction contact between bait stick and rock can be more difficult to achieve.

POST POSITIONED IN FRONT OF ROCK

+ Rock cannot abort its fall by landing on top of upright post.
+ Rock nearly always flips lever and post beyond path of its fall.

NEAR HORIZONTAL LEVER POSITION

(Some variation up or down is OK)
+ Specifically shaped coupling between top of post and underside of lever can be ad vantageous, but not imperative.
+ As listed above, more solid increases surface contact between top end of lever and rock.
- Cord may want to slide up post (Normally correctible by roughening post surface or slightly adjusting angles between lever, cord, and post.

HIGH ROCK ANGLE

- Longer falling time when tripped, thus more time for quarry to react and possibly escape.
- Less % of quarry's body likely to be under rock.
- More tenuous, unstable contact between rock and lever.
- Taller fencing materials required.
+ Bait stick is shorter, choice and spine of suitable materials is broader.
+ Friction contact between bait stick and rock is potentially easier to achieve.

POST POSITIONED UNDER ROCK

- When tripped, rock can begin its fall but actually land atop lever and post (which did not receive sufficient speed or force to flip them out of the way) and remain upright.
- Tripped rock can begin to flip lever and post away but, because of its high angle and thus sluggish start, only knocks them over, often resulting in base of post remaining under front of rock thus blocking its com plete fall.

NOTE: I used this style of deadfall set for several years with adequate success, but I also experi- enced the above two problems occuring more times than I can remember.

DIAGONAL "FIGURE 4" LEVER POSITION

- Requires a carved "no-slip" coupling between top of post and underside of lever.
- As mentioned above, high rock angle in conjunc tion with diagonal lever position creates less stable, less surface contact between lever and rock.
+ Cordage does not tend to slide up post.

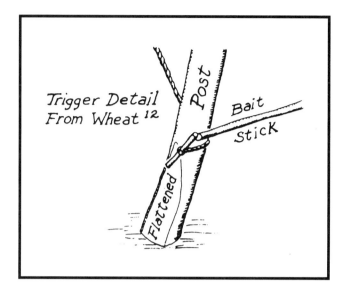

Trigger Detail From Wheat [12]

be affixed to the trigger pin and lever. The above proportions are not gospel-you may encounter sets where more dissimilar lengths of components work better-but I've found it efficient to make up a bunch of matched trigger pieces ahead of time, then choose rocks that suit them.

As previously mentioned, completely functional deadfalls can be spontaneously made and set with little or no modification of materials, but given the choice, I prefer to make some refinements. I normally groove the back end of the lever so the wrapped and tied cordage won't slip and I slightly flatten the top side of the other end to increase its surface contact and stability where the leading edge of the rock will rest.

This second modification can wait until you are matching individual levers to specific rocks. It is also advantageous to shape the top of the post and/or the underside of the lever to prevent sliding or rolling where those two contact each other (see illustration). With sincere thanks to John McPherson for the tip (Why didn't I ever think of this?!?), I'm now a devout convert to selecting posts that have a natural fork or at least a broadened diameter at the base; this configuration retards the post from twisting, greatly increases stability and can make setting infinitely easier.

The trigger pin, stiff, straight, approximately 1-3" long, can be round, partly or wholly flattish, bi-pointed like a gorge hook for fishing or a completely unmodified twig (see illustrations), but I prefer to point at least one end and groove its center. It can usually be slipped through the initial twist loop of your cordage and will hold itself in place in the groove, eliminating need for a bulkier knot.

Since that bait stick remains under the rock when it's tripped, you want something as straight and thin as possible, but having strong enough spine (rigidity) to span the distance between the trigger pin and the rock with out undo bending or finally buckling from the pressure the trigger pin will exert against its butt (non-baited) end. A flimsy, rubbery bait stick just won't work. In the Great Basin I generally use dead willow or rabbitbrush shoots or basal stem sections of giant wild rye

grass. Always initially cut bait sticks a few inches longer than you believe necessary. Unless you've found one of those perfect rocks uniformly gritty enough to grab the tip of the bait stick anywhere you position it, you can't predetermine its final working length until you locate a solid friction contact point. I do this by "feel" with the tip of the bait stick probing for a spot as far under the rock as possible. When a spot is found, I note where the back end of the bait stick should be cut or snapped to abut with the trigger pin. Since I am actually setting the deadfall when I determine the working length of the bait stick, I usually snap it with my teeth rather than cutting it because my left hand is already occupied in holding the trigger pin to the post to prevent the rock from falling. The final moves are first relocating the friction contact point with the tip of the bait stick, then very slowly allowing the free end of the trigger pin to swing slightly forward until it contacts, and subsequently is applying all its pressure against, the butt end of the bait stick. If all goes well, the bait stick does not slip from the rock and the deadfall is set!

When you attempt to set your first Paiute deadfall, you may question my labeling it as "simple". You may even scream loudly and profanely at the deadfall components (or at me!), especially after several aborted attempts in which the rock smashes your hands! Please persevere. It is a delicate trigger mechanism; familiarity and success require practice. Hopefully the following tips and troubleshootings will round out the previous descriptions and discussion and ease your initiation into the Paiute deadfall.

Side view of a "demonstration set" showing positions and suggested effective angles of component parts. Bait is Biscuitroot bulb.

Tips & Troubleshooting

The most commonly encountered problem beginners face in setting the deadfall is the lever and the post wanting to swing or twist to one side. Counteract by: 1.) Making sure there is NO wobble in the rock when front is lifted to working height. Trim or shim if necessary. 2.) Reposition or reshape top end of lever for more solid meshing/contact between it and rock. 3.) Use a post with a forked or broader base instead of a dowel-shaped cylindrical base.

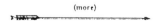

(more)

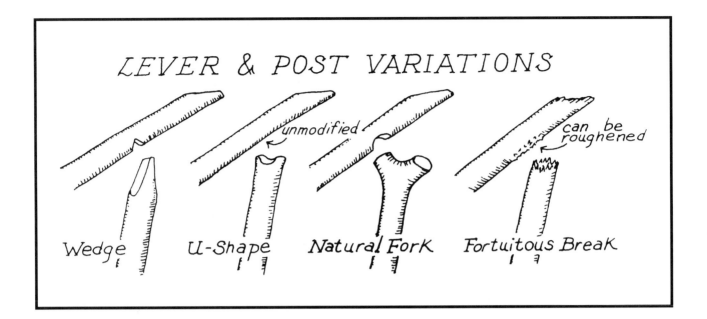

LEVER & POST VARIATIONS

Wedge   U-Shape   Natural Fork   Fortuitous Break

unmodified

can be roughened

If the cordage and trigger pin want to slide up the post: 1.) Lightly rough up the post surface. A naturally weathered surface will grip the cord better than smooth bark or a cleanly peeled stick. 2.) Flatten the area of post and /or trigger pin where the two contact each other. 3.) Alter the angle that the lever and cord "pull" on post by slanting the post more (moving its base slightly further from rock) or try position the post more vertically and lowering the cord end of the lever. 4.) Ascertain if you possibly need a shorter or longer working length of either cordage or lever.

If the free end of the trigger pin where it abuts the end of the bait stick wants to swing downward toward the ground, try: 1) Flattening the portions of post and trigger pin to create more surface of contact between the two. 2.) Shortening the trigger pin. 3.) Abutting end of bait stick against trigger pin closer to the post.

NOTE: The above three most common problems are often interrelated; frequently one simple adjustment can eliminate all of them.

Sandy, dusty, wet of other soft ground can ineffectualize a deadfall. Some compensations include: 1) Place a base piece, a thin flat rock, wood or bark chip, under the post to stabilize it and prevent it from sinking into the ground. 2.) "Pave" the ground beneath the deadfall rock, especially where the quarry's head and chest should be, by slightly imbedding smaller flattish rocks or a few hard straight sticks laid paralleled to each other to create a more unyielding surface. 3.) Set the whole deadfall on bedrock or on top of another flat rock or bark slab that you can move to where you want the set to be.

To prevent crushing your hands under your own deadfall (which can be serious with a heavy rock) place a fist-size or larger rock or chunk of wood under the deadfall rock but not obstructing the space where you'll position the bait stick. This will block the complete falling of the deadfall rock should it slip while you're setting it. Of course, remove the block once the deadfall is set. I offer thanks to the long-forgotten person who suggested this improvement. For years I just figured having a perennial case of "bloody deadfall knuckles" was part of the game!

Bait: If you happen to have such goodies as nuts, raisins, candy, cheese, peanut butter, carrots, doughballs, etc., your success is almost predestined. Of course, with all that on hand, why would you need to kill small furry animals? I normally have tried to rely on finding adequate bait within the natural environment-wild rose hips, berries in season, seeds extracted from pine or fir cones, a succulent bulb, root or mushroom-anything your quarry might eat that it finds more easily obtainable on the end of a bait stick than by working for it (as via digging, climbing, traveling far, etc.). Normally herbivorous critters can also, perhaps more through curiosity that hunger, be attracted to meat-grasshoppers, fish innards, jerky, etc., and these baits can attract other potential quarry as mustelids, raccoons and opossums. Woodrats especially can be enamored by items other than actual food (see below). In most primitive living, even survival, situations one frequently has on hand some pregathered or "brought-with" foodstuffs. You then must decide whether you're better off to eat this yourself or to gamble on expending some for bait to potentially catch something greater. Whatever your available bait, affix it solidly to the bait stick. If the bait is not strong enough to thread onto the stick and stay there, wrap and tie it on with cordage, plain fibers or even a couple of your own hairs (harder for survivalist skinheads). Your success rate will increase with the bait as far under the rock as possible and with the bait as far under the rock as possible and with the lowest angle of the deadfall rock to the ground that still allows just enough clearance for the quarry's head to reach the bait. When tripped, the contact between the falling rock and the most vulnerable anatomy of the quarry is almost immediate

Forked post increases the stability of the set.

this is little problem, but with a line of more than a dozen or so it's easy to do. Figure out a system to mark or remember each and every set. Check traps at least once a day; twice is better, although the most appropriate times can vary according to the particular quarry's habits. Especially in hot weather you'll want to collect your catches as soon as possible before bloating occurs, yellowjackets have carved away half or you suddenly notice myriad vultures circling overhead! At the same time/you don't want to check in the midst of the quarry's highest activity period or so frequently that you alter their behavior patterns. I normally make an early morning and a mid-late afternoon round, and vary that if circumstances warrant. One deadfall may catch a nocturnal woodrat overnight and, when reset early in the morning, catch a diurnal squirrel later that same day. If nothing happens at some traps over two whole days and nights they're probably not in lucrative spots and should be moved. Always take down all traps before leaving an area; it is irresponsible and unethical to leave baited deadfalls set if you'll not be there to make use of any catch.

Knowing where to set traps and what kinds are most appropriate for any particular critter or habitat grows with experience. You have to begin somewhere. Its advantageous to read up on the natural history, ecology, animals and their habits pertinent to any wild area you frequent. With that information as a base, your best trapping successes will come from directly observing live animals going about their repetitive daily patterns. Note their species, numbers, sizes, times of activity, routes taken, habitual runways, foods eaten, locations of burrows, nests or forms, interactions with each other,

(more)

and immobilizing and the quarry has almost no time to react and pull away.

Blocking or "fencing" the sides of the deadfall rock takes little time and can further insure success. The object is to guide or channel the quarry into the set from one side near the front so that when its head reaches the bait, most of its body is also under the rock. However, don't fence so completely that the critter is apt to bump the trigger pin or bait stick before reaching the bait. Use sticks, bark slabs, smaller flat rocks, etc., leaned against the sides of the deadfall gently enough not to trip it. Make sure the fencing materials are long enough to reach above or overlap the top side of the deadfall rock so they can't accidentally fall underneath nor inhibit the rock when tripped.

Don't forget where you set your traps! With only a handful

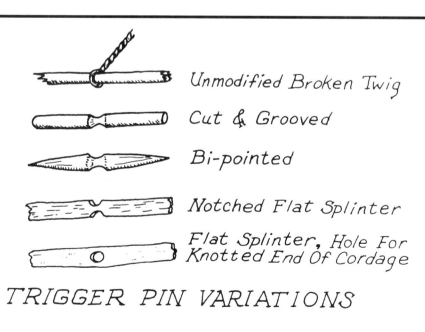

Unmodified Broken Twig

Cut & Grooved

Bi-pointed

Notched Flat Splinter

Flat Splinter, Hole For Knotted End Of Cordage

TRIGGER PIN VARIATIONS

"FENCED" DEADFALL

ad infinitum. When animals remain unseen, investigate likely habitats for tracks, scat, food storage spots-any signs revealing their activities. The scope of this article can only minimally introduce some ways and means for learning animal habits, but an old adage sums up the goal worth striving towards: "The fundamental principle of successful trapping is to determine what the animal you with to trap is going to do, and then catch him doing it!"

While a sprung and empty deadfall does not supply you with any meat, it can potentially supply you with some extremely useful information if you can learn to read what actually happened, then make necessary adjustments to the set. When you approach a downd deadfall, but see no obvious catch, pause a moment, study the scenario and snap a mental photo. Note position of rock, other visible components and any obvious tracks or signs (If the ground surface around or near the deadfall is accommodating, I like to deliberately smooth over a patch of dirt just so I can see what tracks may appear). Then carefully lift the rock--often you will have been successful. A "pancake" deermouse or chipmunk is not much, but it's food. Congratulations! If nothing is there, your personal interpretive phase begins. Note position and condition of bait stick--does bait remain or is it gone? Any signs of hair, blood or struggling animal? Did the rock fall "in line" or is it askew?...might be bigger quarry than the rock could handle. Any cattle tracks around? Any fencing material under the rock? Just a few "baited questions " here to get the aboriginal Sherlock Holmes in you activated! In twenty years of teaching this trap to hundreds of people in field conditions, I've noted that beginner deadfalls found sprung but quarryless the first few times have most commonly self-destructed due to inadequate strength, stability or positioning of components or set so tenuously the slightest

breeze or raindrop could trip them. I close with a personal "what Happened here?" vignette entitled:

A Packrat Tale

During the final living-with-the-land week in one of my Aboriginal Life Skills courses in Oregon's Wallowa Mountains I had set a Paiute deadfall one afternoon along the sheltered base of a rimrock where woodrat tracks and scat were obvious in the dry dust --a sure catch I thought. It was baited with a fresh biscuitroot Lomatium sp. and the cordage portion of the trigger apparatus was two-ply dogbane Apoynum cannabinum string. Upon checking it the next morning the deadfall was sprung but empty, bait and bait stick still under the rock. Strangely, the dogbane cord had been nibbled and frayed almost through in two places. It was a good set--I didn't understand how the rat was escaping. I reset it with a new length of cord and same bait, not yet having really discerned the nature of the failure. The second morning the deadfall was again sprung., empty, bait stick under the rock as before, but the entire lever-cordage-trigger pin apparatus was completely gone. After a couple minutes of incomprehension, the cartoon light bulb (Aboriginal hand drill burst into flame) brightened my mind. (1) I had twice missed the rat because it was never under the deadfall rock when tripped, and (2) The rat was not at all interested in the biscuitroot bait; it wanted the dogbane cordage! OK. This time I made a new lever and pin and substituted a thin buckskin thong for the cordage piece. I removed the biscuitroot from the bait stick and in its place tightly wrapped a generous length of dogbane cord. Finally, the third morning I had solidly caught that fat packrat! We feasted on three rats that day, as another participant's deadfall was successful and I had caught a second rat in a pole snare actually set for a chickaree (red squirrel).

Except where otherwise credited, this article is presented as my own opinions, assessments and experiences. Comments and feedback are welcome. While my information is definitely not exhaustive, for some this may be more than you ever cared to read about the Paiute deadfall! Hopefully for others it will stimulate field application or even research into the physics of weight distribution throughout the trigger components. To each his own. Me? Really, I'm glad I know how to catch a critter when I need one!

REFERENCES

Cressman, Luther S.
1977   *Prehistory Of The Far West, Homes of Vanished People,* University of Utah Press, Salt Lake City, pg.108.

Dalley, Gardiner F.
1976   *Swallow Shelter and Associated Sites,* **University of Utah Anthropological Papers,** No. 114, Univ. of Utah Press, Salt Lake City. pg. 62-63.

Fowler, Catherine S. (Compiled and Edited by)
1989   *Willard Z. Park's Ethnographic Notes On The Northern Paiute Of Western Nevada, 1933-1944,* Vol. I, **University of Utah Anthropological Papers,** No. 96, Univ. of Utah Press, Salt Lake City. pg. 23-24.

Jamison, Richard L. (Compiled by)
1982   **The Best Of Woodsmoke,** Chapter 11, "Deadfall trapping" by Larry Olsen, pg. 71-76, Horizon Publishers, Utah.

Jennings, Jesse D.
1978   *Prehistory Of Utah And The Eastern Great Basin,* **University of Utah Anthropological Papers,** No. 98, Univ. of Utah Press, Salt Lake City. pg. 47.

Kelly, Isabel T.
1932   **Ethnography Of The Surprise Valley Paiute,** University of California Publications in American Archaeology & Ethnology, Vol. 31, pg. 87-88.

Loud, Llewellyn L., & Harrington, M.R.
1929   *Lovelock Cave,* **University of California Publications in American Archaeology & Ethnology,** Vol. XXV No. 1, pg. 154-155.

Lowie, Robert H.
1924   *Note On Shoshonian Ethnography,* **Anthropological Papers Of The American Museum Of Natural History,** Vol. XX, Part III, American Museum Press, pg. 199.

McPherson, John
1988   **Makin' Meat - 2, Obtaining Subsistence in Nature, Deadfalls/Snares, etc.** PO Box 96, Randolph, KS, 66554, pg. 21-22.

Olsen, Larry Dean
1973   **Outdoor Survival Skills,** Fourth Edition, Brigham Young University Press, Provo, Utah, pg. 78-79.

Steward, Julian H.
1933   *Ethnography Of The Owens Valley Paiute,* **University of California Publications in American Archaeology & Ethnology,** Vol. 33, pg. 254.

Wheat, Margaret M.
1967   **Survival Arts of the Primitive Paiutes,** University of Nevada Press, Reno, pg. 72-73.

THE SAMPSON POST DEADFALL
By James Andal

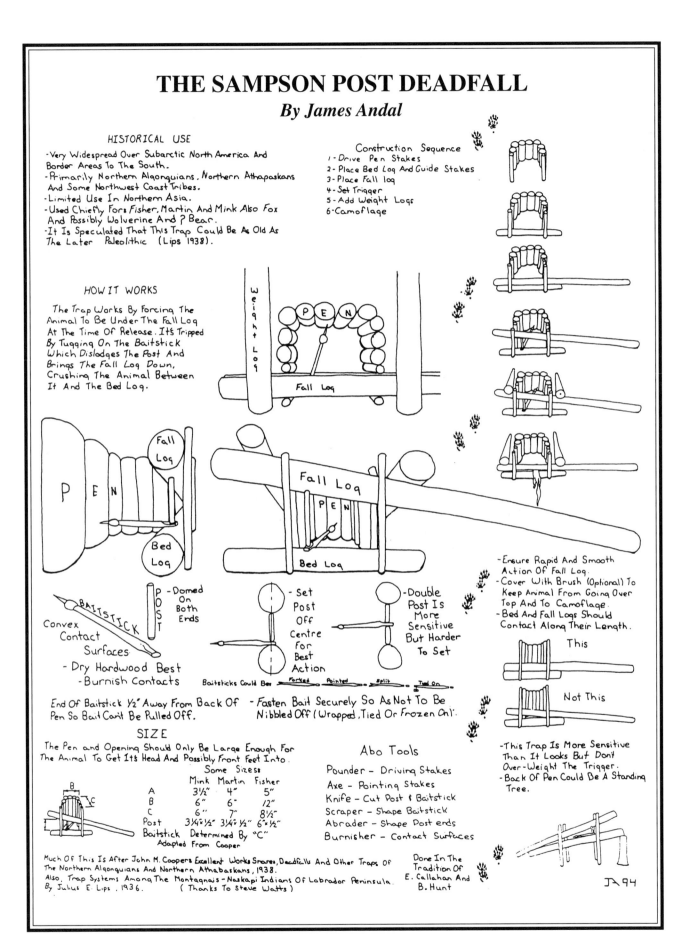

HISTORICAL USE

- Very Widespread Over Subarctic North America And Border Areas To The South.
- Primarily Northern Algonquians, Northern Athapaskans And Some Northwest Coast Tribes.
- Limited Use In Northern Asia.
- Used Chiefly Fors Fisher, Martin And Mink Also Fox And Possibly Wolverine And ? Bear.
- It Is Speculated That This Trap Could Be As Old As The Later Paleolithic (Lips 1938).

Construction Sequence

1 - Drive Pen Stakes
2 - Place Bed Log And Guide Stakes
3 - Place Fall log
4 - Set Trigger
5 - Add Weight Logs
6 - Camoflage

HOW IT WORKS

The Trap Works By Forcing The Animal To Be Under The Fall Log At The Time Of Release. It's Tripped By Tugging On The Baitstick Which Dislodges The Post And Brings The Fall Log Down, Crushing The Animal Between It And The Bed Log.

Weight Log

PEN

Fall Log

Fall Log

PEN

Bed Log

Fall Log

PEN

Bed Log

POST — Domed On Both Ends

BAITSTICK

Convex Contact Surfaces
- Dry Hardwood Best
- Burnish Contacts

End Of Baitstick ½" Away From Back Of Pen So Bait Can't Be Pulled Off.

- Set Post Off Centre for Best Action

- Double Post Is More Sensitive But Harder To Set

Baitsticks Could Be: Forked   Pointed   Split   Tied On

- Fasten Bait Securely So As Not To Be Nibbled Off (Wrapped, Tied Or Frozen On).

- Ensure Rapid And Smooth Action Of Fall Log.
- Cover With Brush (Optional) To Keep Animal From Going Over Top And To Camoflage.
- Bed And Fall Logs Should Contact Along Their Length.

This

Not This

- This Trap Is More Sensitive Than It Looks But Don't Over-Weight The Trigger.
- Back Of Pen Could Be A Standing Tree.

SIZE

The Pen and Opening Should Only Be Large Enough For The Animal To Get It's Head And Possibly Front Feet Into.

Some Sizes:

	Mink	Martin	Fisher
A	3½"	4"	5"
B	6"	6"	12"
C	6"	7"	8½"
Post	3¼"×½"	3¼"×½"	6"×½"

Baitstick Determined By "C"

Adapted From Cooper

Abo Tools

Pounder — Driving Stakes
Axe — Pointing Stakes
Knife — Cut Post & Baitstick
Scraper — Shape Baitstick
Abrader — Shape Post ends
Burnisher — Contact Surfaces

Much Of This Is After John M. Coopers Excellent Works Snares, Deadfalls And Other Traps Of The Northern Algonquians And Northern Athabaskans, 1938.
Also, Trap Systems Among The Montagnais - Naskapi Indians Of Labrador Peninsula. By Julius E. Lips, 1936.   (Thanks To Steve Watts)

Done In The Tradition Of E. Callahan And B. Hunt

JA94

Reflections On The Rabbit Stick

By Jim Allen

I first tried using the rabbit stick in about 1986. I still remember my initial reaction being one of amazement. I was amazed at the amount of power and force that could be delivered by an 18" wrist-thick chunk of wood. I hunted occasionally with such a stick, but usually with minimal success. I didn't become seriously interested in the rabbit stick until about two years ago. I would like to share some of my observations regarding "The Stick."

As I began to explore the use of the rabbit stick in earnest, the first thing I did was to go out and cut a massive piece of dead Osage, as thick as my forearm. I then shaved this down with a draw knife to an elliptical handle to fit my hand, then sanded the whole thing. It was a work of art. I gave it some tung-oil until it shined in the sun. Then I tested it. The first thing I discovered was that after about four throws, my arm felt like a piece of rubber. **Lesson #1:** the rabbit stick must be light.

I went back to the woods. This time I selected a thin but strong piece of Osage (both the these sticks, by the way, were "V" shaped). The thinner stick worked fine. I experimented extensively with it, and it was with this stick that I discovered some of the interesting secrets of the rabbit stick.

First of all, I found that my success rate depended mainly on how the stick was thrown. If the rabbit stick is thrown overhand (end over end), much of the area covered by the stick is "wasted." The following illustration might help explain this point. *Illustration 1* shows a typical "overshoot." The illustration is from the thrower's point of view. The thrower has thrown his stick a little too high. But in order to have hit his target, he would have had to throw it so that the rotating ends pass between 1 to 8 inches above the ground (target zone). Anyone who has thrown a rabbit stick more than twice knows that this is very hard to do! If the overhand throw is a little low,

the stick will hit the ground and "kick up" sometimes jumping 10' into the air. To make matters worse, the overhand throw must be "dead on target" in terms of "right to left" trajectory, because the stick's coverage zone right to left is only as wide as the stick itself: almost 1". Slim chance!

Now let's turn the stick "sideways" and see what happens! The sidearm throw changes everything. Look at the *Illustration 2*. Again, we are using a 3-foot rabbit stick. Now our left/right coverage zone is a little less than 6 feet wide! If the stick is thrown anywhere within the 5'10" zone your target will be hit. Also, I discovered that it's relatively easy to control the flight "elevation" of the stick with the sidearm throw. In other words, its relatively easy to sail the stick from one to eight inches off the ground. What's more, a "low throw," rather than bucking wildly into the air, will often skip or slide at a low trajectory right into the target.

It should be added here that at any time when using the rabbit stick, it may "rotate around the target," even with a nearly "dead on" throw. This is due to the nature of the weapon and is almost unavoidable.

When I began teaching wilderness skills I was amazed at the skepticism and disbelief of my students regarding the killing power of the rabbit stick. As a way of convincing them, I asked them to tap the stick lightly against their forehead. Later, I spoke with another wilderness skill teacher, and was surprised to find that he used the same convincing technique! Try it.

In the eastern woodlands, I've found the rabbit stick to be of limited effectiveness against rabbits. It's more effective on

Rabbit sticks and throwing club.

(more)

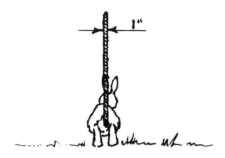

Figure 1

Figure 2

groundhogs, birds, squirrels, and other game animals that are often out in the open. But rabbits are generally found in dense cover, where a rabbit stick doesn't fly well. In dense cover, a shorter, heavier rabbit stick might be more effective. It may not be a coincidence that most of our museum rabbit sticks come from open scrub (or "bush") lands of Australia, and the open tundra of the North. By the way, if you throw your rabbit stick in the woods, you'd better be accurate with it. I've got two cracked rabbit sticks to prove it! **Lesson #2:** don't throw your rabbit stick at trees; the trees always win.

Photos and Illustrations by David & Paula Wescott

Throwing with a side-arm release.

I make no claims to being expert with the rabbit stick. For those seeking expert advice on "the stick" I recommend you turn to those instructors who have years of experience in its use. However, I hope that my observations will be helpful to the beginner and I hope you have as much fun as I do in learning about what may be the simplest of all human weapons: the rabbit stick.

Jim Allen is the author of Sleep Close To The Fire. Available from TRailhead Press, PO Box 4717, Elkhart, IN 46514-0717

Southeastern Indian Rabbit Sticks

"Throwing Club" - Recent information ...now establishes the former existence of the throwing club among the Catawba as a means of killing rabbits...Particulars are as follows: material, green saplings of hickory stock peeled of bark approximately half their length to form the handle or light end, each weighing one pound, respectively 15 1/2 and 18 1/2 inches total length, and 2 inches and 1 1/2 inches in diameter at the thick end, round in cross-section throughout, not curved. Their function is simply that of a cudgel--to knock down and kill small creatures in a set or on the run.

...Men used the weapon for hunting in a "fire patch", as an area of burnt over brush is called. Four or five hunters generally went together, each armed with three clubs to throw, and accompanied by dogs. When a rabbit tried to make its escape from the fire-patch they would throw clubs at it.

The throwing club for rabbit hunting as employed by this people has significance in the study of the distribution of weapons in the Southeast and Southwest of the continent. Hitherto unrecorded in literature outside of the latter zone, the round-sectioned throwing club is to be included among devices of tribes in a limited area of the South Atlantic Slope cultural horizon. In the Powhatan area of Virginia its former use for killing rabbits has been described for the Rappahannock (see below).

From: Catawba Hunting, Trapping and Fishing, by Frank Speck, University Museum, Philadelphia, PA, 1946.

"Throwing Club" - The throwing club, as mentioned before, is chiefly for killing rabbits in the autumn rabbit drive. About two feet in length, it is fashioned from the base and trunk of a dogwood sapling. The club end is the thick end of the trunk near the ground. The bark is not scraped off. In experienced hands, the club becomes an effective weapon, being thrown in an overhand-sidewise manner which sends it spinning at the victim.

The dogwood club is heavy as a whole, the striking end outweighing the grip end. It was never hurled at a rabbit until the animal had started to run. A call or shout was given to start a rabbit when one was spotted in the grass. As the rabbit bounded forward, the club was thrown to intercept it, which it invariably did when launched from the hands of an experienced club slinger. Two or three clubs thrown at a victim left little chance of escape.

The rabbit drive took place in the autumn after the harvest time and was participated in by a group of from 10 to 15 men with dogs in a two or three day excursion.....in a communal hunt under a "leader". The club is hurled by a sidewise arm motion to hit the ground ahead of the running rabbit flushed by the men and dogs.

From: Rappahannock Taking Devices: Traps, Hunting, and Fishing, by Frank Speck, Royal Hassrick, and Edmund Carpenter, 1946.

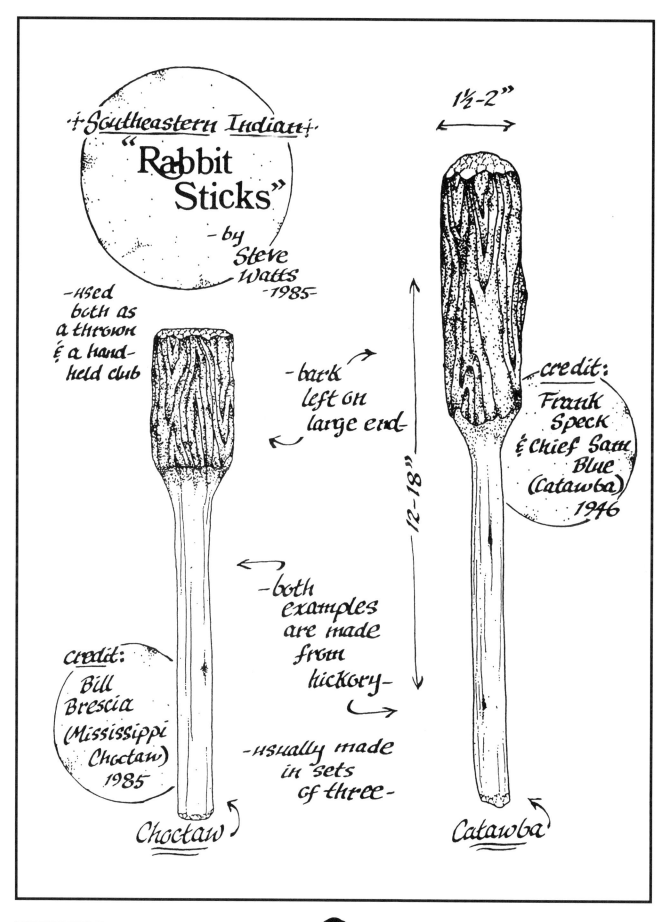

† Southeastern Indian †
"Rabbit Sticks"
– by Steve Watts
–1985–

–used both as a thrown & a hand-held club

–bark left on large end–

1½–2"

12–18"

credit:
Frank Speck & Chief Sam Blue (Catawba) 1946

credit:
Bill Brescia (Mississippi Choctaw) 1985

–both examples are made from hickory–

–usually made in sets of three–

Choctaw

Catawba

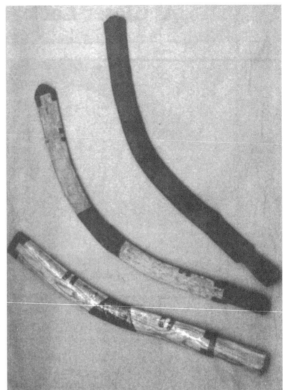

More On Sticks
Specimens from the
Museum of Northern Arizona

The sticks on the left are older (lenticular) design. The newer ones on the right (plano-convex) are painted and varnished. They both possess the characteristic 130°(+-) angle. One interesting fact about the rabbitstick, according to the orientation of the handle, curve, and plano-convex surface, the majority of sticks on display are left handed. That is, if the top is curved and the bottom flat, it should be easy to distinguish the orientation of the stick in use. Most sticks I have seen are oriented to the wall in whatever way makes a pleasing pattern for a display, not how the stick would be held in use. Designs painted on were fairly consistent among obvious Hopi sticks. They believe the stick was brought to them by Sparrowhawk. He kept it under his wing, and threw it when it was good. The stick was a formidable weapon even for the hawk. The marks on the margin of the sticks are rabbit ears.

Section 3

CONTAINERS
Holding It All Together

INTRODUCTION TO CERAMIC REPLICATION

By Maria-Louise Sidoroff

Archaeological ceramic replication, information must be obtained from many sources. Ceramic technometric procedures such as X-ray diffraction, spectrographic analysis, petrography, neutron activation, the use of binocular microscope, and the scanning electron microscope are some laboratory techniques that provide quantitative information about ceramic artifacts. This includes paste composition (clay and temper), as well as method of manufacture and decoration, atmosphere and temperature of the firing. Additional information can be obtained from the project report of the field archaeologist who evaluates the relative placement through time and space of the artifact. Typologies and assemblages of ceramics from the site are constructed, and relationships to material from other sites are evaluated. Ethnographic accounts of contemporary traditional potters can offer technological information about paste composition, construction techniques, firing methods, breakage patterns, and the trading and function of ceramics within a society.

The search for natural clay should be concentrated along cuts in the surface of the earth such as: rivers, streams, landscape or construction excavations, eroding hills and cliffs. After a good rain, the clay appears quite shiny in contrast to the duller surface of the larger grained soil. Clay is formed from the decomposition of igneous rock into tiny particles during ancient geologic times and naturally occurs in most parts of the world. **Primary clays** (Kaolin and Bentonite) remain at the place of origin and have larger particle size than **secondary clays** (earthenware and stoneware) which are transported by erosion. The smaller particles size of secondary clays and the minerals gathered in transport create conditions of greater workability. These clays are also the most abundant.

A hand ax or a shovel can be used to scrape away organic material mixed on the surface of the clay deposit, and to hack out chunks of the most pure clay. Sometimes, the clay is moist and needs only to be wedged (a type of kneading that re-aligns the clay particles and eliminates air pockets) and then used immediately. Other clays require blunging (to knead the clay in water to make it more workable). Exposed clay veins in an arid climate can be hard and dry but will soften quickly when set in water. Some clays function better if they are sun dried, ground into a fine powder and re-moistened. This procedure is common when a fine, thin walled pot is made and then decorated with a slurry of clay (sometimes mixed with mineral pigments) called slip.

A simple test in the field can determine the workability of the clay. To understand the quality of plasticity, a pencil thin coil is squeezed out of the clay and bent into a ring. Sufficient plasticity exists if the ring holds its shape when set on end; if the ring does not slump flat there is also good self supporting strength to

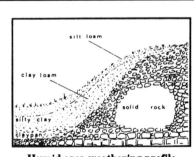

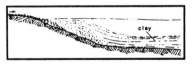

Humid area weathering profile.

Graduated lake bed deposition.

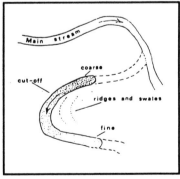

River Oxbow distribution.

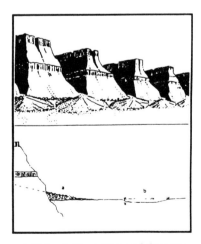

Arid land alluvial fan and deposits.

build a pot. Successful functional ware can be made from poor clays and clays can be adjusted by weathering and aging but, for the beginner, the time is well spent in locating a good source for the first try. Studio clays, which are cleaned and blended by ceramic supply houses, do not function well in open pit firing. It is possible to add a small amount (20%) studio clay to an imperfect natural clay to improve workability and still have a paste which functions well in the stressful rapid heating of an open fire.

The next test at the source involves an egg size lump of clay formed into a small cup. The ease with which the walls are thinned and self-supporting strength of the cup can provide important information on the potential of the clay. After the cup is air dried, a test firing can be conducted in a campfire, home fireplace, or charcoal grill. These are fires which typically have an oxydized atmosphere, that is, a free flow of oxygen and duplicates a firing atmosphere common among pre-industrial cultures for functional earthen ware. The pot will harden and turn buff or reddish according to the amount of iron in the clay) after a few hours in the fire. Often there will be dark smudges somewhere on the pot - "fire clouds" where carbon was absorbed into the clay. These smudges will not wash off and can only be removed by re-firing. Many potters value the placement and shape of these "fire clouds." In the completely oxydized atmosphere of an electric kiln these spots never occur. A reduced atmosphere in a smokey firing with dung, grass, peat, or sawdust for fuel, provides a black or grey pot - sometimes with a red "fire cloud" where a flash of oxygen occurred.

Usually, additions are made to the clay to create a paste for pottery fired in an open pit or simple kiln. Purposeful organic or mineral additions to the clay are called temper. Sometimes temper is naturally occurring, such as sand or fine volcanic ash, and no more need be added. The purpose of temper is to improve the workability of the paste, to prevent cracks in the pot while air-drying, and to counteract thermal shock to the pottery during firing and use. Technometric analysis can indicate the type of temper used in ancient pottery. There is a wide variety of documented temper ranging from organic materials such as blood, bone and goosedown among the Inuit to crushed quartz and shell among the Woodland Indians. Once a good source of

clay has been located and tested, a large supply can be gathered. Temper is wedged into the moist clay in batches with proportion of about 1 part temper to 4 parts clay for workable paste.

Temper identification can be important to the archaeologist in order to place the artifact within a particular assemblage. However, some fine organic material such as cattail fluff or milkweed fluff can decompose in the wet clay during aging and leave no evidence for chemical or physical evaluation to describe. For replication experiments in association with an archaeological site, the search for clay, temper and fuel should concentrate within a 2 mile radius of the excavation where the ceramic artifacts were retrieved. The conservative attitudes of contemporary traditional potters have been well documented in ethnographic accounts and while sources of raw materials are often kept secret among potting families they are known to continue to utilize these same resources for generations.

For successful replications of handbuilt earthenware, too little emphasis has been put on the importance of the pottery-making skills of the experimenter. An individual with limited experience with clay will have a difficult task making the simplest pot. The ease with which an experienced potter can hand-build a pot comes with years of experience. One way to perfect technical skills of pot making is to take a ceramics course, attend sessions in a private studio or study with traditional potters in their own village.

A studio that concentrates on instruction on the potters wheel can provide the opportunity to understand the fundamental properties of clay. The instructor may be interested in hand building and open pit firing, but due to public interest, limits instruction to modern ceramic methods. Such a potter can be the greatest ally in the search for natural clay, preparation of a functional paste, learning technical skills, and providing support facilities.

Once we come to the most challenging phase of all - the application of intense heat to the air-dried pottery. Even the most experienced potter feels excitement, apprehension and anticipation at each firing. In my next article I will discuss types of fuel, causes of success or failure, what to do with broken pots and how to cook in great pots.

PRIMITIVE POTTERY FIRING

By Maria-Louise Sidoroff

On SATURDAY MAY 11, 1991 we conducted an above the ground pottery firing within a full size replicated Lenape Village on an island in Waterloo Lake, part of the Waterloo Foundation for the Arts, Stanhope, New Jersey. The village has long houses, women's quarters, burial ground, carvings and artifacts to bring to life the culture of the N.J. Indians at the turn of the 17th century. Curator John Kraft invited a small group to fire some potter replications made from New Jersey clay and to begin to develop a pottery making area within the village.

Figure 1. TIME: 12:30pm - Pottery set close to fire, warming to 200-300° F (hot to touch).

Figure 2. TIME: 1:00pm - Setting up wind break against prevailing south-westerly winds.

Figure 3. TIME: 1:30pm - Burning logs and hot ashes moved to the side, platform of greenwood laid out on the ashes (large broken pottery fragment could also be used instead of greenwood platform to raise up pottery)

Figure 4. TIME: 2:00pm - Circle of fire around pots continues to slowly draw moisture from the clay.

Figure 5. TIME 2:30pm - "Tipi" of wood placed around very hot pottery. Circle of fire pushed inward until flames touch edge of logs in "tipi." Temperatures as high as 1700° have been documented through reading of thermocouples placed in the center of the fire. The fire felt very hot at this point, predominant wood: oak and ash.

Figure 6. TIME: 3:30pm - Pottery exposed.

Figure 7. TIME: 4:00pm - Fuel completely burned to ash.

Figure 8. TIME: 4:15pm - Sharla Azizi rolling hot pottery out of ashes.

A Method For Firing Primitive Pottery

by Evard Gibby

For those who have been experimenting with primitive pottery and are ready to fire some pieces, the following method, adapted from his booklet **HOW TO MAKE PRIMITIVE POTTERY,** is a simple and fairly successful technique.

The last step in making pottery, prior to using it, is to fire it. However, a fair warning is in order! This step is where your pottery is very vulnerable to breakage! But unfired pottery is of little use. So don't give up, keep trying and you will be rewarded with success at least part of the time!

Primitive peoples' firing methods ranged from simply building a fire over the pottery to using several kinds of kilns. This is a more common and practical method used for small pieces, such as cooking and eating bowls. Here is how to do it:

Scrape a shallow depression in the ground, about one inch deep and two feet in diameter. Place three pebbles on the ground on which each overturned pot will be suspended. Or lay a row of thumb-sized sticks under the pots. Lay a piece of cordwood, the same diameter as the height of the pots, on each side of them and across the ends in order to completely surround the pots with a heavy wood foundation. Leave a little space between the logs and the pots.

Next, a few dried cow chips are crumbled up in small pieces and added to cover the pottery. Then carefully lay a few more small logs across the foundation. Build a tepee fire on top of these logs and let the whole thing burn down to coals. The pottery should be allowed to cool slowly, but cooling down can be sped up by periodically scraping some of the coals away, and eventually lifting the pots out with some sticks. For best results firing should be done on a day with very little or no wind.

Pottery glowing bright red in the coals of a fire should indicate a firing temperature from 1300 to over 1600 degrees Fahrenheit. According to the **Chemistry And Physics Handbook's** Color of Heat Chart, an object heated to a dull red will be at about 1300 degrees Fahrenheit, and as it heats up to about 1600 degrees it will glow bright cherry red. Also according to Frank Hammer's **The Potter's Dictionary of Materials and Techniques,** the minimum temperature to accomplish a successful firing of pottery is 1112° F. So with this in mind, once the pottery reaches the glowing red-hot stage it can be assumed that it has fired hot enough to mature, and it can be allowed to start cooling down. This sort of wood firing with a few small pots should take roughly two hours or less, from start to finish.

The following chart shows the different stages of firing, and the appropriate temperature (degrees Fahrenheit) as each stage takes place.

TEMP.	COLOR OF POT	DESCRIPTION
0068		Water smoking begins. Pore water is driven off
0250		Water smoke complete
0390		Decomposition - vegetable matter begins to break down
0660		Ceramic change begins
	Clay changing to pottery	
1112		Minimum temp. to accomplish a f iring
1300	Dull Red	Ceramic change complete. Vitrification begins -body shrinks
1600	Cherry Red	
1700	Orange	
1830		Anything above this temp, alumo-silicates fuse into mullite crystals which strengthen the pot.
1850		Red Clays mature.
2100	Yellow	
2200		Red Clays melt
2300		Stone ware matures
2960		WhitePorcelin matures

Pottery glowing bright red in the hot coals of a wood fire should indicate a firing temperature of somewhere between 1300 to over 1600 degree fahrenheit, and according to the above information, should be adequately heated to mature the clay.

Various Containers

How To Cook In Primitive Pottery

In the summer of 1975 an experiment in replicating and utilizing a Middle Woodland Indian material culture was conducted. One goal in that experiment, besides manufacturing and utilizing many of the known tools of that time, was studying ceramic wares and cookery.

Almost all of the food that was cooked over the duration of the project was either roasted in coals or boiled in large clay pots. Although seemingly limited this allowed for considerable variety and was no great handicap. Variety was attained by eating many different foods, raw and cooked, and by cooking staple foods in different combination with other ingredients.

Our 14 primary ceramic pots were used for various jobs over the course of the project. Cooking and storing water were the most practical uses; hence these were the main functions. The third most common use for them was drawing water. This, however, was not very practical as they were hard to carry, fragile, and easily spilled.

The pots were kept together in close proximity to the hearth. The largest pot, because of its cumbersome size (5 gallon), was kept permanently in the top of a volcano-like mound of dirt with a ditch for a hearth encircling it. Fire could be positioned completely around the pot. This way the pot would not have to be elevated above the fire in a precarious manner. This container was too large to suspend on rocks, as most of us considered it too large and fine to risk having it fall over. Our solution however was not the best. The base of the pot was insulated by the dirt so the fire did not contact the base sufficiently enough to heat it without making a huge fire, wasting excessive fuel and human energy.

The pots, when used, were taken from the storage area to the hearth and propped up above the fire on three oblong rocks sunk into the dirt. This technique allowed for much greater contact area with the fire than with any other method and was definitely our favored way. Another method that was slightly inferior to this was placing the pot in a narrow ditch with

a fire built beneath. The pot made contact with the sides of the ditch to hold it in place. A fire could then be built up on either side of the pot and coals could be pushed underneath the pot to heat it *(see illustration)*.

Anywhere from one to four pots were used during a single meal. The ones that were not used for cooking were left permanently in the pot storage area and used for storing water.

Some of the pots that were broken during the project were repaired by various techniques. Some pots were cracked from firing and were too fragile to use for cooking. We applied a hot resin-wax mixture to these cracks with a crude brush made by chewing the end of a small twig. This did not add much strength to the pots but it did waterproof them so that they could be used as water storage jars.

One pot was repaired by drilling a hole on either side of the crack, lacing with gut, and then sealing the crack with hot resin-wax mixture. This was more time consuming but a much superior method.

Only a few of the pots we made exceeded the average hardness of the Indian pots we were replicating. If enough care were taken to choose the hottest burning woods and to dry them throughly, one could consistently make pots harder than the Middle Woodland pots.

In an effort to recognize research that has not been widely published, this paper fromThe Experimental Archeology Papers #4: The Pamunkey Project, Phase I and II (June 1976. p. 359-375), has been excerpted and reprinted by permission of the editor, Errett Callahan, PhD. The Pamunkey Project was a multi-phase experimental program in living archaeology concerned with Middle and Late Woodland Indian subsistence living. Ceramics and Cookery At the Pamunkey Site, Phase II, by Charles Paquin. Virginia Commonwealth University.

Wear

As far as evidence of use goes, breakage from handling and cracks from thermal shock during usage were definitely the most radical alterations that occurred to our pots. The only other types of wear that I noticed were slight pits on the bottom of the cooking pots caused by the hearth stones they were placed on, minute scrape marks on the insides of some pots caused by shells used for eating, stirring and cleaning, and heavy blackening on the outside from the fire.

I wanted to see what would happen if I had each person rate all the cooking pots in terms of their preference. I noticed that the pots that appeared to be the best replicas were the most preferred. Pots that were not shaped well, that were thinner or thicker than their Indian counterparts and thus more fragile, and pots that were smaller than average were not favored for use. This held true for all the pots except for one especially well-built small pot and the largest one which, while being one of the better replicas, was too large to be practical.

For most of our boiling needs, our team of 7 to 8 adults required pots of around 1 gallon capacity. Except for smaller individual eating bowls, we had little need for pots much smaller than a gallon volume.

We had almost exactly 1/3 the breakage during Phase II as Phase I. Through discussion and reflection, the following criteria were determined to be the major factors in our improved success rate of use:

During Phase I -   8 of us broke 16 pots in 4 weeks.
During Phase II -   7 of us broke 4 pots in 3 weeks.

1- The pots were thinner
2- The coils were more thoroughly joined
3- The exteriors were more extensively paddled
4- The pots were more carefully pre-heated and fired and thus harder and without hair-line cracks
5- The pots were more carefully handled

Table A	Phase I	Phase II
Major pots made	25	32
Pots taken to site	23	22
Made at site	1	
Pots broken at site	16	4
Broken prior	2	8
Returning whole and usable	7	19

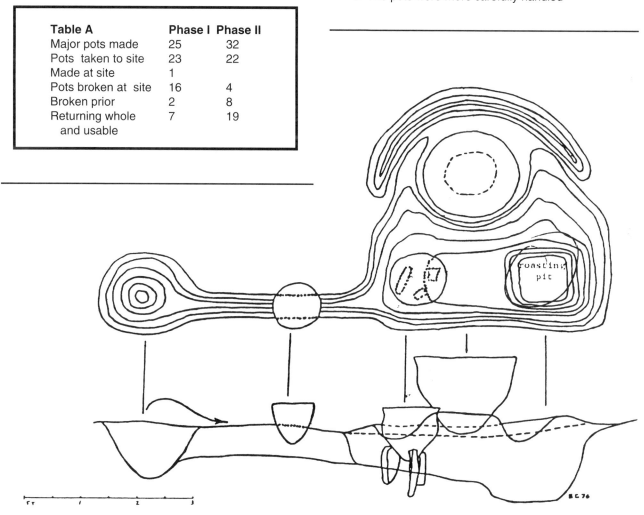

Figure 1. Phase II Open Hearth System

A similar project was undertaken this spring at *Boulder Outdoor Survival School.* 14 students used one 4 gallon pot to cook all of their meals for a period of 11 days. Instruction on preheating, handling, and general use was given to make sure that a consistent method was used to reduce the chance of breaking. We used a superbly crafted Anasazi corrugated pot provided by John Olson and Duane Stout of *Prehistoric Pottery Replicas* in Hurricane, Utah. We also used some low-fire tea pots and bowls that ended up exploding from the thermal shock of the combined heat and moisture. **The following tips and guidelines come from our experience which gave us considerable insight into the skill of cooking with primitive ceramic pots**.

- *One person is responsible for the use, care, and handling of the pot for each meal. Too many cooks can literally spoil the pot.*
- *Never lift the pot by its rim-empty or full. Always use two hands to support it from the bottom, especially when hot and/or full.*
- *Fill the pot with about one half more water than you expect to use. Boiling and loss of water that transpires through the pot will reduce the final amount of moisture left for the cooking process.*
- *Always set the pot in a depression in the sand and never in a location where it might be kicked or knocked over.*
- *A small flamming fire of small twigs will heat the pot in minutes. Use only finger-sized sticks to produce maximum heat efficiency and less charcoal residue.*

-Use a key-hole fire(as in the left half of Fig. 1) if you wish to boil and bake at the same time. Willow fish wickets may be propped over the pot fire to broil fish and meat while the pot boils.
- Firmly place three stones in the fire pit to support the pot. The pot must be suspended above the ground and fire, as the sand and damp pot do not adequately conduct heat for efficient results.
- Preheat the pot of water next to the fire before putting it on the support rocks. Wait for water to be visible on the lower portion of the pot, and let it warm slowly before putting it into the fire.
- Use your hands to place the warmed pot on the fire. This lets you feel the temperature of the pot and demands care in placing the pot on the support stones.
- Tip the pot sufficiently to one side so that you can keep an eye on the contents without constantly having to lean over the fire pit.
- Keep a stir stick handy incase the water overheats and begins to boil over. Stir down any boiling to keep food from spilling over and burning to the outside of the pot.
- Use a pair of lifting sticks and a steady partner to lift the hot pot from the flames (lifting sticks are two stout green sticks (willows) cut down with stone blades). They were laid along the sides at the bottom of the pot and gently maneuvered underneath by a team of two people. At a given count, the sticks were lifted slightly and held under the pot only high enough to clear the edge of the fire pit.
-Do not leave leftovers in the pot overnight. The moisture will seep out, leaving a dried-on mess. Place all leftovers into a gourd or wooden bowl. In case you must leave food in the pot, cover the top with a sandstone or bark slab to keep the contents moist until morning.
- When cleaning the pot, place it into a depression in the sand to give support to the walls and reduce stress on the pot as it is scrubbed. Burned-on foods may require scraping with a bone to dislodge large pieces, and sanding with a sandstone scouring stone to clean the pot. A final cleaning can be done with Equisetum (Scouring Rush).
- Prior to packing it into the pack basket, scrub the outside of the pot with dry sand and bark to remove excess soot.

INTRODUCTION TO NORTHWEST COAST WOODWORK

Text and Illustrations By Gregg Blomberg © 1992

When Captain Cook visited the Northwest coast of North America in 1778, he commented on the natives' "great dexterity in works of wood . . " Cook was surprised by the quality and quantity of the wood work he found. He was paying tribute to what were perhaps the world's premier wood craftsmen.

The art and craft of the people of the coast was easy to admire. The natives wove wonderful and complex blankets of mountain goat wool mixed with domesticated dog hair or finely worked cedar bark. They crafted gracefully designed beautifully imbricated basketry, including wonderfully woven hats and baskets tight enough to hold water. These artistic people worked cooper, stone shell and bone into objects from hunting and fishing equipment to jewelry and healing charms. Almost every article they used was decorated by painting and/or by working into sculptural form. The designs used usually represented clan and family crests and personal spirit helpers, mostly mythical animals.

For all of the coast natives' diverse skills, woodworking was their forte. Their houses were great wooden structures 100 feet and more in length with mortised beams and huge carved supporting poles.

Of all the carvings, the totem poles displaying their family crests and their wonderfully carved seaworthy canoes are the best known. Living on the salt water fjords and inlets of the northwest, their form of transportation was by canoe. The graceful boats they built were worthy of a people born of the sea. Some of the larger craft were 65' long and could hold 2 or 3 dozen people with ease. The style of their canoes varied from group to group along the 1200 mile long coast. In the southern part of the area the Westcoast or Nuu-chan-nulth took 8-man 36' long craft far out to sea in search of whales. It was common for them to take 50' gray whales. For these seafolk hunting for seal on the high seas and fishing the halibut banks out of sight of land was routine. The northern groups would often undertake journeys of hundreds of miles for trade and plunder.

The coast people had a great sense of drama and made a wide variety of masks that ranged from portrait masks to mythical beasts and birds with 5' beaks.

Many of the masks were animated: eyeballs rolled, tongues wagged, flippers propelled them through mythical waves, beaks and jaws clacked and bit. Some of the masks fit right onto a performer's face, but forehead masks and frontlets that allowed vision underneath were at least as popular. Some of the complex masks would open to reveal another mask inside, hardly a project for the beginning carver.

To truly appreciate the effectiveness of these dramatic performances, it would be necessary to attend one. The whirl of the dancers in the center of the great cedar house as the flickering fire illuminated the fantastic beasts, combined with the shouts, singing and beat of the drums, makes for high excitement indeed. These performances are very sophisticated. The mood may change from serene to intensely dramatic to comic. Varied rhythms add even more texture. Spectators may be threatened by a grotesque beast or join in taunting a cosmic clown.

The Coast aboriginals staged elaborate feasts, enjoying as they did the abundance of the Northwest coast. The treen in which these foods were served became another area of carver's excellence. Bowls, spoons and ladles often resembled the canoes with raised ends and graceful sheer. Many bowls were made to resemble animals, a seal perhaps, head and flippers extending from the ends with a fat hollowed-out body. Some bowls have inlays of abalone, operculum or coppper and/or are covered with incised Northern Formline designs. Many feast dishes were 6' or more long. Ladles and bowls were sometimes made of steam-bent and carved mountain sheep horn in place of the more familiar wood.

Another area of interest and excellence on the Northwest coast was bent-corner box making. Bent-corner boxes have their sides made from a single plank which has been kerfed, steamed and bent into a box. The open corner is then pegged or sewn together, a bottom board is added and a top made if desired. The native peoples of the northwest coast used these boxes for storage, as water buckets and even boiled food by dropping red hot rocks into them with tongs. The height of box making was reached by the northern peoples who made huge chests, often with massive lids and fully carved and painted sides. Some of these chests have figures projecting from them so realistic one expects they will jump free of the box and begin to dance around the fire. These boxes born of water and fire have the special magic common to objects from the Northwest coast.

The woods selected by the natives varied according to the item and its use. Certainly red cedar was the most important and has the added advantage of rot resistance invaluable in this rainy climate. It was used for houses, canoes

(more)

Gregg Blomberg is the owner of Kestrel Tools, specializing in tools, books and classes on Northwest Coast carving techniques. His dedication to the art and culture of the northwest are admirable. For a catalog, contact him at: Rt 1, Box 1762, Lopez, WA 98261. Complete reprints of the adze, bent box, ladle, and other articles are available for a small fee. Please honor all copyrights.

and totem poles. Even the bark of the cedar was important for use as clothing and cordage. For masks some tribal groups used cedar extensively. Its light weight made it the obvious choice for the larger dance masks. Red alder was often chosen as a mask wood for portrait masks and frontlets. Alder is fine grained and relatively easy to work. Yellow cedar, maple and yew were other woods of importance. Carvings were usually made in green wood and cured after.

Prior to the wide-spread availability of iron, the wood working tools used on the NW Coast included wedges of antler, adzes with stone and bone blades, and knives of fragile but extremely sharp mussel shell, flakes of jadite and other stone. Beaver teeth were hafted and provided a very effective cutting edge. Chisels, hammers, mauls and drills of stone and bone completed the tool kit.

Iron tools were not unknown prior to white contact. At the Ozette site on the Olympic peninsula, evidence of 28 iron tools was recovered, this from a site dated 440 years BP. The origin of the iron is subject to conjecture but it could have come from the orient and been traded in a series of exchanges across the Bering Strait and eventually down the coast. Other objects of aboriginal trade were known to make journeys nearly that tortuous. It is also likely that small amounts showed up in boat wreckage and other flotsam from the Orient via the Japanese current which even today brings glass balls and Chinese light bulbs to the beaches of the Northwest coast. Captain Cook in 1778 noted that iron was not scarce in Nootka sound. He described some of the iron chisels in use as being eight to ten inches long and 3 or 4 inches broad.

There are curved knives not wholly unlike the present coast tools in the Japanese tool tradition but there is no reason to suspect that the crooked knife was not an independent invention of the woodworkers of the Northwest coast. These are, after all, sculptor's tools and especially adapted to hollowing. Northwest Coast craftsmen were supreme sculptors and many if not most of their carvings required hollowing. Since Northwest coast craftsmen were very inventive and competent designers in every other realm, it follows that tool design was another area of their excellence. Captain Cook's journal goes on to describe the knives. "The blades of the knives were crooked something like a pruning knife . . the most of them were about the breadth and thickness of an iron hoop and were certainly of their own forming and helving." In Dixon's 1787 account of the knives at Nootka Sound, he states "a fondness for carving and sculpture was discovered amongst these people by Captain Cook: iron implements were then also in use; and their knives are so very thin that they bend them into a variety of forms which answer their every purpose." So it seems crooked knives were part of the aboriginal carvers' kit at least from the earliest white contact.

An interesting hafted knife was recently found at Hoko River not far from Ozette that dates an impressive 2800 BP. Its curved blade is quartz crystal. This elegant little knife may represent a real predecessor to the modern crooked knife.

For about 100 years after the coming of the Anglos, the Northwest coast cultures experienced a florescence of art. This was due in part to the material prosperity brought about by increased trade. Ultimately the original peoples were all but destroyed by the diseases of the whites and by missionaries and other zealots who banned tribal ceremony and burned masks and totems to otherwise "civilize" the natives.

Fortunately today there is a new renaissance of art and energy. The popularity of collecting contemporary coast art is actively energizing coast craftsworkers to produce new works of art. The work draws heavily on the traditions of the past with plenty of vitality to create new directions and adapt to new media. Today NW coast art is becoming more widely known. Wood carvers everywhere are challenged and intrigued by the imagination shown by the old NW coast sculptors.

The inspiration left by the early northwest cultures is available to us through thousands of examples in museums and private collections located throughout the world. Almost every major US and Canadian museum has a collection of NW coast art. The museums of the northwest have fine collections. Wonderful examples can also be seen at the Museum of Civilization, Ottawa; The Heye Foundation, NYC; the Museum of Natural History, NYC; the Smithsonian, Washington DC; the Field Museum, Chicago; the Peabody Museum at Yale, the Milwaukee Public Museum; the University Museum, University of Pennsylvania; and the Denver Museum of Natural History. For those not fortunate enough to live on the northwest coast or within reach of one of those museums, there are books. Luckily literature on NW coast art has flourished along with the renaissance of the art.

There is no worthy how-to-do-it book covering all aspects of Northwest coast art. In fact the commonly available book **How To Carve Totem Poles** advocates carvings that could be called folk art but which bear little resemblance to classic Northwest coast work. Those carvers with a real interest must use their ingenuity to learn. Any serious student will eventually need to master the northern formline design. This design system is the basis for northern art and provides a useful background for the art of the southern coast as well. Bill Holm's landmark book **Northwest Coast Indian Art** has been the standard for over thirty years on this subject.

There are classes in various aspects of the art available on the coast. Novice carvers typically begin by replication of pieces in books and museums. Beginning with ladles and bowls will aquaint the student with the tools and techniques used. Careful study should eventually result in pieces of your own inspiration made in the northwest coast style. For aficionados, the exploration of this intriguing art form and culture is full of excitement and delight. That there can be so much adventure still pervading this art is yet another tribute to these original peoples.

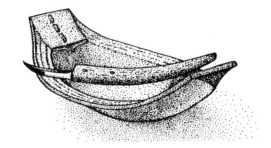

Bent-Corner Box Making
Text and Illustrations By Gregg Blomberg © 1991

STEPS IN KNIFE KERFING A BOARD

1. Lay out lines. It may help to diagram kerfs on the edges of the board too.
2. Cut to depth with a knife. Take care not to go too deep. Keep knife vertical. Do not cut overwide or joints will be sloppy. If you need to, use a straight edge to guide knife.

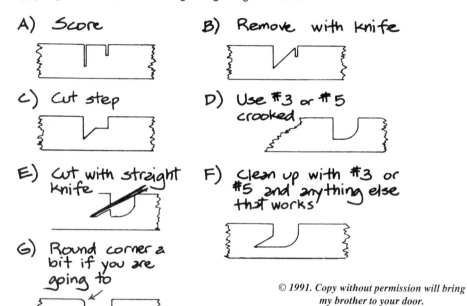

A) Score

B) Remove with knife

C) Cut step

D) Use #3 or #5 crooked

E) Cut with straight knife

F) Clean up with #3 or #5 and anything else that works

G) Round corner a bit if you are going to

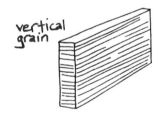

vertical grain

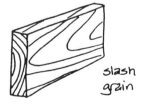

slash grain

Vertical grain lumber (top) usually bends better than slash grain. Woods that work best have a long fiber grain (red cedar, Alaska cedar, spruce, and hemlock). **Experiment.**

KERFING ALTERNATIVES *

Alternatives to kerfing with a knife are using a router, a radial arm saw, or - my favorite - hand sawing with a Japanese Azebiki flooring saw. To do that, clamp a depth stop to the side of the saw. A piece of plexiglass works well.

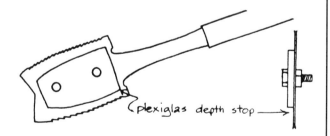

plexiglas depth stop →

I slotted out the saw and drilled holes through the depth stop for the bolts. Be sure to make the cut perpendicular (90 degrees). You can saw the full depth side and knife-cut the rounded side. Use of the Azebiki will insure a uniform depth of kerf. A radial arm saw will make these cuts as well.

KERFS FOR BENT-CORNER BOXES

At right is a corner (shown open and closed) used as a wider rim for inlays. Of course the larger the kerf the larger the radius of the bend. Most aboriginal boxes had corners that were quite square. 1/4" is about as small as is practical to cut. A 5/16" kerf is quite common. It takes a hot-wet steam for 45 minutes. Bending the wood very green is helpful.Keep green wood wet until you are ready to use it. The green wood makes it easier to carve out top and bottom boards as well as helping the kerf start to bend with minimal split out. The 90 degree kerf at left is the "southern" corner. The boxes made using these corners are suprisingly strong. A beginner should knife-cut kerfs.

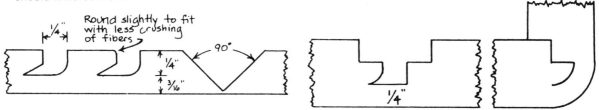

TYPICAL OLD KERFS

Many old boxes have kerfs that are much more crude than these. Bill Holm's research shows that it is the rare old box that comes up tight against the inside plane of the side. Usually the bevel shows inside the corner (below left).

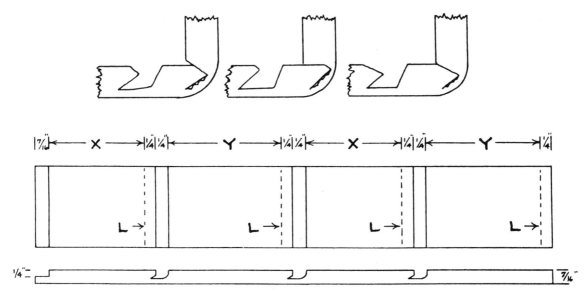

TO LAY OUT A BOARD FOR KERFING

X and Y amounts are equal for a square box. If a rectangular box is desired, make X sides one dimension, and Y sides the other. L- lines show the space that will be taken by the corner laps.

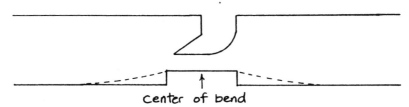

center of bend

Using a thicker board allows a tapering of the sides after bending, thus giving more "life" to an otherwise straight sided box. Cut out the outside as shown or merely score the lines with a knife or the Azebiki saw. The extra wood at the corner will pop out upon bending.

STEAMING THE BOARD

A. By fortuitous circumstance, 6" stove pipe fits right into a #10 can. Use this simple set-up for box sides under 6". A roll of hardware cloth keeps the board out of the water. Stuff a rag into the top to slow the escape of steam.

B. A Simple Box Steamer. Board is propped upon sticks. Cover with a plywood board. Use a 6" to 5" reducer on the top.

C. Box steamer using a propane crab cooker and a gas can for the steam. This works well for boxes up to 10" wide and 6' long. To steam one corner at a time, use separate top boards and fill the gaps with towels.

Opinions vary on how long to steam, depending on kerf, wood, and other variables. Twenty minutes of hot-wet steam will bend green wood beautifully with little or no fray out. It may be necessary to steam longer on dry wood.

David Wescott

Bent-wood box , spoons and tools by Norm Kidder.

FITTING THE TOP/BOTTOM

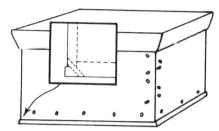

Pegging the bottom on was done through the sides and into the bottom. The joint at the side of the box was done at odd angles for strength. Spruce root was used to sew the boxes together as well. Refer to Hilary Stewart's <u>Cedar</u> for illustrations.

Dome top lid projected over the sides of the box.

Kwakiutl "marriage box" lid. The storage boxes these lids were fit onto often had distinctive texturing rather than carved or painted designs.

Many chest lids were thick with dramatically flaring sides. For weight and wood stability they were hollowed out. Crisscross with a skill saw and finish with adze and knife

Tlingit "red corner" box lid was simply dished out a bit.

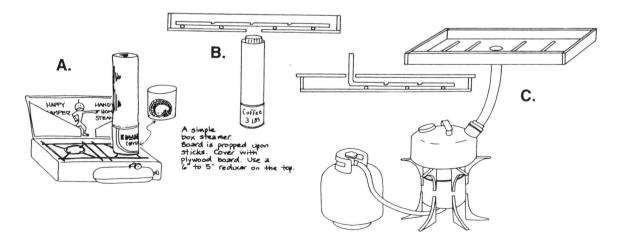

How To Make A Northwest Coast Elbow Adze

The adze and crooked knife form the nucleus of the northwest carver's tool kit. The elbow adze is useful, beautiful and not difficult to make.

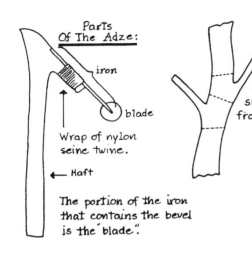

Parts Of The Adze:

iron

blade

Wrap of nylon seine twine.

← Haft

The portion of the iron that contains the bevel is the "blade".

Obtain a suitable crook from a hardwood tree.

To lay out your adze make sure you have satisfied Holm's constant. (explained below.)

Make or obtain your iron before actually cutting out your haft · so as to check relationships

Remove the "cheeks" from the crook.

Layout should be pretty much in line with tree's trunk.

Typical Adze Blades

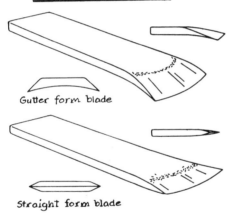

Gutter form blade

Straight form blade

Straight form adze irons are used for shaping and finishing. Gutter form blades have cross·grain cutting ability · so are good for hollowing and roughing. The blade must have some bevel on the top surface. This bevel gives necessary clearance to the stroke and aids in bringing the blade out of the work. Blade angle of 20°-25° is correct for most uses.

No bevel on top· blade will not work.

20°-25°

Make blade of 1¼" × ³⁄₁₆" or 1¼" × ¼" CARBON TOOL STEEL.

Holm's Constant

"The edge of a shaping adze blade must be at right (90°) angle to the first finger." This principle insures a working tool· ie. insures the adze will enter a flat piece of wood and leave it, taking a chip on the way. If the 90° comes too high up the haft all the adze will want to do is bite or jab. If too low the blade will be unable to "reach" the work with a normal in·the·wrist adzing motion.

The principle outlined to the left shows that the angle of the haft and its design are interrelated with the length of the iron and the bevel or drop of its blade. The more acute the angle of the haft, the longer the iron must be and vice·versa. Use a right triangle, make a mock·up iron of stiff cardboard and play with the relationships.

After you have your layout· cut out haft and shape with crooked knife and/or rasp.

Install iron with stainless hose clamp and try the adze. Fine tune if necessary.

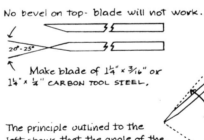

90°

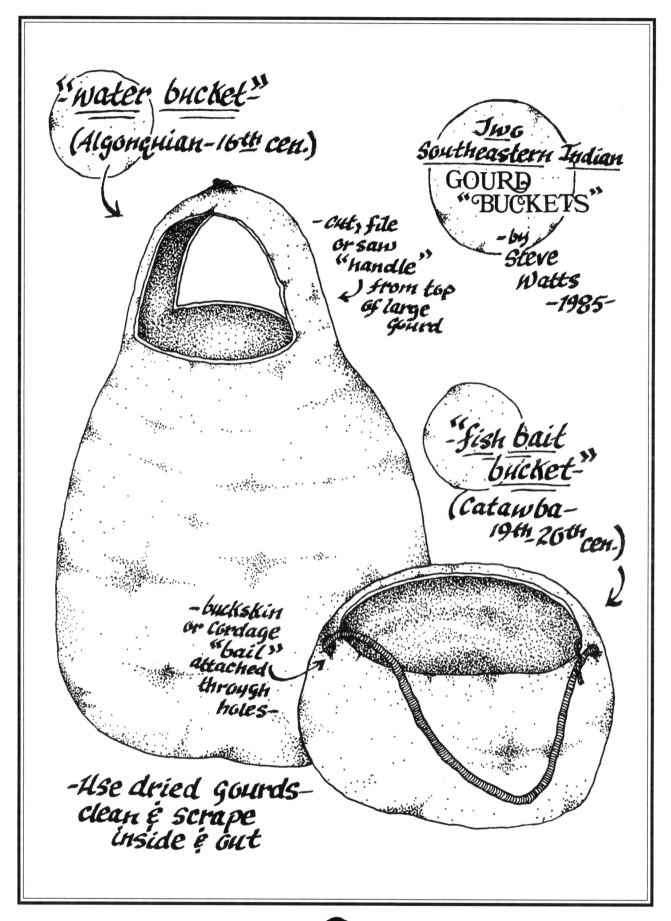

"water bucket"
(Algonquian - 16th cen.)

Two Southeastern Indian GOURD "BUCKETS"
- by Steve Watts -1985-

- cut, file or saw "handle" from top of large gourd

"fish bait bucket"
(Catawba - 19th-20th cen.)

- buckskin or cordage "bail" attached through holes -

- Use dried gourds - clean & scrape inside & out

Barking Up the Right Tree.....CONSTRUCTION OF
THE JUNIPER BARK BERRY BASKET

Text, Photos, and Illustrations By Jim Riggs, © 1993

After attending the 1990 Rivercane Rendezvous in northern Georgia in mid April, I made a trip up into North Carolina to visit my old pal Doug Elliot. Having made dozens of one-piece folded and laced bark baskets using Western Juniper (*Juniperus occidentalis*) here in Easter Oregon, one of my goals while in the Southeast was to gain experience making some Tulip Poplar baskets to note firsthand the similarities or differences in the materials and process. I figured I could find no better teacher than Doug--his house is bedecked with literally hundreds of them, more styles, sizes and forms than any one person could seemingly imagine, let alone produce!

During a marathon day-hike through "his" forest (alien to Western me--"What's this Doug? And this? What's this used for?"), we found a young Tulip Poplar freshly cut and left by loggers (it had been in their way). Later in the hike we fortuitously encountered a hickory

sapling bruised, scarred and bent over as loggers had removed other trees. Doug's eyes lit up (Well, his eyes are really never un-lit!) and he showed me how to strip long narrow lengths of bark from the base to the top of the tree. We then split outer from inner bark, coiled and kept the latter for our lacing material. We also cut through several outer growth rings of the wood proper at the base and peeled away splints for the basket rim reinforcement hoops. It pleased us that all necessary materials for several baskets had been salvaged from other's waste. Back at Doug's place we began the actual basket construction, ... but he's already explained all that.

Aboriginal Bark Containers

In the arid Northern Great Basin and semi-arid interior Columbia River Plateau regions of the Pacific Northwest, most of the Native-produced folded bark baskets I've seen appear to be made of Western Juniper. While I've not experimented with them yet, the Common Juniper (*Juniperus communis*), the Rocky Mountain Juniper (*Juniperus scopulorum*)

and perhaps others should also work. In the moister forests of Northern Idaho and western Montana westward to the Cascade Mountains and coasts of Oregon, Washington and British Columbia, Natives used mainly bark of the Western Redcedar (*Thuja plicata*), occasionally Alaska Yellow Cedar (*Chamaecyparis nootkatensis*), and minimally a few others not identified in my available literature. *(For an illustrated informative article, "Cedar Bark Baskets" by Mary D. Schlick, describing contemporary rejuvination of the craft by a Native Yakima man, see American Indian Basketry magazine, Vol. IV, No. 3, Issue No. 15).*

To my current knowledge the actual antiquity of aboriginally produced bark containers in the Northwest is not known. Standing Redcedars in the Southern Washington Cascades showing old bark removal scars--ostensibly peeled for one-piece folded baskets--having been dated by growth ring counts to a little over 200 years ago. Most museum specimens with data seem to be of post-contract, ethnographic acquisition: although I've not undertaken thorough research, I know of no bark containers of this style that have been found in an archaeological context and subsequently dated. Exhaustive research into aboriginal one-piece folded bark containers is obviously someone's Master's Thesis begging to happen, but if you really want to just make you own bark baskets of juniper, read on!

Jim Riggs is a naturalist, author, and skilled craftsman living in northeast Oregon. He is well known for his knowledge and technical abilities in the arts and skills of the Great Basin Native Americans. He has much to share and say on the suject - here's another example. He may be contacted by writing PO Box 672, Wallowa, OR 97885.

These examples of one-piece folded baskets of Western Juniper bark from the Harney County Museum, Burns, Oregon, illustrating considerable variation in construction and craftsmanship. They are included here as examples from the past that may compliment contemporary construction and reinforce our ties with the past. Burns is within the Northern Paiute culture area, but it is not known for certain if the 2 baskets were of local manufacture. The lacing and trim materials are not positively identified. Age is unknown, but portions of commercial cloth on each indicate at least use during post-contact times. Some measurements are included, but are not complete.

LEFT EXAMPLE
HEIGHT - corner to rim = 15"
HEIGHT - ctr. of bottom to rim = 12 5/8"
DIAMETER - at mouth = 6 3/4"
CIRCUMFERENCE - at middle = 19"

This is a finely crafted specimen showing external scoring at the base and tightly-laced rim. A cloth strip wrapped twice around the body with two-ply, hand-twisted plant fiber cordage tied to that appear to form part of the carrying strap. Another continuous length of 2-ply cordage runs through periodic rim lacing holes and "chain-links" back under itself around the entire rim circumference. The specific function of this neatly affixed cordage is not known.

RIGHT EXAMPLE
HEIGHT - corner to rim = 17"
DIAMETER - at mouth = 7 1/8"
CIRCUMFERENCE - at middle =
                19 3/4"

This is a more crudely made specimen of much thicker bark. The bottom has not been scored, but appears more to have been "mashed and manipulated" to shape as the sides were folded up. The top is not evenly trimmed and the rim binding is not continuously wrapped. A knotted length of 2-ply cloth "rope" affixed to one side of the rim appears to be part of a carrying strap.

Tools For the Task

As an aboriginal process, construction of a juniper bark basket from selection and procurement of the raw materials all the way through to the finishing touches encompasses a number of well-defined sequential steps, each facilitated by the employment and application of appropriate knowledge, tools and action. In my advanced Aboriginal Skills courses I've found it an excellent project involving multiple primitive technologies and skills using only natural materials and replicated aboriginal tools--No steel allowed! So keep that "basket idea lightbulb" (Oops, they haven't been invented yet -- let's try "flame") glowing in your mind, but first you have to manufacture the tools. These include:

1. A percussion flaked hand axe or "chopper" of obsidian, chert, basalt, etc., used to outline and groove through the bark panel on the tree and to initially pry up the bark edges for peeling. While some Acheulian hand axes were works of art, yours need not be as long as it works. Sometimes you can just find a fortuitously shaped and sized rock that, with minimal edge retouching will suffice. Hafted edge-ground axes and celts also work fine.

2. Spalled obsidian flake blades for trimming and scoring the bark, cutting lacing materials, etc. It's a good idea to back these (dull all but the intended cutting edge) so that bark and finger trimmings don't occur simultaneously!

3. A pressure flaked stone drill, usually chert or basalt for strength, hafted with sinew, pitch, hide glue, etc., to a straight shaft for hand drilling side and rim lacing holes.

4. Occasionally a "spud" for prying the bark panel from the tree. This could range from an appropriately shaped, unmodified antler tine to a stick found on the spot and modified to a chisel shaped and using hand axe, flake knives or by simply abrading to shape on a gritty rock. If you're not inclined to be a purist Abo, just employ correspondingly appropriate modern tools. You'll learn less, but you'll still be making a bark basket.

Selecting a Suitable Tree

Unlike Tulip Poplars where most of the bark from a single tree can be utilized, juniper species in general are not noted for growing tall, straight, unbranched nor clear-barked. You may have to scour dozens of trees before finding an unblemished and sizeable enough panel of bark suitable for making one basket. Denser stands of junipers will usually have proportionately more cleaner-barked, branchless portions of trunks than bushier trees growing in the open. It is rare to find any single tree that will yield multiple suitable panels of bark. Trees about one foot in diameter are excellent. On much larger trees both the furrowed outer bark and the cambium are proportionately thicker, harder to cut through and peel from the trunk and harder to accurately manipulate later in the process. However, huge-based junipers often branch into several parallel smaller trunks; you may have to exercise the ape in you to climb up and survey them, but the sides of those facing each other, especially when shaded by dense outer foliage, are often quite free of twigs and knots. Clear sections of larger limbs will also work.

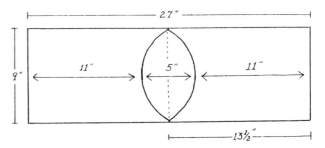

Template for average sized & proportioned Aboriginal Western Juniper bark basket.

To replicate a typically proportioned aboriginal basket you are looking for a clear panel of bark approximately three times longer than wide. While aboriginal examples I've seen have ranged from quart-size and smaller up to baskets that could hold several gallons, the most common initial panel dimensions are 9-11" wide by 27-33" long. The surface should be as free as possible of any branch stubs, major scars or deep "dives" where the bark furrows down into the wood. These irregularities don't mean that cleanly removing the panel is impossible, just potentially more difficult. Since normally only a single vertically oriented rectangle of bark is removed from any one tree, the tree is not completely girdled and thus does not die.

Removing the Bark Panel from the Tree

When I've found what appears to be a suitable panel I strip and peel off the roughest of the flakey-to-shaggy outer bark; it usually comes off in long strips. This sometimes reveals initially unnoticed flaws making the panel less desirable, but it also reduces unnecessary thickness of extraneous outer bark that you'd have to chop through with the hand axe. On most panels you can safely strip the brownish outer bark down to the depth of any furrows, but slow down when the newly exposed layers of bark begin to show a more reddish-purple color. The white cambium lies just beneath this. At this stage you needn't remove all extraneous bark; more can be cosmetically peeled later after the basket is bent to shape.

Using a chert hand axe to score the bark

Depending on the style and sharpness of your hand axe, you might want to wear a glove. Using glancing, chopping, overlapping blows, outline the perimeter of your panel. If possible, make the panel an inch or so wider than necessary so a longitudinal strip can later be cut from along one entire edge to be used for the rim reinforcement hoop. Once you have the panel clearly delineated, use your hand axe as a grooving tool. Hold it with both hands, apply pressure and side it back and forth in the cut to connect all the chop marks and deepen the groove all the way through the cambium to the wood proper. The cambium will be whitish and the wood more a yellow-tan. It is especially important to make sure the cambium is cleanly grooved through to the wood in the top and bottom horizontal cuts; any still-connected spots there can cause splits in your panel if you're a bit careless in peeling it from the tree.

Using hands and arms to "fist" a panel of bark from the tree.

Loosen the bark carefully using fingers and tools, beginning at the corners.

Begin at or near a corner in one side groove and, with fingers or the point of the hand axe, gently pry under and lift the edge. Work fingers or axe up and down, sliding under the bark, until an inch or so along the entire edge of the panel is free. If you're peeling during an optimal sap flow and the bark seems to be separating easily from the trunk, just continue shoving your fingers and hands further under the bark, then up or down toward each end. On a large panel, if working under from only one side becomes awkward, repeat the initial edge-lifting along the opposite side and work back toward the already-freed area. If the bark is being a bit stubborn and finger and hand pressure are insufficient to cause separation, use a "spud" or pry bar, but carefully! Prying too forcefully at any one spot may easily split the bark. Also be extra careful when freeing the panel at the top and bottom cuts (end grain of the bark) where splits are most likely to occur. Never try to just pull the slab off from one side or to back-bend it severely-it will split for sure. Sometimes a few splits are inevitable. Short ones at the ends will be held in check later when the reinforcing rim is laced in place. Longer splits can be laced closed before the basket is bent to shape, but splits that extend more than half the length of the panel, even when laced closed, can make folding the bottom difficult without worsening them.

The main ingredient in successfully removing the bark panel reasonably undamaged is to begin slowly and carefully to "get the feel" of the material, then proceed accordingly. When the sap is extra juicy I've had panels literally pop free with very little coaxing. When more finesse is required, it is similar to carefully fisting the hide from a deer. Steel knives, axeheads, flat pry bars, etc., will of course work, but cause more unnecessary bruises, gouges, slices and splits in the bark than "kinder and gentler" methods.

In my experience in Eastern Oregon I've found June into early August the optimal period for peeling bark without much difficulty. Years of drought or excessive moisture can vary those parameters. Typical Western Juniper habitat is a fairly arid environment though, and by late August many trees are too dry to peel. There are alternatives however, and one failed attempt need not mean another won't work. Moisture content can vary considerable between individual trees. Try trees growing more densely, thus more shaded, higher elevation trees, trees growing closer to a direct water source or the north side of a tree instead of the sun-baked south side. Conversely, in earlier spring, the "pre-warmed" south sides of lower elevation trees may be ripe for easy bark removal.

Your freshly removed bark panel is best scored and bent to shape within a couple hours of peeling or it may dry too much and become brittle. Sealing slabs in your standard large-sized aboriginal plastic garbage bags can keep them malleable for several days. Panels that have dried too much can be soaked in water until pliability returns, or even more quickly reconstituted by thoroughly wetting, sealing in a black plastic bag and placing in direct sun for a few hours.

Scoring and Folding the Bark Panel

If you planned your rim reinforcement to come from your bark panel, lay the bark out, cambium side up, and cut that approximately one inch wide strip from along the entire length of one side of the slab (Other rim options are discussed later).

Now measure and mark the midpoint of the panel's length with a straight line across its width (I use a piece of charcoal from the campfire). You don't need a tape measure; just stretch a piece of cordage to the length of the bark, then fold it in half to mark the midpoint. Now draw a symmetrical "bipointed ellipse" (this is a contradiction of definitions that says exactly what I mean, "eye-shape" or "football-shape") with its points and midline aligned along the midline of the bark (I hope you're not feeling overly maligned by my instructions yet!) The tips of the points should barely reach, or remain a hair short of, the bark margins. The width of the ellipse will be the width of the bottom of the basket. The width and shape of the ellipse, in relation to the width and length of the bark panel,

will largely determine the shape or style of the finished basket. A narrow ellipse will dictate a flatter, more "flask-like" shaped basket; a broader ellipse will produce a rounder, more cylindrical basket. Either way, the ellipse must come to a point at each side for the ensuing fold to bend and overlap properly. Most of the aboriginal juniper bark baskets I've seen were of the broader-bottomed, more cylindrical style.

The next step is to score or groove the entire circumference of the ellipse to a depth of approximately one third to one half the thickness of the cambium layer. Be careful not to cut all the way through! I use a sharp obsidian flake (large enough to hold securely) and cut a V-shaped "trough", slicing out the cambium from inside the "V". The V-cut or kerf allows the sides to fold up with less binding. Inside scoring appears to be the prevalent method on the aboriginal juniper bark baskets I've looked at, but the two examples illustrated here from the Harney County Museum, Burns, OR differ. One is neatly scored from the barkside (outside) as is most commonly done with poplar baskets. I personally believe the smoother, more uniform outer poplar bark lends itself to outside scoring more efficiently than the shaggier, more uneven-thicknessed juniper or even redcedar bark, where it is easier to error in determining appropriate cut depth. The other basket is much cruder overall, and appears to have not been scored at all, but more "mashed and manipulated" to adequate shape as the sides were bent up. An intermediate method on some abo bark baskets (that I've not tried yet) involves no actual cutting, but rather delineating the foldline along the ellipse by deeply compressing the cambium fibers with a wedge-ended stick used as a stylus. I imagine the spud, or similarly shaped antler, bone or stone would work as well. These variations illustrate that no single method is prescribed, even within a single culture area, nor considered "the only right way" to insure the bark will fold exactly where you want it to.

By whatever means, method or madness you've scored your panel, you are ready to form the basket by folding the sides up. Remember, the bottom is not going to be flat--as the sides are bent upward, the points of the ellipse must be free to bend downward. Thus, laying the bottom over a rounded such as your leg or a small log gives you a solid surface to press against without inhibiting downward movement of the

Apply pressure evenly and provide support with whatever means you can devise.

points. To begin the fold I like to spread one hand across the ellipse, thumb at one point and remaining fingers evenly spaced across to the other, and apply downward pressure, more concertedly at the points, as the other hand gently coaxes one side panel upward. Evenly distributed support and pressure from your hands, fingers, and arms contacting as much surface of the bark as possible gives you more control and lessens chances of lengthening existing splits or causing new ones. Bend slowly, a little at a time, and make sure the fold is following the score line, especially at the points. If the panel really fights you and just does not want to bend, you may have to deepen or widen the score line and/or strip off additional outer bark that could be inhibiting flexibility. Juniper bark does not often just "flip" into shape; it takes some manipulating and training. As you bend you may hear some cracking and popping. This may scare your ears, but normally it is just brittle sections of outer bark breaking and should not adversely affect the process or result. When you have won with one side let it relax but keep it at least slightly up-curved as you repeat the folding process with the other side. During this phase you may wish you had an extra arm and hand to help support, brace, hold and bend, and you may have to invent some interesting new holding positions to get both sides folded up evenly.

When you have trained both sides to fold up freely to a vertical position, you want to bring them together to form the basket so the edges along each side overlap about an inch. Overlap will be less, of course, down at the corners, but if you drew and scored your ellipse well at the points, there at least shouldn't be any opening there before the overlap starts. If you are not quite satisfied, you can usually improve them with some specific pinching and manipulating.

At this stage I tie a buckskin thong around the basket to hold it to shape, then strip off any remaining raggedy outer

bark that may have popped loose at the folds. I also check the evenness of the top circumference; if one side is taller than the other, or other irregularities exist, I mark with charcoal what to trim off. You can either open the basket back out flat to trim (easiest, I think), or wait til the sides are laced up and trim just prior to applying the rim reinforcement strip.

Drilling Holes and Lacing the Basket

The holes for lacing are drilled in two parallel rows up each side of the basket about an inch in from each edge, or just beyond where the overlap stops, and thus through only a single layer of bark. The lacing will run back and forth through the holes to encase the double layer overlap. On the very first juniper bark basket I made, having no instruction nor experience with the medium, I started punching lacing holes with an awl, but soon realized my error when all the holes started to connect by a long split. Switching to the stone-tipped hand drill, employing abrasion rather than punching, eliminated the splitting problem. Holes can also be successfully burned in.

The number, placement and spacing of holes depends on the size of your basket, your esthetic whim and the style of lacing you choose. The two most common are a single lace that spirals around and around through the holes from bottom to top, and a double lace (can be one long lace begun at its middle through the bottom two holes) where each end crosses back and forth through the holes. This creates a pleasing X-pattern to the lacing. The sides can also be simply tied closed through corresponding pairs of holes rather than continuously laced. This could be advantageous in situations where long laces are not available.

Holes can be drilled while you have your basket temporarily tied to shape, although the edges tend to bend downward from the drill pressure unless you prop them in place with a couple of short sticks wedged inside. You can also shove your foot or a conveniently sized chunk of wood inside to serve

as a backing brace for drilling. Or, you can just mark your desired hole placements with charcoal, then open the bark and lay it out flat on a more stable surface for drilling. If you already have your rim strip sized, you can measure its width in from the top edges of the basket panel and drill those holes too, though I normally wait til the sides are all lace up because some rim holes may have to be drilled through the double thickness overlap at each side.

Lacing material can be whatever you have on hand or can find in the immediate environment, including buckskin thongs, wet rawhide thongs, two-ply dogbane or other fiber cordage, sinew, long strips of willow bark, whole or split thin willow withes, pliable roots or vines as honeysuckle orClematis, shreddy barks as big sagebrush, strips of peeled juniper cambium, tule stems, cattail leaves, ad infinitum! While lacing material of high tensile strength is easier to use and to cinch tightly, super-strength is not imperative. The main function of the side lacing is to hold the overlapped edges in place while they're still pliable; as the whole basket dries, the bark becomes quite rigid and retains the shape it was trained to.

Lacing the Basket Rim Reinforcement Hoop

The main functions of the rim reinforcement piece are to protect and prevent splitting or other damage to the top edge of the bark sides, to hold the basket mouth to desired shape while the rim and basket body dry and take on a set and to increase overall durability of the basket. I prefer the convenient availability, flat configuration and "neatness" of the juniper bark strip for the rim, but I've also frequently used green lengths of willow or red osier dogwood shoots split in half. The flat side lays in contact with the basket. Functional rims can be laced around either the outside or the inside of the basket mouth, or on both sides. Aboriginal baskets exhibit all three variations, and some have bundled rims that appear to be willow shoots, bark strips or other fibrous material laced on.

The term rim "hoop" is slightly misleading in that I've never seen nor made a bark basket where the rim piece was first separately bound into a hoop shape before being laced onto the basket.

To prepare a juniper bark strip for the hoop, trim it to a uniform width (about an inch), then "pre-bend" it in your hands or over your leg to relax stiffness and train it to better conform to the curvature of the basket mouth. Lay it around the basket and cut it an inch or two longer than the actual circumference so that, when it's laced in place, there will be some overlap of the two ends. Measure the rim strip width's distance down from the top of the basket, mark that, and drill your lacing holes roughly 3/4" - 1" apart all the way around. Begin lacing on the strip near one end (the distance in from the end that the other end will overlap) and continue lacing all the way around the basket mouth. Your final lacing stitches will bind down the overlapped area and end at your point of origin. Leading ends, splices and finishing ends of your lacing material are normally not tied off, but simply tucked under a previous or forthcoming stitch; once dry, they shouldn't come loose. Actual rim material, number of holes you drill, lacing material and technique can be whatever you choose to experiment with, as long as they work! The more baskets you make, the more you'll come up with interesting variations and refinements. For example, you can thin or "feather out" each end of the rim strip prior to lacing so that the over lap is hardly noticeable.

Finishing Touches and Variations

A freshly completed juniper bark basket should still be somewhat malleable and, if desired, you can do some cosmetic manipulating to adjust the shape of the mouth, flatten or round out the sides, etc. When I get one to the configuration I want, I place a short stick or two inside to prop and hold it in that position while it dries. Kept in the sun, sufficient drying should take only two or three days, depending on thickness of the bark.

The final step is attaching a carrying strap long enough to loop over one's neck and shoulder so the top of the basket hangs at about waist level. I usually affix a buckskin thong loop to each side of the basket through a pair of lacing holes, then tie a longer shoulder strap to those. When I first began making bark baskets I marvelled at the simplicity of the one-piece folded design, but the inevitable inverted U-shaped bottom (typically deeper on the standard aboriginal more cylindrical forms that were my only models) seemed impractical. Then, while picking currants, one day I suddenly realized that the curved basket bottom meshed perfectly with the opposite curvature of my upper thigh. This use-position, with the strap around neck and one shoulder, props the mouth of the basket upward and forward and frees both hands to rapidly and efficiently strip berries into it. How neat! However, I've found no documentation that this handy position was either intended during aboriginal construction or practiced during use.

While the aboriginal use of juniper bark appears limited to constructing the basic berry basket type described here, I find it to be nearly as versatile as poplar bark, but much less efficient to harvest in quantity. Once you have made a basket or two, you learn to visualize exactly what size and shape of bark panel you need to construct specifically dimensioned baskets or containers intended for other uses. Juniper bark makes an excellent lightweight but sturdy quiver that provides more arrow protection than skin. But, bark cylinders too narrow to reach one's hand into do offer a creative challenge for getting them laced up! Flat-bottomed free-standing containers can be made from one or two panels laced up to form the sides and a third circular or oval slab laced onto one end to form the bottom. Various lids for containers can also be created. There is evidence that Redcedar bark baskets were occasionally sealed with pitch along all seams and holes and used as water containers and/or for hot stone boiling, although I've not yet tried this with juniper (there's always more to do!). A successful experiment I did recently try was substituting frame-stretched and dried elk rawhide for bark. The only significant construction difference I found was that the rawhide folded easier when scored on the outside.

A "Pretty-Up" basket of elk rawhide, colored with red and yellow ochre and charcoal. Rim is of Red Osier Dogwood with buckskin fringe.

A simpler style of folded basket I've seen pictured of cedar but not juniper bark eliminates the elliptical bottom and is simply scored in a straight line across the midpoint of the panel. Then, proceeding as normal, the sides are bent up, edge margins overlapped, drilled and laced and finally the rim piece affixed. Because this style has a V-shaped bottom produced by the straight-line fold, it holds less, but capacity can be increased by forming the mouth to a circular shape, gently spreading the panel sides apart to their limit and propping these both in place until dry.

Whether you are surrounded by Tulip Poplars in the East, live in the land of Western Junipers, somewhere inbetween or beyond, where other trees may work just as well, one-piece folded and laced bark containers are fun to make and muti-functional for the modern Abo. So, when Spring rolls around, your blood's flowing, the sap's up, the weather turns hot and you experience uncontrollable urges to begin peeling things off, embark on a new kind of basket project--bet you can't make just one!

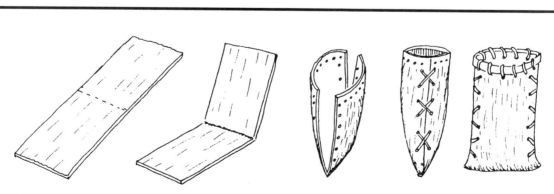

Construction Sequence for Single-Fold Style Bark Basket

MAKE A MOUNTAIN BARK BASKET

By Doug Elliott, © 1992

Jim Riggs

**Traditional Tulip Poplar bark baskets
made by Doug Elliott**

The traditional Appalachian tulip poplar bark basket, all laced up with the smooth inner bark of hickory is about as beautiful, useful and easy to make as any basket you'll ever find.

I was first introduced to bark basketry by my mountain neighbor, Paul Geouge, who has been making them for years. I was enchanted by the way he explained their simple practicality.

"So you've been out fishing all morning, following the creek up into the mountains. You're catching a few of them native speckled trout, but after a while the stream gets too small. So you call it quits and head up to the ridge for the long walk home. There you run onto the biggest patch of ripe huckleberries that you've ever seen! You'd love to haul some of them berries home, but you ain't got nothing to carry 'em

in. "How could you do it?", *Paul asks, with a twinkle in his eye.* "Well, if you knew how to make a berry basket, you'd just find you a young tulip poplar tree, make a poplar bark basket and tote them berries home, buddy! Now they'd taste mighty good after a fish dinner!...."

A simple bark basket can be made rather quickly. An experienced person can make one in half an hour (though beginners are lucky if they can do it in half a day). There's no end to their usefulness and adaptability - I've made them into backpacks, daypacks, fruit baskets, purses, and clothes hampers. I even have a large flat one I use as a briefcase!

Gathering and Preparing Materials

The best time to strip the bark from the tree is in late spring and early summer "when the sap's running." The new moon in June, according to Paul, is the period when the sap flow is highest. He uses the bark of tulip polplar trees for the basket and the inner bark of hickory for the lacing. If tulip poplar trees don't grow in your area, white ash works well, and Basswood can be used for the lacing as well. Quaking aspen (*Populus tremeloides*) is also useable but is brittle. Out west similar style baskets are made out of cedar and juniper (see the article by Jim Riggs). Experimentation will probably reveal others that work as well. The sooner the basket is made after it comes off the tree, the more workable the bark will be.

To gather bark for the basket, locate a young tree (three to five inches in diameter is good). Fast growing, second growth trees are best. Find a smooth area on the trunk and mark off a section twice the depth of the proposed basket. Cut through the bark into the sapwood and carefully peel that piece of bark off around the whole circumference of the trunk. Use your knife or axe blade to pry under the bark. (Yes, this does kill the tree. For this reason I usually choose a tree crowded in a thicket or one that's about to be cleared and I usually fell the tree in order to get several baskets from each tree. The debarked tree will dry quickly and will be great for kindling.)

Some trees work better than others. Don't be discouraged if your bark splits: you can still sew up the cracks when you lace up the basket. Remember, your chances of removing the bark smoothly and easily are best if the tree is young, has

Doug Elliott is a naturalist, herbalist and storyteller. He lectures, teaches, conducts workshops and storytelling concerts throughout the country. He is a collector of plant and animal lore. This article is from Doug's book Woodslore, *available from Doug Elliott, Rt. 1 Box 388, Union Mills, NC 28167.*

Jim Riggs

few branches, and you are doing it in June on the "coming up" (waxing) moon.

To gather the lacing bark, first locate a young hickory (or basswood). A piece of bark about an inch wide is cut loose at the bottom of the trunk and pulled firmly up toward the top of the tree.

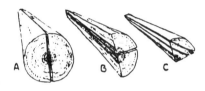

This first strip might only be a foot or two in length, but with each strip that is taken, the length will increase. Some strips might be the whole length of the tree. Then each strip must be peeled in half and the portion with the outer bark discarded or used in other craft projects. These wide strips of inner bark are then cut into thin strips suitable for lacing. For the best results the knife should be very sharp and the strip you are cutting should be pulled taut with its end held securely (like under your foot). Rugged scissors can also be used. This lacing is ready for immediate use or can be coiled and allowed to dry for storage. It need only be soaked for half an hour or so before using.

A hoop is needed to reinforce the rim of the basket. This can be made from any wood splint or flexible sapling. I often split a two inch diameter section of the hickory tree that I stripped for bark. Using a large knife, small axe, or froe, I split it in half (Diagram above). Then I split each half into quarters (B). Then I split one or two splints from the outer portion of each quarter (C).

Take the bark and carefully lay it out flat with the bark side up and mark a line across the bark halfway between the two ends. From here mark two curved lines so that you have what

Clockwise from top left: Initial cuts in bark, peeling hickory bark, removing poplar bark from a sapling.

looks like an elongated football shape. Take your knife and score or cut just through the outer bark along the two curved lines. (Illustration) Then carefully fold the bark along the cuts and you will see the basket's shape come into being! (Figs. 1,2,3) Take your awl or leather punch and make your holes opposite one anther along the edge where the two sides will be laced together. (Figs. 4) Make sure the holes are a good inch from the edge. Use the lacing and lace up each side like you would shoes. (Fig. 5,6)

Then once the top edge is whittled smooth, take your flexible hoop and bend and carve it into shape and set it into the rim. (Fig. 7) Punch the rest of the holes around the top and lace it in. (Fig.8) I usually like to put two loops of lacing along the edge of the basket to which I can fasten a carrying strap.

There you have your basket! It's ready to use. As it dries, it will get lighter and more ridgid. Mr. Geouge showed me some baskets that his family has used for more than twenty years, picking berries with them every year. Not only are they rugged and long lasting, but the ones he makes are so beautiful that he can sell any extra he makes at the local fair. "You know, " he once confided to me with a grin, "some folks that buys 'em aren't even intending to pick berries in 'em. They're just buying 'em for the curiosity!"

Can you imagine that?

(more)

Fig. 1 Lay out bark and scribe lines

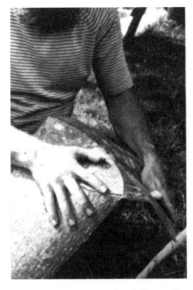

Fig. 2 Gently bend bark inward

Photos from *Woodslore*, by Doug Elliott

Fig. 3 Allow sides to curl & overlap

Fig. 4 Punch holes along each edge

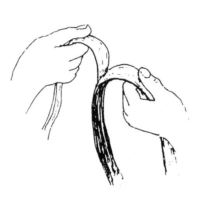

Split and seperate inner and outer
bark for lacing

Fig. 7 Trim top and punch holes

Fig. 5 Place holes 1" from edges

Fig. 6 Lace as you would your shoes

Fig. 8 Lace hoop into top of rim

Variation On A Theme - Aspen Bark Containers
Photos By David Wescott

Designs can be incised into the bark to create attractive containers. John Olsen creations.

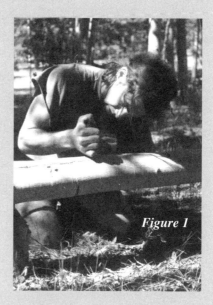

Figure 1

- Using a stone flake, Matt scores the bar (Fig, 1).
- He uses his thumbs to gently pry open the incision (Fig. 2).
- A fid made from a branch is used to separate the bark from the trunk (Fig. 3).
- Once it is released, the bark can be easily removed (Fig. 4).

This exercise took place in early spring immediately after the snow had receded from the meadow.

Figure 2

Figure 3

Figure 4

BARK CANTEENS:
Carrying Water Primitively

By Anthony Follari

An important requirement that should be taken into consideration when traveling in the outdoors is a water supply. Even if there are several water sources along the way, it is preferable to be able to carry some water with you. I enjoy testing and experimenting with primitive gear, and prefer to travel using only what I have made. I didn't like the idea of using a modern plastic or metal canteen as the rest of my gear is restricted to stone age technologies. So I set out to search for a primitive canteen design that I could construct myself.

I considered gourds, tightly woven root containers, pitched basket containers, animal stomachs and bladders, ostrich eggs, bamboo sections, etc. However, they all seemed unsatisfactory as they were either not available in my geological area, were hard to procure when needed or required a significant investment in material preparation and construction time. I was in search of something that could be made easily from readily available resources enabling me to make (or repair) it when needed, not when time or materials presented themselves. So I set out to experiment.

For my first attempt, I borrowed the Indian bark rattle design. The bark rattle always reminded me of a drinking flask. In fact, the first time I saw a picture of a bark rattle I thought it was a canteen. One day while I was processing some pitch to seal some bark containers, I fashioned a small bark rattle out of some leftover scraps. I pitched the sides, filled it with water and tested it. This experiment worked successfully and lead to the basic design I've used for several years with only one modification. I discovered that, upon drying, the bark inside the mouth of the canteen would curl, sometimes curling so tightly that it would stress or pull loose at the side seams. Prior to reuse, the mouth of the canteen would have to be soaked to rehydrate and unfurl the bark inside the mouth. Additionally, this is the same area subjected to the most wear from constant removal and installation of the cork. To solve the problem, I constructed a wooden plug to fit inside the mouth of the canteen similar to a big cork. Then I drilled a hole through this plug and pitched it inside the mouth of the canteen. The cork used to seal the canteen was reduced in size and placed inside this plug/collar as opposed to directly contacting the bark. This refinement is a nice option and significantly increases the longevity of the canteen. If you need a canteen quickly, I would eliminate this step, or add it later. For long term use however, it is a worthwhile consideration.

Although the canteen I was using was serviceable, I was still not satisfied, as the volume for its size was less than I had hoped for. Sometime in 1993 I began to experiment again.

I redesigned the bottom like a berry basket. This substantially increased the depth of the canteen, thereby increasing its volume without increasing its overall length or width.

The berry basket bottom solved the volume problem, but created another. The bottom of the canteen now took on an arch, forming two points at the corners. The weakest and hardest area to seal were now subjected to more abuse, as you can't put the canteen down without placing it on the two corners. This problem recently was solved during a primitive campout. I was contemplating the problem with my friend Barry Keegan, while in a rain shelter we had made. We were discussing constructing some type of guard or cap that would protect the corners. When we looked down we saw hickory nuts. The solution was right in front of us. We split a nut in half, pitched it on and solved the problem. The final result - a primitive canteen that could be made quickly, from a wide variety of readily available materials. It is durable and holds sufficient volume. I have personally used these canteens for days on end and both Barry and I have been using them in our advanced courses where six people rely solely on them to carry water for five days. The use and abuse they receive is a testament to their durability. My original canteen is over six years old and is still going strong.

To construct a one quart canteen similar to the ones pictured in his article you'll need a sheet of ark about 7" wide by about 20" l ng (obviously you can reduce or nlarge your dimensions based on the size canteen you need). A branch about 4" in diameter will serve nicely. The type of trees I have personally used are elm, hickory, and white ash but based on other bark projects I have completed, I am sure birch, pine, serviceberry, and tulip poplar will work equally as well (and probably many others). In selecting a piece of bark, choose a section that is straight and has few to no branches or imperfections in the bark for the length you need.

Anthony Follari is a naturalist, a craftsperson and teacher. This article first appeared in its full form in Bulletin # 10, Pages 63-68. It is edited for this compilation to reduce duplication of information contained in previous articles. Anthony and former business partner, Barry Keegan have contributed a variety of informative articles that appear both here and in Primitive Technology: A Book of Earthskills.

Once the bottom is formed, tightly roll one side inward and the other side around it.

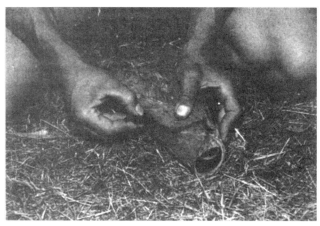

At this stage, the canteen could be dried and sealed, but I prefer to reshape the sides, giving the canteen a more finished look.

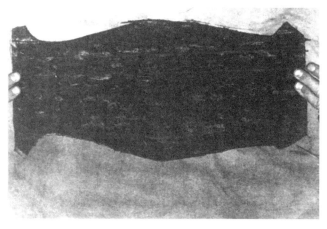

The finished shape of the bark after reshaping the sides and top.

Once the bark is removed from the tree, it will want to curl up. Gently flatten it out, rough side up. Find the mid point and scribe a reference line (using the reference line as a guide, scribe two symmetrical arcs forming what looks similar to a bi-pointed football [see illustration]). This is the same layout you would use to make a berry basket. You may want to review Doug Elliott's and Jim Riggs' Berry Basket articles in the 1993 spring issue of the *Bulletin of Primitive Technology*. I recommend that you have the ends of the two arcs intersect and form an "X" about 3/16" before reaching the sides of the bark. This will overlap the bark at the corners when the canteen is folded up giving you tighter and easier to seal corners.

Once the layout is complete, score about 1/3 of the way through the football shape from the rough side. Although many berry baskets are constructed with the score on the smooth or cambium layer side, our intention is to maintain the integrity of the inner bark for maximum waterproofness, so be sure to do all your scoring on the rough or outer side of the bark. To shape the canteen, gently work the bark, slowly bending and folding it along your scored lines. Allow one top half to roll tightly inward and the other half to roll around this inward roll, forming the basic shape of the canteen. You'll have to adjust the tightness of the roll to regulate the final shape. You can let it dry and seal the sides at this point, but I found it nice to reshape the sides and top.

By reshaping the top and sides, you remove all excess bark from the final shape of the canteen. This excess bark serves no purpose and only traps debris, makes drying out the canteen between uses more difficult and reduces its volume. There are many ways to shape the sides, be creative. The objective is to have 3/4 of an inch overlap remaining around the side seams.

To reshape the sides, mark with a piece of charcoal the outer sides of the canteen. Reopen the canteen and trim off the excess, refold and mark again, this time marking the inner rolled edge. Reopen and trim, leaving about 3/4 inch overlap. I prefer to reinforce the mouth of the canteen by overlapping the bark completely around the collar or cork. If you didn't reduce the overall thickness of the bark by scraping and the outer surface is rough, it is a good idea to shave off the outer bark where the seams are to be sealed.

When all your trimming and reshaping is completed, refold the canteen, striving to have the corners fit as tightly as possible. Tie up the canteen with cordage and place a stick the size of your cork or wooden collar in the mouth of the canteen and let it dry. While the canteen is drying, you can process your pitch and construct the collar if you decide to use one.

The collar needs to be a round tapered cylinder of wood with a hole through its center. Using only primitive tools, softer woods like basswood, cedar, sassafras are easier to work or woods with a "pithy" center will facilitate making the hole (ie. *sumac* and *alanthus*). I have, through trail and error, come to prefer harder woods. They may be more difficult to fashion

(more)

Letting the canteen dry, be sure to tie the bark in position and install a stick the size of the cork or collar you are using in the canteen mouth.

Preheating and coating the collar and canteen mouth To facilitate handling the collar, insert a stick into it as a handle.

Insert several small sticks to wedge open the sides prior to applying the pitch.

After the top and sides are sealed, abrade a groove around the top and secure it tightly with cordage.

into the correct shape, however they seem to swell less, subjecting the canteen mouth to less fluctuations between use and drying, increasing its longevity. The actual shape of the collar should be slightly tapered matching the taper of the mouth of the canteen.

The next step is to prepare the pitch mixture. The mixture I use for canteens is 60% filtered and rendered pitch and 40% fine ground black charcoal. Don't get too concerned with percentages as you can mix anywhere between 15 to 60% charcoal and still have a good quality seal. The charcoal supplies grit and aggregate for extra bonding and holding strength. For best performance and appearance, the charcoal should be ground as fine as possible. You can also add rendered fat (be careful, a little goes a long way) or beeswax to help maintain the flexibility of the pitch and make a more forgiving bond. Although I have experimented with many pitch additives, I have come to prefer plain charcoal for canteens. Pitch adheres best if the surface it is to be applied to is preheated. This way the hot pitch will flow and disperse itself facilitating the sealing and adhesion process. If hot pitch is applied to a cool surface, it will harden before it gets a chance to flow and adhere.

To seal the canteen, preheat the canteen's mouth and collar and apply the pitch to the outside of the collar and the inside of the canteen mouth as uniformly as possible. Then spread the canteen's mouth open enough to insert the collar and heat the whole area up near the fire liquefying ail the pitch so it flows and coats all the surfaces completely. I place my finger in the collar and twist and swirl it in place spreading the pitch evenly. Once the collar is in position, remove it from the heat and let it cool.

The next step is to preheat the side seams and seal them with pitch. I insert small sticks along the edge spreading the seams apart slightly. I then paddle pitch under the seam with

Removing the excess pitch from the seams.

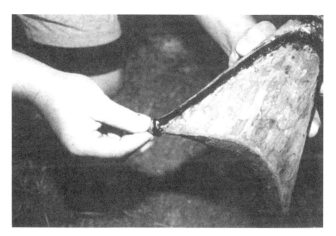

Installing the protective hickory nut caps.

The berry basket bottom canteen we just completed next to a flat-bottom canteen.

a wooden spatula, maintaining enough heat to liquefy and coat the overlapped surfaces uniformly. Once the seams are filled, I remove the small sticks used to hold the seam open and paddle pitch on the seam building it up slightly on the outside leveling the difference between the two overlapped bark surface. Then remove the canteen from the heat and let it cool.

I next abrade a groove about an inch below the top, completely around the mouth of the canteen with a stone blade and tie some cordage in place around this groove. Although this is another optional step, it helps hold the bark in place better and the seams are subjected to less stress, especially in hot weather and in direct sunlight where the pitch may soften slightly. I also coat the cord with pitch to prevent it from absorbing water and/or becoming loose.

Now chip and scrape off any excess pitch, then sand until the seams and top are neat and uniform. To smooth the sanded pitch, preheat again, this time only enough to liquefy the outer surface and smooth the pitch.

Once cool, I like to test the seal by blowing into the mouth of the canteen to see if there are any major leaks. If all is well, I fill the canteen with water and let it sit, filled, for approximately three hours, continually checking for leaks or seeps. If one appears, mark it, empty the canteen, dry it out and reseal that area. Once the canteen is waterproofed, the next step is to make protective corner caps.

To make the protective caps, split a hickory nut in half, grind out the inside, preheat it and fill it with pitch, preheat the canteen corners and push it on letting the excess pitch ooze out. Remove any excess pitch while you shape and smooth the corners. Lastly, carve a wooden plug that fits snugly for the cork and make some cordage to wrap around the canteen forming a carrying strap. At this point your canteen is complete and ready to be used.

The canteens described in this article are durable, but normal care and common sense must be exercised in their use. They are not meant to be laid on their sides or upside down when filled but, instead, carried or hung upright. When no longer in use, dry them upside down with the cork removed. When using these canteens I recommend carrying a pitch stick with you to perform any in field repairs. If a chip or leak does appear, it is not necessary to completely dry the canteen, but dry it the best you can before attempting to reseal it.

You may notice a slight coloring or taste change in the water when using your canteen, this is normal and fades with use. I find the added flavor pleasing reportedly nutritious (I prefer elm's flavor the best).

In closing, I hope you derive the same pleasure in making and using primitive equipment that I do and that this article encourages you to make your own canteen. If you do, I would appreciate any comments, suggestions or refinements. Until then, may the wind always be at your back, the sunrise to meet you and your primitive canteen be forever full.

The Uses of Birch Bark
By Jim Miller

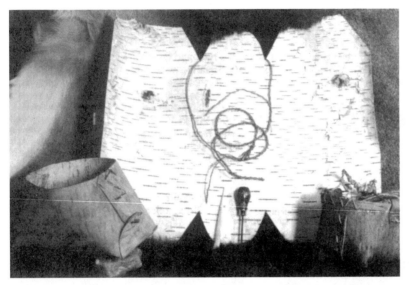

Tools of the trade...Birch bark worked with an awl and tied with finger twisted string, forms beautiful and functional containers.

During the spring of each year, you have an opportunity to touch a part of history. If you live in the Great Lakes region springtime is a time of gathering, harvesting from the garden of Mother Earth's Bounty. The beautiful white birch tree comes to life as her sap begins to flow offering drinkable liquid and a refreshing sweet tea from the twigs of her branches. The beauty of the bark is like no other tree. It's a privilege to be able to use the functional pieces that come from its bark. A birch-bark basket just feels good to hold and, as you will find out, is surprisingly sturdy.

Centuries ago, tepees and wigwams, baskets and bowls, cups and dishes, arrow quivers, even cookware were all fashioned from the bark of this forest beauty. Removed in large sheets in the spring, the white skin is flexible, waterproof and lightweight. In days past, this tree was given an offering out of respect, because removing the bark would shorten its life.

Today the opposite is true. Just a stone's throw from my home, one-hundred acres of young woods was cleared last fall. The very woods in which I tracked my first fox and deer so that I could learn their ways. Two miles from there another parcel of land was cleared for one more shopping center. The trees still lay in piles to be burned. Our salvage of the birch bark when collected in the wake of chainsaws and bulldozers is bittersweet, but it is a reality these days.

Although the bark of any size tree is usable, the older trees offer thicker, sturdier material.

Begin by looking or feeling (if the tree is down) all the way around the tree to locate any long or deep gashes and scrapes. Avoid these unless you just need a few thin small layers for writing on or to add to your fire starting kit.

With knife in hand, make a deep cut into the bark running the length of the tree. In the early part of the spring, I use my knife or a thin wooden wedge to begin to pry the bark away from the wood of the tree.

In late May through June, the bark will pull off with very little effort other than the initial cut! But I harvest bark year-round whenever I see a patch of woods that has been leveled. You can too, and you'll never have to cut a live tree. After removing a couple pieces, you'll be an old hand at it.

Soak the bark in warm water a few minutes. This will help keep it from cracking and/or the layers from separating.

To make a container (like the one pictured) choose a fairly thin piece and fold the edges up. Now gently crease the bark where you want it to bend using your thumbnail or a butter knife. I fold and crease the ends much the same way my mom used to fold wax paper around my school lunch sandwiches.

A little hint here: It really helps to make a cardboard pattern first, especially if you are working with a limited supply of birch bark.

Once your folds are made, you can hold them permanently in place by punching a hole through the bark and inserting twigs. I use cordage made from bass wood or stinging nettle fibers to hold the larger baskets and plates together.

This is a God-Send in a survival situation. No special tools or skills are required. If the bark is fresh it will bend without cracking and will hold water in, if it's a bowl, or out, if it's a canoe. Although a little pine pitch will be needed on the latter.

Water-filled containers can be placed directly on the fire bed for cooking purposes or hot rocks can be placed in them to bring the water to a boil--truly amazing stuff! Remember to say ...thank you trees.

Removing bark with an antler handled knife.

RUDIMENTARY "FIST" POTTERY
(PREPARE A MASS OF CLAY FIRST)

BEGIN BETWEEN HANDS BY ROLLING A LUMP OF CLAY THE TWO PALMS OF THE UNTIL YOU CREATE A LARGE "MARBLE."

TAKE THE OTHER HAND (NOT HOLDING THE "MARBLE" OF CLAY AND SMASH A LARGISH STONE INTO THE CENTER, CONTINUE THIS MOTION UNTIL THE MARBLE HAS A LARGE HOLLOW IN THE CENTER OF ITS MASS. ROTATE THE "BOWL" NOW IN THE LEFT HAND AS YOU "DAP" THE STONE INTO THE HOLLOW.

TAKE A SMALLER STONE AND "DAP" THE INTERIOR OF THE BOWL TO THIN THE BOTTOM AND SIDES. AVOID THE RIM STILL HOLDING THE BOWL IN THE LEFT HAND. CAREFULLY TAKE A "WET" STONE DIPPED IN WATER TO FINISH THE RIM WITHOUT ENLARGING IT BY WORKING THE EXTERIOR RIM THICKNESS.

-FINGERS → SUPPORT INTERIOR WITH — OF RIGHT HAND. LET DRY AND FIRE.

© '94
CHAS. SPEAR

CLAY and POTTERY

SEARCHING FOR CLAY

WHAT TO LOOK FOR →

LOOK FOR "SPIDERING" of GROUND

DRIED CLAY APPEARANCE

↑ FOUND IN LOW LYING RUN OFFS, STREAMS AND CREEKS (DRIED) AND OTHER SOURCES OF WATER MOVEMENT AND SILTING, OR SEDIMENTATION

DIG OUT THE CLAY TO THE DEPTH OF THE SPIDERING... PACK INTO CLOTH BAGS AND TAKE BACK TO CAMPSITE.

CRUSH DRIED LUMPS TO A POWDER USING A STONE

CLAY POWDER   CLOTH TARP   WHEN CLAY IS

FULLY POWDERED: ADD WATER AND WEDGE INTO A CLAY LUMP

ADD PULVERIZED

MUSSEL SHELLS (FOR TEMPERING) ONLY ABOUT 1/4 AMOUNT OF CLAY MASS.

MUSSEL SHELLS.   NORTAR & STONE PESTLE

CLAY + SHELL TEMPERING IS NOW SHAPED INTO "FIST" POTS.

SMOOTH WITH GOURD-PORTION AND WATER.

LET DRY IN SUN 2 DAYS AND "FIRE" IN A GROUND KILN (DISH SHAPED)   STONES   DRY WOOD STACKED 3 FT. HIGH

STONES

FIRE ON A DRY, WINDLESS DAY LET COOL OVERNIGHT.

CHAS. SPEAR © '94

Section 4

PROJECTILES
Bows and Arrows

YOUR FIRST PRIMITIVE BOW
From Live Tree To Finished Bow In 6 Days
By Tim Baker

Unless you live in the driest of deserts, your first bow could be resting just under the bark of a nearby tree, probably only a short walk from where you are now. Extracting it is a simple process, and takes just a few hours work using even the most primitive tools.

A fast, durable bow can be made from virtually any wood. Weak-wood bows simply need to be wider than strong-wood bows. A fifty pound osage orange bow, for example, may be only one inch wide while Eastern red cedar needs a full two inches. Completely serviceable bows can even be made from very light woods, such as pine. Their three inch widths are a bit ungainly however. Most North American hardwoods yield a safe and efficient 40 to 50 pound bow at 1 1/2 inches of width.

Choosing A Design

There are dozens of bow designs. The one selected here is likely the first bow ever made. The ancestor of all bows.

It is a good choice for many reasons. It is the simplest bow to make. It is durable. It is fast and it is beautiful. Instructions for it's design appear in the night sky each month: the silvery light of the new crescent moon.

Even though this is the easiest made bow, it is not inferior in any regard. With its full draw and un-jittery release it shoots a heavier, more penetrating arrow faster and more accurately than short draw primitive bows in present vogue.

Variations of this design appear repeatedly in the historic and prehistoric record. Eight thousand year old versions survive in the bogs of Europe. Depictions of it abound in Egyptian tombs. Plains Indians used such bows

"...to learn ever more of the bows' endless secrets". So says Tim Baker in reply to why he has spent just about every minute of the last three years studying and making primitive bows ... 430 as of last count. Reading everything available on the art of bowmaking, critically appraising and testing, breaking the rules to discover just what the rules are. "Out of paleoanthropological nostalgia."

Splitting log.

before they acquired the horse. Eastern woodland Indians relied on this bow until rifles replaced them. Spanish armor was easily perforated by this weapon. Armed with such bows the English routinely marched at three to four-to-one odds against crossbow armed French armies. This simple, un-temperamental, rugged bow will do all you could want a bow to do.

Selecting Wood

For your first bow, it's best to avoid osage, locust and mulberry, The white sapwood of these trees must be removed down to the heartwood, a task that can easily take longer than making the bow itself, and which can endanger the bow, as will be explained .

Choose any heavier than average wood. Some good choices are elm, ash, hickory, oak, hop hornbeam, birch, maple, acacia, dogwood, beech and any of the wild or domestic fruit or nut woods.

Cutting The Wood

Find a four inch or larger diameter straight, untwisted trunk. Ideally one with a 4" by 70" knot-free area; 3" by 66" is minimum. A larger area will let you place the bow in more favorable terrain once under-bark irregularities are revealed.

Cut from the more parallel portion of the trunk, above where it swells before entering the ground. But first cut a half inch wedge of wood from the tree and inspect it's growth rings. If closer than 15 per inch, find another tree. Tight grained hardwood is often weak. Large diameter trees usually have tighter growth rings, so 4 to 8 inch diameter trees are the best candidates.

will work too. After a half hour of steaming, the inner bark will pull free in strips exposing the untouched wood surface.

Debarking without tools is highly preferred. The outer growth ring is left un-marred, therefore as strong as it can possibly be. This is valuable because the outside surface of the tree will be the back of the bow (the side facing away from the shooter), and bows break at their backs. Any severing of back fibers or growth rings increases the chance of breakage. This is another reason for first-timers to avoid wood whose sapwood must be removed.

If debarking with tools, use a drawknife or spokeshave only on the outer bark. Use a scraper to work through inner bark to surface wood.

Tools and Equipment

Here are four suggested tool kits. Choose your level of technology.

1) The sharp, straight edge of knapped stone (preferably flint, chert or obsidian) and a flat piece of sandstone.

2) A hatchet, rasp, file and glass or sheet-metal scraper.

3) A hatchet, drawknife, spokeshave, coarse and fine rasp, glass or sheet-metal scraper, and sandpaper.

4) Bandsaw, spokeshave, glass or sheetmetal scraper, coarse and fine rasp, and sandpaper.

A bathroom scale is useful for judging the bow's weight at different stages of tiller. If you wish to use totally abo methods, rely on your best guess instead.

Make a tillering stick from a 1 by 3 or 4 inch, 36 inch long board. Any wood will do.

Problems

First time bowmakers generally have the following problems: 1) The bow breaks. 2) The bow has too much local or general set (looks as if strung when unstrung). 3) The bow shoots slow and flabby. 4) The bow starts out to be, say, a 40 pounder, but mysteriously ends up a 25 pounder (a lot of heads are nodding right now).

Causes

1) Broken bows result, in order of likelihood, from A) too narrow wood, B) wood fibers or growth rings violated on the bows back, C) removing too much wood in one place or D) overstraining the bow while tillering. Decayed wood, or wood

Avoid dead wood. Osage, yew, black locust and mulberry are rot resistant, but we're avoiding these for now.

Using antler, wood or steel wedges, split the log in half. If these halves measure ten or more inches on the outside curve, split them again.

Remove the bark. If cut in spring, summer or early fall, the bark will peel fairly freely from the staves. If winter-cut, scrape the surface bark off and place the stave in a hot shower or a steam box. Burying the stave in damp soil beneath a long fire

(more)

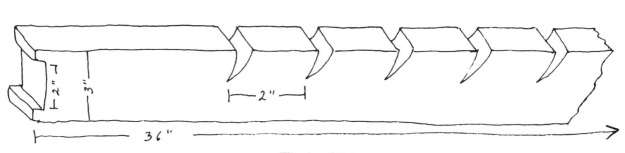

Tillering Stick.

with hidden imperfections is rarely at fault.

2) Local set is caused by removing too much wood in one area of the belly (the belly faces the shooter). Excessive general set is caused, in order of likelihood, by A) making the bow too narrow for the strength of wood, B) using incompletely dried wood, or C) by overstraining the bow while tillering.

3) Slow shooting bows generally result from excessive string follow (set). But severely whip-ended, and excessively round-in-the-handle bows shoot slowly too. Whip-ended bows bend mainly towards their ends. Limbs that are too massive, due to poor design or poor tillering, will shoot slow too.

4) Bows end up weaker than intended when too much wood is removed from all parts of the belly.

Solutions

Following just five rules will virtually guarantee a fast, unbroken, efficient, proper strength bow:

1) Be certain the bow is wide enough for its intended draw weight and the strength of wood used.

2) Be certain that the wood is dry.

3) From the very beginning to the very end of tillering, ONLY remove wood where the limbs are bending least.

4) Avoid over- straining the bow while tillering by pulling to given weights at various lengths of draw.

5) Avoid taking too much wood from the belly by pulling, as above, to given weights at various lengths of draw. These tillering weights/lengths are given shortly.

Making The Bow

Select a debarked stave and pencil a 2" by 66" bow blank on its outside surface (photo left). Now that the bark is off, small knots may be visible. Before penciling out the bow blank, "move the bow around on the stave" to avoid as many knots as possible, especially larger ones. A stave with punky or rotted knots should be discarded.

Work down to, but not through, the pencil lines. Cut square sides. Save the largest stave scrap for a drying test.

Using the stave's back as a finger guide, draw lines on both sides of the blank. Start at 1/2" thick at each tip, gradually widening the line to 7/8" thick at mid-stave. Let your fingers follow the dips and rises of the back. This will cause the pencil line to do the same.

Work down to, but not through, this line. Make the belly surface fairly flat.

If using a bandsaw, hold the stave at a slight angle while cutting so that when both sides have been cut a low peak is created mid-belly ... this prevents under-cutting the opposite line. Then remove the peak.

The stave at this point will look somewhat like a bow, but everything done to it so far has been CARPENTRY!

Bowmaking begins with TILLERING. Tillering is the selective removal of wood from the belly, the aim being to cause the limbs to curve evenly and equally.

Luckily, instructions for doing this come built into the wood. *REMOVE WOOD ONLY WHERE THE LIMB IS BENDING LEAST AND PERFECT ARCS WILL AUTOMATICALLY RESULT.*

Penciling-in the outlines of the bow. Lines indicate width and thickness of the preform.

Floor Tillering

With one end of the blank on the ground and the other held in one hand, press forward at the center of the belly with about 35 pounds of force.

Sight down the arc as if checking an arrow for straightness. Note which areas are bending least, or none at all. Make pencil marks at these places. Scrape off the pencil marks and a good bit of wood along with them. If the blank is too thick to bend, remove wood everywhere until it will. Maintain a fairly flat belly.

Floor tilleing.

Continue removing wood **ONLY WHERE THE BOW IS BENDING LEAST** until both limbs are curving evenly and equally. Continue until about 35# of force against the grip will bend the blank about 5 inches.

Drying

Unsplit logs, bark intact, can take several years to dry. Quarter-split, debarked staves can take a year or more. Even 2 x 2 inch staves can take several months to dry. This is fine if you have geologic patience, or make bows for a living and have a pipeline of drying wood.

The method used here, working the stave down to near finished dimensions before drying, takes only a few days ... and it reduces the danger of warp, checks and compression damage associated with drying larger dimension wood.

The bow made to illustrate this article was taken from growing tree to well cured bow in six days.

In normal room conditions of 70° and 50% humidity, your floor tillered blank will dry in two weeks if the density of slippery elm. Three weeks if like white ash. Four weeks if like hickory.

At 100° and 40% humidity, drying time about halves. Some good drying places are an attic, a heated closet, under a dark tarp during the day, inside a hot car during the day or in a box or tube with lightbulbs inside.

How to know when your bow blank is dry? ... take a stave scrap at least one foot long and reduce it to the width and thickness of your blank at mid-limb. Weigh the scrap on a postage scale or similar. Let the test scrap and bow blank have identical drying conditions.

Note the scraps weight every day or two. Weight will drop 25% or more the first day, then taper off. Note how long it takes to appear to be losing no more weight. Then wait 25% longer and it, and the blank, are dry.

If no scale is available, make a crude balance beam, The scrap on one end, an equal weight on the other. As the scrap dries, balance will shift, requiring occasional adjustment. As with a scale, note how long it takes to appear to be losing no more weight ... then wait 25% longer and it, and the blank are dry.

The slippery elm stave used to illustrate this article was felled, split, cut down to a blank and floor tillered the same day. The wood was dripping wet, its moisture content well above 30%. It weighed 2# 6oz after floor tillering. After 24 hours in 100 °, 40% humidity

(more)

air, it weighed 1#13oz, with an average moisture content of 19%. On day four, weight was 1# 10.5oz, Average moisture content 11.5%. On day six, weight was 1# 10oz, with a uniform 9% moisture content, perfect for this area. Dry! No warp ... no twist ... no checks.

The blank had been left 2" wide its full length because narrow limb ends would likely warp while drying. Being so thin relative to width, lateral warping is insignificant. In the rare event twisting becomes evident while drying, de-twist the stave and clamp it in place to a two by four. Put small spacers under the blank.

The blank may have some natural twist unnoticed on the tree. If less then 10° from end to end, ignore it. If greater then 10°, de-twist and clamp as above.

If you're using only primitive tools, use a wide jawed wrench made of wood instead of clamps.

Regardless of the drying method used or care employed, some twist may remain when dry. Ignore it. Performance will not suffer.

Penciling Out The Bow

The center two feet of the bow's length will be 1 1/2" wide. From this width let it narrow in graceful curved lines toward a 5/8" tip. Draw a shape that is pleasing to the eye. Pencil the bow out freehand. This will let you follow, to some extent, the natural meandering of the grain, especially as it widens around the knots. This gives the bow immense character and increases its safety. Just make sure that a straight line drawn from tip to tip crosses the center of the grip. Work down to, but not through, these pencil lines. Finish the sides to just short of final- sanding smoothness.

The next few millimeters of wood removal is the heart of bowmaking. This is where weight, speed and durability are unalterably determined.

Final Tillering

It's important to have even and balanced limb curvature at every stage of tillering. No flat or over-bent spots. If one part of a limb bends more than another, forces concentrate creating local, permanent, performance-ruining set.

The dried blank, you will notice, has gained considerable strength. A bit more floor tillering is in order. Remove belly wood again until about 35# push against the grip will bend he bow about 5 inches ... enough to permit a low stringing of the bow.

Make your best effort to have both limbs bending not only evenly, but equally.

Cut or file nocks one half inch from the stave tips.

Make a string of at least 160# strength. Tie or weave a loop into one end (instructions follow).

Tie one end of the string to one nock. A half hitch or any knot will do, but a timber hitch, being adjustable, is preferable (note photo). For now, string the bow only about 3" high.

One limb will inevitably be bending more than the other. With the bow strung, remove wood only from the least bending limb until both limbs are bending equally.

Put the bow on the tillering stick and rest the stick vertically on the scale, bow on top. Pull down on the string until the scale reads about 15#. Rest the string in the closest notch. It's helpful to have inch marks drawn on the tillering sticks face.

Lean this rig against a wall, back up a few feet and inspect the curves. If one limb is bending unevenly, or less than the other limb, make appropriate pencil marks, remove the tillering stick, and scrape away the pencil marks. At this stage, wood shavings can be fingernail thick.

Unstring the bow and adjust the timber hitch bringing the string height to 6.5" from the bows back. This will be the bows finished string height.

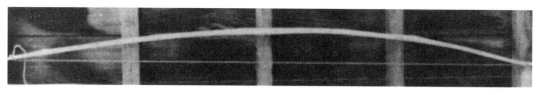

Continue this inspecting-marking-removing-pulling-weighing until you reach about 32# at 20".

Put the bow on the tillering stick and draw to 23" from the bow's back. Inspect limb curvature and balance carefully. Mark and remove wood only where limbs are bending least. Each time significant wood is removed, seat the bow to its true new shape by drawing to 23" several times. Check draw weight on the scale occasionally. Continue this inspecting-marking-removing-pulling-weighing until you reach about 38# at 23".

The bow is almost finished. Shavings should be paper-thin. Leave no tool marks.

Put the bow on the tillering stick and draw 25" from the bow's back. Inspect limb curvature and balance carefully. Mark and remove wood only where limbs are bending least. Each time significant wood is removed, seat the bow to its true new shape by drawing to 25" several times. Check draw weight on the scale occasionally. Continue this inspecting-marking-removing-pulling-weighing until you reach about 40# at 25".

Tillering is now complete.

Sand the sharp edge from all corners. For comfort in the hand, round the grip corners considerably. File or sand the limbs free of tool marks. Use 80 grit, then 120 grit paper ... and even finer if you want a sheen on the wood.

This rounding and smoothing will remove enough wood to increase draw length to about 26" at 40#. Shooting the bow

Proceed With Caution

Now you're entering dangerous territory. This is where most beginners and many veterans go astray   A s you continue tillering, how can you know how far and how hard to pull the bow? How can you know if you're overstraining the limbs giving them permanent, excessive set? On the other hand, how can you know that you're not removing too much wood, making your 40# bow into a 25 pounder?

How can you know if you're ruining your bow without having made a few dozen bows and developing good tillering instincts?

The following weigh-as-you-go figures act as a "tillering template". They show how a capable bowmaker would handle these problems.

Put the bow on the tillering stick and draw the string about ten inches from the bow's back. Inspect limb curvature and balance carefully. Mark only where the limbs are bending least. Remove wood until the bow pulls about 12# on the scale at 10" of draw. It's convenient, but not necessary, to leave the bow strung while removing wood.

Put the bow on the tillering stick and draw to 15 inches from the bow's back. Inspect limb curvature and balance carefully. Mark and remove wood only where limbs are bending least. Each time significant wood is removed, seat the bow to its true new shape by drawing to 15" several times. Check draw weight on the scale occasionally. Continue this inspecting-marking-removing-pulling-weighing until you reach about 22# at 15 inches.

Put the bow on the tillering stick and draw to 20" from the bow's back. Inspect limb curvature and balance carefully. Mark and remove wood only where limbs are bending least. Each time significant wood is removed, seat the bow to it's true new shape by drawing to 20" several times. Check draw weight on the scale occasionally.

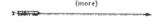

(more)

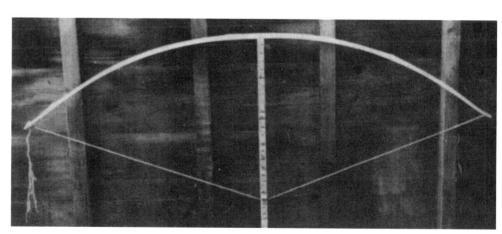

A well-tillered bow shows an even pattern while pulled.

at 27" of draw will seat the bow right in at a permanent 40#. If the bow somehow ends up a few pounds lighter than intended, remove up to one inch from each tip and cut new nocks. This will raise draw weight by as much as 4#. Only the limb ends will need re tillering.

When finished, chances are one limb will still bend slightly less than the other. Let that be the bottom limb. Grip the bow with the top of your hand at dead center. The arrow rests on top of your hand.

For grip comfort you might want to add a padding of leather, wood, or cloth at the back and belly of the grip, covered with a leather wrap.

Because of its width and gentle construction, your bow will shoot fast for its draw weight. At 40#, it should cast a 500 grain hunting arrow about 137fps, almost 150 yards.

If your bow has more than two inches of string follow, the wood was too weak for this width or strength bow. If much less than an inch and one half of follow, a higher weight bow could have been made ... or a narrower, therefore less massive and faster (useful information for your next bow from the same, or similar, tree).

For convenience, here are the "tillering template" figures all in one column.

Floor tiller	5"	35#
Tiller Stick	??"	15#
Tiller stick	10"	12#
Tiller stick	15"	22#
Tiller stick	20"	32#
Tiller stick	23"	38#
Tiller stick	25"	40#
Sand bow	26"	40#
Shoot at	27"	40#

Care and Treatment

If treated properly, your bow will last for decades. Rub the new bow with boiled linseed oil or pure tung oil for fifteen minutes. Rub on additional light coats every few days. Twenty rubbings are needed for a real moisture barrier.

Until fully protected, don't string the bow if it's been in humid conditions for more than a few hours. A permanent, speed-ruining set will result.

Store the bow in normal room conditions ... or as close to 50% humidity as practical.

The biggest threat to safety and performance is someone from the fiberglass tribe innocently drawing the bow past its designed draw length. This will probably break the bow, and will certainly increase string follow. One additional inch of follow reduces cast by several yards, making a bow shoot as if several pounds lighter.

Different Draw Weights and Lengths

For lighter or heavier bows, raise or lower the "tillering template" weights accordingly. For example, a 50# bow is 20% heavier, so add 20% to the draw weights at each stage of tiller.

For shorter or longer draw lengths, use the same tillering draw weights, just adjust where you read them. A 29" draw bow, for example, would be checked at about 10 1/2", 16", 21 1/5", 24 3/4" and 27".

Add or subtract 2" of bow length for each one inch change in draw length.

> *If properly treated, your bow will last for decades.*

For heavier bows, make the limbs about 1/8" wider per additional 4# of draw weight. For lighter bows stay 1.5" wide but narrow the grip a bit. Normally a 40# bow of most hardwoods would only be 1 1/4" wide. 1 1/2" was used here for safety. This extra 1/4" of width increased limb mass about two ounces, costing about three yards of cast. Not a bad insurance investment when working with wood of unknown strength. A future article will show how to determine wood strength before making the bow, letting you choose optimum limb width.

The limbs on heavier bows will become wider than the grip. For strength, the grip must be made thicker. 1 1/8" wide by 1 1/2" deep is a comfortable, safe size. When shaping the grip, the wood must thicken before narrowing.

Making A Bow String

A bowstring should be at least four times the bows draw weight. A 40# bow needs at least a 160# string. That's a hair less than 1/8" diameter if made of linen, yucca, dogbane, true hemp or sinew. A bit thicker if rawhide and thicker still if gut.

Linen will be used for this example. To determine the number of strands needed, first see how many pounds of pull are needed to break an individual strand. Then divide that number into 160.

If one strand breaks at 20#, then 8 strands are needed. But use 10 strands ... no one makes a perfect string. Cut the strands about half again longer than the bow ... cordage shortens as it's twisted. Divide into two plys of 5 strands each. Taper the last four inches of each ply with the edge of a sharp knife. Wax both plys, preferably with beeswax.

Starting about nine inches from the end of the plys, twist up about 2 1/2 inches of standard cordage.

Bend the cordage into a loop, setting one "Y" on top of the other.

Continue making cordage until a bow-length string is made.

The timber hitch is tied semi-permanently to the lower nock. It is easy to tie, and easy to adjust in the field.

Kiln Dried Wood

For those who do live in the driest of deserts, or who have the patience of a mongoose and just ... can't ... wait a few days

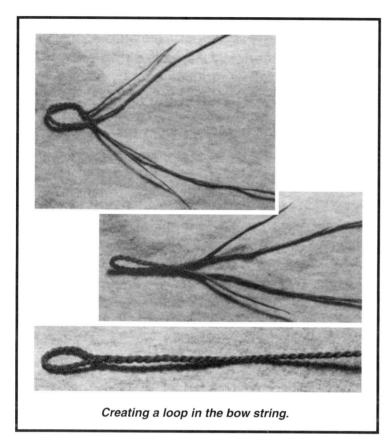

Creating a loop in the bow string.

for wood to dry, spend a few dollars and buy a length of 1 by 2 inch or larger kilndried, lumberyard hardwood. Hickory, maple, ash, elm, birch, white oak or red oak, in order of preference.

Despite oft-repeated, and obviously untested, myths to the contrary, kiln dried wood is as likely to make a good bow as airdried wood ... a slight misnomer since kilndried IS airdried. No matter how it was dried, avoid checked and warped wood.

When making bows from boards, don't think that you're settling for unnatural, processed material. Boards are simply trees that have been treated in a rather undignified manner. You are freeing a thing of dignity from the humiliation of static servitude.

Each growth ring in a board was the under-the-bark surface of a tree some year in the past. Use your spokeshave as a time machine. Scrape back through the board's summers and winters, down to the first growth ring which covers a 2" by 66" area. On some boards this may only involve rounding edges, re-establishing the tree's natural curvature. Choose a board with at least 7/8" of wood left under this first full ring.

About one in fifty boards will qualify if 1" stock ... maybe one in ten if 2" stock.

(more)

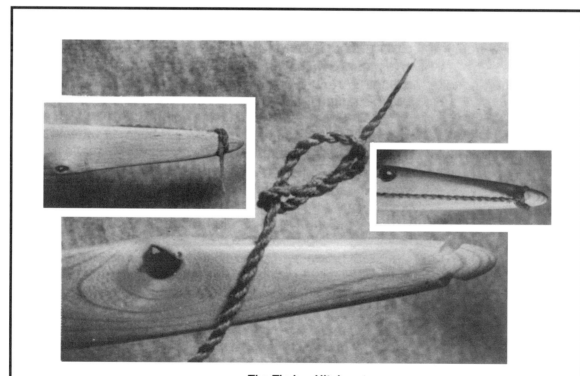

The Timber Hitch.

Reject boards with knots larger than a rice grain. Knots on boards can not easily be left raised for strength, as on a tree's surface.

Notes On Tool Use

Tool motions should be long and sweeping, not concentrated in one small area.

The tool should be in motion before and after bearing down into wood, like an aeroplane practicing landings.

Never start in the same place twice; stagger touch-down and lift-off.

To prevent washboard, change the East-West angle of the tool each stroke, then one pass will remove the crests of the last.

In the early stages of tiller, a lot of wood can come off with little effect ... but toward the end, tissue-thin wood removal will cause noticeable tiller changes. Until you have a feel for this, take off less wood than you want to.

Tim Baker teaching the fine art of bowmaking at the Glass Buttes Knap-In, 1991.

Bowmaking books

The Bent Stick,
by Paul Comstock. POB 1102, Delaware, OH 43015.
The Book of Primitive Archery,
by Jay Massey. POB 429, Girdwood, AK 99587.
Bows and Arrows of the Native Americans,
by Jim Hamm. Bois d'Arc Press, Rt. 1, Box 395X, Azle, TX 76020.
Cherokee Bows and Arrows,
by Al Herrin. Al Herrin makes the bows of his ancestors, the Eastern Woodland bow, sibling to the bow of this article. White Bear Publishing, Dept. B., Rt. 3, Box 172, Tahlequah, OK 74464.
Makin' Meat - 1: The Primitive Bow and Arrow,
by John McPherson. Prairie Wolf, POB 96, Randolph, KS 66554.
The Art of Making Primitive Bows and Arrows,
by D.C. Waldorf. Mound Builders Arts, POB 702, Branson, MO 65616.
American Indian Archery,
by Reginald and Gladys Laubin. Univ. of Oklahoma.

The finished belly should be as smooth as a banister. Nicks and tool marks can't be sanded out locally; a several inch long sweep must be sanded out with each mark. Otherwise a low spot will result, weakening the bow.

Unless wood is flawless, a spokeshave is not safe past the mid-tillering point. It can snag belly wood, especially at knots. Use only rasps, scrapers and files towards the end.

Raised back knots are left untouched, relying on the tree's engineering wisdom.

One of the best bow tools is a beam of hard light. Sunlight, or a single incandescent bulb. When held at certain angles to this light, even small irregularities in the wood stand out like moon craters.

The best single bowmaking tool available is the "bowscraper". It's narrow enough to ride the dips and rises of a stave, and has a vertical blade to prevent snagging. Weight can be brought to bear on the work, removing wood quickly. An occasional pass with a medium rasp helps prevent washboard. **$16.50 includes S/H. Dick Baugh, 490 Gary Ct., Palo Alto, CA 94306.**

If you can't find certain woodworking tools in your area call the **Woodsmith Store, Berkeley, CA (414) 540-6247.**

Wiseman's Frontier Supply handles natural, unbleached linen string. **(616) 828-5558.**

STICKS AND STONES WILL MAKE MY BOW

Text, Photos and Illustrations By Barry Keegan

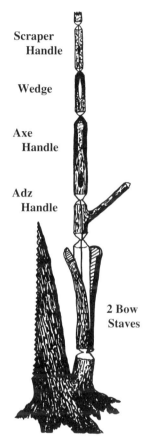

Scraper Handle

Wedge

Axe Handle

Adz Handle

2 Bow Staves

Figure 1. Natural hardware store.

Photo 1. Selecting a sucker growing from the base of a mature tree.

When it comes to making longbows the old way, my first four attempts are in eight pieces. My first "whole bow", which I still shoot, is made of hickory! I've used trickier woods for bows since then but to make a replica of an existing Native American bow by using only stone tools, I wasted no time in deciding what wood I'd use.

The Bowstave

A stave of hickory was cut on a hot day in late July (Photo 1). A summer kill speeds up a process described later in this article. Even when it is green, hickory is a very hard wood. This eight inch diameter tree was cut down in about on hour with a stone axe (Fig. 1).

I seasoned this seven foot long stave in my garage for a year. A thousand years ago it would have seasoned in a shelter; far from the fire but out of the rain, where it could dry slowly without checking.

Making My Tools

The Stone Axe - I made the stone axe blade by flaking a river cobble of Catoctin Greenstone which closely resembled the shape of the desired axe blade (Photo 2). Billets of antler and dogwood were used to percussion flake the blade to shape, and a very hard quartzite pecking stone was used to peck the blade into a smooth, rounded and symmetrical shape. Next, I polished and sharpened the blade on a large flat gritty stone using water and loose sand as an abrasive.

The blade was shaped so the sides were widest at the center. The edges I tapered slightly from front to rear so the blade or celt fit more tightly in the handle with use. The blade had a 60° angle, an angle more acute than this may chip or crumble with use (Fig. 2).

The handle was also made of hickory. Medium to soft woods are easier to shape but easier to break. I kept the top of the handle thick where the hole for the blade was to be. I left enough thickness on the sides of the hole, as well as on the top, to keep it from splitting during use. The hole should tilt slightly down toward the front so, when inserted, there is an 85° angle between the underside of the blade (where it extends out of the front) and the front side of the handle. This angle allows the axe to make a straight, not a glancing cut and reduces unnecessary shock.

The blade must fit tight on the top and the bottom of the hole only, never on the sides, or the blade then becomes a "wedge" and splits open the handle. Within the hole, the celt should contact in the cove of the handle but not on the outer edges or splinters may chip out around the hole. I curved the top of the handle to make little or no contact with the tree as I cut.

The Stone Adz - To make my adz blade, greenstone was also used. I flaked, pecked and ground it to shape the same way that I made the celt. I used a long stone with a corner-like edge (Fig. 3) to grind out the hollow underside of the adz blade with sand and water.

To haft the adz I cut a section of hickory trunk with an angled branch for the handle. I split a two-piece "vice-like" head, the trunk part, and hollowed it out by burning and/or carving on both the top and bottom for a perfect socket to hold the blade (Fig. 4). The back of this

The Widest Part is in the center

60°

Figure 2. Axe - Side view.

(more)

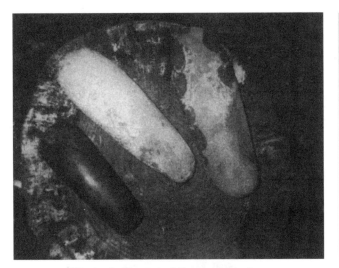

Photo 2. Stages of Greenstone Axe:
from right - flaked, pecked, ground.

Photo 3. Close-up of adz head showing buckskin
"gasket" around Greenstone.

socket was made flat so the blade wouldn't be driven deeperr into the handle with use.

A buckskin "gasket" wrapped the blade to keep it from slipping out. The top or "cap" piece was shaped so the rawhide wrapping was in a protected trough so as not to catch on any wood during use. I used a thick rawhide strip to wrap the top piece to the handle. The rawhide shrink-dried but the blade still fell out with use. I made a wooden wedge and drove it into the back of the adz head and the blade never fell out again (Photo 3). The wedge can be pulled out to remove the blade for re-sharpening. I tested this adz on seasoned black locust and it cut well. I had to round the top edge of the blade a bit because it was flaking. Rounding it cured the problem.

Flint Flake Spokeshave - For my spokeshave handle I cut a branch and split it in half. Between these two halves, I lashed a flint flake wrapped in a buckskin gasket. This heavy duty tool worked much better, as I quickly got sore using hand-

Figure 5. Snapping a flake to create a fast, sharp tool.

held flakes. I lashed a snapped flake (Fig. 5) in the handle and it scraped well. So did a thick fresh water mussel shell that I ground to a 75° angle on the outer edge. Nothing was as durable as the flaked-edge scraper which I made by placing the "edge-to-be" on a smooth wooden surface and tipping it up a bit, then tapping the top of the flake with an antler billet or something hard, I created a smooth row of flakes with little to no serration; smooth flake = smooth scrape (Fig. 6).

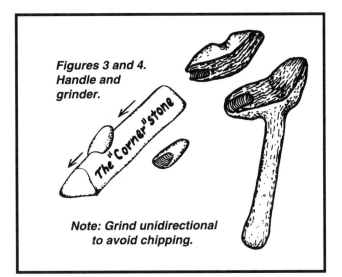

Figures 3 and 4. Handle and grinder.

The "Corner" stone

Note: Grind unidirectional to avoid chipping.

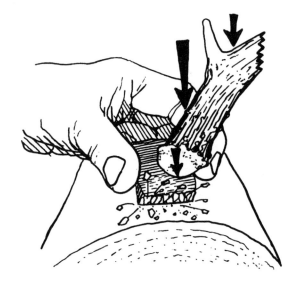

Figure 6. Creating the most permanent edge for a spokeshave. The surface must be flat.

Photo 4. Splitting the stave with the axe head and wooden wedges. Note the wear on the mallet.

Photo 5. "Steering" the split by pulling on the thicker limb, keeping the split in the center.

Obtuse angles last longer, but acute angles cut much faster. An 85° angle is a good compromise. If the angle is too acute it will crumble, leaving tiny flakes in your bowstave.

Fine-tuning the Tools - I spent the winter using and fine tuning my tools while I waited for my bowstave to thoroughly dry .

Splitting the Bowstave - During seasoning, a small crack had formed on the end of my bowstave. This crack was used to help start the split. I popped my greenstone celt out of its handle and placed it into the small crack on the end of the stave, and drove it in with a Rhododenderon mallet (Photo 4). This was very strenuous and difficult because the celt is rounded and tended to pop out of the split. Since then I have used a huge low-angled (15-20 degrees) wedge of Osage Orange (or any hard wood) with a fire hardened tip, which is as wide as the stave. My mallet was much too small.

I used at least four smaller wedges and a partner to hold down the stave as I split it. We guided the split with two wedges on each side. If I split it from one side only, I may have put a "propeller twist" in my bowstave, rendering it useless.

My stone celt was great for cutting through the stringy hickory strips that held the stave halves together. A large knot at the far end required some work to split apart but the celt was THE tool to use; wooden wedges get torn up on their tips by knots and splinter-strips.

My choice of a straight grained hickory made this step and the next ones rather easy. Beware of spiral grained bark because it means spiral grained wood. A slight spiral can be steered in a split by starting a parallel split below or above to create a zig-zagged "staircase" effect which can be cleaned up with the adz, but it is a lot more work (Photo 5 - Fig. 7).

Figure 7.

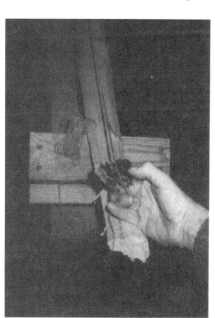

Photo 7. Dogbane chalkline.

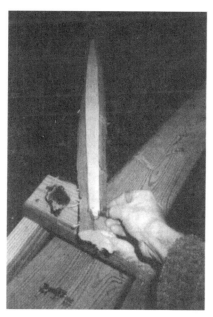

Photo 8. Stenciling the pattern.

Photo 10. Adz to within 1/4".

Photo 6. Removing bark with a bone scraper.

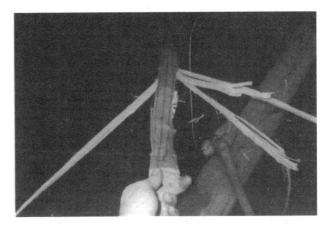

Photo 9. Adzing and pulling splits to the center.

The Back of the Bow - My summer killed hickory peeled easily leaving little work for the bow's back. Even when dried the hickory bark still peeled, exposing a leather-like grain texture on the wood surface. If I had cut this tree in the fall or winter I would have had to scrape off the bark. Hickory is one of the most difficult trees to scrape bark from. A broken or split bone is a great tool for scraping bark from a tree because the sharp edge cuts through the bark but does not dent or cut the surface of hard wood. This tool does require a lot of resharpening (Photo 6).

Blanking Out the Bow - Wedges were used to blank out the bow by splitting and pulling long splints from the stave. I did most of the work this way and it was simple. I then used the adz to roughly shape the bow stave so it was ready to draw the final shape upon.

Drawing the Centerline and Final Shaping - I established the best position to draw the centerline on the back of the bow by looking down its length and width, avoiding knots and looking for the flattest section of the tree.

A primitive "chalk-line" made of dogbane string rubbed well with charcoal from softwood, held tight along the length of the stave and snapped repeatedly, made a clear centerline (Photo 7). Some low areas required drawing in.

I used a stencil of a Native American bow, one of three examples of bows from 1656 AD, Virginia, which are in the Ashmolean Museum of Oxford. The bow is 68 1/2" long, 1 11/16" wide and 11/16" thick. The stencils are made from measurements taken via calipers at measured intervals on the back view and side view of the bow. A thousand years ago I could have borrowed my father's bow to trace.

I laid the stencil on the stave, aligning it to the charcoaled centerline and traced it on with a sharp piece of charcoal (Photo 8). I looked down the bow once again to be sure that I did not trace a twisted or distorted outline.

Adzing the Sides to Final Blank - I then used my adz to work strips loose which I peeled from the handle to the nock ends (Photo 9). The Ashmolean bow is widest at the center or handle; not only from the "back" view but the side view as well. I did not need to worry much about complications of grain direction, as long as I adzed from the widest part to the thinnest, there was no way that I could undercut the grain.

I had to pay careful attention around knots because this is where the stone adz gets chipped! The angle that I swung the adz could do the same damage if I used it carelessly. I split splinters from the knot's bulge and pulled them away from the knot. I abraded the tough parts smooth with quartzite.

Adzing was best done with a soft cushion for the bowstave to stand upon. A hard surface caused the bow to bounce, split or mushroom at the tips. I left an extra inch of length as a good safety measure, until tillering. The cushion also kept soil and moisture off of the bow. The best cushion was of sawdust or bow shavings in a pile with a leather pad covering.

An adz this size is best for bows! For thick parts of the stave, I could use two hands to swing it when I had someone holding the bow for me. I also held the adz with one hand to gently sculpt the nock-ends.

I adzed no closer than 1/4" to the drawing of the bow (Photo 10). The gentle glancing blows of fine adz working tended to loosen the wedge and I had to re-set it a lot.

Photo 11. Using the spokeshave.

Figure 8. Padding on top and bottom allows the stave to be held tight.

Figure 9. Above - The work sequence for making the nocks.

Figure 10. Right - Primitive tillering device.

Spokeshaving and Rough Tiller - That last 1/4" of wood outside of the charcoal outline I removed with the scraper. I call this a spokeshave because it is used like one. To hold the bow still so I could use both hands on my stone flake spokeshave (Photo 11), I had to wedge the far end of the bow under a rock or log. Next, I padded the near end of the bow so it could be wedged into one of my hips. I held the bow quite still by propping my knee under the bow so it laid along my leg, while I leaned all of my weight against it. This kept the bow from flipping over as I worked the top (Fig. 8).

I shaved toward myself, again, from the handle to the nocks to follow the grain. I scraped it down to the charcoal line, which I removed by rounding the sharp corners slightly.

Then I rough-tillered the bow, tapering it gradually and evenly from the handle which I kept twice as thick as the tips. I checked how even the bow bent, periodically as I worked, by pulling both ends back; after resting the bow by its handle, against my bent knee. The bow was bent back about six inches and the arc looked uniform. I needed nocks to tiller it from this point.

Sawing the Nocks - I used my adz to get as close as possible to the final shaping of the nocks and tips. I now

realize how hard hickory wood is. I spent an entire day sawing in the nocks . The bottom of the Ashmolean bow is round with two grooves and at the top is a peg-nock (Fig. 9). I rounded the bottom quite easily with the adz and tapered the peg nock. I had to saw and abrade the square shoulders of the peg nock as well as the round peg. The deep grooves on the bottom were sawn in with a long serrated knife edge (Photo 12). Sandstone blocks made great abraders. A quartzite flake is a combination saw-abrader. When serrated by pressure flaking, a quartzite knife is like a sandstone saw that cuts and widens at the same time; the longer the cutting edge, the better!

Tillering the Bow - To tiller the bow I needed a string. I describe this in depth later in this article. I used a loose string of sufficient thickness at first, so I did not have to bend the bow to string it. I hooked the handle of the bow on a cut off tree branch about four feet from the ground (Fig. 10), which was plenty sturdy enough to allow me to pull the bow back and examine its bend. It helped to have someone do this for me while I watched from a distance, so I could really see the arc.

I finished tillering with the spokeshave. The bow bent very evenly and did not require much work to complete as far as scraping was concerned. Pulling the bow back was a lot of

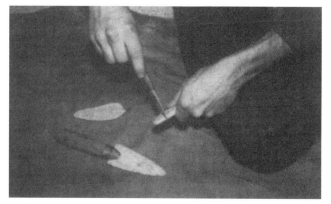

Photo 12. Two quartzite knives and a serrated flake used for cutting nocks.

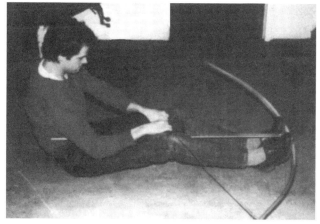

Photo 13. Pulling back the bow.

Photo 14. Finishing the belly with a snapped flake.

work for me because it was a 60 lb. draw at a 29" tiller and I pulled it back fifty times for each inch of tillering. I am no muscle man so I came up with a less exhausting method of pulling the bow back, using my whole body (Photo 13).

The Final Finish - I used snapped flint flakes of acute, obtuse and right angles as "cabinet scrapers" to smooth the bow (Photo 14). These tools were so sharp that I paid little attention to grain direction while removing all of the marks from the sides and belly of the bow. Then I checked the tiller once again to be sure it did not change. My next step was to waterproof the bow. I thawed rendered bear fat, which is stored frozen, and rubbed it into the bow with my hands. I laid the bow in the sun until it soaked in the fat and put on another coat. I repeated this process about four times or until it would not soak in any more fat.

I then used a bone to burnish the entire bow. I laid the bow on a flat surface so I could rest my weight on the bone in my hand. By rubbing back and forth, fast and hard, I heated up the bow and polished it. This closed the pores of the

Photo 15. The author bringing the finished project to full draw.

wood and drove fat into them at the same time; moisture will now be less easily absorbed by the bow.

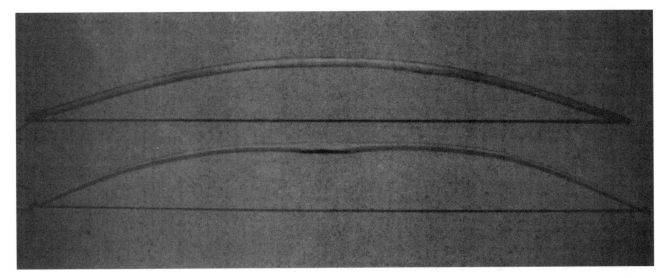

Photo 16. The author's bow (top) with hickory string. Anthony Follari's bow (bottom) with a dogbane string. Both bows were made entirely with stone tools.

Bowstrings

Bowstring #1 - To tiller the bow I twisted a "three strand Flemmish bowstring" of hand spun linen fiber from Sweden. For a 60 lb bow I needed 15 strands; 5 per bundle. I waxed these strands with beeswax, twisted in an eye splice with extra strands to reinforce the nock areas and reverse wrapped the three bundles from one end to the other. I still have this string.

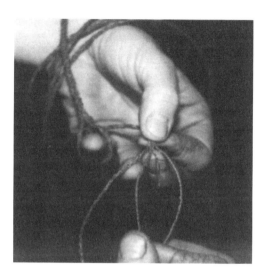

Bowstring #2 - I used the bark that I peeled from my hickory bowstave to attempt a natural fiber bowstring. I soaked the dry bark for two hours until it was impregnated with water. I then split and peeled the outer bark from the inner and then split it again so that all I had were the innermost strips of bark that "touched" the wood - as thin and long as I could peel them. Taking the wet fibers into three separate bundles, I reverse wrapped in the eyesplice and twisted the three bundles down the length of the string. This was a lot like my linen one but I needed to splice in more bark strips to maintain an even thickness.

I quit at half length; before I had invested that much time in building a bowstring that might break a bow that took a lot of work. This string needed to be tested!! I decided that a good test for the string would be a "bow-drill fire"! I used my string on a small bow, and used a set of yucca and cedar. I later broke this string in a bow-drill fire attempt with a Red Oak spindle and fireboard. I had forgotten to soak the string a little while before use: it may have lasted longer if it hadn't been dry and brittle! For a bowstring of bark fiber; oil is a must but a bow-drill string with oil on it is useless.

Bowstring #3 - I used more of my bowstave bark to make a whole bowstring with three very long strands, I added in the extra strips for length, and the eyesplice and lower nock tie area. The string broke when I strung the bow. It was too thin!

Bowstring #4 - I made another string from hickory bark that was much too thick! This was okay though because the bark fiber shrank when it dried - loosing half of its thickness. It dried to be of sufficient size because I strung it to fistmill (6 inches from bow at the grip) and drew it to full draw; a huge risk for my bow - and it didn't break. Success at last.

Bowstring #5 - I made another bowstring of dogbane, with six reverse wrapped threads of thirteen foot lengths. I reverse wrapped these together in pairs so I was left with three strings of double reverse wrapped thread. I then reverse wrapped these into an eye spliced three strand twist bowstring of Flemmish design, adding in an extra double reverse wrapped insert at the eyesplice as well as the tie-off area for the lower nock end. This one broke!

Bowstring #6 - Anthony Follari made a dogbane bowstring using two bundles in a reverse wrap which was as thick as my surviving hickory bowstring. This was for his stone tool bow.

My dogbane string broke during the stringing process. Anthony's string made it to full draw and has not broken yet. Of the two dogbane strings, we were both glad that mine broke! Despite the phenomenal amount of work it took me to make it, I wouldn't want to have to make a bow string that way again. I learned a lot from these bow strings and of the different designs and attempts; I would recommend Anthony's method because dogbane has year-round raw material gathering availability. It takes a little less time than inner tree bark and dogbane is a more predictable fiber. One hickory tree is not always like the other. Mockernut works best for me and hickory is not the best choice of bark fibers for bowstrings. "Basswood is questionable but Red Mulberry is great if you get the right tree." I believe that Elm bark is a possibility because it peels eight months of the year and behaves a lot like hickory bark.

Credits
I would like to credit a lot of my learning to Errett Callahan of Cliffside Workshops, where for two years straight I took all of his classes. It was there that I made my tools and my first bow that did not break. It was at his class that I made the bow in this article! Since I have learned a lot through trial and error, I had to practically make two more bows just to record the data needed to write this article. This includes making tool handles, a whole lot of string, and noting bit reshapenings. I still shoot that same stone tool bow!

WOOD UNDER STRESS

Text and Illustrations By Hari Heath

Few things are at once so simple and yet so complex as the bow. This graceful bend of wood pulled by a string has been used to bring home food, defend against enemies, or conquer new territories for millenniums. Humankind has been shaped by the results of this simple weapon. With passionate inquisitiveness the archers of antiquity have delved into the mystery of wooden springs that fling things.

What are the design principles that make bows work? What happens inside the wood while it is "working?" What has been tried from ancient times to present? How can we make a bow shoot faster without breaking?

Wooden archery is best understood by understanding the rules that allow it to work. Like most rules there are many exceptions, but generally they hold true.

Bows work because stress is applied to the wood via the string. The key to success is understanding stress and the materials ability to handle it. Stress management.

Wood is a complex structure that comes from trees. The diversity of the many species and individual examples of each, especially in relation to the successful application of stress is an immense subject. Available sun, water, and climatic conditions as well as harvest and seasoning processes can greatly affect the individual bowstave. But there remains amongst the diversity some common threads.

Wood is a cellular composition of fiber structures commonly referred to as grain. The grain occurs in several forms on the tree. Vertical grain fibers run up and down the trunk of the tree in each annular grain. Annular grain is produced every year (in temperate climates) over the previous years annular grain. It should be noted that the only "living" part of a tree is the leaves or needles and the inner bark which grows new "wood" each spring until dormancy in the winter. The wood and bark of the tree are essentially "dead" like your own hair and fingernails.

A tree must withstand the forces of nature, especially a lifetime of wind which requires flexibility through repetitive tension and compression cycles. Ideal qualities for a bow.

When a bow is unstrung and assuming it is straight, the length of the back (the part facing the intended target) would be the same as the length of the belly (the part facing the archer). When it is strung and pulled, the back becomes longer (tension) and/or the belly must become shorter (compression). Somewhere between the two forces lies the neutral plane.

The ability of the wood to successfully handle the applied stress of tension and compression and perform efficiently depends on the ability of the bowyer to understand and work with the available grain structure, design as close as possible to the failure point of the material used, and to arrange the configuration of the weapon so that it will have the least amount of moving mass upon release of the string. Often that means compromise.

While stress on wood is the main subject of this article, it is important to understand that the moving mass of the bow limbs affects the efficiency of the bow. Efficiency in this case being defined as the amount of energy transferred to the arrow relative to the amount of energy applied to the bow. How much mass, how far it has to move, the radial distance from the mass to its pivot point (the bow handle), whether it is "working" mass or just going along for the ride, are important considerations in the design process.

Lets add one rule concept and then dissect a few examples from archery's long history. I call it the 2 x 8 rule. If you add twice the width you get twice the strength, but if you add twice the depth you get 8 times the strength. Obviously by adding twice the width you'll double your strength, but how does deepening the bow add so much? By placing the tension/compression forces farther apart.

For a first example lets look at the English longbow. This design existed long before there was an England, but since the English refined it, popularized it, and built a nation with its military results, I'll let them claim the design as their own.

The English long bow is a weapon with a narrow width and a deep rounded belly. To handle the stresses imposed by this cross-sectional design it must necessarily be made from highly stress resistant wood, and it must be long. Especially if it is to be a 100# to 125# war bow pulled to 30" or so of draw.

Figure 1. Mid-limb cross-sections of different bow designs.

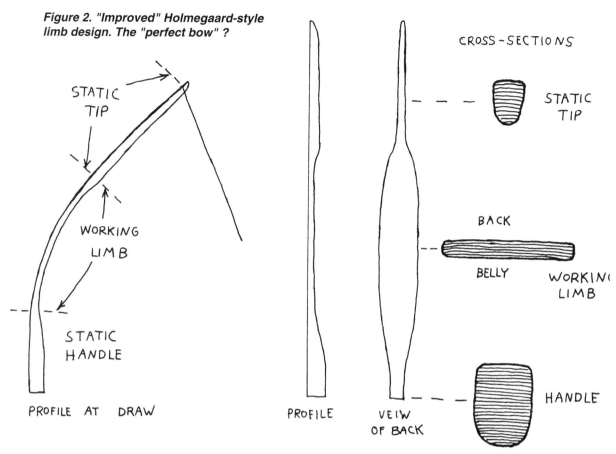

Figure 2. "Improved" Holmegaard-style limb design. The "perfect bow" ?

STATIC TIP

WORKING LIMB

STATIC HANDLE

PROFILE AT DRAW

PROFILE

VEIW OF BACK

CROSS-SECTIONS

STATIC TIP

BACK

BELLY

WORKIN(LIMB

HANDLE

The compromises necessary to pull off this design may not result in a net benefit. Getting strength from increased depth instead of width reduces cast robbing mass, but because the tension/ compression forces are farther apart, the arc of the bow must be more gradual and therefore longer which increases cast robbing mass. The rounded belly design also concentrates stress in the center of the belly.

While there are some negative aspects of this design there are also positive ones. If constructed in the classic D-tillered style all of the parts from handle to limb tips are "working wood" and contribute to the cast of the arrow.

During the first half of this century American target archers popularized the American longbow, a design similar to the English longbow. It retained the flat backed round belly cross-section, the overall length, and often the horn nocks of the English longbow, but had a wider shallower cross-section. A design halfway between the long bow and the flat bow.

Perhaps the best design for a durable efficient high performance wooden weapon is the flatbow. Historically it was found on both sides of the Atlantic and has a known history of over 8,000 years (Comstock, **Traditional Bowyers Bible**, Volume II). It's durability comes from the "wider is stronger" theory, keeping the tension/compression forces closer together. This allows a more radical bending arc and a shorter limb length for a more efficient cast. To optimize performance of the flatbow a rectangular cross-section limb design is often used. This causes an even stress or "work" across the

full width of the limb. This can be achieved by selecting a stave from a large diameter log or decrowning. Decrowning is a careful process of removing the crown from the back of the bow while keeping the annular grain running longitudinally on the back of the bow.

The minus side of the flatbow design is that when you double the width to double the strength you also double the mass. In other words instead of adding a little depth for a small gain in limb mass, you add a lot of width for a large gain of limb mass. This can be compensated for by flaring out to a flatbow design at mid-limb and flaring back to a narrow deep tip.

Another technique used to manage stress is to apply other materials which have greater stress resistance than the wood itself. Sinew backing is one example. In addition to

Hari Heath is the owner of Heathen Arms, and is the developer of The Bow Vise. Hari produces primitive bows and arrows,supplies bowmaking materials, and conducts classes in bow and arrow making. Contact him at: Box 126, Santa, ID 83866.

Support SPT member suppliers and teachers.

being a more durable fiber than wood (under tension forces) it shrinks when it dries and pulls the bow into a more reflexed profile. This has some hidden benefits. First the sinew is carrying a considerable portion of the tension before the wood begins to feel tension stresses, and secondly this "pulls" the neutral plane closer to the back effectively leaving more wood available to resist the compression forces.

For those bow designs which exert extreme forces a composite of sinew backing with a wood core and a horn belly can be used. The sinew takes the tension, the horn is highly resistive to compression, and the wood core acts as a "filler material" to keep the tension/compression forces apart. On the minus side, horn, hide glue, and sinew are approximately twice the density of wood. If the addition of this higher density mass is essential because of high stress factors in the design, then the weapon should benefit from their application. If the design of the weapon is moderate enough to be successful as an all wood selfbow then the addition of sinew and horn will probably result in a net loss of arrow performance. Moisture sensitivity of hide glue and the economy of construction effort also present a negative factor against sinew backing and the addition of horn on a bows belly.

One example of a simple composite bow style is the horse bow found among the plains tribes of North America. It is a short narrow and usually powerful bow used for hunting and war. The sinew backing and horn belly allow it to be pulled to full draw. A narrow and short design like this usually breaks with all wood construction.

The most extreme design to use all natural materials is the Turkish bow. Its long static recurves almost touch together forward of the handle when unstrung. The "working" part of the bow is a relatively short section of the limbs which begin with a reflexed profile and then are radically bent with strong leverage forces from the static recurves. The stresses applied are phenomenal as is the resulting performance. Turkish records for arrow flight exceed 900 yards, although the exact distance of a Turkish yard isn't known. Modern records for "primitive class" flight competition exceed 521 yards (Dan Perry, *Primitive Archer Magazine*, Vol. 2, issue 2, p. 5).

The Nez Pierce horn bow is another example of a unique high stress design concept. Slabs of horn are cut from bighorn sheep, heated and bent to shape for each limb and joined at the handle. The sheep horn forms the belly/compression half of the bow and sinew is applied to form the back of the bow. Both materials are exceptionally well suited for the tasks applied to them, however some replicators of the horn bow design report sluggish performance. Perhaps the denser "filler material" in the neutral plane area inhibits the recovery rate of the limbs.

A simplistic equation that I find helpful in designing a bow is the "longer/wider/weaker" rule. If a bow is designed longer, the stress is spread out over a greater arc. If it is made wider the stress is dispersed across the width of the limb, and if it is made weaker less stress is applied to the bow. The principals can be reversed if the goal is to increase stress and therefore performance. However, if the goal is increased performance with its corresponding stress, narrowing the bow limbs may not be a good idea.

If one were to study the current rage of selfbow technology and attempt to design and build the "perfect bow" (Fig. 2), one would probably craft a weapon with the following details:

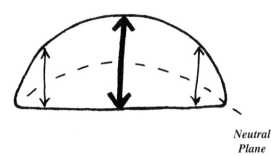

Neutral
Plane

Figure 3. Holmegaard Mid-limb Cross-section. A deeper center carries greater stress. The edges "go along for the ride" and contribute less "work".

A narrowed handle to improve the archers paradox and provide a comfortable grip
Wide flat limbs in the "working" section for efficient durable performance
Narrow deep static tips to reduce mass for increased cast.

The "perfect bow" would be a little over five feet long for a six foot tall archer and the static tips would help reduce stacking at this relatively short bow length.

After crafting our "perfect weapon" (probably with many experiments and refinements) we might happen to turn around and look back about 9,000 years or so and find that we made few if any improvements on the state of the bowyers art. Take the Holmegaard bow for example (Callahan, *Bulletin of Primitive Technology,* issue 8, p. 52) Perhaps the only area that its design could be improved is in the working limb cross-sectional shape. The convex back applies greater stress to the center of the limb than the edges. The use of a more rectangular cross-section would spread the "work" across the full width of the limbs for a more durable stress resistant design (Fig. 3).

How was the bow understood and developed by our ancestors? This is a question that will probably never be fully answered. Wood and cordage do not last long in the elements. The few examples that have come our way from peat bogs and caves have given us glimpses of the past, a past that predates written language and modern objective scientific theory.

The ancient bowyer was at best a subjective scientist. Intuition and "feel" may have played the greatest role in the development of ancient archery. The language and therefore the intellectual thought processes of bowyers past no doubt were much similar, and yet modern technology has done little to advance wooden archery beyond a simple man diligently working with a stick in one hand and an edged stone in the other 9,000 years ago.

THE CAUSES OF ARROW SPEED

By Tim Baker

Accuracy and arrow speed are both important when hunting. Arrow speed can be raised by shooting a heavier bow, but a heavier bow is harder to shoot accurately.

The solution is to design a more efficient bow. Here, a more efficient bow is defined as one which will shoot a given arrow faster per pound of draw weight.

The speed of a given arrow is determined by:

1. **The amount of muscle energy put into the bow as the bow is drawn. This amount of energy is determined by:**
   - **A. Draw weight**
   - **B. Draw length**
   - **C. String height**
   - **D. Bow profile**
2. **Obstructions to the flow of stored energy to the arrow. These obstructions are:**
   - **A. Limb mass**
   - **B. Mass placement**
   - **C. Hysteresis (internal friction in the limb)**
   - **D. String weight**
   - **E. String stretch**

Draw Weight

Consider two bows, identical in every respect except that one draws 40lb at 28", the other 60lb at 28". The 40lb bow will shoot a 500 grain arrow about 138 feet per second, as opposed to 60lb's 162 fps.

500 grain arrows were used in all tests here. Lighter arrows will fly faster, but have less penetrating power. 400 to 500 grain arrows are typically used by hunters shoting moderate weight bows.

Draw Length

Average-length, 50lb bows made from straight staves will shoot a 500 grain, normal-fletched arrow about as follows:

Draw length		Arrow speed (feet per second)
22"	--	133
24"	--	138
26"	--	142
28	--	147

The difference between 142fps at 26" and 147fps at 28", just five feet per second, may seem too small to be concerned with. But for average-design, average-length bows, one additional pound of draw weight raises arrow speed by about 1 fps. This means that a 5fps cast increase raises performance at 50# and 28" to that of a 55lb bow drawn 26". A "free" 5lb performance advantage since both bows are equally hard to pull and hold.

At 22" the above 50lb bow equals the performance of a typical 35lb bow drawing 28". Both 22" ad 28" versions are equally hard to pull to full draw but one performs as if 15lb heavier than the other, a "free" 15lb advantage.

If each of a bow's design features can be optimized the accumulated fps increase can be substantial. Even when comparing similar bow types well designed 35lb bows can easily be made to out-perform poorly designed 60lb bows. It's worth being concerned over one or two fps per design feature.

String Height

If braced 7" high, a given 50lb bow drawing 28" shoots 148fps. If the string is lowered to 4" draw weight at 28" drops a couple of pounds, but arrow speed increases a couple of fps. This result contradicts all expectation. When low-strung the string is limp and weak, and early draw is weak. How can such a bow shoot an arrow faster than when strung tightly?: When braced 4" high, and drawn to 28" the string travels 24". When braced 7" high and drawn to 28" the string travels 21".

The 4" bow weights 13lb when draw to 10", as opposed to 9lb for the 7" bow. This additional early-draw weight more than compensates for the 7" bow's higher late-draw weight.

Bow Profile

An arrow is thrown forward *ONLY BY ENERGY TAKEN FROM THE ARM WHILE DRAWING THE BOW. THE MORE WORK THE ARM IS MADE TO DO THE FASTER THE ARROW WILL FLY.*

Even though drawn to equal distances and weights, different bow designs can cause the arm to work harder. They do so by *MAKING THE BOW HARDER TO DRAW DURING EARLY AND MID PORTIONS OF THE DRAW. A bow's profile, or SIDE-VIEW SHAPE* determines the amount of *ACCUMULATED WORK* needed to draw the bow to length.

(more)

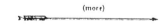

Tim has written more comprehensively on this subject in the "Design and Performance" chapter of The Traditional Bowyers Bible, Volume One, available from Bois d'Arc Press, P.O. Box 233, Azle, Texas, 760220 He also runs the Primitive Archery Switchboard. Information on bow design, construction, and material sources. 510 652-0502. If you have any questions or comments feel free to call or write: Tim Baker, 6609 Whitney St., Oakland, Ca. 94609.

Here are two bows, each drawing 50lb at 28". "Bow "A" is 48" long and made from a straight stave. It shoots a given arrow 142fps. Bow "B" is 48" long, sinew-backed, and highly recurved. It shoots the same arrow 167fps. Even though having the same draw weight these two bow shoot as if more than twenty pounds apart. How can this be?

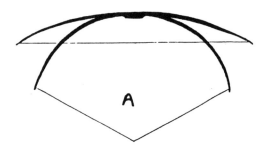

Bow "A" stores far less energy than "B". Note the different weights at various lengths of draw:

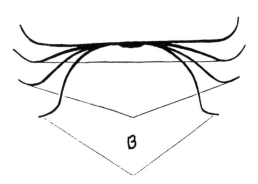

Draw length -- draw weight		
Bow "A" 10" -- 7.1lb		
15	--	14
20	--	24
25	--	38
27	--	47
28	--	52
Bow "B" 10" -- 10lb		
15	--	21
20	--	31
25	--	44
27	--	49
28	--	52

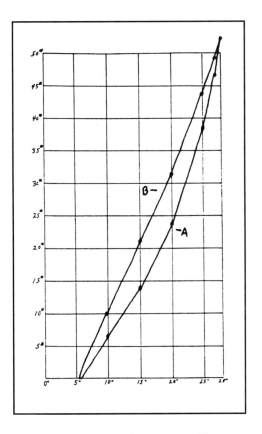

These values are easier to grasp if expressed graphical. The number of squares below the curves represent energy stored.

Bow "B" stores more energy than "A" ONLY because of its profile. If a bow of this side-view shape were made of pine, yew, fiberglass, horn/sinew, or dried spaghetti, energy storage would be the same.

Of course some ideal original, but now degraded profile doesn't count. "As-is," after-being-pulled-a-few-times profile is what matters. If all of the above pine-to-pasta bows were made the same width and thickness the pine and pasta versions would break, or take profile degrading sets. For a given original profile to survive, sufficiently elastic material must be used, or sufficiently wide/thin limbs must be made. Before proceeding the effects of varying string angles must be understood.

String Angle and Stack

Note how bow "A"s f-d line rises more vertically than "B"s during its last inches of draw. This bow becomes suddenly hard to pull toward the end of its draw. Such bows are said to "stack." Bows which stack are uncomfortable and inaccurate to shoot and, as can be seen from their respective arrow speeds, are very inefficient.

A common misconception holds that stack is do to the "fact" that wood suddenly becomes harder to pull just before breaking. We instinctively wince and cease pulling when we feel a bow suddenly stack. But, unfortunately, wood gives no clue whatever that it is about to break. Stack is due to increasing string angle during later stages of draw:

When a straight-stave bow is braced its string rests at about a 20 degree angle to the bow tips. During early stages of draw this angle provides great mechanical advantage: each inch of string movement advances limb tips just some fraction of an inch. A gear effect is at work. Later in the draw, as string angle nears 90 degrees, limb tips are advanced in lock-step with the string. All mechanical advantage is lost. And per-inch weight increase rises abruptly--the hard wall of stacking.

Here is a simple way to demonstrate that stack results from an increase in string angle:

Note the per-inch weight increase at mid draw of a short, straight-stave 50lb bow. Weight will increase about 2lb per inch. Remove the bow's string, replacing it with one half-again too long. This new string droops down loosely from the bow. Note its much greater angle. Again draw the bow, until its limbs are bent as far as when half drawn when strung normally. Now note the per-inch weight increase. It will be about 4lb per inch. And nothing has change except string angle.

Low early-draw weight is an additional, but indirect, cause of stack: Note the low early and mid-draw f-d angle of bow "A". If this bow had the same early draw f-d angle of "B" it would rise to its end point from a higher starting point, and the sense of stack would be diminished.

There are three reasons for the difference in energy storage between "A" and "B":

1. Short, straight-stave bows have high string angles.
2. "B" is a short bow, but its recurves maintain a low string angle. If its recurve had been just two inches long, for example, or set back at a very small angle, average string angle would not change much. If its recurve had been eight inches long and set back at a sharper angle, average string angle would be even lower. Energy storage would be proportionately higher.
3. Measured from point of string contact "B" is a shorter bow when braced than during mid and late draw when strings have lifted free.

Early in the draw, before string lift-off, when deprived of the leverage of its longer limbs, such bows are harder to pull than same-weight straight bows. During mid-draw, when draw weight would otherwise rise uncomfortably high, strings lift off their contact points, letting the retroverted tips WORK AS LEVERS, keeping final draw weight at tolerable levels. In effect such tips work as cams.

Because such recurves are harder to pull during early portions of the draw, total energy storage is very high.

OBSTRUCTIONS TO THE FLOW OF ENERGY TO THE ARROW

Limb Mass

For bows of average length and draw weight one ounce of bow mass effects arrow speed by about one foot per second. Coincidentally one pound of draw weight also effects arrow speed by about the same amount. This means, for example, that if the cast of a 40lb bow can be increased by ten fps it will have the arrow speed of a 50lb bow. Good design and craftmanship can easily raise arrow speed by 10 fps, and more. Lowering limb mass can account for part of this savings.

Double a board's width and its bending resistance doubles. Double its thickness and bending resistance increases eight times. For this reason narrow, thick limbs have less mass than wide, thin limbs. But narrow limbs must be longer to avoid overstraining, and long limbs have their own mass-related performance problems, as will be seen shortly. For a given length limbs should be as narrow as possible, while 1, maintaining a margin of safety against breaking, and 2, not taking a cast-robbing set.

Bows have about the same mass if made of heavy, strong wood or light, weak wood. Simply because less heavy wood is needed to do the same amount of work.

Mass Placement

On an average length and weight bow 65 grains of weight at each tip effects arrow speed by about 1fps. More than one ounce of weight would be needed mid-limb for the same effect (437 grains equal one oz.). One ounce of weight added to each tip costs about seven fps. One ounce placed next to the grip has no measurable effect.

Higher arrow speed will result if limbs are designed with less mass near the tips, more near the grip. If limb tips are made narrow and somewhat thicker they will weight considerably less than if wide and thin. Typical bow wood, 1/2" square by 1 1/4" long, weighs about 65 grains. Limbs with narrowest-likely tips will gain several fps in arrow speed compared to limbs with widest-likely tips.

(more)

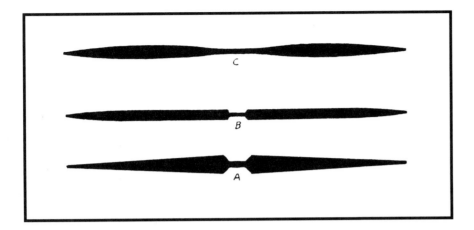

Of the three design extremes above, "A" places least mass near the tips, most near the grip. The reverse is true of "C".

But such wide near-grip wood, as in "A", is not often practical. Wide limbs must be taken from very large diameter trees, otherwise the bow's back will be too crowned.

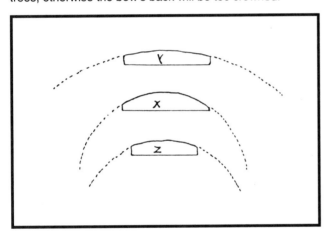

Crossection "X" is shown coming from a 6" diameter tree. "X" may be 3" wide, but because edge thickness is small compared to mid-section thickness less than two inches of its width is doing serious work--wood works eight times harder when twice as thick. This over-worked central two inches will more likely break.

Crossection "Y" originates from a 12" diameter tree. This crossections's entire width is working. This crossection is able to store far more energy.

Wide bow limbs can be made from small diameter trees if the crown is removed, creating a fairly rectangular crossection. De-crowned wood is best backed with sinew, rawhide, or other backings.

In most cases bow "B" is the best compromise between performance and ease of construction.

A two-foot long club is easier to swing than a three-foot long club. This is true for both people and bows.

Short, full-draw bows stack badly, storing less energy. But less energy is needed to throw short limbs forward. Long limbs do not stack, therefore store more energy, but more energy is needed to throw long limbs forward. Obviously some ideal trade-off point exists.

To locate this ideal bow length several bows were made, ranging in length from 47" to 94", each drawing 50lb at 28", each having 1 1/2" set. Each was shot through a chronograph using the same 500 grain arrow:

Length	Fps	Length	Fps
47" --	135	67 --	153
52 --	144	69 --	151
56 --	150	70 --	150
59 --	151	78 --	148
65 --	151	88 --	142
66 --	153	94 --	136

The mid to upper 60's is the most efficient straight-stave bow length at 28" of draw. Ideal bow length rises and falls with draw length. The traditional two-inch adjustment in bow length per inch of draw length is likely about correct.

Test note: Identical limb set was maintained for all tested bows. This required longer bows to be narrower, shorter bows to be wider. For the 47" bow to pull 28" and only take 1 1/2" set required 3" wide limbs, and a perfectly rectangular crossection. Obviously the old rule about not being able to draw farther than half of bow length needs to be erased from the books

Hysteresis (internal friction in the limb)

When measured under conditions of routine use--after being pulled to full draw once or twice--the slowing-down effect of hysteresis is reduced to insignificance.

In the past hysteresis has been measured on cold, un-worked in wood samples, or bows. Using this method cast-robbing hysteresis percentages are common. But this method is incorrect for bows. For all practacle purposes of archery, hysteresis can be ignored.

String Weight

Bows of average weight and length will be slowed by about 1fps for each 20 grains of added string weight. A typical

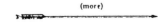

(more)

Following are approximate arrow speeds from various designs. All speeds are based on 50lb bows, drawing 28" and shooting a 500 grain, normal-fletched arrow.

ASYMMETRICAL -- 135fps -- 140 yards.

This may or may not have been the world's first bow. Being a simple, un-tillered branch, it is the easiest to make. It is gripped well below center, as with the modern Japanese bow. This ultra-primitive shoots more efficiently than might be expected. Its lower limb barely bends or moves, so limb mass is not as damaging as would at first seem. Unless made of very strong and elastic wood such bows must be longer than normal, and have lower draw weight.

STRAIGHT-STAVE -- 150 fps -- 160 yards.

If tillered near correctly, and having about 1 1/2" string follow.

DEFLEX TIPS -- 140fps -- 151 yards.

REFLEX LIMBS -- 155fps -- 174 yards.

Reflexed limbs must be bent farther when being braced. Cast is higher because of increased early draw weight. Since more energy is stored limbs must be wider, or made of stronger/more elastic wood or other materials.

NON-CONTACT RECURVES 155fps -- 174 yards.

Energy storage is higher because lower string angles prevent stack, raising mid-draw weight.

CONTACT RECURVES 165-plus fps 190-plus yards.

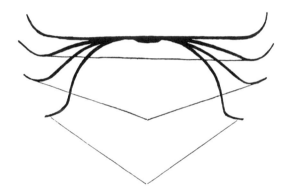

165fps is a medium figure. Depending on the percentage of limb length devoted to the recurve, and severity of the recurve, arrow speed could range from 156 yards to well over 200 yards. Higher energy storage, and resulting increased limb strains generally favor sinew backing for this, and the following two designs.

DEFLEX/RECURVE (Same speeds and text as for contact recurve)

Like the deflex-tipped willow, this deflex design wastes little energy storing capacity. In all lift-off designs energy storage is determined by recurve geometry. Deflexed limbs let a high-strung design nevertheless have high energy storage.

**TRIPLE CURVE (Same speeds and text
as for contact recurve)**

Apart from its striking beauty there is no advantage to this design over a standard lift-off recurve. These "Cupid-bow" shapes are no doubt derivative of early ibex-horn bows. Such bows reflect the horns natural curvature.

SETBACK LIMBS 152fps -- 169 yards.

Almost identical performance with straight-stave designs. Setback limbs start there bend from farther forward, tips therefore approach the string at a greater angle. The resulting slight increase in stack almost offsets gains from this designs higher early draw weight. The most common reason for setting limbs back is to overcome excessive string follow.

**REFLEX/RECURVE 180-plus fps -\
well above 220+ yards.**

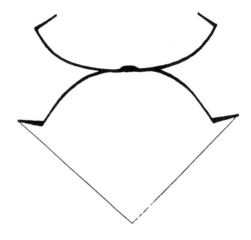

A typical Asiatic composite design. Such profiles are only possible using sinew and horn, usually with a wood core. These bows require extraordinary levels of knowledge and skill. Typically they are used for competitive flight shooting, or for war.

---

string weighs about 190 grains. If 250 grains, arrow speed would drop about 3fps, taking the cast of a 50lb bow to that of a 47lb bow.

Portions of the string near the arrow travel much faster than string near the limb tips. 65 grains of string weight would have to be added at each nock to slow the arrow 1fps. Strings generally break at the nocks, so this portion of the string can be thickened at no cost to arrow speed.

String Stretch

A bow string is under greatest strain not at full draw, but as the arrow is about to leave the bow, as limbs snap the string taught, sending the arrow on its way. Should a string stretch at this moment energy intended for the arrow will be absorbed by the string, slowing the arrow considerably. Low-stretch vegetable fibers, such as flax, true hemp, dogbane, and so on, will cast an arrow a few fps faster than elastic animal-based strings, such as sinew, rawhide and gut. If thickened enough to prevent stretch such animal strings will rise in weight, again slowing cast.

Straight-Stave Profiles

Straight-stave bows are easiest to make and the most accurate to shoot. Since they are also the most commonly made and used subtleties of their design are worth exploring farther here.

We've seen that both short bows and short-draw bows store less energy. Subtle differences of profile in long, full-draw, straight-stave bows also have an effect on energy storage, These differences are largely related to string angle. Tillering a bow so that near-tip string angle is kept as low as possible dampens stack and raises energy storage.

Because bow "A" bends more in the grip than at mid limb it has the most favorable string angle. But excessively round-in-the-handle bows nevertheless have slow cast. Because most of the energy is stored by a much smaller amount of wood the wood must inevitably fail, generally by taking a massive set, and in the very worst place for set to be taken: Even minimal set near the grip projects out to very large tip deflection--string follow. Bows with excessive string follow will obviously have low early draw weight, and will therefore store

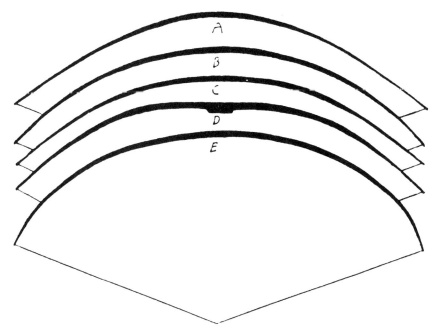

Because it is too flat-in-the-handle bow "D" is slightly less efficient than "C." Most of this design's bending is done mid limb. As a result string angle is higher. Because more work is being done by less wood mid limbs must either be dangerously overstrained or be made unusually wide. If made too wide mass will rise.

This design is required when either bow weight or wood strength requires limbs be wider than 1 1/2". A handle wider than 1 1/2" is too uncomfortable to grip, and two wide for arrows to accurately bend around. Most North American hard woods will yield a safe, efficient 50lb bow using "C"s narrow, bend-in-the-handle design.

"E" is an inefficient design. Its deflexed tips lower early-draw weight, and cause sever stacking. Energy storage is very low. Still, this is the smartest design in some circumstances:

Indians of the South West were forced to use willow for bows, an exceptionally weak and unelastic wood. Willow is capable of storing very little energy.

A stave of wood can only bend so far. It can store so much energy and no more. A third of a willow bow's energy storage capacity may be used up bracing the bow, energy that is unavailable to the arrow.

Deflex tips let a bow be braces without being bent. All of the bow's stored energy is now available to the arrow.

Such a willow/deflex bow will not cast an arrow as fast per pound of draw weight, but net arrow speed can nevertheless be higher.

---

less energy. If such bows bend too much near the grip then by definition they bend too little everywhere else, which means they are too massive everywhere else. Too-massive limbs rob arrow speed. Too round-in-the-handle bows also cause uncomfortable hand shock upon release.

Bow "B"s full-draw profile is a perfect arc of a circle. Limbs are bending equally everywhere along their length. More wood is employed storing energy, so limb set is reduced. In order for mid limbs to bend they must be thinner than in bow "A," lowering mass. "B" stores more energy than "A," and its lighter limbs respond more quickly. Still, this design in not the most efficient.

Bow "C" displays the optimum profile for a straight-stave bow. In order to bend properly a bow's limbs must be progressively thicker moving from tips to grip. A smooth gradual taper. But thicker wood will not bend as far before taking a set or breaking. Therefore thicker portions of a limb can not safely bend as far as thinner portions.

Tillering a bow to satisfy limb safety automatically results in a somewhat elliptical side-view shape, with two refinements: Near-grip set is more costly to performance, therefore, near-grip portions of the limb should be tillered to bend less--just enough to take virtually no set.

In addition, the last six to eight tipward inches of the limb should have little or no bend. Bend here would only raise string angle.

Tips should be as narrow as practical, and thick enough to barely bend. This saves mass where mass is most costly to arrow speed.

Some bows are very wide near the grip, tapering to narrow tips, as in bow "A" under MASS PLACEMENT, earlier. Such limbs do not taper in thickness. Perfect arc-of-a-circle tillering, as in "B," above is correct for these un-typical designs.

A poorly placed arrow from an 80lb bow may see an animal escape to heal its wounds, or die beyond tracking range.

A well-placed shot from a light bow will bring an animal down in sixty yards.

The best weight for a hunting bow is the weight which results in the most accurate shooting at 25 yards. For most hunters this will be between 45lb and 50lb.

The best design for a hunting bow is the design which results in the most accurate shooting at 25 yards. For most hunters this will be a long, straight-stave, full-draw bow, having moderate string follow, As in "Your First Primitive Bow," in the preceding article.

Construction of "Old Time" Southeastern Indian CANE ARROWS

by: Steve Watts -1983-

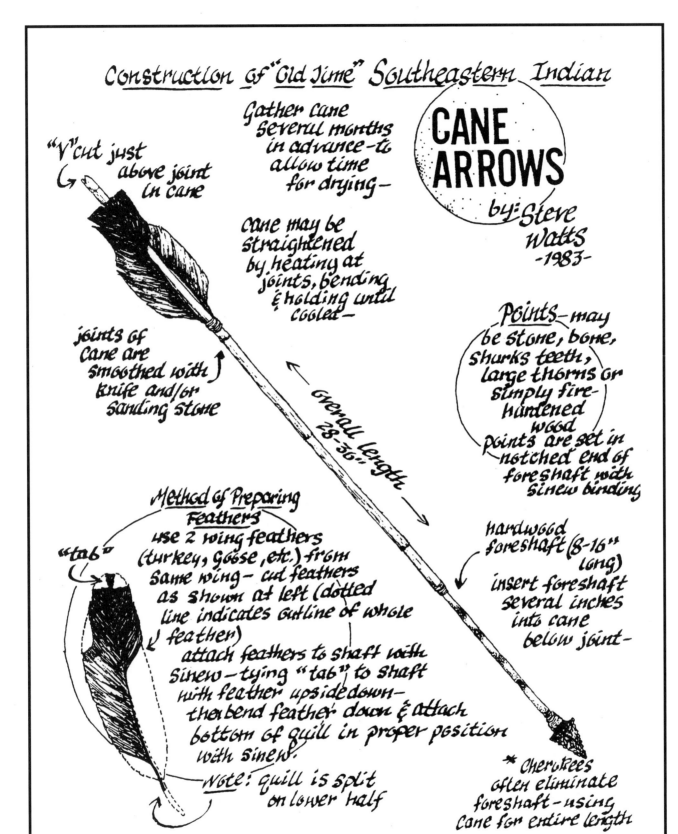

Gather cane several months in advance - to allow time for drying -

cane may be straightened by heating at joints, bending & holding until cooled -

"V" cut just above joint in cane

joints of cane are smoothed with knife and/or sanding stone

overall length 28-36"

Points - may be stone, bone, sharks teeth, large thorns or simply fire-hardened wood points are set in notched end of foreshaft with sinew binding

hardwood foreshaft (8-16" long) insert foreshaft several inches into cane below joint -

Method of Preparing Feathers

use 2 wing feathers (turkey, goose, etc.) from same wing - cut feathers as shown at left (dotted line indicates outline of whole feather)

"tab"

attach feathers to shaft with sinew - tying "tab" to shaft with feather upsidedown - then bend feather down & attach bottom of quill in proper position with sinew.

Note: quill is split on lower half

* Cherokees often eliminate foreshaft - using cane for entire length

SOUTHEASTERN RIVERCANE ARROW NOTES

By Steve Watts

Let us begin with homage to the plant itself — "Rivercane" (*Arundinaria sp.*)

"Cane supplied one of the most important of all raw materials. Besides the use of its seeds (for food), it was employed in making baskets and mats; as building material; in making fishing crails and traps, spears, and arrows; as backing for wattle walls; in making beds in houses and in the construction of corncribs; as a substitute for the shuttle in weaving; as knives and torches; in the 'spiral fire' at Creek councils; in making boxes and cradles, sieves, fanners, hampers, blowguns, blowgun arrows, shields, stockades and fences, rafts, litters, flageolets, counters, drills, and tubes through which to blow into the medicines; as pipes to blow the fire in burning out mortars and in smoking; and sometimes a section was employed to hold braids of the hair."
John R. Swanton, <u>The Indians of the Southeastern United States.</u>
Smithsonian Institution Bureau of American Ethnology, Bulletin 137, 1946.

It's pretty easy to see how those of us here in the North American Southeast find it difficult to conceive of a world without rivercane. It was surely an ace among raw materials for the Native peoples of our area, and remains so for the modern practicing primitive. I believe we could fill an entire issue of the <u>Bulletin</u> with rivercane projects and philosophy. . . but for now, we'll focus on a few brief thoughts about the rivercane arrow.

The Plant and The People

Rivercane is the traditional arrowshaft material of the historic Southeastern tribes: the Cherokee, Catawba, Creek, Yuchi, Seminole, Natchez, Choctaw, etc. Although hardwood shafts were sometimes used—cane was, by far, the material of choice. It is a true North American native hard-shelled giant grass—not to be confused with "reed grass" (*Phragmites sp.*) or the many varieties of imported oriental bamboos.

Rivercane grows across the southeastern United States from Texas, east to northern Florida, and north to the Virginia/Carolina border. It thrives in the rich bottom lands of the area. These are also prime agricultural plots, which have been under almost constant cultivation since the Late Prehistoric. Consequently, rivercane is often pushed to the edges—hanging on along the borders of fields and on the banks of rivers and creeks. To find an unmolested stand of arrow cane, is to find a treasure.

Attractive Characteristics

Arundinaria possesses a combination of attractive qualities that make it suitable for use in arrow manufacture: light in weight, yet adequately rigid with a wide range of flexibility.

Much of this is due to its hollowness and woody, hard shell. These are characteristics that the makers of modern aluminum and fiberglass arrows have attempted to duplicate. And, although extremely well matched arrow shafts can be produced with these contemporary materials, few materials in the bush meet the criteria as well as rivercane.

The abuse these arrows can take is remarkable. I have witnessed them taking violent hits, both head-on and glancing, and come springing back from situations that would have left many a wooden shaft in splinters.

Perhaps one of rivercane's most attractive characteristics as a shaft material is its ease of preparation—no bark to remove, no manipulation of the circumference and its remarkable ability to hold a straightening—being seemingly less responsive to changes in weather than are most hardwoods.

Selection and Gathering

Seek out second-year growth canes without the sheaths which cover new growth. Cut several inches longer than needed, and begin straightening, or bundle to dry. Only when dry will you be able to test for spine—either by feel or with standard spine test apparatus. Remember that with rivercane, rigidity is determined not only by the overall diameter of cane, but by the wall thickness as well. Not all rivercane is created equal. Cut a good selection to choose from. This stuff makes serious arrows. You will be able to find rivercane that can take the power of the most serious aboriginal-style big game hunting bow.

(more)

Straightening

Though it may appear "straight as an arrow" in the patch, once it is cut, rivercane requires straightening. During the early stages of drying (complete drying will take a couple of weeks in the typically humid southeast) you can periodically straighten with hand and finger pressure alone. Completely dried cane will need heat to do the job. Heat the cane over the coals until it becomes flexible. It can then be straightened in hand or over the knee. Hold until cooled. Be careful. Too much heat can cause the air trapped between joints to explode.

Shaft Surface Treatments

Trimming of the joint areas is done by some arrowmakers, but once again exert caution. Excessive trimming can weaken the shaft. Just a slight abrading, sanding or no treatment at all is more typical of Native arrowmakers.

The surface of rivercane can be brought to a smooth luster with a piece of wet buckskin and extra-fine sand used as an abrasive. A mirror-like finish can be created by burnishing with a bone, antler or joint of cane.

The one drawback to rivercane when it comes to fletching and binding is its slick outer surface. This "skin" gives cane much of its strength and spring. However, it is not very porous and does not accept glue as well as do wooden shafts. It therefore becomes necessary to scrape away this skin in any areas to which you may be applying glue—the shaftment area (where attaching feathers) or the nock or pile end where sinew bindings may be applied. But, you should not scrape the whole surface of the cane. It will weaken the arrow and destroy its liveliness.

Nock and Foreshafts

The hollow and jointed nature of rivercane works in your favor when cutting nocks or inserting foreshafted points. Nocks should be cut directly behind the joint for strength. I have never found it necessary to insert a hardwood nock reinforcement as is sometimes done with Phragmites arrows. A good, strong rivercane arrow can accept a nock by itself. With a little bit of sinew wrap reinforcement, I have often cut nocks in the middle of a section without the added support of the joint wall.

The hollow stem is also perfect for accepting hardwood foreshafts. Cut several inches past a joint if possible, reinforce the cut end with a sinew wrap, shave the foreshaft to fit, and insert.

Final Thoughts and Thanks

Many thanks go out to Richard Crowe, Hayes Lossiah, Walker Calhoun, Eddie Bushyhead, Eva Bigwitch and the other Cherokees who have shared their love and understanding of rivercane with me over the years. Whether they use it for arrows, blowguns, baskets or flutes; these folks possess a familiar reverence for this plant from which we could all learn. And, to Claude Medford, Choctaw basketmaker and itinerant scholar of Native Peoples and Places. Thanks, Claude I know if there is a cane patch in the next world—that's where you are now.

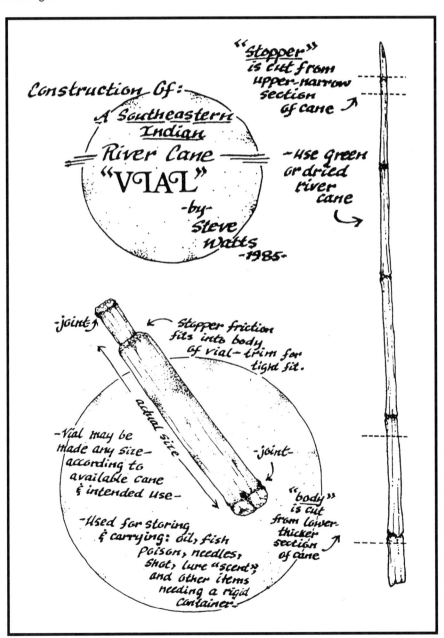

A NOTE ON PRIMITIVE BOW MAKING:
OR THE SECRETS OF SINEW REVEALED
By Dick Baugh

Sinew, the shredded fibers of animal tendon, was used for cordage, binding points on arrow shafts, and for backing material for bows. Why sinew? What are its properties which make it so desirable for these uses? Obviously it is tough and it shrinks when it dries, but how much? A fairly extensive search of the Stanford library, asking professors of biomechanics, mechanical engineering, and archeology yielded no useful information. It looked like I would have to get my hands dirty and do some experiments on the stuff but first, what did we already know about sinew?

Saxton Pope, a professor of Medicine at the University of California in the first part of this century, an intimate of Ishi's, and an ardent bowman, wrote a delightful little book about Indian bows and arrows titled *Bows and Arrows*. He stated that when Ishi made sinew-backed bows he did not worry much about cutting through the heartwood on the back of the bow. This was in contrast to all of the old-time books which describe the fabrication of longbows out of yew, osage orange, or any of the other classic bowyer's woods. The standard caveat when building a self bow (wood only) was to be very careful about having the back of the bow (the part away from the archer) follow the grain of the wood exactly or else it would break where you cut through the wood fibers.

Pope also did experiments with miniature yew bows backed with rawhide or catgut. His conclusion was that adding the backing made very little increase in the cast or ability of the bow to shoot a long distance. Therefore, he concluded, the presence of the backing only protected the back where the grain wasn't parallel and prevented the bow from breaking at full draw. Pope is to be commended for doing experiments but more needs to be done to understand what sinew does.

The Eskimos also made sinew-backed bows but in their frigid and damp climate it was impossible to do anything with glue so their sinew was applied in the form of twisted cordage tied on the back of the bow. The tension in the backing material was increased by twisting after it was bound to the back of the bow [see Callahan, BPT #1 & 2].

Reginald Laubin, in his book *American Indian Archery* described his experiences in replicating Indian bows from osage orange wood and sinew. He stated that as the sinew backing dried it tended to shrink and pull the bow into a deeper and deeper recurved position and contrary to the claims of Saxton Pope, it made the bow more powerful. Laubin's book is full of practical experience but nothing very quantitative.

Another article in *Scientific American* magazine on crossbows (January, 1985) stated that sinew has a tensile strength of 28,000 pounds per square inch. This is useful information but it is only 1/3 of what is needed to characterize sinew.

My own experience with the construction of sinew-backed bows started when I saw a backed bow made by a man living in Oakland. A beautiful job. The replies to my questions were that it was deer sinew applied with Elmer's Glue. Did it shoot well? I didn't ask. Several years later I made a short flat bow out of Santa Lucia fir (initially mis-identified as California nutmeg), backed it with horse sinew applied with Elmer's carpenter's glue. It was a lesson in the fact that even a knotty, poor piece of wood will make an acceptable bow when backed with enough sinew. My next attempt was a very close replica of a 36 inch Yurok bow in the Wattis Hall of Man, Golden Gate Park, San Francisco. This was a yew wood plus sinew combination with very wide thin limbs. Some very elementary mechanical engineering theory says that the only way you can make an extremely short bow such as this and still shoot a reasonable length arrow is to make the limbs wide and thin. Again I glued the horse sinew on the back with Elmer's carpenter's glue. What a disappointment! It looked very nice but didn't shoot worth a darn. After shooting a while and then unstringing the bow, I noticed that the bow followed the string (bent towards the archer) but after being unstrung a few hours it went back to its original shape. In general the bow was "flabby". My last experiment was a plains Indian style bow, made from a 48 inch black locust stave. This time I used hide glue to bond the horse sinew to the back. This bow was dynamite, powerful and fast. Did the hide glue make that much difference?

The engineer in me took over. What are the material properties which will yield a superior bow and how can I measure them? The things which matter are the elastic modulus

(more)

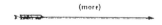

Dick Baugh works amidst the hustle in silicone valley in California. His contributions are well thought out and researched. You can read articles by Dick in most issues of the BPT. We have an upcoming article on California Fire Making Materials. This article on sinew first appeared in Ray Harwoods's Flintknapping Digest. *Dick is an excellent resource. Contact him at 490 Gary Ct., Palo Alto, CA 94306. 415-857-5420.*

(how much it stretches with a given tension), the tensile strength (how much tension is needed to break it), and how much it shrinks when it dries. In addition, it helps to define some other useful terms:

Potential energy: the ability to do work. When you pull the bowstring back you store potential energy in the bow limbs. The available potential energy is equal to the distance you pull the string back multiplied by the average force that it took to pull the string back to full draw. When you release the string the potential energy is transferred to the arrow, giving it . . .

Kinetic energy: the energy of motion. A perfectly efficient bow would transfer all of the available potential energy stored in the bow limbs into kinetic energy of the arrow.

Elastic modulus: a measure of how stiff a material is. Make a one inch cube out of the material and stretch it with a known force. The cube will get slightly longer. The elastic modulus is the force times the length of the block, divided by the area of the block times the distance the block stretched. Steel has an elastic modulus of 30 million psi (pounds per square inch), hickory has an elastic modulus of 2.2 million psi, black locust has 2.1 million psi, and the measurements I have made on yew wood give a figure of 1.2 million psi.

Tensil strength: keep pulling on that one inch cube of material and eventually you will pull it apart. The force per square inch that it takes to pull something apart is the tensile strength. For tempered steel the number is 400,000 psi, for hickory it is 20,000 psi.

For those of you who wonder: yes, it is very impractical to make these measurements on a one inch cube of material. The one inch cube was cited to emphasize the force per unit area nature of the experiment. In actual practice a much skinnier specimen of the material would be tested.

My measurement of the elastic modulus of a dried, solid horse tendon gave a figure of 411,000 psi. Similar measurements on yew wood yielded 1.16 million psi. This said, much to my surprise, that under the best of circumstances sinew had only 21 to 35 percent of the elastic modulus of wood. Put in other words, and leaving out the mathematical formulas, if you make a yew wood bow of 50 pounds pull and add more yew wood on the back to make the limbs 5 percent thicker, the resultant bow will have a 15 percent stronger pull or 57.5 pounds. If, instead of adding more wood on the back of the bow, you make the bow limb 5 percent thicker by adding sinew, the increase in draw with would only be 2.2 percent or an additional 1.8 pounds. **Why bother adding a material to the back of the bow which doesn't add much to its strength? The other 'secret' ingredient must be shrinkage.**

I was pretty well convinced that sinew shrank while it dried and this put the sinew backing under great tension. Did the amount of shrinkage depend on the type of glue used? The experiment to find this out was to glue sinew on the backs of two identical strips of 1/8 inch balsa wood. On the first one the sinew was glued on with hide glue, on the second, the sinew was glued with Elmer's carpenter's glue. The two samples behaved identically. As the sinew dried and shrank it pulled the wood into a curved shape. This experiment showed little difference between the two types of glue, only that sinew shrank as it dried. Again I took two identical 1/8 inch strips of balsa wood and put a thick strip of hide glue on one and a similar strip of Elmer's on the other (no sinew on either). This time there was a pronounced difference between the two. The hide glue shrank and curved the wood just as much as the sinew, and the Elmer's glue did not shrink at all. **Moral of the story: don't use anything but hide glue for applying the sinew.** Furthermore hide glue is 'compatible' with sinew since on a molecular level they are identical. The last experiment with sinew was to see exactly how much it shrank when it dried. I pinned one end of a strip of wet sinew to a piece of plywood, and pinned the other end to the short end of a stick that pivoted at one end. Now, when the sinew shrank, the long end of the lever would move through a greater distance and make the shrinkage easier to see. The result was that the sinew shrank 3 percent upon drying.

In conclusion one can say that the benefits of sinew backing on wood bows come from a combination of several effects acting together. They are: 1. As the sinew dries and shrinks it puts the back of the bow under compression. As a consequence, the wood fibers on the back of the bow are not stressed as highly when the bow is drawn. 2. the sinew protects the back of the bow where it doesn't follow the grain. 3. The back of the bow, which is stretched a great deal at full draw, is now a material which can stretch 5 percent before breaking (wood can only stretch about 1 percent before breaking).

Sinew bundles and bones from one leg of a deer butchered with stone tools.

David Wescott

REFERENCES

Saxton T. Pope
  1980 *Bows and Arrows,* University of California Press.

Reginald and Gladys Laubin
  1923 *American Indian Archery,* University of Oklahoma Press.

ARCHERY IN THE ARCTIC

Part 1

By Errett Callahan, PhD

Figure 1. Test shooting the bow at 30° F below freezing by the Sanikiluaq igloo in which the author slept the night before. (Eirich-Dehne)

Originally published in BOWMEN'S BULLETIN, June 1990. Reprinted by permission of the author, BPT #1, and Bowmen's Bulletin.

It was nearly 50° below the freezing point as I stepped outside. I was decked out in traditional Eskimo clothing and carried a replica of an Eskimo bow and arrows such as hadn't been seen up here in well over 100 years. Here I was way up in the Arctic trying to do some test shooting.

Why am I doing this to myself, I ask, as the 10-15 mile-an-hour winds create a wind-chill close to 60° below freezing, and the air I suck into my lungs turns from ice crystals to ice water? I, a Southern boy from Virginia, who had rarely felt cold much below freezing, suddenly found myself on a lonely, ice-locked island just under the North Star. I felt very far away and completely out of my environment. It seemed as if I had been beamed up to a distant planet, a world devoid of any color except white. Yet I was exhilarated, not alienated, as I crunched my way across the hollow-sounding but tightly wind-packed snow. I walked past the igloo (Figure 1), where I had slept so warmly the night before, past the equally efficient, ancient sod-house and skin tent reconstructions which were insulated well within 6-8' snow drifts. I wandered out over the low hills to a meadow of white for some long-awaited bow shooting.

Preparations for this event had been in the works for over a year. This was part and parcel of a teachers' confer-ence on aboriginal skills put together for selected Baffin Island area school teachers of Canada's Northwest Territories. This conference was masterminded by John Jamieson, principal of Nuiyak School at Sanikiluaq, a community of 200 or so Inuit (Eskimos) on the Belcher Islands in the Hudson Bay. Jamieson, with unprecedented support from the Baffin Division Board of Education, was having resounding success at incorporating age-old cultural skills into the schools, this at a time when modern technology, lifestyles, and "values" are, within a single generation, undermining ancient traditional ways. Not only was Jamieson having the elders brought into the schools as paid consultants to show the youngsters how to make seal skin kayaks, traditional clothing, snow-block igloos and other crafts and skills of Arctic survival and cultural environment, but he was actually studying the ancient skills himself. Now he had brought in specialists from the outside for this landmark conference.

My assignment, besides talking on reconstructive archeology and the "abo" movement sweeping our country (USA), was to demonstrate the long-neglected aboriginal skills of

(more)

flintknapping and bowmaking. Stone toolmaking was one of the first skills to be lost in the Arctic as soon as the whaling ships brought an abundance of metal knives in the 1700s. Archery, however, not only survived but flourished, in part due to the use of these metal tools, for another 200 years until around the turn of the present century.

Hoping to reinstate an interest in archery among the Inuit, Jamieson had the idea of holding an aboriginal hunt during the conference. For this event I had been commissioned not only to be the hunter but to re-create a bow such as had been used during the heyday of Arctic "bowhunting" in the 1800s. (I put "bowhunting" in quotes here because the Inuit did not hunt for "sport" or trophies, as the term implies; they hunted to survive.)

The first thing I did upon arrival at Sanikiluaq, in fact within an hour or so of getting off the plane, was to give an archery exhibition to the community (Figure 2). Jamieson had arranged for the entire settlement to be gathered in the school gym to meet us. He explained to them (in Inuit) why we were here and what we could be doing during the forthcoming week. Then some speeches were given, poems read and awards presented. I was, in fact presented with a pair of seal skin boots and liners made by Silatik Meeko, an elder who immediately claimed me as her "husband", since women only give boots to their mates. (She was a widow.) I wondered why everyone was roaring with laughter, till it was trans-

Figure 2. Archery demonstration in gym at Sanikiluaq. This was the first time an Eskimo type bow had been seen here since the elders were children. (Jamieson)

Shortly after the conclusion of this conference, John Jamieson was hired to teach in another area and departed Sanikiluaq. I was able to stay at his home and hunt seal with the locals for a week. We ate raw caribou and arctic char, and savored the liver of a freshly killed seal while it cooled on the ice flow. The experiences I was able to share with the Inuit in the short time that I was in the north, made it very exciting when I was once again contacted by John to help him with another project in the Northwest Territories. The Candian government has taken an affirmative action to not only protect, but tangibly support the recovery and preservation of indigenous people of the north. The Inuit and Dene have a superb opportunity to regain and /or halt the degradation of their tradional ways. Our Canadian members are growing in number and many are interested in Boreal and Arctic skills. Meeting Don Gardner and Mors Kochanski in Alberta in 1989 was great. Their replications and pursuit of technical preservation is what the SPT is all about.

The Editor.

lated. For a moment I had thought it was serious. . . This was my first introduction to the marvelous and incessant humor of the Eskimo.

To close out the program, I showed them how the bow worked. I wanted them to see that their ancestors' bows were no mere toys but could shoot an arrow with speeds that meant business. I passed around the bow and some arrows while Jamieson explained that not only was this a pure Eskimo bow, but that the sinew braid had been made by their beloved Caroline Kudlarick, who had died just a few months prior.

Jamieson had suspended a burlap "caribou" at one end of the gym. Starting at about 10 yards away, I drew, in classic Howard Hill style, but slowly, so they could take it all in, and sent a rubber blunt whop into the kill area. (Note: The "Howard Hill style" with Mediterranean release has been used in the Arctic for eons. See photo in Claiborne 1973: 108. Also see photo in Jenness 1922: 145.)

Then I took a step back and repeated a shot and so on to the full length of the gym (Figure 2). Not only was this done for a dramatic effect, but I wanted to drive home the impression that this bow could really deliver a punch, that this was a real hunting bow and that a good archer could keep all the arrows in the kill area anywhere within the gym distance. Then the men in the Hunters and Trappers Association, who control all the hunts, might allow bowhunting to creep back into their culture from which it sprang. Not just for our hunt but for their own people in the future.

During the forthcoming week the seed bore its first fruit as Inuit hunters and youth joined me from time to time when I was out roving for practice (Figure 4). Once they spent about an hour at -10° F shooting a lumps of snow they propped up at about 20-25 yards. It simply amazed me how quickly they fell into the proper form and shot with accuracy. And bare-handed too, when our hands were numb without heavy gloves or mittens.

Finding a model for such a bow replica was no easy task. It seems that all the early bows had been hauled off to museums a century ago and that no one in the Baffin Island area today remembers how to make one. A few elders were said to recall seeing bows in their youth, but even these were for children. So I had to start at ground zero and do my own research.

For starters I got out my copies of O.T. Mason (1893), Murdoch (1884), Jenness (1922 & 1946), Claiborne (1973) and Hamilton (1982). I studied these references in depth and quickly came to the realization that although I had been making self wood bows for half a century, the Eskimo bows are in a class of their own. No bent sticks these, Eskimo bows are some of the most intricate wooden bows to be found anywhere on earth (Figure 3). These are classic flat bows with wide limbs and narrow thickened handle. The handles are non-static, meaning that they contribute to the snap when shot and so must be coordinated with the bend of the limbs— unlike the handles of contemporary bows which do not flex. This feature alone requires skilled acrobatics in tillering. To such immaculately worked staves, the Eskimo added a cable of braided sinew, wound from nock to nock along the back. This cable shifted the tension stress beyond the back of the wood into the cable itself, somewhat as modern fiberglass laminations act upon the wood core. The sinew cable, which is not glued in place as are Western Indian sinew-backed bows, also allowed the use of almost whatever kind of driftwood happened ashore to be used for bowstaves. However, the Eskimo usually seemed to have sought out flawless driftwood of spruce or tamarack.

Other types of Eskimo bows are made with drastically recurved ends, akin to the Siberian bows of Asia. A third type is made of spliced and bound (not glued) caribou antler. The sinew cabling along the back of most of these bows is complicated far beyond my understanding. So I chose the simpler "Southern" type of all-wood bow with less complex cabling.

Another thing that hampered me was that most of the bows collected for museums are from the Western Arctic, although the same three types were found all across the North. Within that range the simpler wooden bows were found to the south, and the more complex caribou antler bows were found to the north where, naturally, less wood washed ashore.

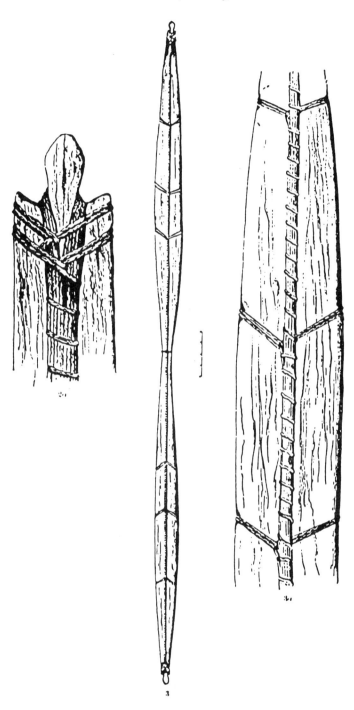

Figure 3. The original sketches of Smithsonian bow #72408 from Mason 1893, Plate LXVI. The nock shown at left does not go with this bow, but the sinew wrapping is identical. (After Mason, 1893)

The bow I selected for replication was about the simplest kind known—the Smithsonian's #72408, shown in Murdoch's figure 3 and Mason's plate LXVI (Figure 3). The writers say that the bows they depicted were "quite old" at the time of their writings, which are now a good 100 years old. So my bow model could well be 140-150 or so years old or from the early to mid 1800s.

It took three tries to get a successful replica. The first attempt was of yew, but it quickly became apparent that the stave I had presented too many problems—oversized knots at the points of greatest stress. And yew, excellent as it is, can be temperamental in the cold. Also I was uneasy with the cardboard template I had made up from the drawings and measurements given in the literature. Nor did I know the all-important cross-section. I just had to see the original.

So I made a trip to the Smithsonian. The staff in the anthropology department were kind enough to retrieve the original bow from the archives and let me examine it in person and in depth. I spent a total of five hours drawing and measuring the original in great detail. Far from being the "simple" bow I had envisioned, this was the finest piece of wooden bowmaking I had ever encountered, old or new. The wood was an immaculate stave, apparently of black spruce or tamarack. It was almost black with age, perhaps from hanging in the rafters of a smokey summer house for decades. I was surprised to note that not only were the sides quite squared, but that a fluted groove ran the entire length along each side from nock to nock. There was also a raised bead which ran down the belly from tip to tip, These features were not apparent in the drawing and underscored the importance of seeking out the original. (Thank goodness a museum had gotten custody of the bow—even though it was not on display—rather than some private collector, who would have died long ago and perhaps had his collection dispersed far and wide to the highest bidder. Such artifacts are impossible to track down 100 years later.) What purpose did these grooves and beading serve? Did they add some unknown engineering function, or were they merely decorative? Why were so many wooden bows so adorned, as the literature states? I also noted the fineness of the sinew braid and how very tightly and systematically it had been applied. I estimated the pull to be somewhere between 60 and 80 lbs, maybe more but not less.

As I drove home, I pondered. Was I capable of replicating such a masterpiece of craftsmanship? It was beyond anything I had yet attempted. I would certainly have to draw up a new template and start all over with a new stave. But where would I get sinew braiding? I explained the dilemma to Jamieson and asked if he might be able to find an elder who still remembered how to braid caribou sinew. He said he'd try. I might be able to braid a little, but I only had enough sinew to make 8 feet of cord. . The literature says from 100 to 300 feet are needed for such bows.

Figure 4. Inuit hunter testing out the bow at -10° F. The hunters loved it. Note bare hands and finger tab. Our hands went numb without huge mittens. (Callahan)

REFERENCES

Claiborne, Robert
1973   ***The First Americans.*** *Time-Life Books, NY [Emergence of Man series.]*
Hamilton, T.M.
1982   ***Native American Bows,*** *2nd edition. Missouri Archaeological (1972) Society Special Publication #5.*
Jenness, D.
1922   ***Report of the Canadian Arctic Expedition,*** *1913-18, Vol XII: The life of the Copper Eskimos. Ottawa.*
1946   ***Report of the Canadian Arctic Expedition, 1913-18,*** *Vol XVI: Material Culture of the Copper Eskimos. Ottawa.*
Mason, Otis T.
1893   ***North American Bows, Arrows, and Quivers.*** *Report of the Smithsonian Institution for 1893.*
Murdoch, John
1884   ***A Study of the Eskimo Bows in the U.S. National Museum.*** *Report of the Smithsonian Institution for 1884: 307-316.*

ARCTIC ARCHERY - *Part 2*

By Errett Callahan, PhD

Meanwhile, not believing that real sinew braid would be forthcoming, I scrounged up some catgut. Real catgut (Australian beef gut actually) is difficult to find now that synthetics have replaced it for tennis rackets. But I did manage to locate three rolls of natural gut (Babolat brand), each 33 feet long at $1/ft. I was $100 in the hole at the outset. I saw that this bow was not going to come cheaply.

Then, over the next several weeks, I prepared a second stave. This was of seasoned sassafras, the bow wood I had available which was closest in characteristics to the black spruce of the original (Figure 7). Using only tools such as the Eskimo would have had 150 years ago—axe, crooked knife and metal scrapers—I honed my replica down to within less than 1 mm of the dimensions of the original. I left only the fluting, beading and the sinew braiding undone. These could be done after tillering.

(I also tested out Richard Baugh's bowscraper extensively. Though, strictly speaking, not a pure Eskimo tool, it is well within the range of their technology. I found this tool to be about the best invention for the traditional bowmaker since the drawknife. In fact, it wins my top award for the best invention of the year. For information, contact Richard Baugh-See the Resource Directory)

When I finally strung up this second attempt, 18 hours of painstaking work flew out the window as the stave shattered into splinters. Actually I had earlier succeeded in stringing it with a low fistmele just a few inches off the handle. This revealed an apparently perfect bend, an unusual   f e a t for a first stringing. I owed this to the skill of the original bowyer, whose dimensions I followed so faithfully, and to an even, flawless stave. I estimated the pull at over 100 lb. This was clearly too much for me to handle, especially with ten-

Figure 6. The author test shooting the bow at home. Note sinew cabling on back. The bow was shot in 500 times before taking to the Arctic and another 500 times while there. The cold did not seem to effect performance any. (David Callahan)

donitis pains. So I thinned it down some more, but it didn't survive the second stringing.

Now about the bowstring. The original string on the bow was of left-twisted sinew. Its thickness varied between 3.5 and 3.8 mm (about 1/8"). The string had sinew-served loops on both top and bottom. The bottom loop was served with a knot on the back side of each wrap, but the top loop had no such knots (Figure 5). The bottom loop was permanently affixed to the lower limb while the top loop was removed from the bow after each unstringing and kept in place with a third loop. Why was the main loop not slipped over and down the limb as with modern wood bows? Because it wouldn't fit. As may be seen by the drawings, the thick tips of the bow coupled with all the sinew cabling won't allow a loop to slip down the limb (Figures 5 & 7). Not a loop the size of the original. I thought a larger loop might work, but when I tried it, I found it to be too wide for the nock, and it kept slipping off the belly shoulders. In replication, one must do exactly as the original when it is known.

I simulated (vs. replicated) a string using linen, and this worked fine (#4 Barbour's flax, 24 strands). I had neither the sinew nor the knowledge of how to replicate this original. Though I had made plenty of sinew strings before, I knew what I didn't know.

An interesting point: the original staring at 54 1/4" long caused the upper loop to lie 3.70 cm (1 1/2") below the upper nock. I didn't measure this fistmele height with my replica, but at my fistmele (about 7") the upper loop was 5.50 cm (2 1/8") below the upper nock when unstrung. Therefore, the

(more)

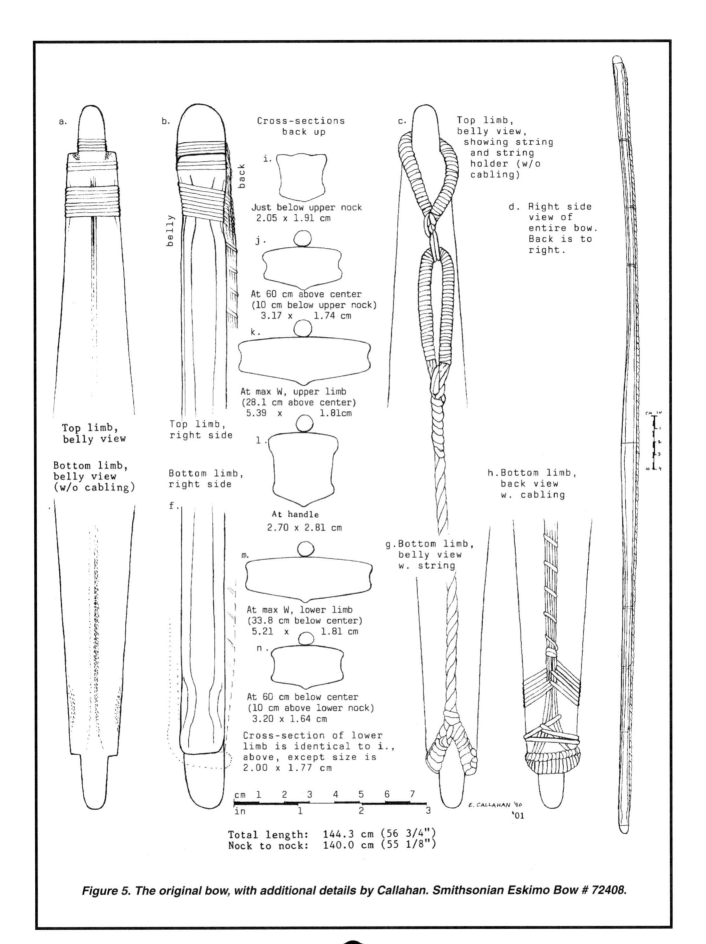

a. Top limb, belly view

Bottom limb, belly view (w/o cabling)

b. Top limb, right side

Bottom limb, right side

f.

belly

back

Cross-sections back up

i.
Just below upper nock
2.05 x 1.91 cm

j.
At 60 cm above center
(10 cm below upper nock)
3.17 x 1.74 cm

k.
At max W, upper limb
(28.1 cm above center)
5.39 x 1.81cm

l.
At handle
2.70 x 2.81 cm

m.
At max W, lower limb
(33.8 cm below center)
5.21 x 1.81 cm

n.
At 60 cm below center
(10 cm above lower nock)
3.20 x 1.64 cm

Cross-section of lower
limb is identical to i.,
above, except size is
2.00 x 1.77 cm

c. Top limb, belly view, showing string and string holder (w/o cabling)

d. Right side view of entire bow. Back is to right.

g. Bottom limb, belly view w. string

h. Bottom limb, back view w. cabling

cm 1   2   3   4   5   6   7
in   1   2   3

E. CALLAHAN '90 '01

Total length: 144.3 cm (56 3/4")
Nock to nock: 140.0 cm (55 1/8")

Figure 5. The original bow, with additional details by Callahan. Smithsonian Eskimo Bow # 72408.

fistmele on the original may have been quite low, between 4 and 5" (?)—unless this was increased by twisting the string.

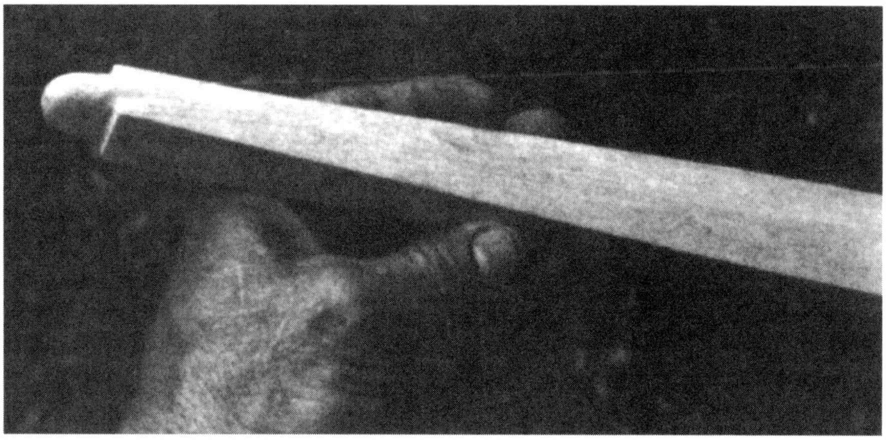

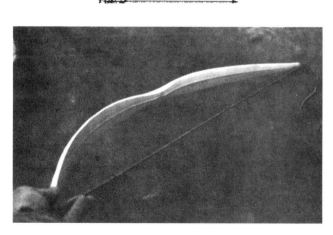

Figure 7. Upper limb, belly view, final preform stage, before beading. Sassafras replica #2. Note limb thickness at tip and squareness of nock, exactly like original. Outside dimensions are within 1 mm of original. (Callahan)

I pondered these things now as I walked over the snow. I crossed a low wind-swept ridge, walking sometimes on snow and sometimes on bare rock, ground smooth by mile-high glaciers over 10,000 years ago. Down into a low valley packed with snow so hard I didn't sink 1/4". No need for snow shoes in the high Arctic. The snow is blown around and then packed so hard by the fierce winds that it's nearly as hard as ice—but much less dense. And it's not at all slippery.

A distant snow bank looks to be a great target. After "warming up" my bow with the traditional eight or ten preliminary pulls, I pause, then ease my bow into shooting position. I draw the arrow with care, listening for tell-tale cracks. I hear the sinew cable creak like a rope on a sailing ship. It's a comforting sound. Though I had shot this bow over 500 times before coming to the Arctic, (and was to do another 500 before I left), this was to be the first test at 15° below zero. But the way I figured it, if it couldn't survive the cold, then it was no replica at all. Form without function is child's play. I draw—20 inches OK; 25, 28 inches. Looks good. Hold; release. It works! The arrow shoots out with terrific snap and slams into the snow bank 30 yards away. I continue roving up and down the valley putting the bow to extreme tests.

This third replica attempt was of white ash. After my second attempt failed, I had too little time left to tinker around with temperamental woods. Now, I know from experience that sassafras makes superb English longbows. It's nearly equal to osage in snap. But it's nowhere near as forgiving. Of the three woods most forgiving under extreme environmental conditions and rough handling—osage, hickory and white ash—the latter is the only wood which might conceivably be found as driftwood in the Arctic. I had personally cut this ash stave myself in New Hampshire two years earlier. So I knew it had all the right growth characteristics.

With only six weeks to go before the expedition, I not only had to make the bow but to become familiar with shooting it. One doesn't take a strange bow on a hunt if one is at all serious. And I also had to make up some Eskimo arrow replicas to match. So I had no more time to waste. Jamieson had come across with a ball of braided caribou sinew. It measured 300 feet and was immaculate—even and consistent from end to end (Figure 10). It had been prepared by Caroline Kudlarick, an elder at Sanikiluaq, just before she passed on in the fall of 1988. There would be no second chance now. (This braid was a little thicker and more coarse than the original.)

To make another long story short, I prepared the ash replica to within 1mm tolerance. But this stave was also far too strong for me to manage. It measured 80lb at only 16 inches. And the lower limb, the one closest to the base of the trunk, was notably weaker than the top limb. (I had noted this characteristic in other woods, leading me to realize that the wood just above the base of the trunk is less compact than the upper part. This area also takes notably more set. Solution: discard the swollen bottom foot or two of the trunk.) Therefore, I had to remove more wood from the top limb than

(more)

Figure 8. Belly view, strung, showing beading on belly before cabling. (Callahan)

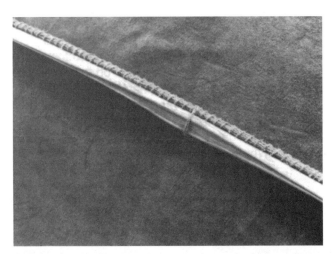

Figure 9. Handle view, showing grooving on sides and sinew cabling on back. Wrap at dead center helps in keeping grip position constant. (Callahan)

the bottom to get a symmetrical bend. This changed the thickness ratios considerably. Note that from this point on, wood was removed only from the belly, leaving the width the same as the original throughout. In this way and for these reasons, I departed from the thickness dimensions of the original. (Any working replica must do so during tillering, for with wood, other factors than thickness enter into the dimensions yielding a perfect bend.)

The next big question was how much weight would be added back on by the sinew braiding? No one knew the answer. The only other Eskimo-type bowmaker I know of, Don Gardner of Calgary, prefers to apply the braid even before stringing it up. But I wanted to see how my bow would perform and weigh in, with and without the braid. This means that the wood alone had to take my full 28 inch draw. In that the maximum bow-length ration is traditionally said to be 2 to 1, a 28 inch draw requires an all-wood bow of no less than 56 inches. Mine was 55 1/8 inches, nock to nock . (This does not necessarily mean the Eskimo pulled 28 inches, but their arrows are typically of that length.)

I made a wild guess that the sinew cable would add 10 to 15 pounds. Knowing that I can handle a 70 pound bow OK, I ordered some appropriately spined cedar shafts. Then I proceeded to shave my bow down to 55 lbs., figuring the sinew would bring it back up to 65 or 70 lbs. At that point I strung it up, adjusted the bend as needed, then shot it in.

My initial reaction was a disappointment. It was a sluggish bow with little snap. And it took on a notable set right away, especially the lower limb. All in all, it shot about like a 45 pound stave of osage. Reluctantly, as it was now too late to start over, I took it in and scraped the fluting into the sides and the beading on the belly (Figures 8 & 9). A rounded corner of a cabinet scraper worked quite well for this, and it went much faster than I had thought it would. After this, I was surprised to find that the bow stave still drew 55 lbs at 28". It had lost no noticeable weight from this "engineering". Further tests in shooting showed that the performance was also

unchanged. So I had to conclude that the fluting and beading may be just decorative after all.

Then I applied the sinew braiding, winding it from nock to nock over the back (Figure 10). (I practiced first with comparable cotton cord on my repaired sassafras stave to get the hang of it.) I'll skip the technicalities involved except to note that 72 feet (14 wraps) of sinew braid were required. I calculated that 100 feet had been used in the original, but that braid was thinner than mine (an estimate 20 to 24 wraps). Because I wanted to have a total cable unit of the same thickness as the original (about the thickness of a pencil), I cut down on the number of wraps. When all was tied off with the proper spiral binding and half hitches in the right places, I strung her up again. The bend was unaffected so, fortunately, no more tillering was required.

The first shock came when I noted that the sinew cable added only 5lbs to the pull! All that trouble for a measly 5 lbs? The second shock came when I took it outside to shoot it. The arrows now zinged out like missiles! The sinew may have added only 5 lbs to the weight, but it added a good 15 lbs to the snap. I now had a 60 lb bow that shot like a 60 pounder (i.e. it shot the way osage or yew would shoot at 60 lbs. I wonder what sinew cabling would do to those woods?) Now it was a joy to shoot the bow. It took on no further set, though I was careful to press the spongy lower limb back to straight after unstringing. Finally I had a bow that was a success and ready to take to the Arctic. First I had to make some arrows to match, but that's another story. As is the hunt.

Figure 10. Applying braided sinew cabling to back of top limb. Half-hitches are worked into cable during nock-to-nock wrapping. Binding of the cable, assisted by bone awl, comes last. Compare with Figure 3 (Callahan)

NOTE: This bow replica took 33.54 hours to make (exclusive of the two rejects) and was valued at $732 (time plus materials). Jamieson personally purchased the bow and some arrow replicas for the Inuit community at about half price. The bow was extensively test shot at minus 25°F at Iqaluit, much farther north without mishap.

Table 1   E. Callahan

DATA ON ESKIMO BOW #72408
IN SMITHSONIAN MUSEUM OF NATURAL HISTORY

Location in museum: area 3, row 208, unit 02, drawer/shelf from top 03C.

Collected by : C.L. McKay at Bristol Bay, Alaska,
at undetermined date preceding 1882.

Published in : Murdoch 1884, Figure 3 and Mason 1893, Plate LXVI.

Length: Total , along back- 144.3 cm (56 3/4")
Nock to nock, along back- 140.0 cm (55 1/8")

Set: 2.4 cm (1"), mostly on top limb.

Warp: 6.9 cm (3 1/8") to right, belly view, mostly on top limb

Center: 72.05 cm (28 5/16"), determined by indentation where cord originally
bound cabling to bow. This wrap may be seen in the Murdoch/Mason
sketch, but it has since been lost or removed.

Balance point: 2.35 cm (15/16") above center.

Maximum limb width and thicknesses at center: 2.81 x 2.70cm (1 1/8" x 1 1/16")

Weight in hand: 1 lb 4 1/2 oz.

Wood: undetermined soft wood, but probably either black spruce or tamarack.

Grain: generally flat to grain but not strictly following grain on back.
Slightly diagonal on belly.

Color: dark brown with a rich reddish-brown hue beneath. Stain comes off on hand.

Finish: very smooth but dull, about equivalent to #240 sandpaper
followed by light #00 steel wool rub at grip. But not polished.

Sinew cabling: 20-24 strands (about 100') of triple braid sinew (probably caribou),
each strand being 1-2 mm (1/16") thick.
Knotted exactly as shown in Mason's Plate LXVI (our Figure 3).

Cable thickness: .59 cm (1/4") at center; .56 cm at mid-limbs; and .56 cm (top)
and .47 cm (3/16") (bottom) as measured 10 cm (4") below nocks.

Bowstring: left twisted sinew 1.38 cm (54 1/4") long, with double- served,
non-identical loops. Upper loop lies 3.70 cm (1 1/2") below upper nock.
Attached to upper nock when unstrung by a third loop and not slipped down
around limb in usual Western fashion.

Estimated weight: 60 to 80 lb at maximum draw, maybe more.

ARCTIC ARCHERY - *Part 3*
Written 12 Years Later
By Errett Callahan, PhD

The Arrows

For this project, I made up 13 arrows. Eight were of the Cook's Inlet type (Figures 11, 12, 13) and five were of the Point Barrow type (Figures 14, 12, 15) (Mason 1893). All of the Point Barrow arrows and four of the Cook's Inlet arrows were tipped with rubber blunts for practice shooting and fun. Four of the Cook's Inlet arrows were hunting arrows with lethal obsidian broadheads. Two had large Ishi points and two had large Puma points (Figure 16).(These points were not Eskimo types, which would have been small triangles or slate points. I did make up such an arrow for the project, with a knapped flint point.) But they were what I felt comfortable with for a serious reindeer hunt. (The "Puma" is a type of my own design.) All four hunting points had wooden caps, based on an Eskimo design, to prevent their getting nicked and dulled in the quiver (Figures 11 and 16). See below.

My records are a bit fuzzy here, but it looks like either two or three of the Cook's Inlet blunt arrows and two of the Point Barrow blunt arrows stayed in the Arctic with the bow, as part of the project. I brought the others home and still have them to this day.

Because of the time limitations mentioned earlier, I had to take some shortcuts in making the arrows. Thus I ordered some commercial Port Orford cedar dowels 23/64", spined for a 60-65lb., bow. Actually these dowels simulated the Eskimo arrows more than if I had gone out and cut some shoots,

for Arctic arrows seem invariably to be made of split and hand-doweled driftwood logs. I have done this many times and must say that when doweling by hand, using a crooked knife, one may follow the grain exactly, whereas machined dowels typically cut across the grain slightly.

Following Mason's descriptions of the two arrow types (of many) which I selected (Figures 11 and 14), I tapered the last eight inches or so of the nock ends. The Cook's Inlet arrows are tapered evenly all around the shaft, ending in a bulbous nock (Figures 11, 12). The Point Barrow arrows are tapered asymmetrically, being flattened on opposing sides, ending in a wide, flat, thin nock (Figures 14, 12). The Cook's Inlet model was fixed up as a sea otter harpoon, but I made mine into hunting arrows for reindeer.

Cresting came next. Mason doesn't mention it, as I recall, but the original arrow artifact shown in his Plate LIX (our Figure 11) is tinted with a red ochre. By the utmost coincidence, as I was wandering around the Smithsonian Museum when analyzing the bow, in December of 1988, I stumbled upon a temporary exhibition of Eskimo artifacts, one of which was this exact arrow I was trying to replicate! Here I noticed the red ochre coloration and other technological details (the feathers are of a spotted gray color, the workmanship is immaculate—no crude quickie arrow here).

When I returned home and made up my arrows, I used a red ochre wash for my cresting. Unlike the original, I restricted

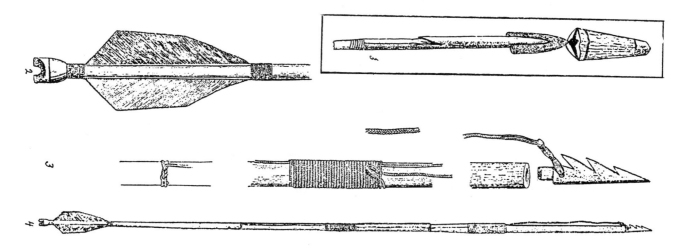

Figure 11. Eskimo arrow from Cook's Inlet. (From Mason 1893, Plate LIX) and point cap (Plate LII).

my cresting to the shaftment, the area beneath the fletching, the area which had been tapered. I applied a watercolor wash from the nock forward, gradually fading out at the end of the taper.

For fletching, I used Canada goose, gray goose, and a found white gull feather. In typical Eskimo fashion, three feathers were used on all arrows.(Sometimes Eskimo arrows had but two feathers.) When shot a few times, these feathers took on an authentic, ragged look typical of the arrows seen in Mason's plates (Figures 13,14,15). Animal hide glue was used to glue down the quills at the sinew binding on each end. (Some were glued the full length for stability, though this probably wasn't necessary. I also bound down the whole fletching on some as shown in Figure 14 and 15) Some of the feathers were used without trimming as they were taken from feathers which naturally laid low and angled steeply back. These feathers had a natural, low, balloon-type taper and looked the most authentic.

The bi-tapered Point Barrow arrows presented a unique problem (Figure 12). Actually the fletching started out being glued and bound to a round shaftment. But at the nock end, the shaft is flattened, not rounded. Where do you attach the quill? As it turned out, I simply attached the two "shaft" feathers to the lower sides of the flattened faces while the cock feather was attached to the top of a narrow side (Figure 12). The hunting points were next attached. The Ishi and Puma types had been knapped out to an average grain weight of 147g (range 140-150g). This is what my experience - at that

time a total of 90 of these obsidian point types for modern bowhunters - had shown to be best for caribou/reindeer-sized beasts.

The points were exactly centered and bound to notches in the end of the shafts using sinew and hide glue. The rubber blunt points were simply slipped over the distal ends of the shafts. The tightness of fit held them in place.

The finished arrows were well rubbed in and burnished with two coats of bear grease. The finished weights of the Cook's Inlet hunting arrows were 507g +- 8g (or 457g +- 3g with rubber blunts temporarily applied for shooting in). The Cook's Inlet rubber blunt arrows were 460g +- 5g, while the Point Barrow rubber blunt arrows were 447g +- 7g.

Before attaching the stone points on the four hunting arrows, I slipped on rubber blunts so I could shoot-in the arrows and see how they flew. The arrows flew superbly and no difference could be detected because of the weights. Once this was done, I removed the rubber blunts and affixed the obsidian points. After that, there was no shooting of these arrows until the hunt so the extremely sharp tips and edges wouldn't be compromised.

As noted earlier, to protect the points until use, I fitted each head with a wooden cap (Figures 11, 16). The original point cap was made of "Two pieces of cedar neatly cut for the blade ...and joined together with a braid of sinew" (Ma-

(more)

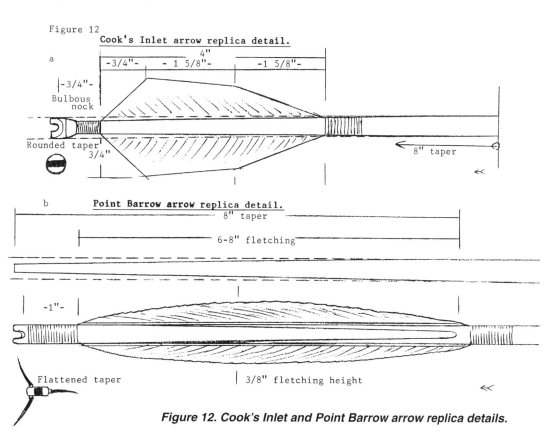

Figure 12. Cook's Inlet and Point Barrow arrow replica details.

Figure 13. Fletching of Cook's Inlet arrow replicas. (Callahan)

son 1893: Plate LII). Mine were made exactly the same except that I used a softer wood (balsa) for added protection. Friction held the caps in place.

My other archery equipment was not Eskimo, but it was pretty basic (and "traditional"). To hold my arrows, I used a quiver I had made of a gray fox pelt. This hung straight down the center of my back by two straps (Figure 2). Such a quiver is, for me, the easiest to put arrows in and out of without looking (though you can't see which shaft you are withdrawing). I used a conventional leather arm guard, especially made up with extra long straps to fit around all that extra clothing. Besides my regular leather finger tab, which I used over thin leather gloves, I glued three pieces of tough leather to the tips of my padded, right glove. Thus I could shoot with or without the thick glove on. In any event, shooting with accuracy was doubly compounded because of all the extra clothing and the bitter cold. It took some getting used to, but shooting a bow in the Arctic was possible and, I must say, uniquely enjoyable.

Back to the rubber blunts, once when I was out roving at 5°F below zero, I had two surprises. For one, I actually hit a football-sized rock at 50 yards; for another, the rubber blunt exploded like glass (Figure 17). Those that didn't explode were wonderful for shooting in the snow, for they don't bury themselves and zip away who knows where under the snow as sharp-tipped arrows do.

Lost Bow, Lost Bowmaker

One of the events the conference participants were invited to by the villagers was a picnic-expedition on Sunday, Mar. 19, 1989, the day before the scheduled hunt. We traveled 7 miles over the ice of Hudson Bay to a wild place called Katapik, a little inlet south of Sanikiluaq. Travel involved snowmobile, or "skidoo" or trailing toboggans, in one of which I bounced around, holding on for dear life. At Katapik, the villagers spent the day dredging up marine foods and fishing. The fishing I saw was done with line nets, but line and hooks may have been used as well. For the dredging, the deep snow was removed to get at the ice, then five feet of solid ice had to be chopped through to make a hole, which immediately filled in with water. A dip net attached to a 20 ft. wooden pole was then lowered down and scraped along the bottom 10-15 ft. below. The net came up with little mussels, sea urchins, sea cucumbers, starfish, and black rocks. The fish, at least, were chopped up and eaten raw. Yum, yum, eat 'em up.

While this was going on, I went roving with my bow and arrows, as mentioned earlier. After shooting my way around the quarter mile area, shooting at lumps of snow and shooting for distance, getting used to the equipment, I returned and let the Inuit try their hands at shooting (Figure 4). They loved it. The young hunters especially took to the bow and I wondered if I'd ever get it back.

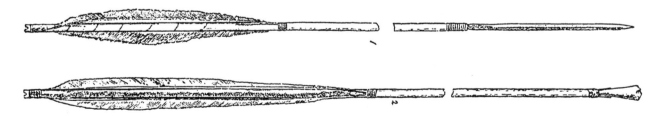

Figure 14. Eskimo arrows from Point Barrow. (From Mason 1893, Plates LVI and LVII.)

Figure 15. Fletching of Point Barrow arrow replicas. (Callahan)

To make a long story short, after the picnic (hot tea on Coleman stoves and sandwiches), the people left, one by one. On the way down, the community had come as a unit, traveling in a long, safari line. But returning was one by one. Finally, I was the last one left. I had been given a "skidoo" and shown, for the first time ever, how to make it go. Someone else had offered to take back my bow and arrows and I saw them safely (?) put aboard a toboggan trailer. After enjoying a short but pleasant period of peace and quiet, and noticing where the last to leave had just skirted the tall island and headed home, northward, I followed suit.

To my surprise, when I rounded the island, I saw no sign of the last snowmobile. It had just vanished into thin air. So I headed off in the direction I thought was home.

In this land of horizon to horizon whiteness, with the shore practically indistinguishable from the broken, tide-tossed, snow-covered ice blocks of the Bay, it occurred to me, after awhile, that I just might be headed out to sea, westward.

With an overcast sky, no compass, and my Southern bump of direction totally disoriented, I figured I'd better stop and think this thing through. So I did. Then I retraced my trail till I discovered where the other snowmobiles had gone off to the left. I had indeed been heading west out across the Hudson Bay. I humbly followed the others' tracks this time, and made it home just before dark. My hands were frozen (it was -5 to -15° F that day) from having to squeeze the handle of the throttle to keep the machine going, nullifying the insulation of the mittens. (Why can't they make foot throttles so your hands won't freeze?)

When I rejoined the others, I was told that my bow had bounced out of the toboggan and the driver had no idea where it was. Just then David Wescott came along and said, "Guess what I found lying on the ice on the way home?" It was my bow.

As a last, near-fatal faux pas, that night I took a long walk out over the snow to get a feel for the vastness and beauty of the Arctic after dark. When I returned, I was reprimanded for foolishness. In polar bear country, no one goes wandering away from the community at night. I got lucky again.

The Hunt That Wasn't

Supposedly, preparations for our reindeer hunt had been made months in advance. Actually these were reindeer, not caribou. They were brought over from Scandinavia ages ago after all the caribou had been killed off the Belcher Islands. The difference between reindeer and caribou is lost to me. They look just the same.

The reindeer herd had been reported in an area about 25 miles to the south. They hadn't been hunted in a long time and were settled down. The chances were good for stalking to within striking distance with the bow (about 30 yards). We were told that the men in the Hunters and Trappers' Association had been appraised of all these arrangements. But a day or so before our expedition, some hunters had gone on a hunt and scared the herd to the very bottom of the island, 75 miles away. Instead of a 25 mile snowmobile ride, we'd have to travel three times that far, the herd was all stirred up, the weather conditions had become dangerous, and, to top it off, it was predicted that I would indeed get frostbite on hands and feet. Have you ever tried to shoot a bow with frostbitten hands? No thanks. I'll stay put. And so there was no hunt.

(more)

Figure 16. Arrow points and point caps used on Cook's Inlet hunting arrows. (Callahan)

(If there had been a hunt, I was prepared to switch from a stone point to a rubber blunt, if the mood struck me, so as not to actually kill the prey. I'd still get to test out the bow and experience the thrill of the hunt but nothing would get killed. This is how I have usually hunted in recent years. See Callahan 2000.)

Since there was no hunt, I gave a bowmaking workshop that day instead. I also had prepared and was scheduled to give a slide-lecture entitled "Reconstructive Archeology and the 'Abo' Movement," showing who was doing what around the world. For reasons beyond my understanding, the talk was cancelled and to this day has never been given. In addition, since we had no reindeer to butcher with our stone tools, as we had hoped,

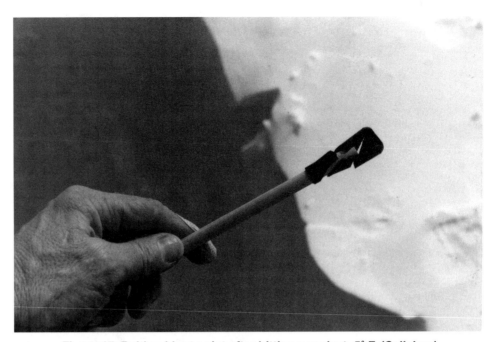

Figure 17. Rubber blunt point after hitting a rock at -5° F. (Callahan)

we were given a freshly killed seal. The seal was partially butchered by hunter Joe Tikivik, who couldn't stop praising the stone knives. "It's the best knife I've ever used...far sharper than any steel knife. It makes less work for the wife" (in cleaning the hide).

Participant Susan Eirich-Dehne, Director of the Manitoga Nature Center in N.Y., took along her video camera to document some of the project. She took a lot of footage of me shooting the bow around the igloos and roving in the outlying area. Apparently at the same time, someone else took snapshots with my still camera from the same positions. These are the photos shown in this article. (In fact I have a whole album of photos taken during this trip.) The video also has a lot of footage of the picnic expedition. (I didn't receive the videotape until years later and only viewed it for the second time the other day, in preparation for this article. There are a few interesting moments.

This event took place during the formative year of the SPT. I had just presented the proposal for such a society the preceeding November. We were not to become on official organization until the following November. But this Arctic project was interwoven into the Society, for conference participants included David Wescott, our Editor, who edited Part 1 & 2 of this article for the very first Bulletins, and Susan Eirich-Dehne, as well as yours truly, three Founding Board Members of what was soon to become the Society of Primitive Technology.

The years have come and gone. The SPT is now a viable international organization, known and respected throughout the world. I don't know where my bow and the arrows I left in the Arctic are now, nor do I know if the "movement" to reinstate hunting with the traditional Eskimo bow and the other old ways we helped to foster has petered out or is still alive somewhere in the NWT. But I still have my wonderful sealskin boots. I put them on every winter when we have our first big snow, and I lay out a "bigfoot" trail through the backyard and the adjacent woods so my daughter, Melody, who was to be born eight months after the gathering, can try to follow my

ADDITIONAL REFERENCES

Baker, Tim
1994   *Bows of the World.* **The Traditional Bowyer's Bible,** *Vol. 3. Bois D'Arc Press: 43-98.*
Baugh, Dick
1992   *A Cordage Backed Bow.* **Bulletin of Primitive Technology** *1(3): 66-71.*
Callahan. Errett
2000   *"Deer Kill".* **Roving Handbook.** *Piltdown Productions: 124.*
Claiborne, Robert
1973   **The First Americans** *Time-Life Books: 108. Emergence Of Man series.*
Collins, Jeff
1998   *Eskimo Bows, Parts 1-3.* **Primitive Archer 6** *(1):26-286 (2): 5-7, and 6 (3): 8-14.*

tracks, as she has done each and every winter since she could walk. We share the cold and I pass on my stories of the far North, where cold is really cold. And where twice I came close to overstaying my welcome.

It was interesting to see that, after the original article came out in the BPT (# 1 and 2), interest in the corded bow was spearheaded, and a whole "string" of corded bow innovations followed (Baugh 1992, Baker 1994, Collins 1998). In addition, a number of Eskimo bows have been made here in my archery workshops, following the template I made up for the bow in this study. Thus the knowledge is passed on. That's what the SPT is all about.

CREDITS

I would like to give foremost credit to John Jamieson, principal of the Sanikiluaq School, and organizer of the conference which gave rise to this whole endeavor. He also assumed the burden of expense for purchasing the Eskimo bow and arrow replicas reported herein. He also deserves thanks for his camera and darkroom work. Thanks also to Chuck Tolley, Superintendent of Schools in the Baffin Divisional Board of Education, Northwest Territories, for not only granting permission for the conference but for participating in it as an active member. Special thanks go to all the Inuit members of the Sanikiluaq community, who received us so warmly and invited us to their community dance, where we made fools of ourselves to everyone's enjoyment. Thanks also to Cindy Ott and Peggy Stanford at the Anthropology Department of the Smithsonian Museum of Natural History for locating and retrieving the original artifact bow and for putting up with me and my questions for hours while I measured and drew it in detail And a tip of the hat to Steve Watts for presenting me with a pair of Eskimo-style wooden snow goggles he made, which were used extensively in my outings. And thanks to Susan Eirich-Dehne for enduring the bitter cold and my many idiosyncrasies while attempting to photo and videotape my archery experiences. Finally, thanks go out to Don Gardner and Doug Stern for their many insights into Eskimo bowmaking. These are the guys to watch in the future.

Callahan drawing his Eskimo bow replica in the Arctic at -25° C. Inuit writing on left is translated on right. Official post card of the conference. (Jamieson)

ON THE CUTTING EDGE:
STONE TOOL BOW MAKING
Text and Photos By Bart & Robin Blankenship, © 1996

The allure of stone tools lies, certainly, in the parallel ridged surface of a precision crafted obsidian knife, in the long, perfectly centered depression running the length of a flint spearhead, or in the delicately serrated edge of a chert arrowhead. These appealing samples of artistry draw most of us to take a closer look at stone tools. When we do, and actually begin to use stone tools, we realize their practical usefulness also means picking up the clunky chunks of debris scattered randomly at the feet of the stone tool craftsman. Mention stone tools and many of us visualize the finely worked blade, hafted to a wood or bone handle and secured with sinew and pitch. "Lovely to look at, delightful to hold, but if you should break it, consider it..." a hell of a lot of work to replace! So as we get down to the nitty gritty of working with stone tools on a regular basis, we often find ourselves setting the hafted blades and finely crafted knives on the display table and reaching to the ground for the forgotten debris.

Photo 1 - Using a wooden wedge and hammer to free up a stone wedge.

A small change in perspective on what a stone tool can be means we can really get down to some serious work with stone tools. For example, splitting a tree trunk with stone wedges, removing a respectable amount of wood with a heavy, hand-held stone chopper, or taking away wood at a critical angle or in a precision amount with a stone spoke shave, chisel or planer. This change in perspective also means that even the "flintknapping impaired", those of us who think a cone is something that holds ice cream, who can't even hit a platform let alone prepare one, and are sure a bopper was something teeny in the '60's, can now stride confidently into the realm of stone tool use.

Our appreciation of the simplest, randomly broken or predetermined one blow stone tools soared after a recent course on which five students made self bows ranging from 35 to 55 pounds in draw weight and 24 to 31 inches in draw length. The average time spent in construction of these bows was 4 days. The wood was partially seasoned Black Walnut and the tools were unhafted stones, and wooden clubs to drive the tools if needed. We all learned a lot about rugged use and abuse of stone tools. By the time we'd finished the bows we were also able to confidently give the most ordinary pieces of broken rock names like wedge, chopper,

chisel and planer. Each tool was quite determinable from the other and everyone had their favorite "set" of tools.

Students were given half logs, six to ten inches in diameter, with the bark still on, that had been cut and split the year before. Unseasoned wood is more easily worked with stone tools, but we used what we had and now know what can be done with partially seasoned wood. (We could have cut our work time in half with unseasoned wood.) The half logs were first split with stone and wood wedges. In the past, we have used antler wedges for much of the wood removal in primi-

Bart and Robin Blankenship are the authors of <u>Earth Knack: Stone Age Skills for the 21st Century</u>. They also operate Earth Knack Stone Age Living Skills. They are currently developing a Stone Age village. Anyone interested in workshops, internships or working on the project may contact them at PO Box 508, Crestone, CO 81131. (719-256-4909.)

Photo 2 - Narrowing the green stave at the handle with a nine pound, two-handed chopper.

Photo 3 - Using a stone planer for removing wood.

tive bow making. However, antler tools take time to grind and they crush and splinter apart quickly, especially when splitting wood around knots. A stone wedge is more brittle and also crushes and breaks, but is so much faster to make or replace. Producing a stone wedge often takes just one blow with a hammer stone.

Our stone wedges were made from basalt, coarse chert, and quartzite. A gradual taper was important, making the wedges easy to start and preventing them from popping out. In first splitting the logs, half inch thick wedges were used. These wedges were more durable, and worked well for quartering the logs. The wedges were driven with crude wooden clubs of locust, hickory and mountain mahogany. Once the logs were split in quarters, wood reduction continued with thinner stone wedges. These thinner wedges were better for careful wood removal. Functional wood wedges were a natural byproduct of splitting the logs with stone wedges. The wood wedges were sometimes a foot or more in length and best used in freeing up a lodged stone wedge or finishing a split that the stone wedge started.

(more)

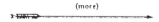

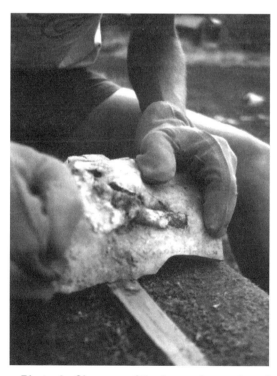

Photo 4 - Close-up of the large planer at work.

Photo 5 - Application of the small planer.

Photo 6 - Close-up of the small planer at work.

One challenge of splitting quarter logs to almost finished bow dimensions with wedges is that the split often dives deeply into wood you don't want to remove. This happens when you try to take off too much wood at a time. To overcome this problem we found it important to remove wood slowly. Splitting less than half of the total wood away at any one time allowed the splits to fade to the outside of the stave. For instance if you had a two inch thick stave and wanted to reduce it on the belly to half an inch you should first remove just under an inch with the first split. The next split would be just under half an inch and the final one under a quarter.

The bows we made were thicker in the handle so it was important not to let the split run into the handle. This was prevented by sawing a notch above and below the handle. The saw was a sharp six inch edge on a fifty pound piece of coarse chert. The bow stave was raked back and forth along this sharp saw edge. Any splits would then terminate at this notch. When using green wood, this notch can be made with a ten pound hand ax. However, seasoned wood crushes with this same ax. So the chert saw was a good answer.

Up to this point the bark had been left on to protect the back of the stave. The bark was now removed with stone planers that were used like drawknives. Random stone pieces from the flintknapping pit served well for this job. Pieces in highest demand were the larger ones of about 8" that were easier to grip with both hands. These planers were brittle and it was important not to use a prying out motion or the edge would chip, ruining the performance of the planer. This bark removal would have been a snap if done while the wood was green. As it was, it took about two hours. It was necessary to leave the stave large here so the dimensions could be adjusted to miss any imperfections discovered once the bark was removed.

The next phase of wood removal relied on heavy planers and some chiseling. The chiseling was a natural evolution from the initial splitting. Often the initial splits made with wedges would taper off, not running as deep as wanted. Because it was necessary to have the limbs taper in thickness it was helpful to use a chiseling technique, starting at the handle, removing wood in focused areas. These stone chisels were the bigger and sharper wedges.

For planing down the staves further we found that a heavy planer greatly expedited wood removal. The fastest planers weighed about 8 pounds. It was helpful to clamp the stave during planing. A simple tourniquet clamp was adequate. Padding the stave under the clamp was important, as well as not letting the clamp rope touch the stave, otherwise the rope would crush into the wood. The most efficient planer angles varied according to the stone used. For basalt sixty degrees was good. Sharper angles crumbled and broke. The chert, being tougher, could hold a steeper angle. Often the planer edge crumbling proved to be a good thing because then only a few 1/8 inch places would be cutting into the wood. This allowed the mass of the planer to bear down on a reduced edge and remove wood very quickly. However, the path of the planer would have to be shifted every pass or two to keep the edge from merely creating a set of trenches in the wood.

Photo 7 - Detail of the finished handle and arrow.

Photo 8 - Finished bow with a 31" draw.

Once the staves were taken down to nearly finished thickness they were set out to finish seasoning. The stresses of final tillering require fully seasoned wood to prevent the bow from taking excessive set, which reduces arrow speed. The work prior to drying the staves took about 2 days. Experimenting on the same wood freshly cut took 3 hours.

After the staves had dried the tips were tapered, first by controlled splitting, with wedges and chisels and then by shaving with planers and spoke shaves. One student using a wedge, split down from the tip toward the handle of her bow to create a taper. She removed too much wood for her desired final shape. To compensate she sawed into the side of the limb where the split hadn't penetrated and popped the split out. This gave that side a concave Holmegaard shape. The stave was large enough that we decided to match the other sides the same way. The result was a very fast bow

throwing a 450 grain arrow 134 feet per second. Her draw length was 24 inches and the draw weight was 35 pounds. Perhaps some ancient forebearer made this same mistake, ushering in that old Holmegaard style?

Final tillering was completed with small spoke shaves having untouched edges. Then the bows were sanded, first with coarse lava, then finished up with scouring rush.

Five beautiful Black Walnut bows were made with one-blow stone tools by novice flintknappers. They now know quite a bit about "the cutting edge." Don't let the intricacies of bifacial reduction or the mysteries of step fracture removal deter you from delving into the stone age! Sit down next to your favorite stone tool artisan and fill your bark bucket with debris, or grab a hammerstone and start bashing. You'll soon have a set of workable tools to rival the Sears "Craftsman " line!

The 30 Minute Bow

By Jim Allen, © 1994

Are you a bow maker? How many bows have you made? 10? 20? If you've made over 20 bows you're doing pretty good. I can visualize you sitting in your shop, carefully scraping away one-hundredth of an inch at a time. Now you're putting it on the tillering board again, painstakingly seeking that perfect balance between the limbs. Measure, scrape, tillerboard, measure, scrape, tillerboard.

Day by day, week by week, your bow slowly emerges. Then comes the sanding and finishing. What you are doing is creating a work of art .. not just a functioning bow. The purpose of this article is to show how little it really takes to make a functional, hard-hitting, smooth-drawing bow. Let me start by saying that too little has been said about this type of bow. Tom Brown has presented one version of a survival bow in one of his books, Larry Dean Olsen demonstrated a simplified bow in his book, and Tim Baker gave it the best treatment of all in *The Bowyer's Bible*. But awesome things need to be shouted from the rooftops, and this is awesome. (Let's just hope your neighbors will understand.)

You start by going out to the woods (seems like a lot of our projects start this way, doesn't it?) Select a straight limb or sapling of any of your bow making favorites: osage, hickory, oak, locust, red cedar, etc. (excuse me for using the word "straight" and the word "osage" in the same sentence). I, myself, use mostly dead wood for bow making. The limb you select should be about 5'-6' long. At the middle between the two ends of your limb, the diameter should be about 1". Of course, the limb will taper at one end while being more massive at the other end.

Now trim off any side branches, if you're so inclined. It will make your bow easier to handle. Using a knife or axe (I prefer an axe) trim down the massive proximal end of the limb to match the taper of the thinner, distal end. HOWEVER, LEAVE THE BACK OF THE LIMB (or sapling) UNTOUCHED. Do all of your trimming (of the proximal end) on 3 sides only. Your bow is now almost finished. Cut nocks in both ends about 1/2 inch from the ends of the bow and ...VOILA, you're done!

Affix a bowstring to your bow and try it out. If you own a scale you can test it for power. If it shoots like a "wimp", cut an inch off both ends and re-cut your nocks. Continue to cut 1" increments until you reach the poundage you desire. My recommendation is to not try to be "macho". Select a draw weight that feels comfortable. As Howard Hill once said, a 40 lb. bow can kill a moose; one of the largest animals on this continent. I have read the writings of many professional archers from the 1950s and 60s who felt that most American hunters were "overbowed" (using bows too powerful for maximum accuracy).

The final step is to take this "stick" to the shooting range and confound the archers using $2000.00 heat-seeking, radar controlled, laser guided, oil-filled, computer assisted shooting machines. They won't understand you, but don't let that bother you.I keep my "crude" bows in the garage. I'm a little afraid of what the ultra-dry air of our gas-heated house will do to a bow without any finish. You can, if you wish, scrape the bark off and put an air-tight finish on your bow.

Well, that's about it! Serious bow makers who have never tried this are in for a real treat. You've overlooked one of nature's true gifts. For the wilderness survival enthusiast, the ramifications of this simple bow are obvious. A good sized piece of flint is all you need to produce a bow in a hurry. Good luck to all who try it. Write and let the rest of us know your successes, failures, or comments.

Jim Allen draws his 35lb., 68" Red Cedar longbow. This bow took about 30 minutes to make.
"The smoothest draw I've ever experienced."

Jim Allen is the author of <u>Sleep Close To The Fire</u>. He is a hunter, trapper, and wilderness skills instructor. Contact him at: 907 Cedar St. Elkhart IN 46514 (219) 293-9570.

Section 5

BUCKSKIN
Enough Brains To Tan Your Hide

Working Hides With Stone, Bone and Antler Tools

By Steven Edholm

These drawings are by Sylvie Beynies from The Center of Archaeological Research of Prehistory and Archeology, Ministry of Research at the National Center of Science Research, France. She attended Rabbitstick in 1994 and interviewed Tamara and Steve along with other tanners on the fine art of brain tanning. Tamara and Steve produced the tools used in these renderings.

At the 1995 Rabbitstick, Tamara and Steve sponsored an ongoing workshop on the process of brain tanning using only stone, bone and antler tools. The resulting hides were as fine as any produced with modern edged tools.

Cannon Bone Fleshing Tool

Serrated teeth in the end of the tool assist in removing membrane and flesh. They must be resharpened frequently.

Tamara Wilder

Wrist thong locks hand in place during use.

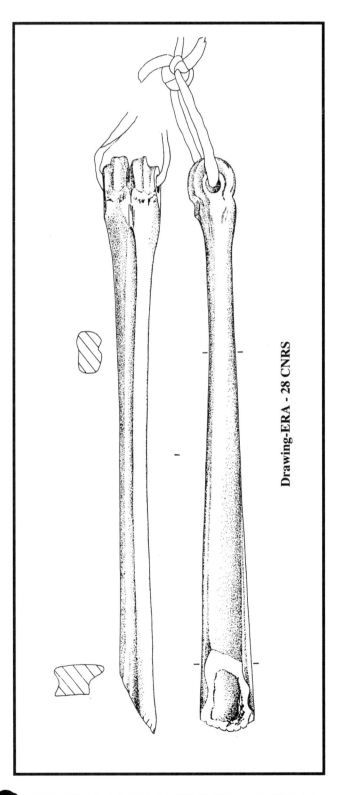

Drawing-ERA - 28 CNRS

Elk Cannon Bone Flesher/Scraper

Used for wet-scraping and fleshing hides in either the pushing or pulling method. Edges must be periodically resharpened with a stone flake.

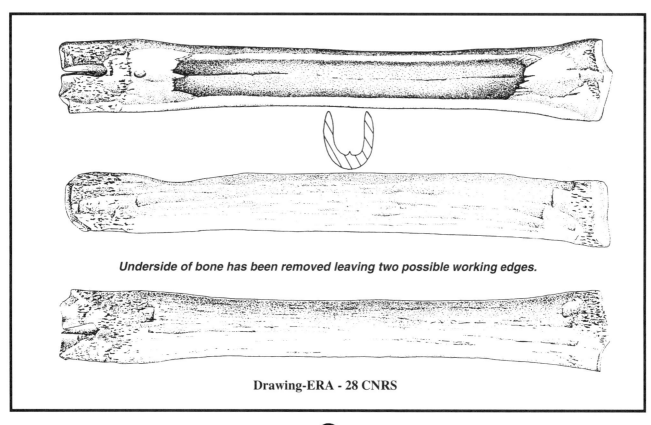

Underside of bone has been removed leaving two possible working edges.

Flint Dry-Scrapers Hafted on Antler and Elk Cannon Bone

The sharply beveled scraper above and left is used to remove hair and epidermis, but not for fleshing. It is common to both the North American plains and African bushmen. It was used for stone-tool tanning demonstrations at both Winter Count and Rabbitstick. The scraper illustrated below depicts a common hafting method for a simple stone blade beveled for the removal of hair and tissue.

Drawing-ERA - 28 CNRS

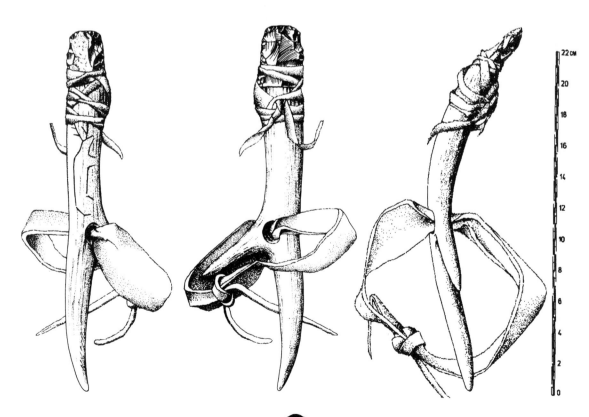

Ulna-Radius Scraper

This tool requires very little modification of the bone to be functional. The edge of the ulna bone which adheres to the radius is already very thin and need only be slightly sharpened with a stone flake. Used for wet-scraping/fleshing hides in the same manner as the elk cannon bone scraper but cannot withstand as much pressure as the cannon bone tool.

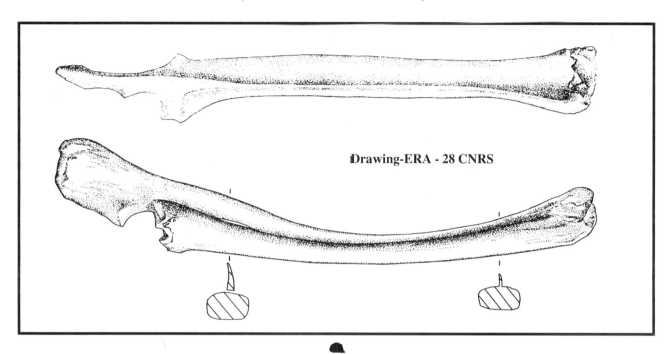

Drawing-ERA - 28 CNRS

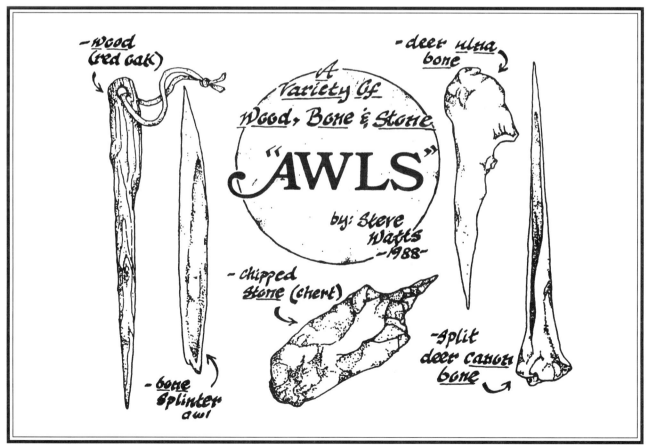

-wood (red oak)

- deer ulna bone

A Variety Of Wood, Bone & Stone "AWLS" by: Steve Watts -1988-

- chipped stone (chert)

- bone splinter awl

-split deer canon bone

BUCKSKIN BABBLINGS

Edited By Alice Tulloch, © 1993

One September evening, during the 1993 Rabbitstick Rendezvous, outside Rexburg, Idaho, some of the top brain tanners in the west "racked their brains." Matt McMahan and Molly Miller had been giving a talk on the care and construction of buckskin garments. Jim Riggs, Steve Edholm, Tamara Wilder, and Dave Bethke soon began giving their input. As darkness fell, they shared their latest tips and discoveries.

Skinning

> **Matt:** *"That shiny new Gerber [knife], it's shiny and brand new, just raging to cut into your big fleshy hide. Don't do it! You don't even have to have the blade touch the hide. Not even once! It's a crime!"*
> **Crowd:** *"Amen! Yes!"*

Everyone agreed that in skinning, it is critical not to use a skinning knife. Avoiding scores and cuts is critical to the ease of processing and the quality of the finished product. After the initial incisions along belly and legs, using a knife is unnecessary. The more the skin is "fisted" off, the better.

A bullet makes a different hole than a broadhead. The bullet hole is neat and easily mended. A broadhead cuts a ragged x-shaped hole, that leaves a more unsightly mend. Sew the holes up, on the flesh side, after it's brained and before you break it dry.

Wet vs Dry Scrape

Most of the tanners present were wet scrape advocates. Riggs prefers the dry scrape method. They had all tried both methods. Two different strategies seemed to be used in processing hides. Riggs and most tanners will dry scrape and finish a skin in two days. But Matt and Molly process up to 80 skins a year in stages. In the fall, Molly wet scrapes all the skins. Matt will brain and break the skins dry later in the winter. Then they're smoked in the calm dry days of spring.

Jim Riggs also told of his experience with freeze scraping. He'd fleshed a skin, tied it into the frame and then set it outside in hard freezing weather. When fro-

Stretched and ready for dry-scraping.

zen and tight, he scraped the same as a dry scrape. He cautioned though that the friction of the scraping blade can thaw the skin after a few strokes, if it's not cold enough. So you have to move around a lot. In a very cold climate, this may not be such a problem.

Steve has had success green scraping. If the fresh skin is soaked in the sun in warm weather, the hide can be ready for the beam in as little as a half day, although it might take 1-2 days. And scraping is much easier. Riggs thought the layers are much easier to see this way, pinkish gray epidermis and white dermis. So you can be more certain that the grain is all off.

There wasn't any agreement on whether or when to remove the membrane on the flesh side. Some tanners remove the membrane as they flesh. Some leave it on and let the rope open it up and remove any excess when drying and breaking the brained skin. Many tanners (Riggs, Edholm, etc.) membrane on the fleshing beam, as a separate step, after epidermis removal and prior to braining.

Braining

Dry scraped hides seem to need only one braining. But these tanners all agreed that wet scraped may need multiple braining. They couldn't agree on why that seems to be so. Wet scrape may be only removing the grain partly through the papillary layer. Dry scrape is more likely to remove the entire epidermis layer down to the bottom of the papillary layer. This may be the reason for the difference in the penetration of the brains.

A short discussion centered on the use of chopped liver in the brains. Some folks use an equal portion of brains and liver in the solution. This was thought to keep the brains from going bad so quickly.

Bart Blankenship offered a "brain" solution that keeps well enough to take out on a long remote teaching course: equal parts of powdered lecithin, soap flakes, and deer fat (1/4 cup each in a gallon of water). Yupik Eskimo women are said to be using Downey fabric softener for the furs for their traditional parkas. But Molly and the group roared back in outrage at these substitute braining solutions. She said that brain-tanned is much softer, stronger and environmentally safer than any other method.

Steve and Tamara, and Matt and Molly, have been experimenting with seasoning their skins. After the skin is entirely wet scraped, they tack it out flat to dry, then store it for 6 - 12 months. They say something happens that lets the brains penetrate better the first time, which helps minimize the need to rebrain wet scrapes. But they report the results aren't necessarily consistent yet.

"Cooking" the brains.

Sylvia Beyfis

Someone in the audience spoke up saying he has tried bringing the skin to the point of fully saturated with brains, then drying and seasoning for 6 months, then resoaking/rebraining and breaking it soft. One needs to be careful though because a brained hide is extremely attractive to critters. Riggs suggested freezing a hide after braining to further open the fibers and get the brains to penetrate as it thaws.

Stretching and Breaking

> Matt: *"There's two theories I have on buckskin. Every hide is different, so that crumbles every theory there ever was. And the second would be that anything you can do at any step of the process to agitate that hide, to keep it moving, to introduce a new direction of stretch that it didn't think was possible is going to make a difference."*

Molly recommended using a small round needle for sewing up holes after braining and wringing. They no longer use a glover's needle for sewing up holes, because it cuts the hide to make the holes. Then those holes open up during stretching They sew the holes with many tiny stitches, using cotton thread. Sinew gets too soft when wet to hold during the stretching process. Artificial sinew can cut the hide during all that pulling. Holes sewn up before breaking will stretch out flat, without puckers.

Matt discussed how to avoid ruffled edges, which seems to be a particular problem when hand pulling a skin. It's important to have your hands doing most of their grabbing and pulling where the skin is thickest in the middle, and much less energy on the thinner armpits and underbelly. Jim has a row of nails on his fence he uses for stretching, to avoid ruffles. He always cuts perimeter holes, even if he doesn't plan on tying it to a frame. So if he pulls the skin dry instead of staking, he'll loop the edge holes on the row of nails and pull a while in the same manner described above by Matt. Then he'll unhook, rotate the skin 90 degrees, and rehang it to pull awhile in the other direction, and so on. That keeps ruffles from occurring. (Jim Miller told me later that a ruffled, hand pulled skin will flatten out if stretched out in a rack for a few days in a dry place.) Matt cautions against overstretching in the lengthwise direction which happens too easily, especially when staking on a frame.

(more)

Preeminent buckskinner and author of
Blue Mountain Buckskin, Jim Riggs.

breaking and drying. Then he smokes with a moist smoke. When done smoking thoroughly, he immediately reworks those stiff spots and finds they then come out soft and fluffy.

Smoking Materials

Tanners in different parts of the country have a wide range of preferences on smoking materials. Most prefer punky wood. Douglas fir punk is widely used.

Matt: *"You don't smell it out here at Rabbitstick. But you take that stuff into town and stand in the bank or an elevator, they think the place is on fire. I've been in buildings where they thought I was on fire."*

Steve advocated the use of a steel cable, instead of a nylon or polypropylene rope which he has melted thru. He cables the skin only on the flesh side. Cabling really opens up and moves the skin. The cable he uses is 1/4-inch diameter garage door cable, anchored tautly on a tree. He also recommends sanding the hair side with pumice quite a bit while pulling it dry to break up any surface crust that inhibits drying and fluffing.

Riggs mentioned that on a skin that he knows is well brained, but the rumps are a little papery as they are drying, he doesn't rebrain. Instead, he finishes the

Jim Riggs also likes cottonwood punk, as well as green boughs of sage, Douglas fir and western juniper. He said "8 1/2 basketballs of green boughs" (or about half a packed gunnysack) are enough to smoke a skin. Most of those using punk recommend popcorn to baseball size chunks. Embers from powdered punk may float up and spot the skin. Everyone cautioned against punk from pitchy trees, due to the pitch pockets that may flare up.

No one agreed on the moisture content of the smoking material. Steve and Tamara use dry Douglas fir punk, with a hot fire, in a direct setup, in a dry climate.

Steve Edholm "cabling" a
freshly brained hide.

Dave Bethke readying a hide
for the smoker.

Tamara Wilder monitoring
a smoking operation.

Some who use a hot fire in a dry climate preferred moist punk to avoid flaring. Those who use cool smoke in tipi or stove pipe setups, used drier punk. Several people keep handy both moist and dry punk while smoking, so they can put on one or the other to help coals that are struggling or cool down a hot bed of coals.

Matt and Molly have been experimenting with light smoking. They wanted to know how little they could smoke and still get away with it. How much smoke is needed to make the miracle occur? They tried very light smoke, even one-sided smoke. These hides did seem to wear well and come back soft after washing. But after one year, they said they noticed that the light-smoked skins were not coming back as soft after washing as the heavily smoked skins they've been wearing daily and washing often for over four years. So, now their golden rule is don't skimp on smoke. Molly said "It's another gift given to us to make skins come back to life." This entire process is really smoke tanning.

Animals

Everyone's steady source of buckskins is the deer. Most preferred it for garments. Although elk is romantic, most felt it was less durable, especially for the much greater effort required to brain-tan them. Riggs said that elk takes three times as much effort as deerskin, and wears out three times faster. The fibers are much larger and looser than in a deerskin. Many folks thought bear with the hair on was a reasonable undertaking for a fur robe, as well as the smaller fur bearers like fox, bobcat, and coyote. Matt recommended that people experiment with domestic animals skins as well, such as goat and sheep.

Matt Richards (right) with Northern Lights organizer, Glenn Charbboneau.

David Wescott Photos

Moose was recommended for moccasins due to its thickness. Jim Miller said the people in the north country have quite a different approach for tanning moose. After the hide is scraped, a couple of tablespoons of melted animal fat is sprinkled over the hide. (Yes, it leaves greasy splotches at this stage.) Then the hide is smoked before braining. Then the hide is repeatedly brained, stretched dry and smoked until the desired softness is achieved, perhaps 4 - 5 times. Of the folks present at Rabbitstick, only Jim Miller had experience brain-tanning buffalo. He said it is a tremendous effort, requiring much scraping, many brainings, and 40-80 hours of work. Buffalo has to be scraped down quite a lot to make it tan-able with the hair on, and a flexible finished product. Then he puts it in a frame and invites the neighborhood kids over to jump on it to break it soft.

The beginner may be daunted by the seeming difficulty in brain-tanning. These tanners are experts sharing with us their discoveries on what makes a successful product, with the least effort. So why wear buckskins in the first place? They're handsome, comfortable, fragrant, strong, warm, breathable and durable. They're even edible in a pinch. They require no harsh chemicals. They are consistent with moral values that honor the gift of the animal's life. And finally, they are not garbage, returning naturally to the earth when used up.

> *Molly: "We were not being respectful to the smoke beings. We were hating smoke."*

Mel Beattie...from start to finish

Dave Bethke wet scraping on a beam.

Making the intitial cuts with stone.

Stretching hides for the dry scrape process.

*Readying a fresh beaver pelt
for the braining process.*

Dehairing a deer hide with a metal bitted tool.

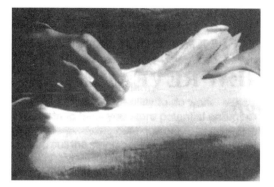

Buffing a hide with a pumice stone.

Wringing out a brained hide on a cable.

Checking the progress.

Wringing out a brained hide on a stake.

The Tanning Process
Photos by:
Upcountry
David Wescott
Ronnie Moss

Sewing the holes before smoking.

Pulling and stretching takes every muscle.

Using group energy to pull a hide dry.

Subcutaneous Stitch For Buckskin

By Chris Morasky

A couple of years ago, I met a German master leather worker while attending a Blackfeet Indian gathering in Montana. We talked about hide tanning techniques and compared the oil-tan leather he uses for making traditional Bavarian costumes to the brain-tan leather that I had. He was especially interested in the holes I had repaired in my buckskin. He examined the way my stitching had loosened, leaving a gap between the hide edges, and how the needle holes had stretched to become visible, also exposing the thread. Looking up from the leather he said, "I really want to show you how I sew up hide cuts!"

What follows is an explanation of his technique, along with a few suggestions from my own experience and that of other buckskinners. I don't recall the name given to this stitch by my German friend, but it is also used in the medical field where it is called a subcutaneous stitch.

Start with a dry, tanned hide, either white or smoked. Trim any stiff edges from around the holes to be stitched. Holes larger than 1/2 inch in diameter should be cut oval to reduce the puckers, or folds, created by stretching the hide during stitching. The puckers that do result will be removed later.

Use the smallest round needle that you can. A glover's needle is easier to use, but the slits created by the needle's sharp edges are more likely to stretch or tear than round holes. Sinew or strong natural fiber thread is preferred to synthetic thread, which may eventually cut into the leather. Tie a figure-eight knot at the end of your thread. This knot is tied by forming a loop, then giving the loop an extra 1/2 twist before threading the end through. It looks like an "8" and will not slip.

To begin sewing, push the needle through the flesh side of the hide to the hair side about 1/16 inch from the edge of the hole. Now sew a short stitch parallel to the hole on the hairside of the hide. The stitch starts at the initial needle hole and does not go through the hide, but dips into the hide then back out to the hair side (Fig. 1).

For the next stitch, start across from the initial needle hole on the opposite side of the hole in the hide. Make another short stitch parallel to the first (Fig. 2). The third stitch begins where the first stitch ended. The fourth stitch starts where the second stitch ended, and so on.

When the stitches are pulled tight, the result is a hidden thread within a seam that could be mistaken for a hide scar, looking at it from the hair side (Fig. 3). From the flesh side, the edges of the hide along the stitch are often visible, but this side of the hide is usually the inside of a garment, so who cares?

The last step is to remove the puckers that form from uneven stretching of the hide along the repaired hole. These wrinkles can simply be ironed out, using an iron at a low temperature setting. Alternatively, a smoked hide may be dampened and stretched a bit to remove the wrinkles.

For extremely large holes, consider cutting out a patch in the shape of a heart, eagle, or whatever to further customize your leather. A dyed patch is quite striking, and turns a hide's detriment into something that looks as if you did it on purpose.

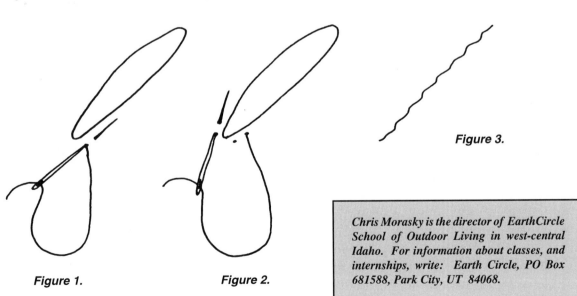

Figure 3.

Figure 1.

Figure 2.

Chris Morasky is the director of EarthCircle School of Outdoor Living in west-central Idaho. For information about classes, and internships, write: Earth Circle, PO Box 681588, Park City, UT 84068.

Tan Your Hides with Nature's Tools

By Jim Miller

Tack the pelt to a board and scrape with hand tools. The end result is a soft, supple hide, free of chemicals and done at home.

Our ancestors lived very close to the circle of life. Thankful always for the food, tools and clothing that came from a successful hunt. Warmth, color, protection and camouflage are shared with us by our four-legged brothers through the giving of their pelts.

Today, one need only walk the roadside to find animals whose lives were taken. Thoughtlessly and sometimes without knowing, left there to become hawk food.

Whether you're seven or seventy, for the beginning tanner a roadkill could become a rewarding first project. Many of these pelts are in perfect condition. My hat is made from the first pelt I ever tanned. The process is an easy one and will start you on the way to eventually using all of the animal. So let's get started.

As much as possible pull the pelt off the carcass. Only use your knife if absolutely necessary. If the animal is a fairly fresh kill and still warm, the membrane and pelt will pull away easily when skinning. However, if the carcass is cold, this stuff acts like rubber cement and must be cut carefully, particularly at the head, neck, and tail. Always leave as much meat on the carcass as possible. It will sometimes want to pull off with the pelt.

To simplify your first project, slice the hide open all the way up the belly to the hair of the chinny-chin-chin. (Sorry, it's

an old butcher's saying.) Now, throw it over a very smooth log or tack it out flat on a piece of plywood.

You can use a fairly crescent-shaped knife held at a 90-degree angle to the pelt. Now push and scrape. Remove all the fat, meat and membrane until you begin to see the pores of the skin. Sometimes hair will pull back through the underside of the skin. Just move on to the next area and keep scraping. The membrane on the head or mask is the toughest to get off, so take your time. The tails generally have a lot of fat on them. Clean them well (soap and water?) but go gently, they can break fairly easily. Fortunately they're so fluffy they can be sewn back together without a sign of the disaster. You've finished the first step referred to as "fleshing." Set the pelt in a warm spot to dry for a day or two.

Pelts and skins used for brain-tanning require a thorough fleshing job. The fine oil that is used is the reason for this. When the animal's life is taken it gives you a complete tanning package as a bonus. It is said that "every critter has enough brains to tan its own hide", except buffaloes (and some people I know). Remove the brain from the raccoon's skull and mix with about 1-1/2 cups of water. Cook this mix for about 10 minutes. Then mash, mix or blend into an oily liquid. This will be divided into two equal amounts.

Buff up the pelt's surface with some sand paper or granite rock. Apply the lukewarm mixture and rub it by hand. Go ahead ladies, it'll make your skin soft. Allow to dry overnight. Buff the surface again and apply the second coat. Now cover with a very warm and wet towel and let it set overnight.

(more)

Jim Miller is a frequent contributor to the Bulletin and strong supporter of the SPT. His articles have ranged from simple gathering to a complete birch bark canoe project. He is an active member of the SPT and teaches primitive technology throughout the country, and primarily in the Great Lakes area. He hosts an annual gathering and runs courses at his home site. Contact him at: 962 F-30 East, Mikado, MI 48745.

Stretch and work the hide over the edge of a board to soften the hide in the tanning process. This should be continued until the hide is dry.

The following morning uncover and begin to stretch your hide. Pull side to side and head to tail. The back of an old wooden chair works well for this. Pull the pelt down over it, stretching and buffing over the full length of the pelt. Take breaks whenever needed, but continue to stretch until dry,

The fibers in the skin are a lot like a baby diaper, crossing and overlapping each other. Applying oil to these fibers and rubbing them together fluffs them up making them soft and airy. When the pelt's dry and no longer cool to the touch, it's ready to be smoked in the tepee. The skin can be hung at the top and rotten wood placed on the fire to smolder and smoke.

At the campfire the pelt can be suspended on sticks downwind but out of reach from a possible wild flame. Remember you want smoke not fire. Moths like tanned pelts of any kind, but smoking deters them allowing you to enjoy them year-round. So clear out a corner of the garage and brain-tan those pelts. A beautiful and respectful memento from the hunt or a well earned reward for salvaging a roadkill.

Hey, honey, stop the car. I think I saw something back there.

Surrounded by the results of "roadside trapping."

Matt Richards Photo

BRAINS, BONES AND HOT SPRINGS:
Native American Deerskin Dressing
at the Time of Contact
Text, Photos and Illustrations By Matt Richards, © 1996

Did I ever tell you that I love braintan? Well, I do. I love making, wearing, smelling, feeling, stretching it. I love it when I'm cold, I slip it on and it warms me up. I get excited when my sweetie wears it. It's great stuff. My love affair with it began eight years ago when everyones friend Jim Riggs introduced me to it. Since then, I've tanned hundreds of deerskins, trying out the methods others used, and the ideas that came to mind during those fertile hours of scraping and softening. Always looking for easier, more direct techniques to accomplish that goal: velvet soft buckskin.

Last fall I started researching every detail I could in ethnographies and explorers' reports of their experiences with the "Indians". Steven Edholm and Tamara Wilder were doing the same thing, and so we traded information. Between us we found over 100 different reports of primitive deerskin dressing in North America, as well as Siberia, Europe, China, Japan, and South Africa. The plethora of different techniques, tools and substances used in the process boggles the brain. In modern days, we often say there are as many techniques as there are tanners, and the same seems true of the past. What we've learned has revolutionized the way Michelle and I dress deerskins, and I have hopes it'll do the same for you.

In this article, I will describe and illustrate most of the recorded approaches to each step in the process. Sometimes a technique is dependent upon other techniques being done or not being done in the same process continuum. My purpose here is not to teach you a process, but to show you the many options that were practiced by Neolithic peoples, and to varying degrees why, so that you may experiment and adopt ones that are appropriate for you. This discussion, however, will be limited to the dressing of deerskins. Because of their durability, softness and availability, they were the most commonly tanned, worn and utilized skin in North America; the most widely used "fabric" of pre-historic times. While many of these techniques can and were applied to the dressing of other skins (caribou and antelope especially) each skin type

Stages of Manufacture - from the hoof to finished product. Buckskin - the most comfortable and durable material available. Just ask the source.

has its own structure that requires specialized methods. All information presented here-in is limited by the materials I was able to find. There are many tribes for whom I have not been able to find any detailed information. Some of these reports would shed a different light on certain details. If you have any, I would like to see them.

(more)

Matt and Michelle like to incorporate primitive skills into their homesteading, hiking and adventures. They tan and sell beautiful deerskins and garments, teach custom brain-tanning workshops and are publishing a detailed "how-to" handbook to wet-scrape brain-tanning. Visit them at braintan.com. You can also contact them at: 10398 Takilma Road, Cave Junction, OR 97523. Or order their oustanding book Deerskins Into Buckskins.

Scraping Set-ups

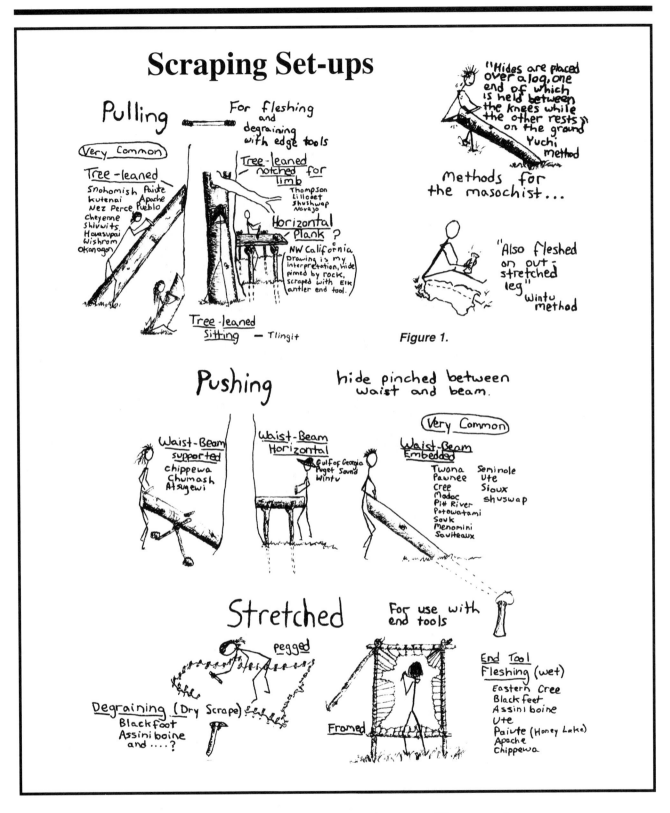

Pulling — For fleshing and degraining with edge tools

(Very Common)

Tree-leaned
Snohomish, Paiute, Kutenai, Apache, Nez Perce, Pueblo, Cheyenne, Shivwits, Havasupai, Wishrom, Okanogan

Tree-leaned notched for limb
Thompson, Lillooet, Shushwap, Navajo

Horizontal Plank?
NW California
Drawing is my interpretation, hide pinned by rock, scraped with Elk antler end tool.

Tree-leaned Sitting — Tlingit

"Hides are placed over a log, one end of which is held between the knees while the other rests on the ground" Yuchi method

Methods for the masochist...

"Also fleshed on out-stretched leg" Wintu method

Figure 1.

Pushing — hide pinched between waist and beam.

Waist-Beam supported
Chippewa, Chumash, Atsugewi

Waist-Beam Horizontal
Gulf of Georgia, Puget Sound, Wintu

(Very Common)
Waist-Beam Embedded
Twana, Pawnee, Cree, Modoc, Pitt River, Potowatami, Sauk, Menomini, Souiteaux, Seminole, Ute, Sioux, Shuswap

Stretched

pegged

Degraining (Dry Scrape)
Blackfoot, Assiniboine and....?

Framed

For use with end tools

End Tool Fleshing (wet)
Eastern Cree, Blackfeet, Assiniboine, Ute, Paiute (Honey Lake), Apache, Chippewa

These deerskin dressing methods will be broken down into subjects in the order of their most common application: **beams, fleshing, degraining, structure openers, brain solutions, softening, smoking and dyeing.**

Dry-Scrape or Wetscrape?

Almost all stone age North Americans scraped deerskins wet over a beam. Even on the plains, where dry scraping was intimately understood for degraining (and thus dehairing) buffalo, evidence points out that most peoples chose to wet-

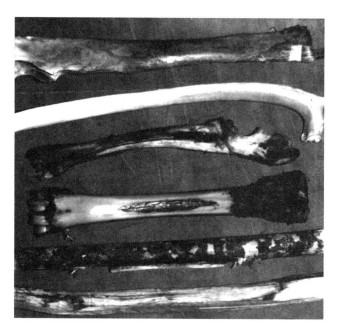

Photo 1: <u>EDGE SCRAPERS</u>- nearly universal, used for fleshing and degraining. Left to Right: Thoracic vertebrae, Buffalo. These extensions of vertebrae form the hump. Very flat, stout tool, with natural edge. Rib, Buffalo (also Deer, Elk, Mtn. Sheep, Moose). Ribs were the most common and wide-spread tool. The flatter ones are the easiest to use. Ulna-radius, Deer. Natural edge. Don't over clean, as sinewy membranes hold it together. Use narrower beam. Used in scattered locales. Cannon bone beamer, Elk (also Deer, Mtn. Sheep). Extensive use away from Plains. Two edges created by hollowing out center. Wood and bone scraper. Bone shard implanted in wood with pitch binder. Common to Eastern Woodlands. Great tool. Split stick, Oak. Various hardwoods. Some use on NW Coast and scattered other locales.

scrape deer. However, the reports of deerskin dressing on the northern plains have been greatly obscured by the focus that buffalo tanning received. It is clear, that the Blackfeet and Assiniboine dry-scraped deerskins. It is probable, that its use extended to other northern plains tribes, <u>at least</u> occasionally, though many of them clearly wet-scraped. My belief is that dry-scrape was primarily used as a thinning technique on thicker hides to render them lighter weight, easier to brain and soften. This use translated occasionally for some tribes and regularly for a few, to deer. Deerskins are naturally thin, readily softened, and easy to de-grain wet with primitive tools. *"Beaming tools are thus identified with the dressing of deerskins and in this respect stand distinct from the adze-tool used in dressing buffalo skins. They seem to be used whenever the dressing of deerskins is prevalent."*
Clark Wissler, Plains Indians anthropologist, 1910.

Beams

To wetscrape, a solid surface is needed to provide resistance to the tool as layers of skin are pushed or pulled away. Almost always these surfaces took the form of logs leaned against a tree or implanted at an angle in the ground with the other end waist high. Both forms were widespread. Other styles did exist. Horizontal waist-high beams were used in the Gulf of Georgia-Puget Sound area, and horizontal planks were used in NW California (Figure 1).

Fleshing

Depending on how the deer was skinned, fleshing was done before or after de-graining. If the skin had chunks of meat or fat, it needed to be fleshed first. There were two basic types of fleshing tools, end and edge. For example, with a cannon bone, the end of the bone was cut at an angle and used as an 'end' tool. While the side of the cannon bone could be modified and used as an 'edge' tool (Photos 1 and 2).

Edge tools were used to push or pull the flesh from the skin, which was pinched between a wooden beam and the

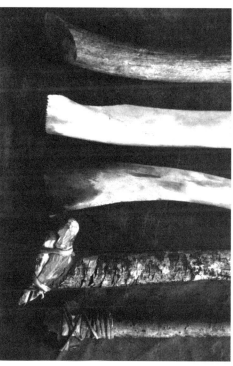

Photo 2: <u>END SCRAPERS</u>- some use for Deer, very common for furs and large hides. Left to Right: Hafted knapped stone for fleshing. Elbow adze, knapped stone on wood, for fleshing and dry-scraping. Cannon bone flesher, beveled edge, wrist thong brace. Most common of the end scrapers. Serrated cannon bone flesher, less common than previous, gained in popularity after contact. Elk antler, beveled edge, for degraining wet-scrape on wooden plank (NW California only). Works, but is it worth the tine?

Photo 3: *SOFTENING TOOLS*- counter clockwise from upper left: Pumice, great for abrading without overly roughing up surface, extensive distribution. Mussel shells, abrades and stretches. Used as found, convenient thumb slot, and very effective. Common tool on west coast. Simple and retouched flint flakes, and slate shards. Many types of stone used including split river rocks (skipping stone types), extensive distribution. Stone and wood elbow adze, used with frame. Abrades and stretches. Used by buffalo hunting tribes. Hafted knapped stone, abrades and stretches. Plateau, Tlingit, Ojibwa, Natchez. Buffalo humerus core, from bulbous end of bone. It is porous and very abrasive, after aging. Plains. Elk antler, beveled. Abrades and stretches. Plateau, NW California. Cannon bone, beveled. Abrades and stretches. California, Plateau, Apache. Deer antler, beveled. Abrades and stretches. Also, anything abrasive or with an edge: turtle shells, sandstone, buffalo tongues!

tool. End tools were used with a chopping motion to remove flesh from skins held under tension in a frame, pegged to the ground or between an object and the other hand. The working edge of the end tool was sometimes serrated to better grip the flesh.

Most tribes used the edge tools for fleshing, the same one that they used to degrain. End tools were used on the northern plains, and filtered into adjacent areas. End tools were extensively used for other types of hides, large ones that were easier to work pegged out, or lashed to a frame, and hides on which the hair was to remain. With hair-on hides, deep fleshing is crucial. This can better be accomplished with end tools because edge tools must be used with a beam, where the cushion of hair limits the depth the tool can flesh, and the hair often gets damaged. End tools were used throughout North America for this purpose, and are therefore common in the archaeological record. Deerskins were predominantly fleshed with edge tools on a beam.

Degraining/Dehairing

The same edge tools that were used for fleshing were used to remove the hair and grain. Many required but slight modification from their natural form. Tool edges were either squared or beveled. Ribs, cannon-bone beamers, and ulna-radii were the most common. Due to their curved shapes, the ribs and ulna-radii require a narrower crown on the working surface of the beam, so that they don't contact too large of a skin surface and lose their bite. I've scraped several deerskins with their own unmodified ulna-radius, and its been easy, though not as fast as with a flat tool and wider beam. I've also been trying out some oak scrapers. So far they've been losing their edge too fast, and not gripping the grain enough to push it off. I would like to try some even harder woods like Mountain Mahogany, and/or fire harden the working edge of softer woods. Amazingly to me, the Yurok reportedly used old Douglas Fir branches, not even a hard wood. End tools, particularly the adzes, were used for dry-scraping. NW California tribes reportedly used beveled elk antlers to scrape

> *... if you can neutralize the ground substance, you can get complete brain penetration with one simple dunk in the brain solution.*

hides, with a wooden plank backing. This was an end tool being used to wet-scrape. I've tried out this combination, and it works.

Structure Openers

Never heard of this step, huh? This is the really exciting stuff! Fresh hides are structurally bound up by the "ground substance", a.k.a. mucopolysaccharides (many sweet mucus). This is something you need to deal with in every hide you tan! Most modern wet-scraping primitives brain and rebrain deerskins until they get soft. This can be very annoying. It is necessary because the fibers are coated with "many sweet mucus" which filter the liquids that enter the skin, and protect the skin, but in tanning they inhibit brain penetration. Stone age Indians as well as ancient and modern old world tanners had ways of dealing with this, and did so consciously with each and every hide, and so should you! The bottom line is that if you can neutralize the ground substance, you can get complete brain penetration in one simple dunk with the brain solution.

> *"...powerful control {is} exerted by the ground substance over the passage of ions through skin. The mucopolysaccharides in ground substance . .. bind water so firmly that few other types of ions can normally reach the fibres. ... Tannage of pelt with the ground substance still present, e.g. the tanning of raw skin, tends to be slow, uneven and uncertain. "*
>
> R. Reed,
> *Ancient Skins, Parchments, and Leathers*

These are some definite, and some speculative, structure openers that I have found in Neolithic deerskin dressing:

Curing dry skins
Alkaline soaks (usually wood-ash)
Tannic acid soaks
Carbohydrate soaks (particularly corn)
Hot springs (opens my structure at least)
Sharp-tool scraping (dry-scrape)
Pre-smoking
Repeated freeze/thaw
Multiple brainings—includes multiple wringings

Curing

"Have you ever noticed that when tanning skins in August, its easy to get the brains penetrated and the hides supple? You think you know what you're doing. . . and then you get fresh hides in September and SLAM it takes three brainings to get them soft." **Matt**

As a dried hide sits over time, it cures. My belief is that the cure involves the mucus bonds weakening and then dissolving. This allows much easier brain penetration. Whether this was consciously used I cannot say, but many peoples had the rhythm of hunting deer in the fall and either fleshing, or fleshing and degraining and then drying and storing their hides until spring or summer. Whether conscious or not, this was and is widely used. In some instances at least, it is likely that the hides were stored in the rafters of dwellings, and were thus pre-smoked (see pre-smoking section) as well as cured. In my experience, partial cures seem to occur in 4-6 months and full cures seem to require 9-12 months, depending on weather, storage conditions, and thickness of the hide.

Alkaline Soaks

"The hide of the deer was soaked in water and ashes and the hair removed, and then the process of tanning continued until the buckskin was soft and pliable."
Geronimo

Many tribes soaked their skins in wood-ash water prior to scraping. The reason for this is often credited to the ashes causing the hair to fall out. The real value of the ashes lies in the alkalinity's ability to disrupt the mucoid bonds. It opens the structure in only two or three days. Michelle and I are excitedly using this method. By simply adding ash to your pre-scraping soak, you can get complete brain penetration in one simple braining with fresh hides. The Comanche used burnt lime rock for the same effect. It was likely intentionally and unintentionally practiced in desert areas by soaking hides in alkaline lakes, pools or creeks. This method was used, at the very least, throughout the plains, Great Basin, California, and northern Mexico, as well as scattered other places; though by no means by every tribe or on every hide. This method was also the predominant one used by American pioneers as well as modern commercial tanneries. Many of the sources emphasize that the lye solution should be weak. Strong alkalis or acids (remember this when reading the tannins, and carbohy-

drates, sections) can change the structure of your hide in ways you may not desire. They cause them to swell and feel rubbery. The ideal alkali content is between p.h. 9.5 and p.h. 10. 5. Pioneers would float an egg or a potato in the lye solution, if it floated so that an area the size of a quarter was exposed above the surface, then it was perfect. The merits of wood ashes were summed up by Andy Schuebeck, an eighty-four year old rancher that I met this spring, who was reminiscing about his youth when his family and neighbors made buckskin, *"They would soak the hide in wood ash water to get the glue out, so it tanned easier. "*

Tannins

Prior to braining the Klallam soaked their hides in boiled fern leaves. Other peoples added tannins to their braining solution in the form of shredded wood barks. This could have two possible effects. Tannins chemically combine with collagen fibers and change their nature, possibly interfering with the mucoid bonds. Acidity alone has much the same effect as alkalinity and would likely disrupt these bonds in much the same way. I have not used tannins in this way, though Steven and Tamara have. They did it with one hide and said that it seemed to improve brain penetration

Carbohydrate Soaks

"Young Indian corn, beaten to a pulp, will effect the same as brains." **John Lawson, describing the *Indians of North Carolina*, in 1709.**

Indians of the southeast, northeast and the southern plains soaked their hides in corn water. Either using mashed sweet corn alone, or ground flint corn and brains to tan their hides. The soaked corn, as it sits, quickly sours, with two possible effects. Yeasts (such as acidophilus) digest the carbohydrates in corn and excrete acids ... and acids disrupt mucus bonds. And, if you remember, our friends the mucoids are mucopolysaccharides. The saccharides, are also carbohydrates that the yeasts will digest, opening the structure. I have tried this in part with one hide, and the structure loosened. It merits more experiments. There is no evidence that stone age Indians allowed their corn to sour for this effect. However, when I tried this, the corn solution soured and bubbled in a six hour soak (during corn season on the east coast where it is 90 degrees, 24 hrs. a day, it's sure to have these effects).

Hot Springs

"Skins were prepared by soaking in water, often hot springs..." **John Price, describing the Washo.**

Modern tannery effluents have been a major environmental problem on many rivers, and so recently I was making a list of the chemicals used. Many of these chemicals occur naturally in hot springs. Many of them are sulfur based and neutralize the mucus.

(more)

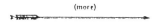

I have tried this with two hides. One came out wonderfully soft in one soak, when it should have required two or three. The other came out better than would be expected, but needed a second soak. The difference was the first sat in the spring outflow for 24 hours, and the second came home in a bucket of water.

This is enough evidence to convince me that something is going on, though not necessarily miraculous. Hot spring chemistry varies a lot, but it does have commonalities. I'm going to try it out some more, maybe do a tour....

Sharp Tools / Dry Scrape

Using a sharp tool allows one to scrape deeper, removing the entire grain and papillary layer where fibers are densely packed and the ground substance is particularly concentrated. It is easier to penetrate brains into the remaining fiber core where the fibers are larger and less tightly packed. Dry-scrape and sharp-edged wet-scrape (a modern hybrid) both accomplish this, and this is their advantage (see Jim Riggs' *Blue Mountain Buckskin* for a thorough account of dry-scraping). They both can result in one soak brainings. The drawback is that you can easily scrape too deep, creating holes and an uneven surface.

Pre-Smoking

A few tribes hand-stretched their hides over a smoky fire after the first brain soak prior to the second, and a few others dried their just-scraped hides over a smoky fire. As mentioned before, this may have also been done incidentally by storing hides in smoky rafters. Smoke changes the internal structure of a hide creating crosslinks which I don't pretend to understand. It is still practiced in Canada by Native Americans on moose hides and by the Dinsmore bros. in N. Idaho on deerskins. They say that pre-smoked hides are easily brained in two soaks, sometimes one.

Freeze/Thaw

"The Shuswap declare that skins are rendered much easier to dress by freezing (after degraining)"
James Teit, ethnographer, 1900.

A few tribes consciously froze and thawed their hides repeatedly, claiming that it made them easier to brain. Brain-tanning friends in Montana have been doing this for years with the same effect. It is not claimed to result in one soak braining, but to greatly reduce resoaking.

Brain/Rebrain

Some tribes, like many of us, simply rebrained their hides once or twice, after working them partly dry, especially large skins. Each time the hide is soaked, brains penetrate deeper, opening the structure more. Repeated wringing and soaking is an efficient form of this practiced by some peoples, then and now. This method is also used when other methods fall short. I've tanned most of my hides with this general method, and have always hoped there was a better way. There is and there are....

It is physiologically impossible for fresh deerskins to brain well in one soak, unless the gound substance has been neutralized. Understanding this can make your tanning predictable and fun instead of unpredictable and irritating. Each of these methods has its ins and outs. I encourage you to experiment and where possible seek out knowledgeable sources for more detailed how-to information.

Brain Solutions

Brains contain emulsified oils, which permeate the water with which they are mixed, rather than separating from it. This quality allows the tanner to coat the fibers with lubricating oils, without <u>saturating</u> every pore of the skin with oil. Nearly all tribes used brains, although there were a few notable excep-

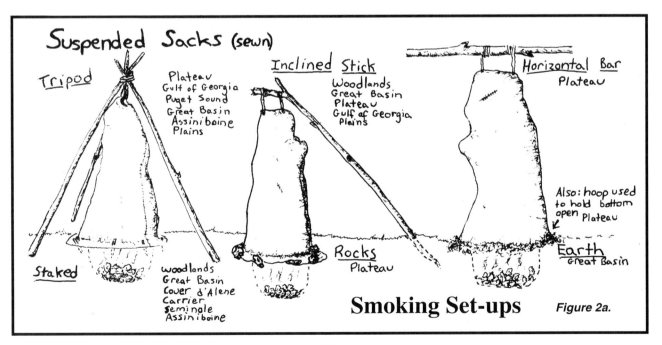

Smoking Set-ups — Figure 2a.

tions. Tribes of the southern Colorado River region sometimes used saguaro cactus seeds instead. The Tonto Apache used jajoba berries, a plant renowned for its emulsified oils. Sometimes, tribes in the southeast used sweet corn. **Peoples from the NW Coast and Fraser River Plateau used fish and sea mammal oils, with a somewhat different methodology. They would completely saturate the skin repeatedly with oils and then they'd degrease it with urine. This would chemically create a different type of leather, known as oil-tan. This is paralleled in modern days, by the tanneries that use cod oil to saturate the skin and then degrease it with sodium carbonate, resulting in what is popularly known as chamois.** These tribes also brain-tanned.

Other substances were put directly into the soak solution with the brains. Some of these, added oils; possibly to improve the *feel* of the finished skin, or at the least, to help the brains go farther. Other additives may have improved penetration by disrupting mucoid bonds.

Additives To Brain Solutions:
Oils: spinal fluid, liver, bone marrow, tallows and fats, fish oils, acorn soup, pine nuts.
Soaps: soaproot lather (amole lilly), yucca
Tannins: wild rhubarb, elderberry, thimbleberry and elm shavings
Ashes, cornmeal
Decomposition: The Sanpoil, Thompson, Wishram and Okanogan purposely decomposed brains for months before using. What this added, besides stench, I do not know, but it was reputed to bring out the oils. *Try this out,* and then tell me all about it.

Softening

Buckskin is stretched from damp to dry to make it soft. Tools are used to aid in the stretching, as well as to abrade the surface of the grain and flesh sides. This abrasion of the outer surfaces, allows the skin to stretch fully, and the texture to be soft. Abrading tools were used by all tribes. There were two types, rough surfaced and sharp edged (Photos 3 & 4).

The sharp edged tools, because of their shape, also stretch the fibers, serving two functions. These are some of the "thumb-nail scrapers" common to archaeological sites. Many people mistakenly identify these tools as dry-scrapers.

Deerskins were softened in frames (woodlands, northern plains, plateau, NW Coast), hanging from horizontal poles (plateau, Apache), over beveled posts implanted in the ground, and with the hands and feet. The stretching post was common wherever the frame was not (Photo 5).

Smoking

"...heated smoke; and by some chemical process or other, which I do not understand, the skins thus acquire a quality which enables them, after being ever so many times wet, to dry soft and pliant as they were before, which secret I have never yet seen practiced in my own country; "George Catlin, from his travels on the northern plains, 1832-1839.

Smoking was not nearly as universal as we imagine. Some tribes did it regularly, most did it situationally, and many didn't smoke 'em at all. Many tribes only smoked moccasins. Next in line was leggings. Others smoked these two items until they were colored, and smoked other hides but not long enough to color them. In drier southern areas (the southwest,

(more)

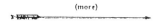

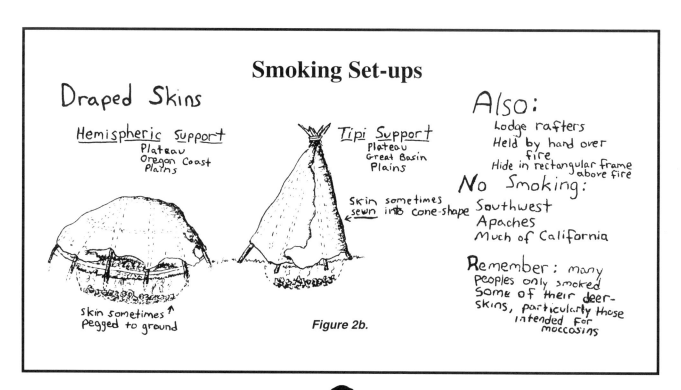

Smoking Set-ups

Draped Skins

Hemispheric Support
Plateau
Oregon Coast
Plains

skin sometimes pegged to ground

Tipi Support
Plateau
Great Basin
Plains

Skin sometimes sewn into cone-shape

Figure 2b.

Also:
Lodge rafters
Held by hand over fire
Hide in rectangular frame above fire

No Smoking:
Southwest
Apaches
Much of California

Remember: many peoples only smoked some of their deerskins, particularly those intended for moccasins

Photo 4: <u>CABLES</u>- left to right: Braided rawhide (buffalo sinew also used). Both mentioned mostly in connection with tanning Buffalo robes. Stretches hide well, a little abrasion, but not very durable (note wear in center). I might try a rawhide thong next time, for same effect, and no time braiding. Buffalo scapula, center of bone removed, working edge beveled sharp. Stretches and abrades, durable. Really shreds! Wild grape vine, lasts longer if used while still living. Some initial abrasion, good stretching. Also, any rough-barked woody sapling, vine, or branch. Comanche, Potawatomi, northern California, eastern Great Basin.

Photo 5: <u>SOFTENING SET-UPS</u>- clockwise from lower left: Wooden post with stone implant. This stone has sharp, squared, top edges, so the post abrades as well as stretches. Couer D'Alene, southern California. Wooden post, hide stretched as its pulled over beveled top. Doesn't really abrade. Very common tool. Suspended hide; hide suspended by buckskin thongs from pole supported by tripods. Allows for easy hand stretching and use of abrading and stretching tools. Plateau, Apache. Frame stretching; frame and hide lashed with rawhide. Allows you to stretch hide larger, thinner and flatter. Also reduces amount of stretch left in finished hide, which is good or bad depending on intended use. NW Coast, Plateau, northern Plains, Woodlands, Southeast. knapped chert hafted to stick; long for two handed softening. Stretches and abrades. Common with frames. Beveled wood frame softening tool. Stretches, little abrasion.

Texas, much of California, parts of the great basin) they never smoked their hides. <u>Why not?</u>

The myth is that if white hides get wet they must be completely resoftened. I've tested this a lot, intentionally and unintentionally. The reality is that when white hides get wet they are somewhat harder to resoften than smoked hides, though not nearly as hard as unworked hides. Smoking does, however, serve a wonderful purpose. The more hides are smoked, the *easier* they are to resoften, especially after multiple wettings. So it was a trade-off.... the effort of smoking vs. the effort of working out stiffness. That is why smoking was more important in northern regions and moccasin hides were the most likely recipients (Photo 6 & Figure 2).

Tannin Dyes

"... yellow and red, some black and russet, and every man according to his own fancy. "

Spark, one of the explorer De Soto's companions, describing the deerskin clothing of the Florida Indians.

It is often stated that pre-contact Indians did not know of the use of tannins on hides. This is clearly not true. The very earliest reports, from nearly all sections of this continent, describe the natives coloring their deerskins with various bark dyes. They do not seem to have used them to create a full bark tan, but even a short soak in tannins will change a hide's nature to some degree. Tannins make skins less stretchy and a bit thicker, great for moccasins. They color skins. They may also make them slightly less water absorbent, long soaks do. I do not know how they effect their ability to go from wet to dry repeatedly.

Dyes were specifically used on white unsmoked hides. The art, and range of color were highly developed in the southwest and the southeast. There use was as widespread as smoking, though not always as commonly used. In some areas, tanners clearly had a choice whether to dye, smoke or leave a hide white, depending on the intended use, and the preference of the tanner. Like smoking, dyeing was particularly mentioned in connection with moccasins.

Tannin dyes used: alder, oak, paper birch, Douglas fir, canaigre, ferns, sumac, hemlock.

Other dyes mentioned, which I do not know if they contain tannin: ironwood, willow, elm, elder, white maple, Mt.. mahogany, indigo bush (*dalea emorii*), ephedra, lemonade berry (*rhus trilobata*), oregon grape, honey mesquite, leather root, mistletoe.

"Once the buffalo became virtually extinct, and deer and elk scarce, hide preparations and use came to an end, and so abruptly that it has not been possible for scholars to reconstruct in complete detail all of the old ways of dealing with hides. "
Thomas E. Malls, referring to the plains cultures.

For those who learned the art of brain-tanning by studying ethnographies and the memories of Native Americans, the record is often unclear and incomplete. Thanks to their efforts, we can learn the basics in a week-end class anywhere in the country. Now that we have some hands-on experience, the ethnographies, European leather technology, and experimentation, can teach us how to recreate processes that are efficient, authentic, in sync with our bioregion and fun. They may also help us understand how different techniques create different types of buckskin, best suited for specific uses. Whether you're an educator, archaeologist or feral human, brain-tan will forever "en-deer" you to its sumptuous softness, and unrelenting strength.

A suggested control for deerskin experiments:

You must know the status of your hide's internal structure if you want to experiment with ways of improving brain penetration. Use fresh, frozen or wet-salted hides, hides which have not significantly dried since the deer's death. When hides dry they start to cure and an unknown factor comes into play: how much is cure affecting your results? Dried hides don't fully resaturate easily, which interferes with any soaking experiments you may try (e.g. wood-ash soaks). Hides frozen with the hair-on, or wet-salted seem to undergo no noticeable curing. They are just as tough to brain as fresh ones. Wet-salted means wet, not damp, almost as wet as it was on the deer's back. I experiment with frozen and wet-salted hides, and use fresh hides for the ultimate test.

Let's define "A Braining"

As we work to simplify our techniques, hide-tanners often discuss how many brainings it takes to get a hide soft, but we have different definitions of the term. For some, it is how many times a hide was soaked in the brains, for others it is how many times a hide was worked until dry. Each time a hide is brought to the ' wrung out sponge' moisture content and then put in the brain soup, brains penetrate deeper. I suggest that if you get complete penetration in one soak, call it one braining. If you wring and resoak four times, call it four brainings. If you don't work the hide dry in between, then you are rebraining efficiently, but you are rebraining. (note: hides brain better damp than dry, there is no advantage to working them all the way dry in-between brainings).

AN ABBREVIATED BIBLIOGRAPHY:
for complete bibliography contact author.

Catlin, George
1913   **North American Indians.** *Leary, Stuart and Co., Philadelphia.*
Geronimo
1906   **Geronimo: His own Story.** *Edited by S M. Barrett. Newly edited by Frederic W. Turner III, E. P. Dutton and Co., New York.*
King, Arden Ross
1947   **Aboriginal Skin Dressing in Western North America.** *Unpublished Ph. D. dissertation, University of California, Berkeley.*
Lawson, John
1709   **A New Voyage To Carolina.** *Reprinted 1967 by University of NC Press, Chapel Hill.*
        Mails, Thomas E.
1972   **The Mystic Warriors of the Plains.** *Doubleday and Co., Garden City.*
Price, John A.
1962   **Washo Economy.** *Unpublished master's thesis, University of Utah, Salt Lake City.*
Reed, R.
        Ancient Skins, Parchments and Leathers.
Swanton, John R.
1946   Indians of the Southeastern United States. **Bulletin of the Bureau of American Ethnology,** *vol. 137, Government Printing Office, Wash. D.C.*
Teit, James
1900   The Shuswap. **Memoirs of the American Museum of Natural History,** *vol. II, pt. VII. G. E. Steckert Publishing, New York.*
Wissler, Clark
1910   Material Culture of the Blackfoot Indians. **Anthropological Papers of the American Museum of Natural History,** *vol. V, pt I, New York.*

Section 6

TRANSPORTATION
Moving Along

PRIMITIVE TRAVEL GEAR

By Matt McMahon

The following article will attempt to outline the basic tools and accouterments carried by a "generic" stone age traveller in a mountain/forest environment. It is well beyond the scope of a short article to describe variations in these components based on region, season and availability. Such an "article" would indeed require several volumes. Therefore, the concepts described below will be concerned only with a few of the more essential components that primitive man may have carried for a short range sojourn into the mountains. Bear in mind also that the writer is a "woodsman" and not an "anthropologist", therefore, what the text may lack in terms of specific cultures, origins of tools or information of a "speculative nature" will instead be supported by directly applied methods and experiences of the author, camping and traveling under primitive conditions in the mountains of western Montana.

The bag'o sticks.

No report on the gear and accouterments of a primitive mountain traveler would be complete without consideration of our most exciting archeological find to date; the Iceman. Here, for our study and research, are the very tools and gear carried by this stone-age traveler, as they were preserved in a Thyroxin glacier for 5,000 years. Whatever the scientific community 'speculates' of the nature of his journey, or the origin of his tools, one thing is certain, he was a seasoned mountaineer and had the tools of his trade close at hand when he lay himself down for the last time.

At the time of this writing, there remains much that we are waiting to see and hear of these tools as only a few media representatives have managed to breech the intense political and scientific red-tape required to view and photograph his belongings. However, we should at least be able to consider the information that has been released on the tools he was reported to have been carrying. Lets begin by identifying the basic categories that have been addressed by mountain travelers of ages past.

Obviously, the ability to ignite and maintain a fire might be the most pressing of all survival concerns. Rest assured, any seasoned woodsman would have the ability to improvise basic tools in the field. Nevertheless, only a fool would venture into the mountains without at least one firemaking tool. The Iceman was carrying a 'flint striker' and certainly this would have been a desirable first choice. 'Plan B' might include a bow-drill or hand-drill components. Depending on space and weight limitations these could include drill, hearths, spindle, cord, bow, etc. For a compact **'survival' firekit** one might consider both a flint stricker and a small hearth and drill 'tips' of proven softwoods (cottonwood, cedar) that can be spliced onto any available shaft creating a 'compound' drill (see Letters to the Editor).

In my research, in areas where firemaking is a life or death concern, (Alpine/Arctic) the bow-drill was considered more 'sure-fire' (reliable) than the hand-drill and thus justified the carrying of one extra component; cordage. In my own experience, the spindle and bow can be gathered or improvised easily and a strong cord of buckskin or softened rawhide can be cut from skin clothing in an emergency or carried around at the expense of an ounce. Achieving a coal from a hand-drill is a fickle method requiring perfect technique and materials. In an emergency situation one might not have the strength or perfect materials and may choose the bow-drill as the more practical method. Of course the set is useless without proper tinder to bring the coal into life. The Iceman carried a **'tuft of fiber'** reportedly used as tinder. This fiber would vary widely by region and season, but as a survival kit component should be as fine and dry as possible. My personal choice would be cattail or thistle down nested in bone dry shredded cottonwood or cedar bark both of which are common in forested mountain environments. All of these items could be protected in a wide variety of containers. The **'everyday' kit** could be housed in a tight fitting wooden box or oiled skin bag. 'Emergency' fiber might be sealed in intestine, dipped in wax or similarly protected in a **hollow vial or bottle** Any amount of birchbark would be worth its weight in gold as even dipped in water it burns furiously at the kindling or flake stage.

Now unless one is burning only "squaw-wood" (branches that can be sectioned without tools) a chopping tool will make life easier. This brings us into the category of **'cutting tools'** and this subject could easily require a volume. From my experience in the field two different cutting operations are most frequently employed. The ability to section or remove wood quickly (chopping) and the ability to sever fibers of cordage or to open the belly of harvested game (slicing). The Iceman was equipped with both. His yew-wood handled **copper ax** was 'state-of-the-art' for his time and he carried also a small ash-handled **'flint dagger'** for medium utility tasks. You would also be wise to carry a pouch of **flint 'blanks'** and an **antler-tipped flaking tool** with which to produce razor-sharp blades for delicate incisions, both of which the Iceman possessed. But flaking tools and flint knives were common in his time and easily replaced or traded items. It was the Iceman's ax that was an indispensable tool representing many hours of laborious primitive forging and crafting, that has so fascinated the media, bringing new insight into the origin of metal tools. Ask any true woodsman which tool would be of greatest importance in a forest environment and he will answer 'my ax!' My personal **'traveling ax'** is a small hatchet of high-carbon swedish steel with a 1 1/4 lb. head and a short (10") hickory handle. With this tool I can section poles or small logs for firewood or shelter building, split shingles, hew boards, strike sparks (with a flint) pound stakes and crack hard nuts, shells or the skull of attacking enemies, predators or prey. The Iceman obviously valued his beautiful and rare copper ax and it was reported that his right hand was permanently frozen into the exact shape and diameter of his handle.

Let us now consider rope, string and other utilitarian **cordage**. The ability to lash or bind poles and saplings is crucial to constructing many shelters. Any number of tasks from mending clothes to producing **snares or fishline** also depend on fine diameter strong cord or thread. The Iceman carried a **'grass rope'** for lashing, hauling or possibly negotiating rock decents. I have twisted similar grass **'cables'** that would easily support a man for such purposes. It is also advisable to carry a **bone needle** and **fine vegetable or sinew fibers** to complete delicate tasks as in suturing or mending broken seams as it was reported the Iceman had done. I can also suggest carrying a stout **hole punching awl**, flint shards for cutting fabric and patches of buckskin from which custom laces or thongs may be cut. **Hide clue, pitch glue** and **rawhide** could complete this sewing /repair kit.

No serious woodsman would venture far without a weapon to procure game or as a means of protection. The Iceman carried a Yew-wood **long bow**, **quiver** of buckskin and **arrows**. The incomplete state of his arsenal suggests he was replacing a lost or damaged bow and tackle. Aside from a modern firearm (and even this is debatable) a reliable bow

and arrows would be the most effective weapon for procuring big game with snares and deadfalls providing a steady source of small game. Add **fishline, bone hooks, net** and **fishspear** and you are capable of securing fish as well. As for cooking your catch, there are countless methods of preparation involving only 'field expcdient tools such as pinning meat to a plank propped near the fire or steam pit cooking. The Iceman carried a birchbark container and this may have been a lightweight 'cookpot' for the 'rock boiling' method of using bent willow tongs to drop red-hot rocks into a stew to boil it. And although water is easily found in the mountains one would do well to carry a **water vessel** of animal bladder, gourd, pottery or skillfully woven and pitch-sealed basketry.

A primitive fishing kit.

Every mountain traveler should consider carrying an **'only-aid kit'**. This differs from a 'first-aid kit' in that when traveling remote regions one might find himself too far from his 'medicine man' to expect help or rescue. The Iceman carried '2 fungi' on a thong as well as a piece of charcoal. Many medicinal properties have been attributed to 'fungi' of various sorts and charcoal has a long history in the cure of plant poisoning. Yet one can only 'speculate' as to whether these were part of his 'medicine chest.' Once again it is beyond the scope of this article to identify all the components of a working 'only-aid kit.' Consider the hazards of your environment and prepare for them. Sterilized (boiled and sun dried) cloth bandages, an antiseptic ointment or salve (spruce pitch/ bear grease) for cuts or burns and pain relieving willow bark would be a start. The identifying of edible and medicinal plants of your region should be high on the list of skills for any woodsman.

Travel foods would be subject to season and availability The Iceman was reported to have carried some Ibex (deer)

(more)

The Paleo Travel Kit

meat and a few berries. The combination of dried meat (jerky) and dried berries, herbs and vegetables is traditional with mountain travelers as they fill the stomach while keeping within space/weight limitations. The addition of animal fat to the pulverized ingredients mentioned above makes 'pemmican' a time honored travel food. Say you were fortunate enough to have killed a deer of 100 lbs. actual meat weight. This could be smoked or sun-dried in as little as 48 hours to a small package of perhaps 10 lbs.. The same holds true of many fruits, berries and herbs. It is no accident that modern military and mountaineering rations are 'freeze dried' for maximum calories at a minimum space/weight ratio. A true woodsman may find a balance between these food items and his ability to hunt and forage food from the wild.

The choice of **adequate clothing** and/or shelter is possibly the most crucial factor of survival in an alpine environment and a lack of preparedness in this category may well have been the reason for the Iceman's early demise. I have found the combination of brain-tanned buckskin (tough, windproof) over wool, felt or fur (warm, insulative) properly exploits the best properties of both fabrics. Buckskin is the ideal fabric to take the abusive scrapes and scratches of mountain travel and effectively cuts wind as it is solid and not woven. It provides the protective 'shell' for more insulation yet delicately woven fabrics. The addition of an oiled (bear grease, mink oil) light skin sheds water effectively and an oiled fur-in skin garment combines all of these features. The Iceman wore buckskins made from the hides of 3 different deer common to his region. His grass cape would have made an effective blanket at lower elevations but for the 10,000 ft. elevation at which he was found a heavy robe of fur or felt might have saved his life.

There are very few **primitive shelters** portable for one man. The secret here is campsite selection in an area abundant in shelter building materials. In the case of winter travel, snow becomes your best friend and a shelter made from a giant, hollowed-out snowball has allowed me to sleep comfortably at -40 degrees F. with no fire or sleeping bag. Lacking snow, a lean-to of moss-chinked poles, covered with birchbark, skin or boughs, slanting 60 degrees or greater will shed rain or snow while providing an effective fire reflector. A crude bed of poles elevated 1 or 2 feet and left open to the fire

allows the reflected heat to come in under you, or hot rocks can be rolled under it. This platform provides the warm sleep that every traveler needs as well as a work area during bad weather and at chair-seat height you need never worry about wet bedding. Thick boughs or woven reed matts under you and a warm robe or grass blanket over you and you sleep in comfort. For intense cold or wet your fire should be 1 step away and made of hot burning small logs as long as you are tall and backed by a non-burning (or very slow-burning) wall of logs (green cottonwood is best) to throw the heat back into your shelter. Most likely the Iceman would have settled for the light of his fire by which to complete work after dark. However, there are several options for illuminating the primitive camp. Torches of various quality can be made, most often by dipping a fiber or bundle into a flammable substance. Dried mullein flower tops dipped in fat, wax, oil or pitch is only one of many combinations. Often, balls of rough pitch were thrown into the fire to provide a few minutes of extra illumination. **Tallow candles** and **'koodliks'** (fat-burning lamps) are very effective. My 'koodlik' has often been our families only source of light through long, dark Montana winters.

The information given in this article is certainly not complete, but should serve as a foundation from which to build your primitive travel kit. Obviously specialized activities will require specialized gear. It should also be obvious that the higher your skill level the less gear you must carry to support you. For instance a native 'scout' or 'messenger' may have fit all his necessities into a small pouch or bag allowing for speed and ease of movement. On the other hand, the addition of a packframe (the Iceman carried one), sled, cart, pack animal or more men, can substantially increase the load bearing capacity. Whatever your activity or skill level I hope this article will help the reader identify some basic components and methods while fostering a respect and kinship for the Iceman as a true woodsman.

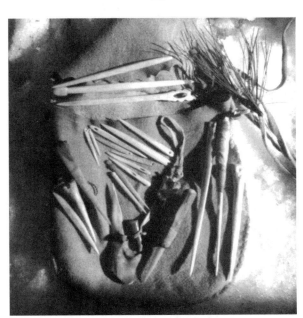

David Wescott photos

PRIMITIVE FIBER BUNDLE WATERCRAFT:
A Materials Primer

By Steve Watts

From the Nile and Indus river valleys, to the lakes of the Andes, to the shores of the Mediterranean, to the backwaters of northern Australia, to the marshes of the Great Basin, to the coasts of California and Mexico. . . Native Peoples have used bundles of rushes, reeds and barks to construct a variety of watercraft. The tropical and temperate zones of the globe yield up an abundance of raw materials suitable for the manufacture of such vessels.

(more)

Sedges & Rushes

These pithy-centered wetland plants with round, square or triangular cross-sections represent perhaps the most widely utilized category of fibers for bundle boat construction. "Bulrushes" (*Scirpis sp.*) of many varieties can be and have been used throughout the world, with the giant "Tule" (*Scirpis californicus & Scirpis acutus*) serving as the raw material for a wide range of raft/boats: from small egg and tool carrying "marsh buggies", to one man boats (as reconstructed by Jamison, Baugh, Kidder, Riggs and many others- see page 34) to large sea-worthy craft (as reconstructed by Kidder - see page 36).

Rush boats are also found in South America, with the Uru and Aymara canoes of Lake Titicaca being the most well known. Africa, still supports surviving bundle boat traditions in the areas of Okavanga Swamp, Lake Chad and Lake Turkana. In France, Hungry and eastward into India, Korea and Japan the interplay of bulrush and humans continues with fiber bundle watercraft technologies appropriate to local conditions.

North Africa yields the famous papyrus sedge (*Cyperus papyrus*) of the Nile valley--most often associated with Egyptian paper making but equally useful as the raw material for the construction of both ancient rivercraft and the modern experimental sea-going vessels of Thor Heyerdahl (the "Ra", "Ra II" and the "Tigris").

> *A note on two confusing terms often encountered in the study of fiber bundle watercraft:*
>
> *The word **"reed"** is used to refer to a multitude of plant stems and fibers used in bundle boat construction. It may refer to rushes, sedges, canes ore other grasses. Likewise, "reed boat" may refer to vessels made from a variety of materials.*
>
> *The word **"balsa"** is used (as in Richard W.Cunningham's California Indian Watercraft, 1989) to refer to "a canoe constructed of multiple bundles of wands, canes, reeds, sedges or bark rolls lashed together and arranged in such a fashion as to create a cavity or hold". "Balsa" used in this way refers to a type of watercraft--not to be confused with the tropical "balsa tree" (Ochroma logopus) found in South America. (This wood, by the way, has its own place in the world of primitive watercraft-- Heyerdahl's "Kon Tiki", which sailed in 1947, was an ocean-worthy raft constructed of balsa logs.)*

Grasses

Certain hard-shelled, hollow-stemmed, segmented plants of the grass family lend themselves especially well to the construction of fiber bundle rafts and boats. While not as flexible or as easily harvested and manipulated as rushes and sedges, these large grasses offer excellent floatation due to their isolated hollow chambers. Being hard shelled, they also resist water absorption and decay much better.

Throughout the Orient and in Pacifica the giant of all grasses, "bamboo" (*Bambusa sp.*) is used for an almost countless number of tasks including the construction of bundled rafts and boats. The large size and strength of some bamboo species allow for vessels capable of transporting great amounts of weight. The spread of bamboo around the globe in historic times makes it an available boat building resource for the modern-day *neoaboriginal* living within its expanded range.

For a bamboo cousin that is native to North America we look to the southeastern United States. Here along the creeks and in the river bottoms we find "rivercane" (*Arundinaria sp.*). Although no contemporary Native Americans in the area have living traditions related to bundle boat construction (the typical aboriginal vessel being the dugout canoe) there are early historic references to the construction of rivercane rafts among Indians of the Gulf

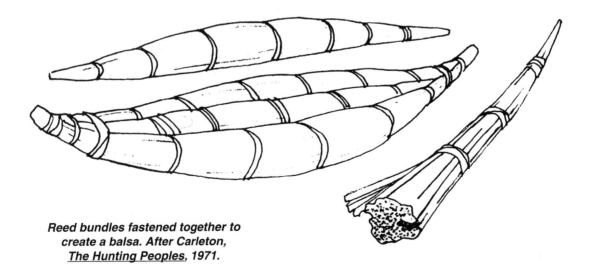

Reed bundles fastened together to create a balsa. After Carleton, The Hunting Peoples, 1971.

region (an experimental model has been reconstructed by Watts - see page 40). In fact, the Spanish invaders who entered the southeast in the 16th century were impressed enough by these rafts to adopt them for their own use. Other Arundinaria species are found in South America.

Another widely distributed grass useful for boat building is "phragmites" or "reed grass" (*Phragmites australis*). The most famous examples of phragmites boats are those constructed by the Seri Indians of western Mexico. These are long and sleek and have been called by Richard W. Cunningham "one of the most graceful watercraft built by primitive man". *Phragmites* does not attain the strength or size of either bamboo or rivercane, yet still possesses more rigidity than any of the sedges or rushes.

Adding a cattail and cane gunwale

Bark

The mention of bark in relation to boats typically brings to mind birchbark canoes or other bark-clad vessels. Yet, in Australia and Tasmania aboriginals used bark in a totally different way. Using the thin peeled bark of Melaleuca or other "stringy" barked trees, several bundles were bound separately then secured together forming a raft/boat with pointed bow and stern (An excellent example is illustrated in **Discovery**, March 1993, *Ten Thousand Years of Solitude*).

Using a windless to tighten cane bundles. A cane balsa containing 646 pieces is replicated at the Schiele Museum, 1993.

Palms

The stalks of fronds from plants of the Palmae family (palms and palmettos) are lightweight, pithy, buoyant and strong. Bundled boats made from these stalks have been documented in the Gulf of Oman and other Mid Eastern locations. On at least one occasion, Heyerdahl used palm frond stalks to reinforce the bottom of one of his ocean-going papyrus craft.

The finished rivercane balsa.

FLOAT YOUR OWN BOAT

Figure 1. Poling a one-man balsa with a turtle harpoon. This is one of the last Seri balsas, circa

...She [the mother of Moses] took for him a basket of Bulrushes, and daubed it with bitumen and pitch; and she put the child in it and placed it among the reeds at the river's brink.... Old Testament, Exodus 2:3

Giant cane (*Arundo and Arunanaria*) is found at common latitudes throughout the world. In **People of the Desert and Sea** (Felger and Moser, 1985) historical accounts of the primitive Seri people using balsas into the twentieth century gives us a living record of what the boats looked like, how they were made and how they were used. Boats were made of simple bundles of cane bound by strong ropes of mesquite (*Prosopis*) root. A replica of such boats may be seen in a small museum at Kino Bay, Sonora Mexico, traditional home territory of the Seri.

"Among the seafaring Seri, probably every able-bodied man owned a balsa. When the owner died, his balsa was burned". They were primarily used for turtle hunting and fishing. Note the turtle harpoon, double-bladded paddle, and pecked stone anchor stowed on the deck of the boat in figure 2. There is also record of Seri men making an emergency boat from dried flower stalks of century plant (*Agave cerulata*).

With this information and brief accounts in local historical records, Steve Watts and crew began an expolration into how rivercane would work as a watercraft. Models were first built by each participant to learn the basic skills needed and to test design ideas. The crew then worked as a unit to create a full-scale craft. The results may not be considered "scientific", but their experiment shed new light on a variety of questions related to southeastern watercraft. Future projects will no doubt continue from this energetic start.

Projects that focus on the technologies that are combined to produce watercraft generally call on a variety of skills, materials and techniques. **Start small**-practice your skills on a project that requires the same processes but produces different results; ie. burned bowls utilize all of the skills used to produce a dugout. **Sample sources and materials** - if you are replicating a specific craft and cultural style, then research your information. If all you want is to get out on the water, don't be limited by what works "best". **Test your ideas** - try a variety of materials and forms. Boats from skin, bark, wood or fiber bundles can be made almost anywhere. **Record your results** - let us know what you discover.

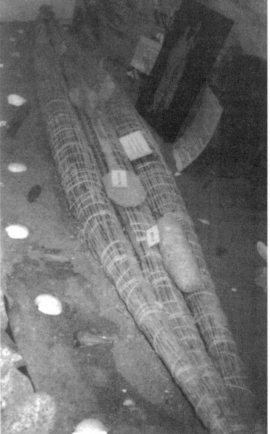

David Wescott

Figure 2. 18' replica made from photos taken at the Smithsonian Institute of a Seri balsa collected in 1895.

TULE BOATS

By Dick Baugh

Tule boats are easy and fun to make. What better excuse do you need to make one? They were used by the Native Americans who lived around San Francisco Bay, Central California and farther east into Nevada. Similar craft can be found in Peru, Baja California and Africa. There are many "correct" ways to make a tule boat. About the only thing you can say that is bad form is to tie it together in such a shoddy manner that it falls apart.

What to Make it Out Of

In California two marshland plants were used for buoyancy, *Scirpus acutus* and *Scirpus californica*. These plants, sometimes called tules or bulrush, can grow up to 8 feet tall. The stems of *S. acutus* are preferred over *S. californica* because the pithy stems seem to absorb water more slowly (private communication from Norm Kidder). *Typha* (cattail) stems are a very poor substitute. One might try doing it with *Arundo donax*, the common river reed introduced from the Mediterranean (see page 41). It wouldn't be authentic but would last a lot longer. Be creative! If you make your boat with freshly cut reeds they will shrink as they dry. You can compensate for this by tightening the bindings.

> *Bulrushes are gathered seasonally, usually at the height of th growing season - early fall or late summer... before rust spots begin to appear. [Then] spread them out in a shady spot and turn them occassionally for even drying.... Fresh rushes are too brittle to use; they crack when they are tied tightly and they soak up water more readily. ...it is better to begin with rushes collected and dried earlier, then dampened again for the project... I recommend testing the leaf by squeezing it betwween your fingers. It should be "spongy" not brittle. If it "cracks" when you squeeze it, it is either too fresh or it has been soaked too long.... The best way to dampen the leaves is to sprinkle them with water and wrap tham in a damp cloth for a couple of hours.*
> **Richard Jamison, *Primitive Outdoor Skills***

Holding It Together

You have a wide choice for cordage to bind the whole thing together also. In California the Native Americans used wild grape vines, cattail leaves, willow withes, and the same tules used for buoyant hull. Being rather stiff the grape vines were simply made into spiral hoops. Cattail leaves and tules can be rapidly twined into 2-ply rope. The most desirable for cordage are the dried stems of the *Typha anjustifolia* (narrow leafed cattail) which seems to be tougher than *T. latifolia*. In a hurry you can even use store-bought rope or binder twine. A single strand of binder twine is too weak and is so narrow that it will cut the tules. It is best to quadruple the binder twine for added strength and to keep it from cutting the tules.

The Design

2, 3, 5, you name it. The number of bundles you use for the hull is not critical. The first tule boat I ever made, about 18 years ago, was the Paiute style, two bundles, all tules pointing in the same direction. The bundles were about 5 feet in circumference and very conical. Another option is to alternate the ends of the bundles to get a boat which is fattest in the middle.

You want the skinny end (ends) to curl up. It looks nicer that way. That can be done in two different ways. First, if you have plenty of strong cordage you can just gradually curl it up as you tie it together. The other way is to cut two branches with approximately the same curvature and imbed them in two of the bundles placed in line with the keel. (One on each side of the boat.)

In binding the bundles together, fashion may vary. In Peru each of two bundles is bound spirally with one long continuous rope. The Paiute method, using cattail rope, is to make separate rings binding each bundle. If you don't have much confidence in the strength of your cordage it's best to have several rings around each bundle. That way if a rope breaks the whole thing doesn't come apart.

Propulsion can be by single bladed paddle, double bladed paddle or pole. You can also do it surf board style. Warning: Never try to pole across a lake that is 20 feet deep with a 10 foot pole.

The illustrations I have included should give you some clues on how the process works. In order to use your tule boat for several months don't let it sit in the water when you aren't using it. Haul it out and let it dry. Otherwise it will rot. If you are thinking about putting some water repellant stuff on your boat look out! Things like linseed oil and other drying oils will spontaneously combust when in large aggregations. I know from personal experience in having almost burned down a hardware store in my youth by forgetting to dispose of some spilled linseed oil in the basement. Don't stick beans up your nose either.

> *The analytical mind of Dick Baugh has given us pause for thought on a number of topics in past Bulletins; corded bows, fire by friction. He is also the maker of a fine bow scraper. He may be reached at 490 Gary St., Palo Alto, CA 94306.*

1.

2.

3.

4.

Deer Scapula Tule Knife

5.

6.

7.

1. Collecting tules from a lakeside marsh in preparation for making a tule boat (Jim Riggs)
2. Bundling fresh-cut tules into equally sized bundles with the tips and butts oriented correctly.
3. Binding two bundles together with twisted cattail-leaf ropes.
4. Pulling the prow into position.
5. Binding the prow with cattail-leaf ropes. Note the bent branch added to the core to stiffen and shape the uplift.
6. Trimming the boat with a deer-scapula tule knife.
7. Adding the tule gunwale to the boat deck (Jim Riggs).
8. Dick Baugh and Norm Kidder wrestling a bunch of tules.
9. The finished boat ready for its maiden voyage.

All photos except 1 & 7 were shots of a demonstration project conducted by Dick Baugh and Norm Kidder at the Rabbitstick Rendezvous in 1992. The tules and cattails were cut fresh and used without drying, producing a very serviceable boat. Sequence photos by David Wescott. Photos 1 & 7 from numerous projects completed by Jim Riggs at Malheur Field Station, OR.

8.

9.

David Wescott

Twisting cattail leaves into a single-ply cord with a twister. Leaves are fed into the cord as it twists.

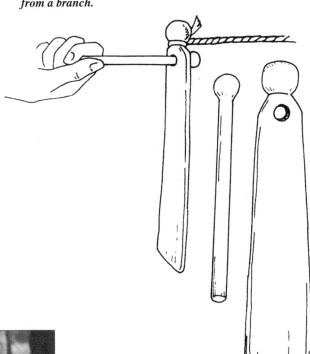

Twister can be made from virtually any wood. The spinner is approximately 12-14' long. The spindle is about 3/4" around and can be whittled from a branch.

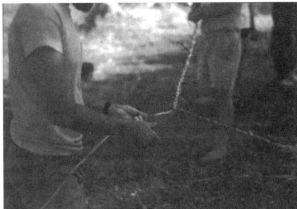

Two single-ply cords are twisted together in the opposite direction to create a counter twist that holds the rope together.

CORDAGE TWISTER

Cattail and tule rope can be rapidly made with a simple rope twisting mechanism. The leaves are wrapped around the top of the twister. It is then spun by one worker while the other holds the free end of the rope and feeds-in additional material. When two lengths of rope are produced, the two are joined at one end and this splice/knot is wrapped around the knob of the twister and spun the opposite direction, producing a strong 2-ply rope.

Jim Riggs

2-ply cord made of whole tules, hand twisted.

THE SCAPULAR SAW:
A STONE AND BONE AGE PROJECT
Text and Illustration By Norm Kidder

Over the years, my job has involved me in efforts to bring a local stone-age culture into the reality of 20th Century youth and adults. Letting people see, feel and use the tools from this time has proven the single most affective teaching technique. The first of these efforts at replication involved a common tool type at our sites called, by archaeologists, a scapular saw. The scapula is more simply known as the shoulder blade, in this case from a deer, elk or antelope. It has been modified to expose a thin area, which is notched to produce a saw-like cutting edge. The first saws were made using power tools, but looked like such. Tools made using hacksaws and files were better, but not yet authentic looking, and gave no information on efficient manufacturing techniques. They did however allow us to test the tools for possible uses. Archaeologists did not list their uses, since that would be specu-

The final step in this Level II effort (see Callahan in the PT Newsletter, Summer 95) was to find the most efficient way to make the tool with the kit available to our ancient craftsmen. The tasks to be performed included: removal of unwanted bone; smoothing of modified surfaces; and filing notches in the cutting edge. The tool kit that was known from the digs included many unmodified flakes of chert and quartzite, and

lation, but trying them on wood, meat, grass, weeds, tules and cat-tails; as hair combs, fish scalers and everything else we could think of left one easy conclusion. The only thing they cut really well is tules and other soft plants, and they cut them more efficiently than any other known tool from that area. The wear and polish patterns on the artifacts also match the replicas. The fact that local Indians built their houses, boats, mats, duck decoys and beds out of tules makes for overwhelming logic for calling them tule saws.

Norm Kidder has worked for the California State Parks since 1972. His main work is interpreting a cluster of archaeological sites dating from 380 B.C. to 1800 A.D., and the Ohlone people who lived there. He conducts Old Ways Workshops in a variety of ancient technologies. He currently serves as the Secretary for the SPT Board of Directors.

various pieces of fine hard sandstone, much of it fire broken. There were relatively few specialized tools. The specific steps involved removing a fin-like ridge from one surface of the bone, and a triangular shaped section of the main piece (see illustrations). Initially I worked at removing these sections by scoring or engraving lines at the desired break points using burin-like edges on the unmodified chert flakes. This was tedious work, and did not always guarantee that the bone would break as planned. Attempting to make a saw as quickly as possible, I abandoned the engraving step and went to crude bashing with hammer stones. After breaking a few in half, I found that I could use a carefully selected anvil stone, and break the bone a safe distance from the final shape, then grind and 'nibble' it to shape. This took much less time and effort, and produced a replica that compared favorably to the originals. If the bone is fresh and soft, engraving in a few problem spots can help avoid disasters. Once shaped, all rough surfaces were smoothed on a sandstone abrader.

A well-used scapular saw.

The final notching step took similar experimentation until I settled on using any thin, abrasive stone edge from hard quartzite to soft sandstone to file at a fairly flat angle on each side. This last step took the most time, about 20 minutes. Using these methods it now takes 30 to 40 minutes to make a finished tool that will last for years of cutting tules. (Over time, teeth break, but can be refiled, giving the tool a more scythe-like appearance found in many of the old specimens.

When demonstrating tule crafts, the saw is perfect as it demonstrates an authentic tool, and is also the best tool bar none at splitting tule stems, as it tears rather than cuts (also a good safety feature when working with kids).

When making the tool, it also demonstrates the importance of unmodified 'found' tools, which are rarely collected by archaeologists or displayed in museums, but which did much of the work in prehistory.

Diegueño Rawhide Sandals
By Paul Campbell, © 1997

These are simplicity itself and very functional. Again the informant was old Jim McCarty, the Southern Diegueño Indian from Campo, who described them to Leslie Spier in the summer of 1920.

A piece in the shape of the sole is cut from any part of a raw deer hide. Two cuts are made on each side near the heel forming two tabs extending up both sides of the foot. Two long buckskin thongs are knotted beneath the sole at the base of the second and third toes and passed through the sole in small openings to the far sides of these toes. The thongs then cross each other over the top of the foot and pass through holes in the tabs. They continue behind the heel and forward under the string on the front of the tab on the opposite sides and back behind the heel again. The finally tie in front of the ankle. Spier's simple drawing is worth all the words.

McCarty cautioned that rawhide sandals may be slippery on wet ground and fiber sandals would be preferred in such a case and on snow.

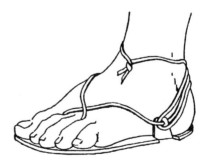

Sketch of Southern Diegueño rawhide sandal and method of tying it. (In Spier 1923)

GÄ-Ó-WO: Building an Iroquois Elm Bark Canoe

Text and Illustrations By Michael Kerwin, © 1992

"Thence we came to a great river, a mile wide, which was not frozen, which made us stay there ten or twelve days, making skiffs of the rind of a walnut [sic] tree. We made good cheer and wished to stay there longer. We made three skiffs to hold three men and one to hold two."

Pierre Esprit Radisson

GÄ-Ó-WO
or
BARK CANOE.

According to Adney and Chapelle (1983), there is considerable evidence documenting the use of elm bark in canoe construction by various North American Aboriginal Peoples. For the most part, these were temporary canoes built when the vagaries of travel required some form of emergency water craft. Generally made using whatever materials lay at hand, elm bark canoes did not warrant a great expenditure of time or labour since they would be discarded once the exigencies of the moment had been overcome.

In the case of the Iroquois, however, elm was used in the construction of a somewhat more permanent bark canoe or gä-ó-wo. These canoes, accommodating anywhere from 1 to 30 people according to early reports, were used almost exclusively for river travel or for sorties outside Iroquois territory by hunters, fishermen or war parties. Despite an alleged awkwardness and lack of grace, these canoes were far superior water craft than most Europeans believed. By the early 19th century, however, suitable bark for canoe construction became increasingly difficult to find. Dugouts, made of eastern white pine, cucumber tree or yellow-poplar, had hitherto been used solely for lake travel; these now replaced elm bark canoes and the elm bark canoe building tradition began to quickly die out (Fenton and Dodge, 1949). Since no original full-scale elm bark canoes remain extant, construction techniques can only be surmised. Information concerning building methods come from four sources: early historical accounts by Europeans, surviving models of Iroquois elm bark canoes, ethnological and linguistic studies of related elm bark industries, and temporary canoes made of spruce and elm by other tribes.

The early European accounts are unfortunately often vague, as observers did not always concern themselves with details of construction. Notable exceptions include descriptions by Peter Kalm, P. Pouchot, David Zeisberger and J.F. Lafitau. Of these four 18th century observers, Kalm was, by far, the most meticulous in his recording of the building process.

The surviving models of Iroquois elm bark canoes provide important information concerning materials and construction techniques. There are, however, two significant facts which must be considered when examining models: they

In 1991 Michael Kerwin and Michael Ketemer built the only existing full-size replica of an Iroquois elm bark canoe. Both are active members of the Ontario Recreational Canoe Association. The replica, at 18' is considered relatively small in comparison to historic records of boats carrying 30-40 people. It is now curated at the St. Marie Among the Iroquios Museum in Liverpool, NY. The Author and Mr. Ketemer are currently building a Beothuk canoe of birch and spruce made by an extinct tribe of Indians from New Foundland. The author wishes to thank Elizabeth Lumley for her assistance in the preparation of this article. For more information on the project, contact 288 Lauder Ave. #5, Toronto, Ontario, Canada M6S 3H6.

were not usually built to any scale and details of their construction were often simplified. Consequently, representations cannot always be trusted to represent their full-scale counterparts accurately.

Ethnological and linguistic studies which pertain to the manufacture of elm bark utensils have substantiated earlier European accounts relating to the removal and working of elm bark. In most ways, these techniques likely remained unchanged, whether or not they were employed in the manufacture of a canoe or a bowl. However, knowledge of the actual processes involved in canoe construction probably died out by the late 19th century.

Temporary canoes of elm or spruce bark, made by tribes other than the Iroquois, provide a final source of information about building techniques. According to Adney and Chapelle:

The theory that the Iroquois type of canoe was very like the emergency or temporary elm- and spruce-bark canoes of neighboring tribes is supported by some statements of the early French writers, as well as by a comparison of the rather incomplete descriptions of Iroquois canoes by later travellers with what is known about the spruce and other temporary bark canoes used in more recent times by the eastern Indians.

Some Abnaki and Malecite building techniques, for example, show a marked resemblance to each other and it is probable that methods used by the neighboring Iroquois were also similar. Not only was there the possibility of cultural influence between tribes, but, in a practical sense, any builder's techniques were limited by the very nature of elm bark itself.

In April of 1991, Michael Ketemer and I began work on a replica of an elm bark canoe, commissioned for the museum at Ste. Marie among the Iroquois in Liverpool, New York. Built over the course of six days at Highland Forest County Park, the canoe measured 17'9" overall with a beam of 37 3/4" and a depth of 18". Since our goal was to construct a replica rather than replicate construction techniques, we used modern tools throughout.

In attempting to build a replica, we relied heavily on the two significant secondary sources mentioned earlier: Adney and Chapelle, and Fenton and Dodge. Yet even with these detailed descriptions of construction processes, much of our work was experimental. As work progressed, techniques evolved or new ones developed; at no time did we hesitate to use what seemed to us to be more practical solutions than those suggested in the literature.

An 85-foot white elm, growing near the park, was selected for the project. The tree was felled onto a bed of branches to prevent damage. Using spuds, wooden poles and hot water, a dozen workers removed a sheet of bark 23' by 6'. With the exception of three cracks and a small hole, the bark was in excellent condition.

The bark was then removed to our work site and laid on a building bed. Unlike the raised building beds used in birch bark canoe construction, ours was simply a level grassy area and, apart from setting up a marquee to provide shade, little preparation was required. The bark sheet was placed with the rough outer side up so that it would be on the inside of the

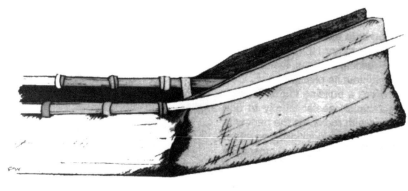

Figure 1. Detail of bark with gunwals lashed in place and crimps produced by elevating the ends.

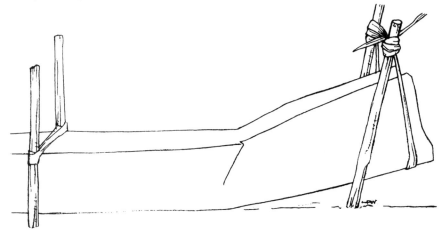

Figure 2. Bark held in place by stakes and lamp wick sling.
(Figures 1-3 by Paula Wescott, after The Bark Canoes and Skin Boats of North America.

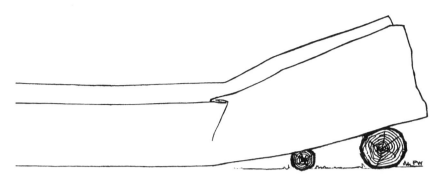

Figure 3. End of bark elevated to produce the crimp and prow.

completed canoe. The bark was cut to size, a center line was marked out, and the rough outer bark was scraped away in those areas which were to be sewn or folded. Finally, a 9" slit was cut along both ends of the center line where the bark was to be bent up to form the stems. During this time and throughout the building process, the bark was repeatedly hosed down to maintain its pliability.

Although we had constructed a building frame, we discovered that it was, in fact, much easier simply to use several planks weighted down with rocks. As the bark was folded up into a hull shape, stakes were positioned on either side of the bark for its entire length and secured crosswise above the hull with lamp wick **(Figure 2)**. As well, long battens were clamped amidships along the upper edges of the bark in order to reduce the amount of warping which occurred once the bark had been bent up to form the sides of the hull.

Unlike birch bark canoes, which use several panels of bark, the elm bark canoe is constructed using only one large sheet. Consequently, in order to produce a canoe with raised ends, the bark must be crimped, or folded, in both fore and aft quarters; to reduce water resistance, the crimps must be made to face aft **(Figure 1)**. This latter detail, dictated by common sense, is found in the surviving models and is recorded in several of the early European accounts.

After some experimentation, we discovered that the first step in forming the crimps was to elevate the ends of the canoe by about 5". Rather than using a sling, as Adney and Chapelle describe, we simply used a short section of log **(Figure 3)**. As the bark began to assume a natural bend, it was scored lightly with a knife. Then, with leverage provided by a short pole, the crimps were made and temporarily secured with clamps. (Unlike the model described by Fenton and Dodge, the crimps were not secured by separate lashings.) The resulting bulge at the crimps was both uneven and unsightly but typical of the elm bark canoe.

HULL	**white elm**
GUNWALES	**balsam fir**
LASHINGS	**basswood**
STEM BATTENS	**white cedar**
RIBS	**cedar, ash, maple**
THWARTS	**maple**
PITCH	**pine, spruce**

"The making of the boat took up half our time yesterday and all to-day. To make such a boat, they pick out a thick tall elm, with a smooth bark, and with as few branches as possible. This tree is cut down, and great care is taken to prevent the bark from being hurt by falling against other trees or against the ground. With this view some people do not fell the trees, but climb to the top of them, split the bark and strip it off, which was the method our carpenter took. The bark is split on one side, in a straight line along the tree, as long as the boat it intends to be. At the same time, the bark is carefully cut from the trunk a little way on both sides of the slit, that it may more easily separate. It is then peeled off very carefully, and particular care is taken not to make any holes in it. This is easy when the sap is in the trees, and at other seasons they are heated by fire for that purpose. The bark thus stripped off is spread on the ground in a level place, [with the smooth side down, later] turning the inside upwards. To stretch better, some logs of wood or stones are carefully put on it, which press it down. Then the sides of the bark are gently bent upwards in order to form the sides of the boat. Some sticks are then fixed into the ground, at a distance of three or four feet from each other, in a curved line, which the sides of the boat are intended to follow, supporting the bark intended for them. The sides are then bent in the form which the boat is to have, and according to that the sticks are either put nearer or further off. The ribs of the boat are made of thick branches of hickory, these being tough and pliable. They are cut into several flat pieces, about an inch thick, and bent into the form which the ribs require, according to their place in the broader or narrower part of the boat. Being thus bent, they are put across the

According to Father Lafitau, gunwales, as well as ribs and thwarts, were often made of "simple branches of tree". Should a more permanent canoe have been desired, the poles may have been split once or twice or even quartered (Adney and Chapelle) **(Figure 4)**. For our project, Ketemer had cut, debarked and split four balsam saplings. Each gunwale was formed of two 9' sections of balsam with the butts lapped and bound with basswood lashings at the canoe's mid length. With the temporary battens removed, the outwales were then clamped onto the hull at a height of 18". Once we had secured the outwales, the excess elm bark was trimmed as far as the crimps both fore an1d aft, thereby establishing the sheer-line amidships. Next, the inwales were added, secured temporarily with braces and clamps. At this point, we could now begin lashing the gunwales in place.

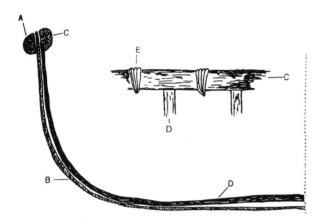

Figure 4. Cross-section of hull amidships: A. Outwale; B. Bark; C. Inwale; D. Rib; E. Lashing.

All lashings were made of bast from the inner bark of basswood. After two days of soaking, sections of bark, 5" wide by 5' long, were scored lengthwise on the inner bark side and split into 1" strips. The outer bark, along with a thin layer of inner bark, was removed; then the strips were cut and split into lashings approximately 1/4"-3/8" wide and 1/16"-1/8" thick. These were coiled and kept in a bucket of water to soak until required for use.

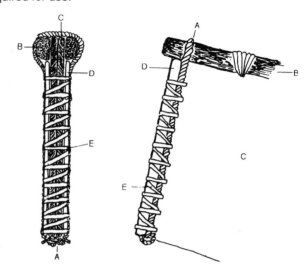

Figure 5. Detail of stem construction: A. Basswood cordage; B. Gunwales; C. Bark; D. Cedar Battens; E. Basswood lashing.

Lashing of the gunwales proceeded from amidships to the crimps and then outwards toward the ends of the canoe. The bast was passed through the elm bark and around the gunwales three to five times, depending on the width of the bast, and then tied off with a square knot. Spacing of the lashings was just over a hand-width, approximately 5"-6". As we worked toward the ends of the canoe, the gunwales were wrapped in wet rags and doused with hot water, and then slowly brought up to the set sheer and propped into position with stakes. At the stems, the outwales were temporarily tied

boat, upon the bark, or its bottom, pretty close together, about a span or ten inches from each other. The upper edge on each side of the boat is made of two thin strips of the length of the boat, which are put close and flat against the side of the boat, where they are to be joined. The edge of the bark is put between these two strips and sewed up with threads of bast, of the mouse wood or other tough bark, or with roots. But before it is thus sewed up, the ends of the ribs are likewise put between the strips on each side, taking care to keep them at some distance from each other. After this is done, the strips are sewed together, and being bent properly, both their ends join at each end of the boat, where they are tied together with ropes. To prevent the widening of the boat at the top, three or four transverse bands are put across it, from one edge to the other, at a distance of thirty or forty inches from each other. These bands are commonly made of hickory, on account of its toughness and flexibility, and have a good length. Their extremities are put through the bark on both sides, just below the strips, which form the edges. They are bent up above those strips and twisted round the middle part of the bands, where they are carefully tied by ropes. As the bark at the two ends of the boat cannot be put so close together as to keep the water out, the crevices are stopped up with the crushed or pounded bark of the red elm which in that state looks like oakum. Some pieces of bark are put upon the ribs in the boat, otherwise the foot would easily pierce the thin and weak bark below, which forms the bottom of the boat. For the better security some thin boards are commonly laid at the bottom, which may be trod upon with more safety."

Peter Kalm

together and the inwales were secured with a figure-eight lashing. Once the sheer had been established past the crimps, the excess bark was trimmed.

The stems of the canoe were bound between two 1" wide cedar battens, semi-circular in section, and a roughly twisted basswood cord **(Figure 5)**. The cordage consisted of 12 strands of paper-thin bast, each about 1/4"-3/8" wide, which had been stripped from the inner side of the bark. The cordage passed up one side of the hull, over the gunwales and down the opposite side and was tied off with a square knot. Lashings, placed at intervals of two finger widths, were then passed through the elm bark and over the cedar battens and basswood cordage. When completed, the stems measured 22" in length.

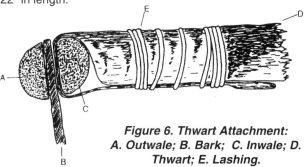

**Figure 6. Thwart Attachment:
A. Outwale; B. Bark; C. Inwale; D.
Thwart; E. Lashing.**

Thwarts were made of striped maple. In many of the old accounts, thwarts were simply made of small saplings or tree branches thinned sufficiently toward the ends to permit them to be bent around the inwale and to be lashed to the underside of the thwart **(Figure 6)**. Our decision, however, was both to remove the bark and to flatten the underside of the thwarts for their entire length. The ends of each thwart were reduced to about 1/8" in thickness with two small kerfs placed at the points where bending would put maximum stress on the wood. The 32" long center thwart was positioned first. Two additional thwarts, each 25 1/2" long, were positioned in the fore and aft quarters.

Typically, some form of flooring was used to strengthen and protect the bark hull. In larger vessels, saplings or split poles were lashed to each rib. For smaller canoes such as ours, flooring consisted simply of a single sheet of bark placed under the ribs, along the middle two thirds of the canoe's length.

Traditionally, small saplings or branches would have been used for ribs, although, on occasion, these were split and positioned so that the flat surface was against the bark. Ketemer, prior to his arrival at Highland Forest, had prepared sixteen ribs of split white cedar 1/2" thick. After being cut to its proper length, each rib was beveled at both ends to ensure a snug fit between the inwale and the bark hull. Next, the ribs were steamed with a portable kerosene and electric steamer, then flexed and positioned about 1' apart inside the canoe. Four of the ribs split so badly during positioning that replacements had to be made. These were fashioned from ash and maple; certainly not the most suitable woods but ones which were most readily available to us.

The canoe was now virtually complete in all structural aspects. Cracks in the bark were stitched with basswood lashings and, in the case of the one hole from the damaged portion of the bark, a patch, approximately 9" by 12", was sewn into place. These areas and the stems of the canoe were then waterproofed using pitch from spruce and pine found in the adjacent forest. Nodules of pitch, collected from the base of broken or cut-off limbs, were melted in a small aluminum skillet. The melted pitch was then applied with a small wooden stick, pushed down into holes and seams and, finally, smoothed with a wetted finger or thumb to prevent the gum from sticking or burning. According to Adney and Chapelle, several materials could be used to make seams watertight: pitch; tallow; or a mixture of grass, shavings, moss or inner bark mixed with pitch or even clay. Although the pitch that we used was not strained or tempered as is the practice in many bark canoes, it nonetheless adhered well to the elm bark. Again, as in all aspects of elm bark canoe construction, circumstance dictated methods and materials used.

With the seams pitched, the canoe was now complete. The building process, based on research, speculation and experience, resulted in what may be the only full-sized replica of an Iroquois elm bark canoe in existence. Lacking the grace and fairness, perhaps, of a birch bark canoe, the replica was nevertheless evidence that the Iroquois elm bark canoe was a remarkable adaptation to existing environmental conditions in pre- and post-contact eastern North America.

REFERENCES

Adams, Arthur T., ed.
1961   *The Explorations of Pierre Esprit Radisson.* Loren Kallsen, modernizer. Minneapolis, Ross and Haines, Inc.
Adney, Edwin Tappan and Howard I. Chapelle.
1983   *The Bark Canoes and Skin Boats of North America.* Washington, D.C., Smithsonian Institution Press.
Benson, Adolph B., ed.
1966   *The America of 1750: Peter Kalm's Travels in North America.* The English version of 1770. New York, Dover Publications
Fenton, William N. and Ernest Stanley Dodge.
1949   An elm bark canoe in the Peabody Museum of Salem. *American Neptune, Vol. 9, #3, pp.185-206.*
Lafitau, Father Joseph François.
1977   *Customs of the American Indians compared with the customs of primitive times.* Edited and translated by Wm. N. Fenton and E.L. Moore. Toronto, The Champlain Society.
Leacock, Stephen, ed.
1932   *Lahontan's Voyages.* Ottawa, Graphic Publishers Ltd.
Liverpool Public Library.
1991   *The Building of an Elm Bark Canoe.* Rick Fensterer, videographer. Liverpool, N.Y.
Morgan, Lewis Henry.
1966   *League of the Ho-dé-no-sau-nee or Iroquois,* Vol. 2. H.M. Lloyd, ed. New York, Burt Franklin.

THE CANOE TREE

By D.R. Doerres

Enclosed is a picture of a canoe tree at Harrow, Ure Australia. In a booklet by the Harrow Historical Society it says of "The Canoe Tree", ...Aboriginals cut the bark from this tree to make a canoe which no doubt was used on the river" nearby.

The American Indians used strips of birch bark for canoes while the Aboriginals cut it in one piece. How they climbed it or tools used is not known.

The tree "Red Gum" has to be over 200 years old, the bark was cut over 150 years ago. The bottom of the cut in the picture is about 6 feet off the ground - making the "Canoe Tree" about 12 feet tall.

There are only a few of these "Canoe Trees" left in Australia.

The Bark Boat*

.... The Australians are quite at home in the water; they are expert swimmers and divers, and most tribes, but not all know how to make and handle several kinds of water-going craft.....but the bark-boat which the Australians also possess, takes us at once to a higher level of development. This is generally made by carefully removing with a stone axe the bark of a single tree, generally a species of Eucalyptus known as red gum; struts are placed inside to open it out and it is propped up by sticks placed at the bow and stern. The ends are ingeniously tied up with string furnished from the bark of another Eucalyptus.

*Ancient Hunters, W.S. Sollas. Macmillan, NY, 1924.

MUD AND FIRE - Tools of the Dugout Canoe Maker

Text, Photos, and Illustrations By Terry Powell

Figure 1. Debry engraving showing the felling of the tree, cutting the trunk to length, and hollowing out the hull, all with fire.

The Friends of the Angel Mounds and the Angel Mounds staff decided to make a dugout canoe as an ongoing educational project for the museum. This was a big decision considering no one at the site had ever made a dugout before. Our project goals were twofold: 1) to illustrate to museum visitors how fire in conjunction with stone tools, was used to fashion a tree trunk into a usable water craft, the dugout canoe, and 2) to provide a project which would begin to make Angel Mounds a "living" and ongoing educational facility for the public. This article deals with the first goal, making a usable dugout canoe. The project was to be carried out by members of "Friends of Angel Mounds", a volunteer support group for the museum.

Angel Mounds State Historical Site is the location of a prehistoric Indian town occupied by the Mississippian people between 1300 and 1500 AD. It is situated on the banks of the Ohio River in the Southeast corner of Evansville, Indiana. The site occupies 103 acres and archaeological investigations revealed a plaza temple, approximately 200 houses and a wooden stockade around three sides of the site with the Ohio River serving as the fourth boundary. Also, within the fortified town are ten earth mounds. It is estimated that 1,000 to 3,000 people inhabited the site. Dugout canoes have not been found in the area but the inhabitants of the site undoubtedly used many as a means of travel and trade with their neighboring communities up and down the Ohio River.

Terry Powell is a professional archaeologist, museum educator and interpreter. While working as a consultant to the Angel Mounds State Historical Park in Evansville Indiana, he helped found a festival of primitive technology. For more information write 2053 Robinson Dr. N, St. Petersburg, FL 33710.

Figure 2. The Tombigbee dugout found in Alabama, dates to 1345 AD. Top and side views.

In order for the dugout project to contribute to the ongoing educational program at Angel Mounds beyond the demonstration of construction techniques, we had to produce a dugout that worked - one that would float and carry people! We knew that research on dugout construction was critical to answering our questions for making a successful dugout. However, we had one question that research could never answer--could a successful dugout be constructed on the first attempt by a group of people who had never made one before? With the determination of our group I knew the answer to that question was "yes", providing our research produced sufficient information.

One of my roles in the project was to conduct the necessary research on how to make a dugout. We had many questions for which we needed answers. Among them were: What did Mississippian dugout canoes look like in AD 1100-1200? How large were they? What tools were used? How did Mississippian people control the fire? After all controlling fire was the secret to using fire as a tool. I knew from past research projects that I would not find complete answers to all of our questions. As a primitive technologist, I would have to rely on my technological ingenuity to provide more complete and plausible solutions to questions not answered in the literature.

An excellent single source for written accounts of early explorers is John R. Swanton's book **Indians of the Southeastern United States.** Swanton's book is a secondary source and compiles information on many topics, including dugouts, from original early writing (see Swanton 1946: 592-597). Swanton relates information from early writers, namely Beverly, Lawson, Timberlake, Strachey and DuPratz. This secondary source was adequate for our project. Another excellent source is Harriot's description of dugout canoe making in early Virginia, along with DeBry's excellent engraving. Harriot's description, from the 1500's, is the earliest account of dugout manufacture. Another important source of information comes from Pericouts description from Biloxi Bay Mississippi in 1699 (McWilliams 1953 in Stowe, 1974: 194-195).

Archaeological reports of dugouts actually recovered from swamps, rivers and lakes in the eastern United States were utilized to get a more complete picture of the size and shape of dugouts.

Size and Shape of Dugouts

Most dugouts were basically a hollowed out log with both ends blunt or pointed, tapering upward from the bottom to the edge (Figure 1). The size of dugouts reported by early writers may be somewhat exaggerated.

Dugouts from 30-40' long and up to three feet in diameter were reported by several writers. Smaller dugouts are rarely mentioned, possibly because they were overshadowed in the writer's mind by the larger ones.

Archaeological reports provided information on smaller dugouts, more in line with the size of our log. Nearly 100 preserved dugouts have been found in Florida, a world record for the number of prehistoric and early historic dugouts found in any one locality (Newsome and Purdy 1990: 164). The earliest dugouts are nothing more than hollowed out logs with blunt ends.

Outer surfaces and ends were largely unmodified with bow and stern indistinguishable. They averaged 15 feet long and 16 inches wide. Sometimes branches were not completely removed (Barbara A. Purdy personal communication, 1982).

Another style of canoe which replaces the older style is more refined inside and out with both ends somewhat shaped by beveling the ends upwards. These average 18 feet long and 16 inches wide. They range in length from 11 to 30 feet.

A dugout from Ohio, dating to 3550 +- 70 BP by radio carbon test had blunt ends that tapered upward from the bottom to the top. Small platforms were on both ends, created in part by the upward tapering of the bottom.

The most pertinent dugout to our study was one found in Alabama in the Tombigbee River. Both ends taper from the bottom to form the platforms that form overhangs on both ends. The platform measures 1.0 feet by 1.2 - 1.3 feet wide. The dugout is 20 feet long, 1.7 feet wide with 1.25 feet interior width and 8 inches deep (Figure 1). This dugout was dated by the C14 method to 605 BP (1345 AD) which indicates the dugout was made during the late Mississippian period, the same period during which Angel Mounds was inhabited. We ultimately modeled our dugout after this one.

Types of Wood Used To Make Dugouts

Dugouts were made from a variety of woods. The type of wood utilized depended largely upon what type of trees were available to the dugout makers. Swanton states that early writers and explorers observed dugouts made from cypress, pine, poplar and black walnut in the Southeastern United States and the lower Mississippi River Valley. Cypress was apparently the most common reported type of tree used for dugouts, when it was available. The largest dugouts used on the Lower Mississippi River were made of poplar. For our project a large poplar log was donated by on of the "Friends", Mr. Bruce Eisterhold.

All but a few of the prehistoric dugouts recovered from Florida lakes, streams and swamps were made of pine. The earliest dugouts were all made of yellow (hard) pine. The Ringler dugout recovered from Savannah Lake in Ashland County, Ohio was made from white oak (Brose 1982:248). The Mississippian-age dugout from the Tombigbee River in Alabama appears to be made of cypress (Stowe 1974:197), but wood identification has not been conducted.

The descriptions by early explorers and the recovery of prehistoric dugouts tell us that many types of wood were satisfactory for the manufacture of dugouts. However, some woods such as cypress and poplar, were preferred when they were available. The characteristics of the tree type undoubtedly had an influence on the type of wood utilized. Trees that grow large, straight, and tall, such as cypress and poplar, would have been ideal for a dug-out canoe.

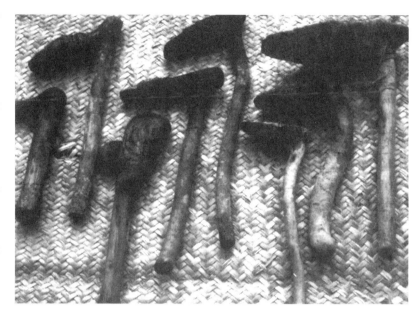

Figure 3. Tools used in dugout construction - adzes, celt (3rd from left) and chert hoe (far right).

Accounts of Dugout Canoe Manufacture

The following is a description of dugout canoe making based on the information provided by early writers. A tree of the proper size was selected, and a small fire was started at its' base to fell the tree. Native stone axes were sometimes used to help fell the tree. These axes mashed the wood more than cut it, producing wood fibers. The fire more readily consumed the fibers than the solid wood and thus hurried the process.

Once the tree was felled additional fires were used to "cut" the trunk to length and to burn off the limbs. According to Harriot large shells were used to remove the bark. Next, the shaping process began. The ends, as well as hollowing out the hull, were shaped by fire. According to DuPratz before the burning began a pad of clay was made for both sides and each end which was not to be burned away. As burning continued down into the hull additional clay was added to areas where burning was completed. Penecaut and DuPratz observed that the hollowing process began with starting a fire on top of the log. Periodically the char was scraped out and the burning and scraping process is repeated until the log is hollowed out.

DuPratz and Penecaut relate that shells were used to scrape out the charred wood. Both of these writers observed Indians living on the coast where large shells were readily available. DuPratz implies that some sort of a wooden tool was used for scraping the char. Lawson is the only writer that mentions stone tools. He states that before the natives had metal tools they scraped and chipped the burned dugouts with oyster shells and stone hatchets (Swanton 1911:592). The words "chopping" or cutting appear only in this one account while "scraping" occurs in many of the accounts. Thus it

appears that burning and scraping was used almost exclusively to shape the dugout.

DuPratz points out that scraping the charred wood away allowed the fire to burn better. He also noted that small pieces of wood were always used for fuel, presumably as another way to control the fire. Harriot states that water was used to quench the fire before the scraping began. Penecaut writes that the burning and scraping process made the hull as smooth as they (the French) could have made it with their (metal) tools. The burning and scraping process was continued until the desired slope was attained. The famous engraving by Theodore DeBry very clearly illustrates the major steps in the dugout construction process (Figure 1).

The Project Begins

The research indicated that mud and fire were the two most important tools. Stone tools were rarely mentioned and sticks and shells (on the East coast) were used instead of stone tools for tasks such as scraping char.

We chose the dugout from the Tombigbee River as an appropriate model (Figure 2). It was constructed by people of the Mississippian culture, the same people who inhabited Angel Mounds and dated approximately to 1300 A.D., the time Angel Mounds was occupied.

The Tools

The first step was to construct tools which would facilitate our work. The most important tool that we needed besides fire and mud was one with which to scrape out the char. Shells were not appropriate for southern Indiana, so we decided to use a stone adze instead of sticks or shells for removing the char from the interior of the hull, as one of the goals of the project was to demonstrate the use of stone tools with fire (Figure 3).

Next, we needed a tool with which to remove the char from the hull once it was loosened by the adzes. Scoops were fashioned from the bark of a dead pecan tree (Figure 4). Water containers were fashioned from large gourds. Water would be needed mainly to mix with the clay to form the proper consistency. However, I did not believe that water would be needed to extinguish the burning coals. They could be scooped out while still hot. A gourd dipper was also fashioned for pouring water on out-of-control hop spots (Figure 4). A celt was also on hand for any unexpected situations (Figure 3). A

Figure 4. Tools used in dugout construction - Bark scoops, fans, water bottle, water dipper and wedge or glut.

large "hoe", typical of those used by Mississippian people in the Midwest, was made to dig clay. These hoes were used by the prehistoric Mississippian people to dig storage pits and house wall trenches, as well as for cultivation (Figure 3). Handles were very short, 18-20 inches long, and the tool was used like a hand pick for digging. The length of the handle is illustrated by a Mississippian figurine which shows a women on her knees using a short handled hoe (Emerson 1982:6-7).

Construction Begins

As the tools were being constructed the log for our future dugout was allowed to dry for a few months. We believed drying would facilitate burning. We noticed minor checking or cracking all over the log but hoped this would not cause later problems. Drying the log was the biggest mistake that we made, as we shall see later.

Our research indicated that the hollowing process started with a fire on top of the rounded surface of the unaltered log. I had figured that the entire process would take more time than our volunteers, and public were willing to contribute to the project. Thus, to speed up the process we cut away the top half of the log before our program started. This would cut down on the amount of time to complete the project and would in no way affect our main purpose which was to demonstrate the use of fire as a tool. Besides, this method made the whole process look less intimidating for our first dugout project.

Our log was placed adjacent to a little stream on the wooded edge of the Angel

Tool Performance

One of the most interesting aspects discovered during our project is the few tools which are needed to make a dugout. The accounts by early writers on dugout canoe manufacture mentioned few tools used in the construction. Specifically, stone tools were rarely mentioned which, based on the results of our project, was no omission by the writer. From felling the tree to completed dugout only three tools are essential - fire, mud, and a tool such as a stick or shell, to loosen the char from the dugout. Other tools are useful, such as a scoop to remove the char from the hull after it is loosened, and a tool to dig clay. The char scraped away very easily and a long stick sharpened to a chisel edge would have worked just as well as our stone adzes. Although our stone adzes were not necessary, they performed well and were low maintenance. Those with more of an acute angle, were excellent for the scraping action utilized.

The bark scoops were very useful tools. After the char was scraped loose with adzes, the char was scooped up from

the bottom of the hull and removed. The handles on the scoops are noticeably a European solution to a situation. Probably a more appropriate form would have been a long rectangular piece of bark held in two hands. However, the handles were useful in performing a very hot and uncomfortable task. The bark scoops also served as fans for encouraging the fire to burn. As the hull became deeper from burning the air flow was restricted more and more. With restricted air flow the fire did not burn well until the fire was well established and created its own draft. The beginning fire was often fanned for lengthy periods to hasten the fire to a mature state where burning efficiency was optimum.

The hoe proved to be a very effective tool. With a short handle of 18-20 inches in length it was swung like a pick to excavate chunks of clay from the stream bank. The hoe was also used in a "hoeing" motion to perform a preliminary mixing of clay and water before it was mixed with hands. A digging stick would have also worked for digging clay but would not have been so efficient.

Mounds property which proved to be an ideal location. Limbs from dead trees provided plenty of fuel for the fire. We also discovered that a bed of clay was exposed in a small bend of the stream which was ideal for controlling the fire. Below the clay outcrop was a pool of water which we hoped would remain for most of the summer while the remainder of the stream dried up to a trickle. Here, within approximately 50 feet of the dugout, we had fuel, clay and water, all in a natural setting, perfect for our demonstration!

On the first day we were ready but nervous. We had completed a test run on the burning a week before to establish the basic procedures of the initial process. We dug a small hole in the ground near the log in which we mixed the clay to the proper consistency, which was an additional interpretive element for our demonstration. From our test run we gained great confidence in the ability of the clay to control the fire. The performance of the clay in controlling the fire was critical to use fire as a tool.

In this test run we instantly realized that there was more to using fire as tool than lighting a fire and watching it burn. There were many things we needed to know to add additional control to using fire as a tool. Penecaut had stated that after the burning was completed the hull was very smooth. I also assumed that he meant it was very even and level in the bottom. Well preserved dugouts from lakes and rivers exhibit smooth and relatively level floors and sides to the hull. We wanted to attain this quality by controlling the fire and not by using our stone tools or modern tools. In order to do this we

had a lot to learn about using fire and most of our education would be gained in front of an audience of several hundred people a day!

We decided to burn the hull out before shaping the ends as that is the most interesting part for a demonstration and we would shape the ends later. The dugout log was elevated by placing two smaller logs 4-5 inches in diameter, beneath it. The extra height made it easier to work on. Wooden "gluts", or wedges, were made to wedge between the round bottom of the dugout log and the logs upon which it was resting (Figure 4). This kept the dugout log from rocking back and forth and disrupting the fire inside. The next step was to form a clay dam on top of the log in the shape that we wanted the opening of the hull to take. Clay was dug from the stream with hoe and mixed with water in the shallow pit beside the dugout. When the clay was of the proper consistency a dam, or ridge of clay approximately 2-3 inches high and about two inches wide, was formed (Figure 5). The width of the clay on the sides defined the thickness of the sides or gunwales. In the end the gunwales ended up to be approximately 1 1/2 inches thick.

A fire was then built in the entire length of the area encircled by the clay. The fire was kept to a moderate size. We believed that a larger fire would burn too quickly and we would loose control. We did not want to demonstrate how to patch a hole in the side of a dugout! After the burning seemed to slow we used sticks to move the burning limbs from one half of the dugout to the other half. Scraping with the stone adzes the hot charred wood easily popped away from the unburned wood

Mud as Insulator

Mud was second only to fire as the most important tool in constructing the dugout. When the proper consistency of mud was attained, burning was controlled very precisely. The proper consistency was found through trial and error in mixing. The clay had to be moist enough to adhere tightly to the wood to prevent drying before the burning cycle was completed, but firm enough to remain in place. When the mud became dry before a burning cycle was complete, it would crack and release from the wood, allowing burning to take place beneath the clay. If burning became too severe beneath the mud, then the burning cycle was terminated early and fresh mud repacked throughout before burning was resumed.

Occasionally a depression was burned into the floor of the hull from uneven burning. If additional burning cycles were completed the depression would burn deeper at the same rate as the rest of the bottom and the depression would continue to exist. To remedy the situation the depression was filled with mud to the existing floor level. The mud kept the bottom of the depression from burning through with suc-

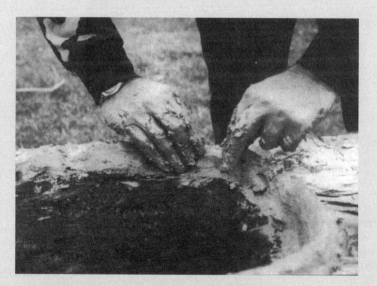

Figure 5. Applying clay "dam" to define the shape and thickness of the dugout.

cessive burnings. Whenever the mud in the depression became too dry it was replaced. After several burnings the bottom of the hull was burned to the same level as the bottom of the depression. The depression no longer existed and burning was continued as usual.

beneath. The heat from the burning charcoal instantly told us that the handles on some of the adzes were too short! From this time on the long handled adzes were definitely preferred. A pulling or scraping action was all that was needed to loosen the char. The bark scoops were then used to remove all of the loose char and ashes. The cracked and partially dried clay ridge surrounding the burned area was also removed and new moist clay was added. We were afraid that another burning would dry the clay too much and allow burning to start beneath the clay and through the cracks. The fire in the half still burning was then moved to the recently scraped portion while the unscraped portion was cleaned out. (Figure 6). By cleaning out only one half at a time there was no down time in restarting a fire. The only potential problem in not cleaning out the entire area all at once was that irregular burning may occur where the two fires met in the center of the canoe. However, by slightly overlapping the burning, this problem was overcome. This process was repeated until the intended depth of the hull was reached.

Figure 6. Fire was moved to one end of the dugout (front) while the char was scraped out and new clay applied in the other half.

As the depth of the hull increased from the burning, extra care had to be taken to protect the sides from the rising heat. Mud was plastered along the entire exposed sides down to the juncture desired with the floor to prevent additional burning. This method worked perfectly. The thickness of the sides was attained at the juncture of the floor with the sides. The 3-4 inches within this zone is where maximum control over burning of the sides is accomplished. As soon as the desired thickness was reached it was plastered with mud. The mud protected the sides from excessive heat as well as actual burning. Excessive heat could cause the sides to crack and split. Thickness of the sides was estimated by eye and was monitored continually. Once the burning came within about 2-3 inches of thickness at the bottom we had to be very cautious. The actual thickness of the bottom is difficult to determine by the eye because both the inside and outside cannot be seen at the same time. Also the dugout was too large around to wrap your arms around it and judge the thickness by feel. Thus we left the bottom thicker than we needed. The floor of the hull had burned smooth and level through every burning to within a couple of inches of the desired thickness of the bottom. With another couple of burning cycles one of our fears was realized. The burning had reached the cracks which were created during the drying period. On the outside surface the cracks were rather long but very narrow, from 1/16 to over 1/8 inch wide. They were assumed to be very shallow also. However, the fire burned down into them which enlarged the cracks to some extent. Additional burning would make them larger. Since we wanted to actually use the dugout we did not want to continue burning and render the dugout completely useless. We decided to terminate burning on the interior and complete the dugout and deal with the cracks later. Hopefully they would swell shut once the dugout was in the water.

The next step was to shape both ends. We were attempting to produce a platform on both ends like on the model (Figure 2). Thus we had to create a short steep slant towards the end and then level off. After completing what we thought was the most difficult portion of the dugout, burning out the hull, shaping the ends, we thought , would be an easy and quick task. We built a fire beneath the end to burn it into shape, which seemed to be the easiest, fastest and most logical approach. However, problems quickly arose. After a couple of burnings it was apparent that burning progressed too quickly. This method created too much heat, producing deep cracks in the ends. Another method had to be used. The dugout was turned over, bottom up, and the fire built on top of the area to be shaped (Figure 7). Burning was much much slower but more controlled, and the cracking ceased.

Keeping the fire from rocking off of the slopes and slightly rounded ends proved to be quite a challenge. As a result shaping of the ends took much longer than we anticipated. Our "platforms" were crude compared to those on the Tombigbee dugout.

After shaping of the interior and exterior was completed residual char was removed from the interior of the dugout to provide a much cleaner interior for passengers. Sand was added to the interior and scrubbed around with a sandstone block. After a considerable amount of char was removed the and char was washed out with water. This process was repeated 2-3 times when most of the char was removed. Now the dugout was completed and almost ready to be launched. The last step was to determine if the crack in the sides and bottom, enlarged by the burning, could be repaired. The dugout was placed in a pool of water for a couple of days. many of the cracks swelled shut, like I thought they would, but some did not. Too much water collected in the bottom and the cracks had to be filled.

Figure 7. Shaping the bottom ends with fire.

We had limited time to repair the cracks before the launch date. With what did Native Americans patch leaky dugouts, or did they? A little research revealed that the Maskwake and Menomini Indians used cattail root as a natural caulking for canoes (Smith 1928:269, Smith, 1923:77). The sources did not state what type of canoes they were used on nor did they give any details as to exactly how the roots were used. With our public launch date coming up soon I did not have much time for experimentation. I had time for one chance to use my ingenuity to figure out how the roots were used. I dried the roots to the point where they were dry but pliable and leathery. I figured that the partially dried roots would absorb water, swell and seal the cracks. The roots were tapped into the cracks with a wooden wedge and mallet. This worked well for the few larger cracks, over 1/8 inch wide but the roots were difficult if not impossible to tap into finer cracks. We decided to test the canoe in water to see how badly it

Fire as a Tool

From my previous study of burned prehistoric Mississippian Indian houses (Powell 1980), I gained a good understanding of the burning process and the critical elements involved in making a fire burn. Now I just had to apply these concepts to regulate a fire so it could be used as a constructive force instead of a destructive force. Many of the basic principles are presented in a brief and condensed manner by Kochanski (1991:19-22 and Powell 1980:46-64).

We soon learned there are three major aspects of fire which are crucial in controlling fire as a tool. The critical elements are 1) size of the fire, 2) size of the fuel, and 3) the arrangement of fuel. A large fire is difficult to control. The heat is so intense that one cannot get close enough to monitor the burning and intense heat dries the wood, allowing it to crack before it can burn. Thus the fire can readily get out of control and you will be forever correcting mistakes, if they are correctable. The best intensity of burning, we found, is one with glowing coals and little flame similar to glowing charcoal in a barbecue grill. A glowing fire produces more than enough heat and all burning surfaces are visible and can be monitored properly.

Just like a charcoal barbecue fire the color of burning material indicates what is happening in a fire. The white ash indicates that past combustion was efficient. The red glow of coals indicated that those areas are burning efficiently now and the black areas are burning inefficiently. Black areas occur whenever airflow is restricted which produces a lack of oxygen. This usually occurs when two pieces of fuel meet, or where fuel and dugout touch. Black areas burn more slowly than the rest of the canoe and therefore may produce high areas on the floor or sides of the dugouts. The fire must be kept burning efficiently in all areas to produce even surfaces throughout the dugout. The arrangement of fuel was the single most important element in achieving a smooth floor. If fuel as spaced too closely together then air flow would be slowed down, or stopped, and burning would not occur, producing the tell tale "black areas". If fuel was arranged too far apart then there would not be enough heat transfer from one piece of wood to another, and the fire would go out. Thus, the burning was constantly monitored and fuel arranging was a constant duty. A crib structure is nothing more than a criss-cross stacking of fuel. This structure of fuel is the ideal fuel arrangement for maximum burning efficiency. We sometimes used this arrangement but usually a modified crib or just parallel pieces of wood evenly spaced across the bottom of the hull was sufficient. Arranging the fuel properly for maximum burning efficiency is a simple concept but the "proper way" changed as the fire burned down and new fuel was added. The diameter of fuel was also found to be important in the evenness of burning. Large diameter logs produced larger black areas than smaller pieces. The ideal diameter branches were approximately three inches in diameter for our narrow dugout. Large logs covered too much floor area and restricted air flow too much.

To Scrape or Not to Scrape

As the burning progressed through each cycle, the big question was "when is it time to scrape out the char? Changes in characteristics indicate when it is time for removal. First, small cracks appear in the char. As the dugout burns the cracks become larger and rough squares and rectangles of charred wood form between the cracks. Finally, as the burning progresses the squares and rectangles become well defined and the edges and surfaces become rounded and the cracks wider. At this point burning efficiency is low and monitoring becomes difficult because of the deep char and ashes. It is at this stage the fire should be moved and the char scraped out.

The char must be removed to promote efficient burning. Charred wood which adheres to unburned wood provides insulation from the fire. The thicker the charred wood is, the slower the wood burns. Char adheres more tightly to some types of wood than others.

leaked. The dugout was test launched into a shallow beaver pond on the Angel Mounds property (Figure 8). Naturally the dugout filled with a couple inches of water. We decided to leave the dugout in the pond for a couple of days and many of the cracks closed from the swelling wood. Some cracks, however, still leaked. Safety was of primary concern and a leaky canoe was not wanted for the river launch. Regrettably, a modern solution was used to caulk the cracks. Unfortunately a native method of repairing the cracks had to wait until after the launch.

The Launch

Finally the long awaited launch on the Ohio River came (Cover). Two experienced canoeist, myself and another person were the "test pilots". Not knowing anything about the stability and performance of a dugout we approached all of our moves very cautiously. Boarding the canoe happened without an embarrassing capsize. I was amazed at the stability. I instantly realized we were no longer dealing with a log but a watercraft. After we were on the open water for a while I continued to be amazed at the stability. With two canoeist and a combined body weight under 300 pounds, the dug-out had about eight inches of freeboard which was adequate protection against the small to moderate waves on the river. Some of our body weight was below the waterline which helped stabilize the craft. In essence, we were sitting in the water, not on it. It easily survived waves from a passing motorboat without capsizing.

A portion of the squared off and flattened ends were submerged below the waterline. I believe the flattened underside of both ends helped stabilize the canoe by lessening the tendency to roll. The ends of the Tombigbee River dugout were flattened more severely than ours, were much thinner, and the undersurfaces were more parallel to the water surface. If the purpose of the flattened ends was to help stabilize the craft, then the Tombigbee craft would have been

more stable than ours. The dugout also maneuvered surprisingly well. Turns were negotiated rather quickly. Paddling was not as sluggish as was anticipated based on the weight and bluntness of the craft.

Since authenticity of canoe paddles was not a subject of interest for the project, we decided to use modern wooden canoe paddles. The log from which our dugout was made had a slight bend to the port side. I thought a slight curve in the hull might hinder the dugout from maintaining a straight course. After canoeing for several minutes, I did not detect any pull to the port side. As an additional test I ceased to use the "J" stroke, a canoeing stroke which keeps a canoe traveling in a straight line, and used a straight stroke. I adjusted my stroke so both of us were exerting the same amount of force. Still the canoe kept a straight course. The slight curve in the hull did not affect the navigation of the canoe. After canoeing for approximately a half mile we turned around and went back to the launch site. We considered our dugout a success and were ready for a long trip.

REFERENCES

Brose, David
1982 *An Archaic Dugout from Savannah Lake, Ohio.* **Midcontinental Journal of Archaeology**, Vol. 7, No. 2.

Emerson, Thomas
1982 **Mississippian Stone Images in Illinois.** Illinois Archaeological Survey, Circular #6, Univ. of Ill., Champaign-Urbana.

Harriot, Thomas
1972 **A Brief and True Report of the New Found Land of Virgina,** from 1590 Thoedor DeBry Edition, Dover Pub., NY.

Kochanski, Mors
1991 *Understanding Wood Fire.* **Bulletin of Primitive Technology.** Vol.1, No.1, pp 19-22.

Lorout, Stephen
1946 **The New World the First Pictures of America.** Duell, Sloan and Pearce, New York.

Newsome, Lee Ann and Barbara Purdy
1990 *Florida Canoes: A Maritime Heritage from the Past.* **Florida Anthropologist,** Vol. 43, No. 3.

Powell, Terry J.
1980 **An Archaeological Study of Burned Structures at the Orendorf Site, Fulton Co., IL.** Masters Thesis, Department of Anthropology, Southern Ill. Univ., Carbondale.

Smith, Huron H.
1923 *Ethnobotany of the Menomini Indians.* **Bulletin of the Public Museum, City of Milwaukee,** Vol. 4, No. 1.
1928 *Ethnobotany of the Meskwaki Indians.* **Bulletin of the Public Museum, City of Milwaukee,** Vol. 4, No. 2.

Swanton, John R.
1946 **Indians of the Southeastern U.S..** BAE Bulletin #137, Smithsonian Institute, Wash.

Stowe, Noel R.
1974 *A Preliminary Report on four Dugout Canoes from the Gulf Coast.* **Journal of Alabama Archaeology.** Vol. 20 No.2.

A CARVED BOAT FROM THE NORTHWEST COAST

Text and Photos By Gregg Blomberg

The thought of carving a dugout came naturally to me, living as I do on an island on the Washington coast. Canoes were as vital to the people of the northwest coast as horses were to the people of the plains. The dugouts the Coast natives built were beautiful, sophisticated and seaworthy. Steve Brown, a fine north-west coast artist and a friend, built several of these craft for the Makah Cultural and Research Center at Neah Bay, Washington. Displayed as they are surrounded by other rich West coast cultural materials, they are an inspiring sight indeed.

> *I chose to build a boat in the tradition of the peoples of the west coast of Vancouver Island and the northwestern corner of Washington. West coast (Nootkan) boats have a reputation for seaworthiness.*

were for use in protected waters or for river travel. The size ranged from small craft for clamming across the bay to sixty-plus foot craft capable of carrying a formidable array of men and weapons off to capture slaves hundreds of miles away.

I chose to build a boat in the tradition of the peoples of the west coast of Vancouver Island and the northwestern corner of Washington. West coast (Nootkan) boats have a reputation for seaworthiness. Unique to the West coast people was an active whaling complex in which crews of eight men would whale using 36-foot boats and sophisticated equipment,

Donald Stiff preparing the log for halving.

Steve Horn

Gregg Blomberg and bow of nearly completed canoe.

The idea of building one of these craft soaked in my brain. The first thing to do was to procure a suitable red cedar log. Since buying a log was out of the question, that meant waiting for one to drift in on the beach. Years of beachcombing told me it might be a long wait, and indeed it was several years; but as the bard had said, "All things come to him who waits," and finally my log chose me. Had I been able to choose, it would have been a log with more breadth and less heart rot and knots. However, the log was a fine old grandmother cedar. Growth rings told it was nearly a hundred years old when Captain Cook "discovered" the northwest coast in 1778.

The styles of canoes built by different groups along the over-thousand miles of coastline varied considerably. Designs were adapted to use and convention. Some designs

Gregg Blomberg is an artist and craftsman specializing in the material culture of the Northwest Coast Indians. He is the owner of Kestrel Tools, makers of fine traditional carving tools; ie. crooked knives, adzes, and inshaves. For a catalog, send $4 to Kestrel Tools, Rt. 1 Box 1762, Lopez, WA 98261, or call (206) 468-2103.

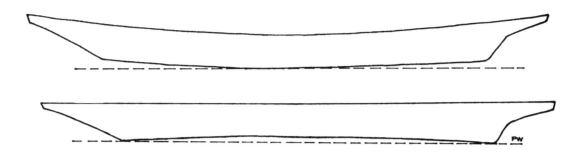

Profiles showing the reverse rocker of the boat bottom prior to steaming, and the resulting rocker created by the spreading of the sides. After Holman from <u>Historical Salish Canoes.</u>

It may be a bit of a digression, but all this stuff about "I'd rather be cut by a sharp tool" seems a bunch of bananas. I am a real believer in sharp tools, but a really sharp edge doesn't believe in anything short of bone. Certain kinds of injuries aren't much fun no matter how sharp the tools are: chain saws for example. Probably the best injury-preventative is being alert to tool run-out. Where does this tool end up it if it goes as far as it can in the direction it is pointed? For power tools this dictum is reversed: the runout to watch is that of your hand (or whatever) as it presents the work to the machine. Perhaps more mystical but just as real is paying attention to the little voice within that says just before an accident that you are working dangerously. Ignoring this voice even for a single stroke can mean a gouge in your palm or something equally unpleasant.

combined with rigorous ritual.

The first step in making the boat was to roughly halve the log and carve the outside. The style chosen is the basic idea, but the log itself can exert limitations, and finally the builder must consider the steaming process that will take place later. Carving the outside involves some educated guesswork as to how the shape will alter during the steaming process.

After shaping the outside, 1/4" thickness gauging holes were drilled at intervals of two hand-spans longitudinally and a hand apart transversely. Into these gauging holes cedar plugs of varying lengths were driven flush with the outside surface. The plugs for the sides near the gunwales were 1 finger width, 1 1/2 fingers width near the turn of the bilge and 2 fingers width on the bottom. [Some are charred or of contrasting color so that they are more visable when they are exposed].

The inside was begun by removing large chunks of waste wood with chain saw and wedges, finish work being mostly done with adzes and inshave. When the ends of the gauging plugs were even with the inside surface, the carving in that area was complete.

While working near the bow on the inside, I got into boat on my knees with a largish gutter hand adze. Without a single overshot stroke, I undershot the first blow, whacking myself in the knee smartly (can one use this adverb in this case? Man, it did smart!) The sequence of picking up the adze, getting into the boat, whacking myself in the knee and getting out of the boat, all without removing a chip, seemed almost ceremonial. Well, the only thing smart that day was the blow. After getting sewed up, I came home and went back to work. Fifteen minutes of that convinced me it was the wrong thing to do and I spent the better part of the next two weeks lying on my back.

After taking time to heal and to finish the interior, the boat was ready to steam.

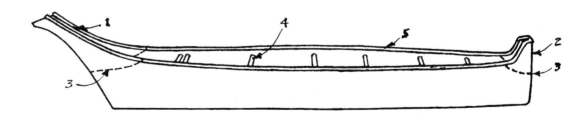

Diagram illustrating the parts of a canoe: 1. Carved bow piece; 2. Carved stern piece; 3. Joints or "scarfs" where carved pieces are joined to the hull with glue and lashing; 4. Thwarts; 5. Gunwale strips pegged to hull. After T.T. Waterman from <u>The Whaling Equiment of the Makah Indians,</u> 1920.

Working with inshave on the outside of the hull.

The log has been scored with a chain saw to block out the inside. The chunks were split out with wedges.

Steaming the boat. The heat was intense.

At this point the carving more closely resembled a cattle trough than a boat. The sides were straight throughout much of the carving's length and the bottom had 1 1/2" of *reverse rocker* in anticipation of the steaming process. For steaming, a fire was built on either side of the boat as close as comfort allowed. From the fires we loaded red hot rocks into the partially water filled carving. The water was kept boiling vigorously for about three hours. As the process progressed, we drove increasingly longer wedges into the hull at the gunwales.

The potential for making two boats out of one at this point can easily be imagined. Cedar is not much embarrassed by splitting, as is attested to by the "handsplit" cedar shake roofs that abound in the northwest. In this regard, having a log too clear and straight-grained can be disadvantageous. I was hoping to move the sides out 10", and although that amount was reached, the boat began to develop cracks at the turn of the bilge. We backed it off to 8". Subsequently the cracks were "sewn" together with copper wire.

The steaming process turned the trough into a boat shape with a nice flare, pretty shear and a slight rocker (as the sides went out the ends came up).

Finally fir thwarts replaced the temporary bracing, and bow and stern pieces were carved of separate pieces of cedar and carefully fitted. To protect the cedar gunwale, strips of fir were pegged into place, and the canoe was painted in the traditional colors with iron oxide pigments - red inside and black outside - with the gunwale strips and thwarts left natural. A striking color combination.

The finished canoe weighs about 150 lbs. It is 16 '4" long with a beam of 34". The carving took about two months, spread over about a year to complete. My own modest ability and knowledge would have been insufficient for the task without the help and encouragement of Bill Holm, Steve Brown and others who have preceded me.

For sea trials a friend and I helped get together a journey to the outside of Vancouver Island. What better place could we take the canoe than to the waters from which the design originated. The others on the venture were all in kayaks. My previous cruising in this area had been in an Eskimo style kayak, but the canoe was a major departure from that. For one thing, gear stowed in a kayak was protected from rain and spray; the open boat would likely often be wet. To our dismay we discovered we had only about 4" of freeboard when fully loaded. Despite this and our novice status as dugout drivers, the canoe performed quite well. We had it in interesting combinations of swell and wave but the

(more)

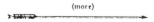

only problem was that of a following sea on the quarter. In that case occasionally the waves would run up the side of the boat and their tops would fall into the canoe. While on the trip we rigged up a sail and had some wonderful downwind sailing in rough waters.

While on the "outside" we visited an Indian village where the canoe obtained the approval of the older folks. Although a friend some years earlier had visited with a man of this group who was using a dugout converted to take a small outboard, not one boat of this type was left in the village. At one point during our visit, three children accompanied by a young man took the canoe out for a spin. For a few minutes there, it actually was an Indian canoe.

Thwarts and gunwale strips in place.

The scarf joint for the stern also shows pieces added to replace rot. This joint could be drawn for greater clarity.

Boas mentions the following rules observed by the canoe builder: He avoids contact with the opposite sex, otherwise he finds rotten places in the wood from which he is shaping the hull; He does not comb his hair, otherwise the ends of his canoe become split; Also, he does not permit anybody to look when he is heating the hull and spreading the sides, for that may cause the canoe to split open. Similar rules are scrupulously observed by the Makah.

T.T. Waterman,
The Whaling Equipment of the Makah Indians

It floats!

Northern canoe-style feast bowl in alder.

Note paddles of Alaska cedar in traditional shape.

DANISH NEOLITHIC BOAT PROJECT

Text By Errett Callahan, Photos By Søren Moses

Søren Moses and dugouts made with Neolithic stone tools in Denmark, 1982 - 87.

Roughing out the hull with adze and ax.

Shaving the gunwales with blade tools.

Final shaping on the exterior.

Detail of the stern showing extremely fine workmanship.

All boats were made with appropriate tools....These canoes are way ahead of anything I've seen in the states. Not only in use of stone tools but in the thinness of the walls. All U.S.. dugouts I've seen are way too thick...

Søren Moses also collaborated with Thorbjørn Petersen in 1987 on a canoe that was 30' long. It was part of an educational program and was paddled around much of Denmark

Mesolithic antler and core axes were used to replicate a beautiful prehistoric Danish dugout in 1986 as well.

Stern with end block in place prior to sealing.

Søren Moses, Denmark, 1986.

Ready for the maiden voyage.

THE ANCIENT CORACLE

A coracle is a small round river craft constructed of leather tightly stretched over ribs of reed, willow or other flexible wood and steered with a wooden paddle. Used throughout time to navigate or fish in streams and rivers, the coracle can drift quite a distance and would have to be carried home at the end of the day . One essential of the coracle is that it can be carried by a lone individual. The little craft is still used today, usually covered with treated canvas rather than leather, in the British Isles and many parts of the Middle East where it is called a "guffa" [they have been used in Tibet, Vietnam, Iraq, Wales, and many other countries]. **Maria Sidoroff**

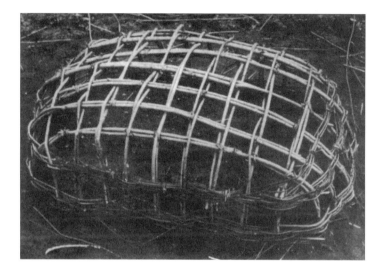

Information from the **National Coracle Centre**, *Dyfed, West Wales suggests a number of similarities in the design, construction and use of coracles found around the world:*
1. Most are circular or oval in design.
2. They are small and light enough to be carried by one person.
3. Coracles are made from local materials; flexible branches, large animal hides. The size of the boat is determined by available materials.
4. Raw hides were put on hair side out to aid in waterproofing.
5. The frame is a simple grid that allows construction of the entire boat to take only a couple of hours.
6. The design and construction produce a very rugged craft that is capable of carrying tremendous loads.

from *Stick Your Oar In!* **by John Fenna found in** *Survival and Outdoor Techniques,* **September 1992.**

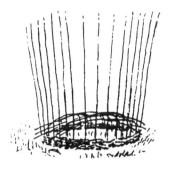

Insert 32 hazel rods (or other flexible thin stems) about 10 feet long in an elliptical oval marked on the ground. The gunwale (edge) is woven first, then opposite rods are bent over and lashed together to the frame. Stones placed on a plank for some days to flatten the bottom. Then canvas is tightly stretched over the lashed rods attached to the gunwales.

from *The Irish Curragh Folk* **by R. MacCullagh**

YUCCA AND AGAVE FIBER SANDALS
OF SOUTHERN CALIFORNIA
Text and Photos By Paul Douglas Campbell, © 1997

Size 11 Yucca sandals made by Paul Campbell from ethnographic reports.

These most ancient sandals of the Southwest were of fiber and until this century the preferred footwear of Southern California and Northern Baja California Indians. The first yucca fiber sandals I ever saw were Diegueño, collected from Mesa Grande in San Diego County, California around 1900; of pristine condition, they were probably made for a collector. I later found examples of this thick protective sandal in many Southern California museums but was unable to uncover the exact manner of manufacture. Fiber wrapped around a twisted fiber loop tied at the toe I speculated, others felt an additional two heavy warps were used. Both ideas turned out to be wrong.

Normally, no foot covering at all was employed by Southern California Indians who went about most daily tasks barefoot, reserving the use of sandals for special purposes. It must have felt like pure luxury, however, when they did put on their thickly wrapped fiber sandals.

Examples of the true Southern California style extended from the Panamint Indians in the Great Basin, where they protected feet from mountain snow, through the Cahuilla east of Los Angeles, who called them *chawish* and where D.P. Barrows described them in constant use among the old people in 1900, to the Kiliwa of the northern Baja California San Pedro Martir mountains where they functioned as expedition sandals when traversing rough ground. This was the same function described for yucca-fiber sandals of the Gabrielino of Los Angeles. In the scant account we have of them from the Chumash, Fernando Librado told J.P. Harrington he wore them when the ground was hot so he would not blister his feet. Captain Newton H. Chittenden observed around 1901 that the Cocopah men of the Hardy and lower Colorado River wore rawhide sandals for ordinary service but made noiseless sandals of mescal (*agave*) fiber for deer hunting.

The Shivwits of Northwestern Arizona seem to have done it backwards. Made of the fibers of the yucca or Spanish bayonet, the two tie strings which normally came off the heel, came off the toe, passing one to the left and the other to the right of the second toe and pulled through a rear loop (the front

Paul Campbell has been following a personal goal of conserving the arts of the Pai people of the southwest before they are gone forever. He has collected over 40 traditional skills. His book, Survival Skills of Native California is th culmination of this collection. Available at the SPT Trading Post at primitive.org.

loop in the standard Southern California version) and back to the instep where they were tied. The heel rested against the rear loop as well as on the wrappings which normally formed the toe. Such sandals were worn on snow by men and women. In winter, bark was tied over the foot to the sandal by means of loops. If a man chased mountain sheep all day in the rocks, the sandals would be worn out by nightfall. Otherwise, they lasted longer it was said.

These are modern ethnographic accounts, but the idea of the fiber sandal was very old.

Antiquity of the Fiber Sandal

We shall find the Southern California fiber sandal known to ethnographers was constructed from a two-warp base. The archaeological record for two-warp fiber sandals in the Southwest is fascinating in itself, but the variety of materials and variations on the basic theme uncovered in cave excavations also suggest ways we might reproduce these sandals today in a field or survival situation.

Mashed yucca sandals somewhat similar to those of Southern California were described from Mogollon caves of west-central New Mexico during 1952 excavations conducted by the Chicago Natural History Museum. In the four caves dug, two sandals of this type were uncovered one of which was actually of grass. However, earlier excavations of Tularosa and Cordova caves, also Mogollon, had yielded other examples of these mashed yucca "two-warp wickerwork" sandals. In fact, at Tularosa Cave they came from all levels, down through the pre-pottery layer (probably before 200 AD). They were most common in the earlier strata. The warps were a

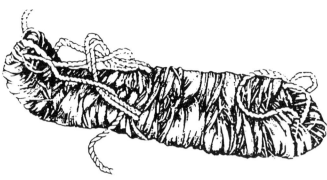

Cahuilla sandal collected in 1875. From Bean, 1978.

loop of yucca leaf knotted at the heel and toe in square knots; according to excavators those ends at the toe were then brought up to form toe ties. The ends of weft elements terminate on the undersole, frayed and provided added cushioning (as in the museum Diegueño examples). The most common sandal at the Mogollon sites, however, was of plaited yucca leaf.

The Hohokam two-warp wickerwork sandals found by Emil Haury in Ventana Cave were also made of yucca leaves; they were the most prominent sandal at the site and are considered the norm for the Hohokam. For warp, leaves were bent at the toe and tied at the heel. Other of the long, narrow yucca leaves were then woven back and forth, over and under the warp like a figure-8 and closely packed, the ends protrud-

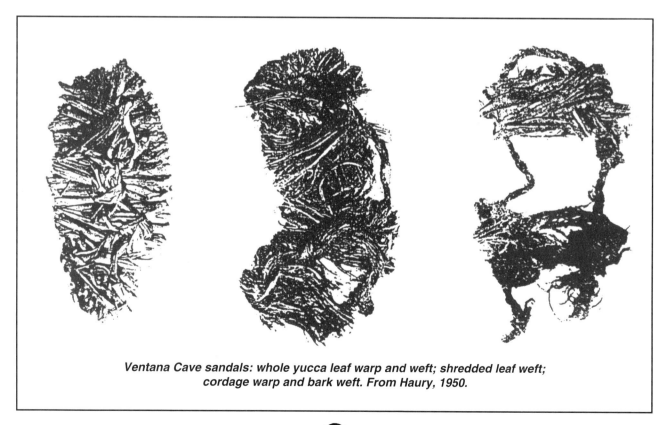

Ventana Cave sandals: whole yucca leaf warp and weft; shredded leaf weft; cordage warp and bark weft. From Haury, 1950.

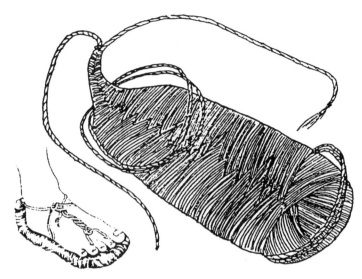

From Meigs, 1939.

ing on the underside. Most of the sandals used a whole yucca leaf weft although some were of macerated yucca leaf, a few of shredded wood and even two of bark strips. Cordage warp was also found with mashed yucca weft (4 examples) and one each of shredded wood, bark and gut weft. The evidence suggested that two-warp style sandals were worn as early as San Pedro times (which has been estimated to have lasted from around 1500 to 200 BC).

Anasazi Pueblo III sites have yielded a few two-warp wickerwork sandals but of a more rigid appearance with the ends of the weft elements extended over and frayed at the sides of the sandal.

Incidentally, Haury describes two other very different styles of sandals from Ventana cave. Fragments of a complex yucca sandal of rows or ovals of chain stitches, superficially like braids, sewed to a matted fiber sole and reinforced with cords at right angles to the "braids," heel and toe rounded in the general shape of a foot, were unique in Southwestern foot gear and apparently distinctive to the Hohokam. The other was as simple as this one seemed complex, being merely pads cut to the shape of a foot from the outer covering of the stem of the mature yucca. Yucca leaf stitching helped reinforce the tendency for the pads to pull apart into individual fibers or separate into layers. As ties for the foot, two shredded leaves of Yucca were stitched through the pad, one through holes a few inches apart in the front and another in back. Haury observed that these along with the other sandals demonstrated the Hohokam "willingness to improvise and test any possible raw products."

From Newberry Cave in the California Mojave Desert, archaeologists in the 1950's excavated split twig figurines dating to 3,500 years ago. The twig models of deer or sheep likely had been used in the magic of an old and far-flung hunter culture. Fragments of sandals of these hunters were found in the cave and were of the two-warp, figure-8 weft style. One was entirely of slender willow (*Salix exigua*)—the warp, a split twig twisted into two-ply cordage .8 cm in diameter and weft,

strips of bark .5 to 1.4 cm in width. Two-ply yucca cordage (.4 to .6 cm in diameter) formed the warp of other fragments with shredded juniper (*Juniperus*) bark weft. Two-ply Indian hemp cordage attached to one of the pieces probably served as binding to tie the sandal to the foot.

Fiber sandals of this sort were extremely ancient and widespread. At Etna Cave, Nevada, shredded yucca sandals of two-cord warp and figure-8 weft extended from the later Paiute occupation back to early Desert archaic, a spread of some eleven thousand years.

Chris Moser, Riverside Municipal Museum archaeologist, described to me two-warp wickerwork sandals from caves of the Mixteca in Oaxaca, deep in Mexico where he has conducted excavations. The loop sole frames were made of agave rope. He found that the remoter villages still manufactured such sandals. he also described the Mixtec process of releasing the maguey fibers. They would soak the leaf for perhaps a month, allowing the pulp to rot away and then scrape the leaf with a "turtle back" stone, such as found in archaeological sites; the stone has a rounded upper surface, a natural handhold and a sheared-off bottom, flat, like a plane, for scraping away the pulp. Afterwards, they returned the leaf to the water for another week or so to complete the rotting process until only clean, white fibers remained.

Precise Methods of Manufacture of the Southern California Fiber Sandal

Information on the Cahuilla from the early years of this century in J.P. Harrington's notes indicate that the Mojave yucca (*Yucca schidigera*) was an ideal source of fiber for coiled rope soles of sandals. Barrows found leaves of this as well as desert agave (*Agave deserti*) known as Mescal, were soaked until the pulpy part and the outer sheath came off; the resulting fibers were buried in mud to whiten them and combed out ready for use. The best fiber came from young green leaves.

In 1908 Alfred Kroeber wrote of a field trip to the Cahuilla, Serrano and Gabrielino east of Los Angeles and described sandals of mescal still in use, especially on the desert. He was told they were worn mainly by men outdoors at night. He admitted he could not understand their construction, but by 1925 Kroeber, who found no clear report of indigenous sandals north of Tehachapi, summarized the Southern California form of the southwestern sandal as untwisted bundles of mescal fiber woven back and forth across a looped cord forming a pad nearly an inch thick. While clear and concise, this hardly comprised a step by step description. Other anthropologists gave even less. How exactly were the sandals made?

It was not until I turned to an ethnographic account compiled by Peveril Meigs in the 1930s on the remote Kiliwa Indians, who are related to the Diegueño, that I found something resembling a complete process—from fiber preparation to sandal manufacture. Meigs wrote:

The most important plant fiber was extracted from the leaves of the mescal. It was used for making nets, footwear, and cordage for miscellaneous purposes.

In the preparation of the fiber, a pit is dug and thoroughly heated by a fire built in it. The hot coals are raked out and green mescal leaves are placed among the ashes in the hot pit and covered with earth. After baking for two or three hours, the leaves are removed from the pit and the outer husk is taken off. The fiber is then scraped clean by being pulled between a wooden surface and a small rounded piece of wood (a spoon in now used) which is pressed down upon the fiber. After being cleaned, the fiber is allowed to soak overnight in water and is then ready for use. While a fiber article is being manufactured, the supply of fiber is kept on dampened ground with damp earth piled upon it, and is

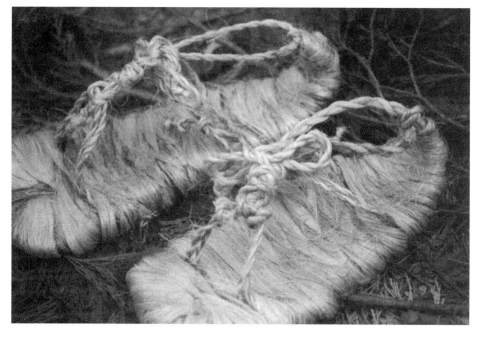

extracted from the pile as needed. The fibers are twisted into strands by being rubbed upon a piece of rawhide on the thigh of the operator. Two of these strands, still damp, are twisted together on the thigh to form a cord.

Maria, the old Japokelkawa mother of Emiliano, demonstrated the manufacture of mescal sandals. She showed great skill and produced an article of high workmanship. She first tied together the ends of a piece of two-strand cord, making a loop to serve as the framework of the sandal. Then, holding the loop to serve as the framework of the sandal. Then, holding the loop taut with fingers and great toe (keeping the knot under the toe), she wrapped a mass of fiber around the end of the loop nearest her, making a bulky ridge as wide as the foot, to serve as the toe of the sandal. Into this ridge she also wound the end of a heavy strand of fibers from which to make the sole of the sandal. She passed this strand around the middle of the toe ridge and wove it back and forth from side to side around the framework cord, keeping the sides of the

framework as far apart as the ball of the foot for which the sandal was intended. When the strand was woven as far as the base of the toes, she bound in a string loop, which would hold the toes of the wearer. When she had woven the strand as far as the beginning of the heel, she bound in a second double string loop. She then finished weaving the heel of the sole, making the heel part narrower than the ball part. The sole completed, she removed the cord from her toe, untied the knot, and with the two end pieces of cord took half-turns around the sides of the second string loop. To wear the sandals, the whole foot is thrust through the rear loop, leaving the outer toes outside of the front loop. The free ends of the framework cord are carried forward through the front loop, then brought back and tied together behind the ankle. The finished sandal is strong and symmetrical, with thick upturned end to protect the toes.

But even Meigs' wonderful description leaves questions unanswered. Leslie Spier's 1923 report on the Southern Diegueño who made similar sandals fills in most of the gaps. Spier learned from a very old man, Jim McCarty, living in Campo, California, near the Mexican border, that both men and women made agave sandals. They did not wear them around camp but for such things as collecting wood or embarking on journeys. Extra sandals were not taken when they traveled since they could make them quickly along the way—only about two hours for a pair.

Sandals (hamnyau´) are of two types: woven, the most used, and rawhide. The woven sandal is made of the long dry leaves of mescal (ema´l), which are pounded and soaked in water to remove the connective tissue. The separated fibers are thoroughly dried on a rock. For use, they are dampened and gently pounded with the mano. For the needed foundation and tie-cords, bundles of fibers are rolled on the thigh into loose strings (ikwi´p) about 45 cm. long and 1 cm. in diameter. To roll into a two-ply cord, two of these are placed side by side, the butt end of one opposite the tapering end of the other. Holding the two in the left hand, they are rolled separately on the right thigh by a single movement. of the right palm; when the left hand is released, the torque in each springs to the left causing them to twine as a two ply cord. Four loops of this cord, 40 cm. in circumference, and a fifth, 95 cm. in circumference, are tied with a square knot (these dimensions are for a child's sandal).

(more)

As the weaver sits on the ground, the large loop is stretched between foot and hand. The proximal end, destined for the toe of the sandal, is wrapped over a length of 8 cm. with bundles of loose fiber until it is 2 cm. in diameter (hutcuwa´wa, the beginning). The loose ends are fastened by twisting together. At this stage the work may be temporarily held by slipping the loop over the knee of under the heel of the disengaged foot. One of the small loops, intended for the toes (mixanuke, foot loop, mi, foot), is passed over the foundation cord, as shown (**Fig A**). A loose bundle of fibers is placed against this loop a second lapping it in the opposite direction, the two are woven together alternately over and under the foundation cord, and the whole pushed tightly against the toe portion. New bundles of fiber are added in pairs. The butt ends of the fibers are lapped; these ends protrude on the sole. The sandal is made the width of the palm. When the heel is neared a second small loop (miatiksaxanuke, heel loop) is introduced in the same way as the toe-loop. The weaving (we´kwil) is continued, but the sandal is made narrower, introducing but one bundle of fibers at a time. When the length is completed, the wefts are forced up on the foundation cord as tightly as possible. A sandal must not be too long, else it will slip and chafe. The ends of the foundation cord are then half-tied and carried through the heel loop, drawing the heel sharply upward (**Fig. B**). To tie on the sandal, the ends of this tie-cord (miuso´la) are brought forward around the ankle, through the toe loop, wrapped twice about itself, and tied (**Fig. C**).

Study of the Kiliwa and the Diegueño accounts reveals expected variations in fiber preparation, weaving, and tying the sandal to the foot, and yet they are essentially the same. Perhaps most amazing, Spier's informant told him that the agave sandal is reversible! In fact, it must be turned over frequently to prevent its wearing out. To accomplish this the toe and heel loops are pulled through the sole and the tie-cord retied to them on the opposite side.

These accounts together supply enough detail to allow

us to actually duplicate the ancient fiber sandal of the Californias. From the Kiliwa comes the function and the construction of the toe, from the Southern Diegueño the importance of forcing the wefts up tightly on the foundation cord. Spier wrote that so tight were they woven that neither stick nor thorn could puncture them We might add Kroeber's observation that Cahuilla toe strings passed either on the two sides of the second toe or to the sides of the second and third toes and that the sandal was tied to allow the foot to slip in without retying each time the sandal was worn.

Still certain other details eluded me. For example, were the bundles of fibers used each equivalent to a single agave leaf? Did the foundation cords taper to a slightly smaller diameter as they became tie cords? Museum examples look as though they do. The complete answer seemed so close and yet so far. I should have been born one hundred years ago. Then a miracle happened. I found in the summer of 1993, in the Pai Pai village of Santa Catarina, a woman who still remembered the old ways. The lower California Pai Pai are closely related to the Southern Diegueño and intermarry extensively with the Kiliwa. When I mentioned agave fiber sandals to Manuela Aguiar Carrillo she effacingly tried to think if she knew anyone who could still make them. Eufemio Sandoval had overheard my question and said, "Why *you* Manuela know how." A little coaxing and she agreed to make a pair for me. These turned out to be very different indeed. They were *made* as the sewed sandals of Ventana Cave only appeared: true braids of agave fiber were stitched together with agave cords into an oval sole. Very ingenious and perhaps an important discovery. The Southern Paiute of the upper Colorado River, known for their love of distance travel for its own sake, make bark or yucca sandals of similar long looped braids; these were held together with open twining.

A few weeks later I tried again. I found an ancient Diegueño woman in the mountains of Baja who still gathered acorns, ground them in bedrock mortars and sifted the flour in coiled juncus baskets she made herself, but when asked of fiber sandals could only reply, they are all dead—those who knew how are all dead.

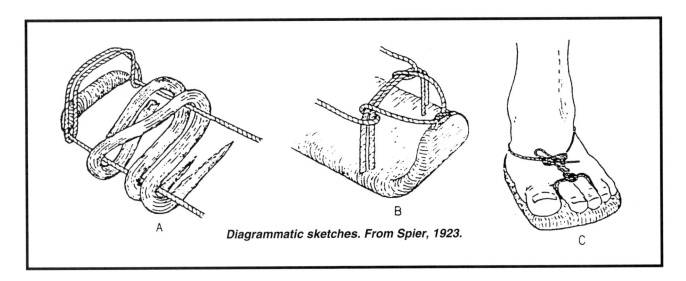

Diagrammatic sketches. From Spier, 1923.

A   B   C

REFERENCES

Alvarez de Williams, Anita.
1975   **Travelers Among the Cucapa.** *Dawson's Book Shop, Los Angeles.*

Barrows, David Prescott.
1900   **The ethno-botany of the Coahuilla Indians of Southern California,** *University of Chicago Press, Chicago.*

Bean, Lowell John.
1978   *Cahuilla,* in **Handbook of North American Indians, Vol. 8 California,** *Smithsonian Institution, Washington.*

Davis, C. Alan and Gerald A. Smith.
1981   **Newberry Cave.** *San Bernardino County Museum Association, Redlands.*

Haury, Emil W.
1950   **The Stratigraphy and Archaeology of Ventana Cave Arizona,** *University of Arizona Press.*

Hudson, Travis and Thomas C. Blackburn.
1979   *The Material Culture of the Chumash Interaction Sphere.* **Vol III: Clothing, Ornamentation, and Grooming.** *Santa Barbara Museum of Natural History, Santa Barbara.*

Johnston, Bernice Eastman.
1962   **California's Gabrielino Indians.** *Southwest Museum, Los Angeles.*

Kelly, Isabel T. and Catherine S. Fowler.
1978   *Southern Paiute,* in **Handbook of North American Indians, Vol. 9,** *Smithsonian Institution, Washington.*

Kroeber, A.L.
1908   *Ethnography of the Cahuilla Indians.* **University of California Publications in American Archaeology and Ethnology.** *Vol. 6.*
1925   **Handbook of the Indians of California.** *Bureau of American Ethnology, Washington, DC. Bul. 78.*

Lowie, Robert H.
1924   *Notes on Shoshonean Ethnography.* **Anthropological Papers of the American Museum of Natural History. Vol XX, part III.**

Martin, Paul S. et al.
1954   *Mogollon Cultural Continuity and Change: The Stratigraphic Analysis of Tularosa and Cordova Cave.* **Fieldiana: Anthropology, Vol 42.** *Chicago Natural History Museum, Chicago.*
1954   *Caves of the Reserve Area.* **Fieldiana: Anthropology, Vol 42.** *Chicago Natural History Museum, Chicago.*

Meigs, Peveril III.
1939   *The Kiliwa Indians of Lower California.* **Ibero-Americana 15.** *University of California, Berkeley.*

Spier, Leslie.
1923   *Southern Diegue~no Customs.* **University of California Publication in America Archaeology and Ethnology 20.**

Wheeler, S.M.
1942   **Archaeology of Etna Cave,** *Lincoln County, Nevada. Nevada State Park Commission, Carson City.*

The Kon Tule crossing San Francisco Bay.

Norm Kidder

LIGHT ON THE SUBJECT OF CAVE ART
By Maria-Louise Sidoroff

Could a lamp made from a fist-size chunk of stone with a natural depression to cradle a lump of animal fat and a lichen wick throw enough light to allow an ice age artist to create his magic design on a cave wall? Sophie de Beaune, University of Paris, designed a fascinating series of experiments to explore this question. She first examined hundreds of stone lamps from 105 different upper Paleolithic sites with dates between 40,000 and 11,000 years ago. They had all been excavated from caves, rock shelters and camp sited in Southwest France, a region of spectacular cave art from the same period. Next de Beaune created working replicas of the ice age fat burning stone lamps "in order to analyze their effectiveness as a light source and to learn about their design, function and use."

Dr. de Beaune's methods and results are detailed in a **_Scientific American_** (March 1993) article co-authored with Randall White, Associate Professor of Anthropology at New York University.

The lamps were most commonly carved out of limestone or sandstone and can be separated into three main categories. Open-circuit lamps were unaltered slabs of rock in which the melted fat runs off through the natural crevices of the rock. This category was found to be wasteful of fuel. Closed circuit lamps, the most common types, consisted of entirely natural, slightly modified or completely fabricated bowls holding up to 10cc of melted fat. Closed circuit lamps with a carved handle were the most intricate with a finely shaped bowl and formed extensions which served as handles.

Chemical analysis of residues in the lamps proved that animal fat, not vegetable oil, was the source of fuel. De Beaune replicated each type of lamp and conducted experiments to clarify how those objects were used in Paleolithic times. The closed circuit lamp with gently sloping sides in the bowl was optimally efficient and wicks made of lichen, moss or juniper bark worked best. Fat from seals, horses and cattle proved most effective in the experiments because they melt quickly and at a low temperature allowing the wick "to absorb the melted fat by capillary attraction and conveying it to the free end without too rapidly consuming itself."

The light output of the replicated lamps was measured in a laboratory and a single lamp proved to generate distinctly less light than a standard candle. This indicated that torches or some other source of light provided additional illumination within the deeper caves. De Beaune's work demonstrated that it would take 10 or 15 stone lamps to provide minimum light for an artist to see clearly enough to paint, perhaps a bison, on the irregular surface of a cave wall. The very dimness of the light may have enhanced the drama of the picture.

Let us imagine an ice-age audience, accustomed to noticing subtleties in the low light of caves, standing before the wall. The tiny flames from several carefully placed lamps play light and shadow on the drawing giving the animal the appearance of vibrating with life. As de Beaune suggests "the dim illumination produced by the flickering lamps may well have been part of the desired effect of viewing art deep within a cave.

LAMP DESIGNS fall into three main categories. Open-circuit lamps (top) consists of largely unaltered slabs of rock. When the lamp is lit, melted fat runs off through natural crevices in the rock. Closed-circuit lamps (middle) have carved depressions to contain the runoff. Carved-handle, closed-circuit lamps (bottom) also have large, shaped fuel chambers but are more finely finished and have formed extensions for easier handling. Burn marks indicate that the wick was placed away from the handle.

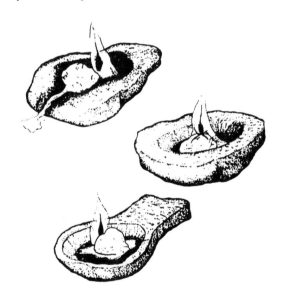

Drawings from <u>Scientific American.</u>
Reprinted by permission of the author.

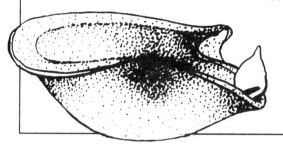

THE CLAY LAMP
By Maria-Louise Sidoroff

This very ancient style of clay lamp designed to burn olive oil was used in the Middle East up until 20 or 30 years ago. Similar lamps, found in excavations dating as far back as 4,000 BC, were modeled by hand and later formed on the potter's wheel. For thousands of years the basic elements of this elegantly simple design remained the same. A small fired clay bowl contains about 1/2 cup of olive oil with a pinched lip to channel the wick.

Step 1 - Form a lump of clay, about the size of a large orange, into a smooth ball.

Step 2 - Press a thumb down through the center of the clay to create a shaft while supporting the ball in your hand.

Step 3 - Use only your thumb to enlarge the lower section of the shaft, thin the walls but be sure to leave a thick ring of clay at the rim.

Step 4 - Place the clay on a flat surface and gently stretch to form a low, wide bowl keeping the rim thick.

Step 5 - Stretch the thick rim into a ledge all around the bowl with the thumb and pointer finger. Eliminate any cracks in the clay with a slightly moistened shell or smooth stick. Excessive water softens the clay and it will not hold a shape.

Step 6 - (This is the tricky part) To stretch the ledge into a spout, first slightly moisten the area that you plan to shape into the channel to hold the wick.

Step 7 - Coax the ledge and the upper part of the bowl into a spout with two fingers of one hand. Support the rest of the ledge with two fingers of the other hand to prevent distortion.

Step 8 - Set the lamp aside to air-dry for about a week.

Step 9 - Heat the lamp next to a campfire to drive off any excess moisture and then roll it among the hot coals, stack wood around in a teepee shape and cook for an hour. This firing can also be done in a fireplace or a cast iron stove.

Step 10 - Allow the lamp to cool in the ashes, fill with olive oil, place one end of the wick curled in the oil and the other end projecting along the channel . . . and light up your cave.

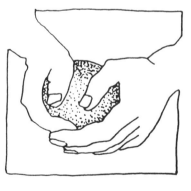

STEP 1

STEP 2

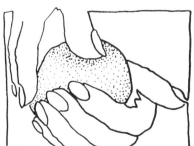

STEP 3

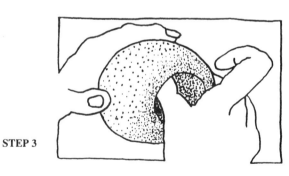

STEP 4

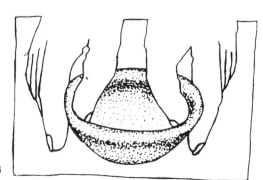

HOW TO MAKE A WICK
By Pamela Janus Weiland

I would suggest the resinous bark of the red cedar or basswood for wicks in experiments with oil or fat burning lamps. Bark is easily removed in the spring, before the sap flows. However, stripping trees completely of bark will kill the tree, so look for uprooted dead trees at construction sites, contact tree surgeons or local tree trimmers. Some bark remains in good condition long after the tree dies. Bark can be worked fresh or dried for storage and then soaked for use. The bark of red cedar can be soaked in water or pounded with sticks to soften the fibers. Soaking will not leach out the resins which make the bark especially suited for wicks. The prepared bark can be twisted or braided into cordage which should serve well as a wick for a fat or oil burning lamp. The fibrous, thick leaves of yucca might also be a good choice for experiments.

Pamela Janus Weiland, owner of Ozark Basketry Supplies, P.O. Box 599, Fayetteville, Arkansas 72702, Phone: (501) 442-9292, will send you her new catalog for $1.00. The catalog offers many types of bark, including red cedar and basswood, along with a wide selection of basket making supplies.

Errett Callahan

"These photos are from a project done by art students at Virginia Commonwealth University in 1974-75. The style was similar to European cave art. We tested a variety of techniques and materials: oil paints, home-made paints using powdered pigments and animal grease, charcoal with and without grease, and pecked indentations. We followed the lines and humps in the rocks wherever we could, using our artist's eye to guide us. Some printings were huge. As these were exercises and not experiments, no records were kept.

NOTE: All our work was done on the walls of modern (post Civil War) rock quarries, usually granite, in Richmond, VA. The walls were exposed to weather. I checked on them every few years and watched them fade, until on my last visit, about 10 years after, no trace was left".

Errett Callahan

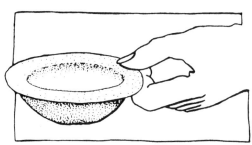

STEP 5

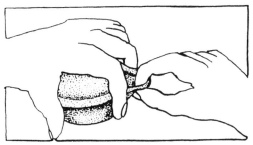

STEP 6

Errett Callahan

Conquering The Darkness:
Primitive Lighting Methods
Text, Photos and Illustration By Benjamin Pressley

Photo 1: Author Benjamin Pressley exploring cave with Bamboo torch made from materials found in the wild.

The archaeological record abounds with evidence of prehistoric cave exploration throughout the Midwest, Mid-south and Northeastern U.S. and throughout the world. Pre-historic people went deep into the interior of the longest cave in the world. They gathered resources and sometimes just explored. During the latter part of the prehistoric period it is apparent that some caves became sacred places where ceremonies were held.

In many caves, such as Wyandotte Cave in Indiana, burned fragments of bark torches, bound with bits of cordage are found strewn along a path where chert nodules for stone tool making have been removed. Fragments of cane torches and bark fibers that have been burned are found beside bare footprints that are said to be 3000 years old or more in Mammoth Cave. Evidence is apparent that minerals such as gypsum and various sulfates, perhaps for paint, were gathered by explorers of old.

How did ancient people light up the night or how did they conquer the rule of darkness in the cavernous depths of the earth? It is evident that indeed they did, for on cave walls all around the world they have left a legacy of artwork still spectacular even to this day. Magnificent frescoes depict a world gone by, yet they have never seen the light of day.

Whether exploring a cave or needing to light a trail or camp in the dark, a knowledge of primitive lighting methods is a valuable skill to know. Intrigued by the possibilities of exploring yet another skill of the past, not to mention the usefulness of such a skill in a survival situation, I began my own experiments into ancient lighting methods. Making light, like making fire, requires drawing upon a practical under-standing and skill with fire. As any good fire builder knows, you must keep a constant supply of good, dry tinder, kindling and fuel on hand to nurture a fire, if you are to keep a fire burning. It is no different when using fire for light.

Pine pitch is very useful as a lighting fuel. Pine pitch is easily gathered as it oozes and solidifies on the trunk of injured pine trees. James Parker came up with a handy way of collecting pitch by cutting short lengths of River Cane, sharp-ening a point on the open end and leaving the other end solid. Drive this gathering container under the bark of a pine tree at an angle and into the cambium layer of the tree. You can come back at a later date for a container of useful pine pitch. However, pine pitch does smoke a lot and it will drip and

(more)

Ben Pressley is the host of the Primitive Technolgy home page at http://ic.net/~tbailey/Primitive.html. He is an ac-tive networker with other primitive technologists, and dedicates a great deal of time to the field through teach-ing and experience.

seriously burn anyone unfortunate enough to get it on their skin. In fact, I have even seen it burn through a leather shoe. For this reason a stick coated on one end and built up by dipping the stick in hot, melted pitch and cooled, until you have a ball of pitch built up on one end (much like making candle), and then lighting this mass and carrying it like a torch is NOT a good idea. A better use for pine pitch, whether torch or campfire, is mixing it in with some other fuel as a tinder to keep a fire going. One very handy application I discovered from my early experiments is a combination of cedar bark rolled up into a ball with fresh pine pitch. This combination ball may then be placed in a lamp made of shell and is easily blown into a flame from an ember. It casts a lot of light and the compactness of the ball seems to slow down the rate of burning to the point I was getting 45 minute burns out of a golf ball sized piece. Rolling it in cedar bark after kneading in fluffy cedar bark also makes them less messy to carry. If you want to keep them pliable so you can pinch smaller pieces off of them, add some bee's wax to the mixture. These little balls are also great for fire starters under wet conditions.

A lamp may also be fashioned by pecking a hollowed depression into a stone. Pecking is done by striking a soft stone with a harder stone until the depression you need is achieved. A Quartzite or Diabase pebble will usually do well as a tool for pecking. Soapstone or Steatite are probably the easiest stones to use for pecking out a depression (Photo 2). Hundreds of lamps made of limestone and sandstone have been excavated from Paleolithic sites in Southwest France, where some of the most spectacular cave art is found. Limestone is a good choice because it conducts heat poorly, so lamps of this material don't get hot enough to burn the user. Sandstone on the other hand conducts heat very well. Perhaps this is why most Sandstone lamps found archaeologically have handles carved onto them. Often, a rock may be found with a natural depression. Just make sure it is a closed circuit depression - it doesn't have crevices where melted fat could run out and be wasted. You can use other containers, such as a gourd, if you have any. Filling this depression with rendered animal fat or vegetable oil and adding a wick into it makes a lamp that works very well. Vegetable oil burns much cleaner and with less smoke than animal fat. I particularly like burning olive oil in my lamps. Chemical analysis from Paleolithic lamps examined always revealed the use of animal fats, never vegetable oils. Fat from seals, horses and cattle prove to be the most effective. The consideration here is that the particular fat being used melted quickly and at a low temperature allowing the wick to absorb the melted fat by capillary action all the way to the burning end at a rate faster than the wick consumed itself. So, for maximum efficiency, make sure the wick in your lamp is just long enough to have one end in the fuel, not coiled up in the fuel. You must keep the flame from being drowned by excess fuel. Pecking out a slot for the wick to lie in while one end dangles down into the fat and the other end is lit, works very well. A wick may be as simple as lichen or a piece of moss that will absorb the fat as it floats. A wick also may be fashioned by simply hand-twisting a two-ply strand of cordage from cedar bark you have stripped from the

side of a tree, rubbed between the palms and fluffed up. If you have cattail down to cord in with it, all the better. A Mullein leaf that has been dried and rolled up works unbelievably well as a wick, also. Alternatively, like the modern Inuit people still do, a piece of fat may be burned on a stone slab; fast, effective, but inefficient. As far as light goes, stone, fat-burning lamps generate less light than the average candle. Steve Watts came up with a wick idea that works as well as any wick I've tried and it is very simple and a variation on the Paleo clump style wick. He takes a pinch of Cattail fluff saturated in the oil and then pinches it above the surface of the oil and lights it.

A torch I particularly like to use is a Hickory bark torch. I have seen this torch burn for as long as 2 hours in cave exploration. This torch is a combination of green and dry strips of hickory bark and a core of an easily combustible material that keeps a constant supply of tinder furnished to the torch. I use broom sedge for my tinder in this particular torch and bind it at various intervals (Photo 3), tight enough to keep it

Photo 3: Preparing a torch made from Hickory bark strips with broom sedge as a tinder in the center.

from burning up too quickly. It is lit easily with a small flame and can be blown on when more light is needed. This torch performed very well for me in Langdon's Cave, near Wyanndotte Cave in Indiana. Another version of this torch can be made by using lengths of River Cane instead of bark. If wide lengths of dry bark, such as are easily obtained from a birch or poplar tree, are available, just roll up a dried length and stuff it full of the tinder. You may find that the bark of the birch may burn fairly easily without stuffing it full of tinder. I like the extra insurance, myself. Bark may also be folded accordion-style and secured in-between a split green stick and tied. This type of torch is used among the far northern people as a

Photo 4: Two torches made from materials found in the wild. Left: Bamboo, beaten on one end and stuffed full of broom sedge and bark, then bound. Right: Lengths of Rivercane bound with broomsedge and barks in the center.

night fishing torch. Strips of River Cane bound together or just hand-held, without any additional tinder, work very well (Photo 4). They light easily and burn very brightly. As they char at the top this is easily knocked off without putting out the flame. That these type of torches were used by primitive peoples in cave explorations is apparent, for there are burned cane fragments found in cavern floors and burned places on the ceilings where they knocked the charred material from the burning ends of their torches, in caves such as Mammoth Cave.

I have also used a mini-torch made from an 8 inch section of Bamboo with another 6 inch section for a handle, open on both ends. Filling it with melted pitch, does not work very well. When lit, it will burn until it gets less than an inch below the lip of the Bamboo section and goes out, starved for oxygen. It also drips badly for all torches must be held at an angle and away from the body, to some extent. What I found that works better is to use pine pitch that is full of pine bark fragments and heat it to the point that it is just clumpy, or gather it fresh, not worrying about cleaning it out. After cutting the bamboo, beat the end that will receive the pitch and bind it around the middle to keep it from splitting all the way down as you beat it. Take a stick and stuff this clumpy mixture into the beaten cavity and then further bind the section containing the pitch. This leaves 'vents' and when lit with a small flame it burns for a length of 45 minutes or more! A larger version of this torch may be made using a longer length of Bamboo and using less pine pitch and

mostly some easy burning tinder like broom sedge, grapevine or other dry barks. I remember exploring Langdon's Cave with the pine pitch mini-torches. Like prehistoric people of old, they left a trail of little lamps glowing behind us as if to light our way back and once when dropped in a puddle were easily re-lit by the flame from another torch.

It was fascinating to explore a subterranean world lit with torches fashioned only from what nature had to offer. An adventure we all will not soon forget and will repeat in other caves.

Steve Watts came up with a torch that I really like (Fig. 1). He cut a length of bamboo leaving two sections connected. one end was left open and filled with oil (olive oil works well, but any oil or fat that burns will work). A dry cattail seed-head was then saturated with the same oil and forced down into the reservoir of oil. When lit, the cattail head makes a very fine wick and altogether makes a very neat torch that does not drip and burns very cleanly, depending on the oil you use.

Cattail and Mullein seed heads perform fairly well when dipped in animal fat or bee's wax or even paraffin. This is allowed to cool and when lit, burns like a candle of sorts. The soft, pithy core of some plants works well as wicks or as candles. Plants that work well for this purpose are Mullein, Elder and soft rush stalks. The pithy center of the soft rush was once dipped in tallow and sold commercially as cheap rush-light candles (Photo 5). To make one of these 'rush-lights', pick tall, mature stems and cut them into sections the length you wish, one foot works well. Carefully peel away the tough outer part leaving enough at one end to hold the tender pith together. Dry these stems and then immerse them in grease, melted fat or any suitable oil that does not evaporate. Set aside to cool, and they are ready when you need them. A one foot length will burn for 10-20 minutes. During Medieval times strips of enriched pine (fat lighter) were lit and held in the mouth for light to read by.

As with any skill, take time to experiment in advance. Try out some of these lights. Have fun with them and you will have a good working knowledge when you need it.

Photo 5: Mullein Candles made by James Parker.

PRIMITIVE LIGHTING METHODS
By Benjamin Pressley
--1996--

Dry Cattail Seed Head Wick
Saturated With Oil

Oil Reservoir

Length of Bamboo

Paleo, Clump Style Wick
Saturated in oil and pinched above surface of oil. Wick can be as simple as Cattail fluff or can be an absorbent moss that floats and soaks up oil as it burns or a wick can be twisted from Cedar Bark or Jute and hung out of oil and lit.

Pecked Out Depression
Filled with oil

Pecked Out Stone Oil Lamp

Oil Lamps

Photo 2: Various Lamps
Left to right: Shell with twisted wick in animal fat; Shell with ball of Pine pitch and cedar bark; Soapstone with pecked out depression with wick made from twisted Jute in vegetable oil; Shell with ball of Pine pitch and Cedar bark; Soapstone with pecked out depression with wick made from twisted Cedar bark and Cattail fluff in vegetable oil.

Section 7

BACK TO BASICS
Tools Through Time

THE LOWER PALEOLITHIC
2,000,000 YEARS AGO

Vignette By Steve Watts, © 1996

*More and more often now, they came down from the trees.
Driven by a rising curiosity which surfaced again and again in
an ever expanding brain. Down...down to the ground with its tall
grass. Risking it all...for food and fascination.*

*Armed with cleverness and the ability to stand alone with eyes above the
swaying seedheads, they ventured out. Pushing back the boundaries of their
unknowns, moving further and further into the dark domain of the Big Cats.
They
watched from hilltop, boulder and sandy rise. They knew the sabertooth's gifts...
the Power and the Edges.
The power of shoulders, legs and paws to climb, and run and grab and hold.
The power of jaws to crush and splinter. A power far beyond their own.
And the edges...teeth and claws to stab and rip, to sever and slice.
Edges...edges of power far beyond their own.*

*Only on the ground could they have discovered the Key. Only here...the place
between Ape and man...here within their sight, within their grasp,
lay...the Stone. Lifting it up, they forged their futures and wrote our pasts.
Striking one against another, they exposed the keenness within.
Talisman and tool were born in the same instant.
The Power and the Edge was now theirs.*

HOMO ERECTUS

Bipedalism...First tools fashioned by man...Bipolar and percussion stone working techniques used to produce simple flake tools, choppers and hand axes...Expedient digging,
hacking and cutting tools of stone, bone, shell and wood...Scavenging, gathering and
hunting of plant and animal resources...Earliest known evidence of simple wood-frame
shelters...Beginnings of control of fire...Earliest throwing sticks and stones...Expedient,
chopped, scraped, ground and firehardened spears...Nut cracking and smashing of bone for
marrow extraction...First evidence of organized big game hunts...Habitation of Old World
tropics and temperate zones.

THE FIRE WATCHERS
By John J. Shea

On the Deceptive Simplicity of Lower Paleolithic Tools

The Lower Paleolithic began around 2.5 million years ago in Africa with hominids whose behavior does not appear far removed from that of chimpanzees. It ended around 200,000 years ago with large-brained humans distributed throughout Africa, Europe, and Asia. By any standard, the Lower Paleolithic is a crucial period for understanding the course of human evolution. Most archaeologists divide the Lower Paleolithic around 1.7 million years ago into an earlier "Oldowan" phase characterized by assemblages of pebble cores and their by-products and a later "Acheulian/Developed Oldowan" phase during which larger, more symmetrical, and more extensively flaked tools augment the more basic range of Oldowan forms. Because of their durability, stone tools comprise the primary documents for the Lower Paleolithic period, and archaeologists who work on the Lower Paleolithic employ ethnographic analogy, contextual clues (lithic microwear, stone tool cut marks on bone), and feasibility/replication studies to wring behavioral information from the lithic archaeological record (Isaac 1986; Schick and Toth 1993).

Replicating Lower Paleolithic tools is an experience shared by virtually everyone who flintknaps. Detach a few flakes from a stream cobble, and violá, you have created a chopper, discoid, or polyhedron that could fit comfortably among any of the thousands of stone tools excavated from Lower Paleolithic sites in Africa, Europe, or Asia. In fact, as an archaeologist teaching in a university, I often illustrate the principles of Lower Paleolithic stone typology by having students bash away at quartzite cobbles for a few minutes, then classify the products of their labors using one of the typological frameworks for describing archaeological stone tools (Leakey 1971). Students generally find this a valuable experience, notwithstanding the occasional bruised finger or broken fingernail, and it is a perfect occasion to instruct conchoidal fracture mechanics, typology, technology, refitting, spatial patterning of debitage, and any number of other issues relevant to an archaeological curriculum.

Increasingly, however, I have observed that such "hands-on" exercises with stone tool technology subtly reinforce an overly simple view of the hominid behavior behind the Lower Paleolithic archaeological evidence. The lesson many students take away from these experiences is that if the tools these early hominids produced were so simple, then it follows that the mentality, technological repertoire, and ecological adaptations of early hominids must also have been relatively simple as well. Such an assumption implies that (1) early hominids were just as much obligatory tool-users as we are, and (2) that the most durable elements of their technology (stone tools in most cases) accurately monitor the maximum degree of technological sophistication of which these hominids were capable. Applied to a Lower Paleolithic archaeological record in which basic tool forms persist for millions of years, these assumptions support the hypothesis that lithic technology is largely irrelevant to questions about early phases of hominid behavioral evolution. If these assumptions are correct, then we may profitably move on to other lines of evidence about hominid behavior, such as the spatial structure of archaeological residues (Potts 1991) or the faunal record (Stiner 1993), but if these assumptions are wrong, then we risk erroneously excluding a potentially valuable class of archaeological evidence.

Even a superficial examination of the physical anthropological evidence allows one to reject the assumption of parity between modern humans' and earlier hominids' need for stone tools. The cortical bone thickness of earlier hominids (*Australopithecus, paranthropus*, and early forms of *Homo*) are much greater than those of living humans when scaled for body size (Trinkaus 1987). From these anatomical contrasts it follows that Early and Middle Pleistocene hominids were also much stronger than living humans. Given that tool production adds cost (time and calories) to the performance of any task, it seems reasonable to suppose that earlier hominids used their great strength to accomplish many tasks for which modern humans must use complex tools.

The nature of the relationship between cognitive sophistication and stone tool technology is more problematical. Inasmuch as tools theoretically improve one's ability to manipulate the physical environment, one would expect strong natural selection for increased dependence on tools and increasing technological complexity. Yet, this expectation is plainly at variance with the imperceptibility of Lower

(more)

John J. Shea is Assistant Professor of Anthropology at the State University of New York at Stony Brook (NY 11794-4364). His research focuses on lithic evidence for human behavior during the Pleistocene. He is currently excavating the Lower Paleolithic site of 'Ubeidiya, in Israel. He may be reached at: Anthropology Department, State University of New York at Stony Brook, Stony Brook, NY 11794-4364.

Paleolithic technological change over the course of millions of years and across widely-varying ecosystems ranging from tropical savanna to arctic tundra. For many prehistorians, explanations for the "overwhelming monotony" of the Lower Paleolithic (Jelinek 1977: 28) focus on a degree of cognitive conservatism categorically different from that apparent among modern *Homo sapiens* after 40,000 BP (Donald 1991; Klein 1995; Lieberman 1991; Mithen 1995). These hypotheses cannot be rejected, but neither, unfortunately, can they be tested with the archaeological evidence. Before we can accept such hypotheses as explanations for the stability of Lower Paleolithic technology, it is worth considering alternatives hypotheses.

What behavioral factors might militate so strongly against technological change for millions of years among small, isolated hominid populations? One possibility is that Lower Paleolithic technologies emphasized versatility at the expense of efficiency. As such, Lower Paleolithic tools would be deceptively simple, their form reflecting conscious design compromise, tools designed to function adequately in a variety of tasks, rather than optimally in a narrower range of tasks. One benefit of a technological strategy emphasizing tool versatility is that by using fewer tools it minimizes energetic costs associated with materials procurement, manufacturing time, transport, and repair. The time and energy saved by such a strategy could then be shifted to subsistence, mating, and child-rearing, activities with direct evolutionary fitness consequences. If such a re-allocation was possible, then one would expect there to have been powerful natural selection reinforcements for this technological strategy. The latter consideration may play a significant role in the millennial stability of Lower Paleolithic technological adaptations.

Admittedly, one major cost of such a strategy is that tools perform sub-optimally in certain tasks, but this is only a significant consideration if tools are being used constantly and to the extreme outer limits of their mechanical tolerance. If tools were being used constantly, one would expect to find preferential selection of high-quality raw materials, to find these materials transported from one foraging range to another, and to find evidence for prolonged use. Instead, Lower Paleolithic assemblages consist overwhelmingly of whatever conchoidally-fracturing rock is most immediately at hand, and evidence for movement of raw materials more than a day's walk from geological sources is vanishingly small. Acheulian handaxes with extensive flaking suggest some degree of curation, but in this respect they virtually stand alone among Lower Paleolithic tools, and it is important to keep in mind that Acheulian bifaces actually comprise only a small percentage of the stone tools recovered from Lower Paleolithic contexts. Pebble-cores and simple flake tools comprise the overwhelming majority of Lower Paleolithic stone tools. The fact that pebble cores and flake tools essentially indistinguishable from Lower Paleolithic tools continue to be part of lithic assemblages through the Middle and Upper Paleolithic, into the Holocene (Gamble 1986: 278; Rosen 1996) and are still made in many parts of the world today (Gould 1980) is testament to the persistent need for versatile technological strategies.

The principal objection to such a view of the Lower Paleolithic as the product of versatility-optimizing technological strategies is that such strategies demand greater cognitive sophistication than those of which we suspect early hominids were capable. After all, it is arguably a far more complex problem to devise a tool suitable for future tasks whose eventuality can only be evaluated probabilistically that to match an existing tool to a task whose requirements are immediately at hand. Yet, the presumed link between changes in hominid cognitive abilities and variation in hominid brain size/structure rests largely on endocasts of hominid crania that provide only a rough guide to the actual neural circuitry of hominid brains (Deacon 1992; Holloway 1985). Indeed, one analysis of Acheulian technology using a Piagetian model of cognitive development has suggested a modern degree of operational intelligence was well in place nearly 1.7 million years ago (Wynn 1991). This conclusion suggests that differences between Lower Paleolithic tools and those of more recent Paleolithic periods may reflect shifts in strategic goals of technological adaptations rather than necessarily profound changes in hominid cognitive abilities. If the interpretation of the evidence advanced here is correct, and if complex technological strategies were already in place at the very beginning of the Paleolithic, then we may need to cast about elsewhere for the ultimate causes of Lower Paleolithic industrial variability. Experimentation with "primitive" technology can contribute to this search by reminding us just how much can be accomplished through the clever, dexterous and intelligent use of simple tools.

The Handaxe.

David Wescott

Paleo 'Bashed' Tools - A Story

Text and Illustrations By Chas. Spear, © 1996

Pick up a rock. Any rock will do. Well, almost any rock. Soft rocks such as grainy sandstones will not work very well. That's the beauty of this type of tool. Half the fun is searching for the best rocks until you learn by sight what will make good bashed tools.

What is a bashed tool? Webster defines "bash" as- to strike; to strike with a violent blow; to smash. A "tool" is any object apart from the body used to perform work or a specific task. A bashed tool is a tool created by striking a violent blow. The object of this bashing is a stone.

Let's look at a scenario. You are thrust into an environment similar to that of paleo-man. It is the first day. You have very little in the way of belongings. You are either naked or clothed minimally with plant fibers stripped and woven or the skins from animal you killed with your bare hands. You are in need of a shelter to avoid the eventual elements. Your tool kit lay in a stream in the form of smooth water-smoothed stones and pebbles. (A)

You walk down to the stream and pick up several random stones. With each you strike the end against another larger stone in the stream. The end of the cobble

flies off, revealing a sharp edge and a corresponding flake with a sharp edge. (B) Until now you have not created a tool until you pick up the flake and use it to cut into the bass fibers of a nearby tree, pulling off the long soft plant fibers scarping away the outer bark as you proceed. (C) These you roll and twist into cordage. When you have prepared enough you begin to pull two saplings together and bind them into an arch. This process is repeated until you have created the framework of a 'wickiup'.

When this is completed you take the bashed stone and strike it again on the same end but on the opposite side near the first flake scar. You reverse it

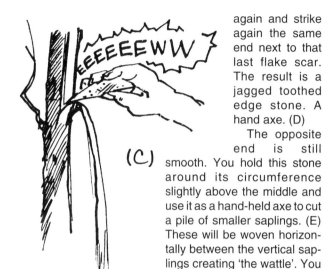

again and strike again the same end next to that last flake scar. The result is a jagged toothed edge stone. A hand axe. (D)

The opposite end is still smooth. You hold this stone around its circumference slightly above the middle and use it as a hand-held axe to cut a pile of smaller saplings. (E) These will be woven horizontally between the vertical saplings creating 'the wattle'. You are done with the hand axe so you discard it. The two additional new flakes (F) are kept to cut handfuls of grasses that are woven into a shingled thatch roof between the frame work supports, starting at the lower end of the roof and progressing towards the peak or top. The wattle spaces are then loosely filled with debris such as leaves and humus litter. This will provide insulation. A small opening is left in the hut to provide a draft for the fire which will vent through a smoke hole near the back of the dwelling. This opening is of equal area to the door opening. Later, you will weave a door to adjust the amount of draft created between the ris-

OOH!

(F.)

ing heat and the door opening and exhaust. The two flakes are no longer needed so they too are discarded The remaining stones are laid nearby, but are basically discarded until needed. (G) You are tired and fall asleep.

The need for food has now gotten your attention on the second morning. From experience a spear used singly without other hunters is of less value than a snare. You go about collecting plant fibers. In order to do so a cutting edge is required. You pick up one of the stones you collected earlier and strike it with a violent

EERRR

(G)

force to release another new ready sharpened flake. (H) You began collecting plant fibers until have enough to make several small snares which will be set on game trails as spring

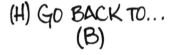

(H) GO BACK TO...
(B)

traps. You use a flake that you discarded earlier to cut several stakes which when driven into the ground with a smooth stone hammer act as triggers. A second stick is inserted between the stake and the springy sapling. (I) A noose is spread on the trail above the ground so that the animal will catch its foot and pull the trigger stick releasing the sapling with the connected noose.

After some thought, you decide you want a weapon to dispatch the animal quickly, because you cannot afford an animal bite. After the traps are set you return to the shelter and knock loose a flake from a finer grained stone. (J) The second flake is struck to cause the energy to travel more into the stone releasing a longer, thinner flake. (K) With the first flake you notch a

(I)

sapling at the base and break it off. Again this is repeated at the narrower end. (L) The shaft is six feet long. Now you take the first flake and cut a channel into the sides of the shaft near the top, cutting from both sides until you have cut a full channel. Into this channel you wedge the flake, rocking it from side to side until it is snug in the channel. With left-over cordage you wrap the channel end of the shaft pulling with your feet and teeth causing the channel to tighten onto the point. (M) The end is then tied off. And the second day comes to a close. You sleep still hungry.

In the morning you awake with a starved feeling in your stomach. You grab your spear and crawl out of the wattle hut and stand and stretch. As you pass a bush you stop and pick some berries you missed seeing the first and second day. You eat just a few to conserve your hunting instincts. On the third snare you have caught a small porcupine. Standing in an opportune spot you thrust the spear tip into the animal to dispatch it. After you

1ST

2ND.

(J)

TIMBER!

(K)

(L)

have pulled the sapling down you untie the noose and carry your prey to the shelter.

You have a choice to butcher the animal right then or build a fire and burn the quills off. On and on choices are made and simple tools are created but are readily discarded. The inability to travel light is a hindrance, yet your bashed tools make all this possible. The rule of thumb: Create and discard.

(M)

FROM THE MIND of
CHAS. SPEAR
© '96

THE BIPOLAR TECHNIQUE:
The Simplest Way To Make Stone Tools
For Survival

By Errett Callahan. Adapted from Callahan 1987

In my opinion, the most practical technique for making stone tools for survival is the simplest way of all—bipolar reduction. Bipolar knapping has been taught to orangutans (Pfeiffer 1972: 333), to Bonobo chimps (Savage-Rumbaugh and Lewin 1994), and even to capuchin monkeys (Okie 1995). The technique is well-known to wild chimps of the Ivory Coast of West Africa (National Geographic Society 1992), though they use their hammerstones for cracking nuts rather than flintknapping. Slip a nodule of flint in where the nut should be and presto you've got a flintknapping chimp.

In 1987, I dubbed bipolar reduction the "nutcracker technology" and predicted that it was mankind's first lithic technology, preceding the Oldowan level by probably several million years. (See Callahan 1987 for detailed discussion. The figures and ideas below derive from this work. Most of the figures and descriptions herein refer to real artifacts from prehistoric sites in Middle Sweden.). That means we were probably Ramapithecines when bipolar flaking first came about (cf Leakey and Lewin 1978). Bipolar percussion is, without exception, the way children attempt to make stone tools when not instructed otherwise. So, for a survival situation, bipolar percussion is what we should be teaching our students, not how to make sophisticated, bifacial "arrowheads."

To do bipolar flaking you simply place the core on a large, hard stone called an "anvil", squeeze the core between the fingers, and strike straight down on top of the core with a hard hammerstone (Fig. 1). Note that, in the figure, there are three variations of bipolar reduction. Usually only the first variation is mentioned.

Bipolar cores (Fig. 2, 3) may be of any size or shape, but if it's much larger than a tennis ball, you can't hold it without bashing your hand as well. (For larger cores, you drop or throw the hammerstone on the core.) The core may be a smooth river pebble, a conical core, an angular chunk, or a thick flake—about any shape will do. It's especially useful for spalling rounded cobbles which you can't get into by any other means. Bipolar works well on any material from obsidian to flint to quartzite. Bipolar cores may be worked to utter exhaustion, until they are too small to squeeze between two fingers (Fig. 4). Nothing could be more economical - - the ultimate recyclable.

For most survival situations, you just need small flakes and cores - - one to two inches in length (Fig. 2, 8). And don't let's forget, the core itself can be one of your most useful tools. Its obtuse edges are excellent for woodworking. Peter White has documented in New Guinea the use of bipolar cores being used to make bows of black palm (cf. White 1968). (They also used adzes to chop down and rough out the staves). I just finished making a mulberry bow using bipolar cores and flake scrapers extensively. (I hafted the flakes into a primitive Baugh-type bow scraper I devised. These tools worked perfectly.)

(more)

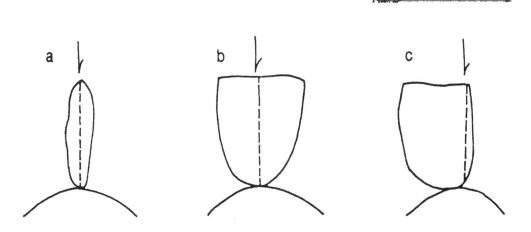

Figure 1. Schematic representation of bipolar percussion: a & b = splitting from center out (a=thin core; b=thick core); c=spalling from outside in.

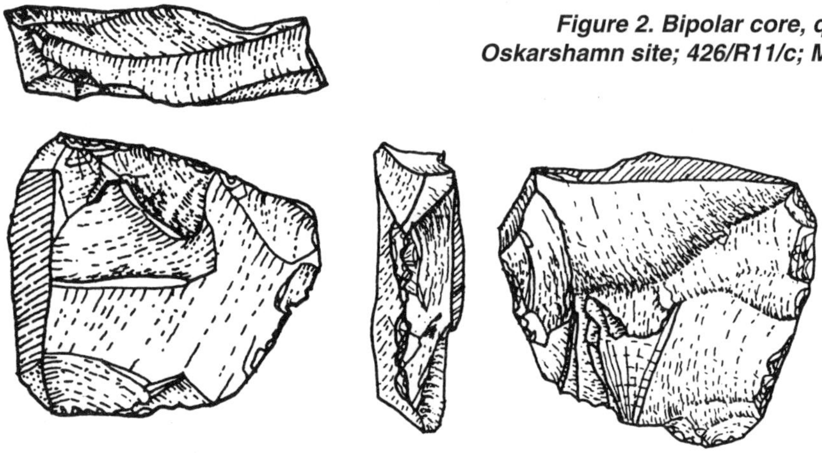

*Figure 2. Bipolar core, quartzite.
Oskarshamn site; 426/R11/c; Mesolithic zone.*

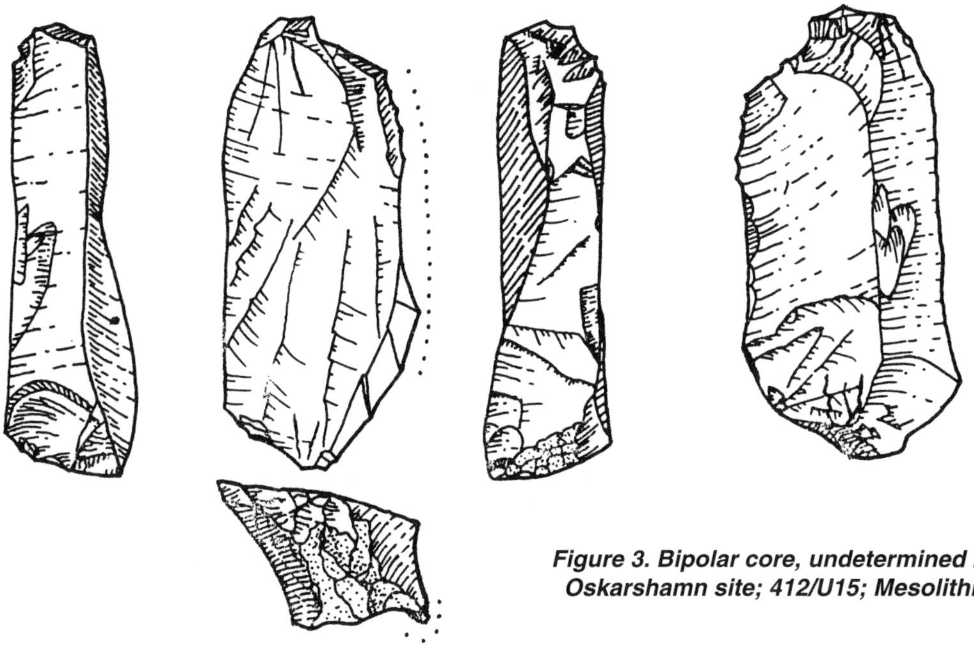

*Figure 3. Bipolar core, undetermined material.
Oskarshamn site; 412/U15; Mesolithic zone.*

Bipolar percussion is often confused with anvil percussion (also a good survival technique). In bipolar percussion you employ rectilinear impact directly downward into the anvil (Fig. 1:Callahan 1987: 20). With anvil percussion, the force is oriented obliquely away from the anvil (ibid) (Fig. 5). The resultant flakes are usually completely different from bipolar flakes.

Bipolar flakes may be of a wide variety of shapes depending upon whether the core is a block, a nodule, a cobble, or a pebble, upon whether the core is worked from the "outside in" or "inside out", or upon whether the flake splits perpendicular, parallel, or at odd angles to the plane of the core face. Flakes removed from the outside of a block-like bipolar core (cf. Fig. 1c) may be indistinguishable from some anvil flakes (cf. Fig. 5) and so cannot be described at this time. Flakes removed

from the "inside out", that is, from the outside of pieces split from the inside of a core (cf. Fig. 1a, b), are unique and may be described. Such flakes, where they do not shatter, are typically thin and flat, in both dimensions, on the ventral surface. They usually exhibit a sharp but crushed platform, this being a function of platform collapse upon impact by a hard hammer (Fig. 8). Crushing may or may not be exhibited on the opposing end. The sharp lateral margins are usually the portion employed for functional use. (Quoted from Callahan 1987: 31, 34.) (See Figs. 6-9.)

In bipolar percussion, the flake may be released from either the top or bottom of the core - - whichever gives the least resistance. It is <u>never</u> released simultaneously from both the

(more)

Figure 4. Bipolar core, quartzite.
Oskarshamn site; 467/J21; Mesolithic zone.
Note extremely small size.

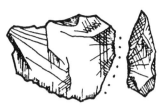

Figure 6. Bipolar flake, quartz.
Oskarshamn site; 425/R10; Mesolithic zone.

top and bottom, as so many writers erroneously state (cf Callahan 1996: 84).

The unique thing about classic bipolar flakes is that they are usually thin, flat, and quite straight. Freehand and anvil flakes are typically more curved. Bipolar splitting occurs because the Hertzian cone is bisected. That's why flat faces develop. Thus there is a notable absence of positive and negative bulbar scars.

Bipolar flaking also frequently yields "triangular splinters". Such flakes (Figs. 10-12) exhibit strong, steep-angled margins, which, like the obtuse edge (Crabtree 1974), can stand considerable pressure during use without damage to the edge (Callahan 1987: 34).

Freehand percussion, mentioned above, is the "usual" way to remove flakes from a core. Though it may seem simple to us, it is far too complex to be taught to primates today (Savage-Rumbaugh and Lewin 1994). It was not until the Oldowan era of some 2-3,000,000 years ago that our ancestors (Homo habilis ?) were first able to control this technique systematically (Oldowan choppers).

This model allowed virtual freedom of movement across the landscape, with any size and kind of lithic material being suitable for use. The evolution of a system dependent upon rather small flakes of predominantly local material and an informal, fluid tool typology may have been a master stroke

of wisdom unappreciated by the makers of large, formal tools (Callahan 1987: 61).

It's a good model to start knapping from in survival situations today.

(more)

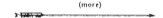

CREDITS: Drawings by Alicja Grenberger, Helena Knutsson, Kjel Knutsson, Marina Matsson, or E. Callahan. Research for the 1987 "Silver Book" was funded by the Swedish Council for Research in the Humanities and Social Sciences, as facilitated by the Archaeological Society of Uppsala, Uppsala University, Sweden. Special thanks to Kjel and Helena.

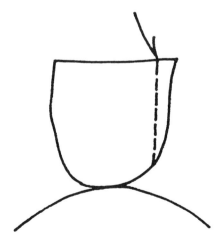

Figure 5. Schematic representation of anvil percussion.

REFERENCES

Callahan, Errett
1987   *An Evolution of the Lithic Technology in Middle Sweden During the Mesolithic and Neolithic.* (The Suilver Book) AUN 8. Societas Archaeologica Upsaliensis, Uppsala, Sweden. ISBN 91-506-0623-9.
1996   A Review of Whittaker 1994. In **BULLETIN OF PRIMITIVE TECHNOLOGY** 11, 82-85. Society of Primitive Technology.

Crabtree, Don
1974   The Obtuse Edge as a Functional Edge. **TEBIWA** 16(1): 46-53.

Leakey, Richard E. and Roger Lewin
1978   **PEOPLE OF THE LAKE: Mankind and Its Beginnings**. Anchor Press/Doubleday, NY. **National Geographic Society**
1992   Secret World of the Chimpanzee. TV special aired Mar. 15.

Okie, Susan
1995   Monkey Think, Monkey Do: Meet a Capuchin that Makes Stone Tools. **Washington Post**, 12 APR 95: H1, H5.

Pfeiffer, John
1972   **The Emergence Of Man**. Harper and Row.

Savage-Rubaugh, Sue and Roger Lewin
1994   Ape at the Brink. **Discover**. Sept.: 91-98,

White, Peter J.
1968   Fabricators, Outils Ecaillés or Scalar Cores? **MANKIND**, 6 (12); 658-666.

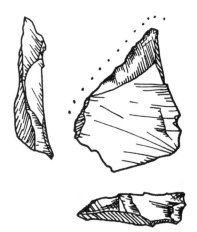

Figure 7. Bipolar flake, quartz.
Oskarshamn site; 398/X12; Mesolithic zone

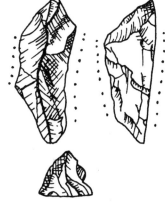

Figure 10. Triangular splinter (bipolar), quartzite.
Oskarshamn site; 458/R51; Neolithic zone.

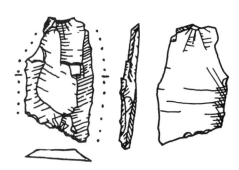

Figure 8. Bipolar flake, quartz.
Oskarshamn site; 20/J31; Mesolithic zone. This is a
classic bipolar flake, but not necessarily a typical one.

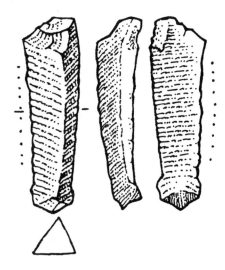

Figure 11. Triangular splinter (bipolar), quartzite.
Oskarshamn site; 224/N49/c; Neolithic zone.

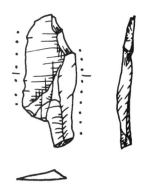

Figure 9. Bipolar flake, quartz.
Oskarshamn site; 108/d17/c; Mesolithic zone.
Another classic bipolar flake.

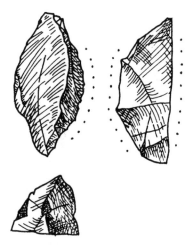

Figure 12. Triangular splinter. (bipolar), quartz.
Oskarshamn site; 442/S15; Mesolithic zone.

Easy to Make "Pebble" Tools

By Paul Hellweg, © 1979, Photos By David Wescott

`Stone tools are frequently desirable and occasionally essential in emergency situations. Their functions are limited only by the scope of the imagination - they help scrape hides, dress game, make fire sets, prepare cordage, and so forth. Unfortunately, stone tool-making is usually discussed as a technical skill similar to that of pressure or percussion flaking. These are highly desirable skills to acquire, and many students justifiably seek to master them. But these techniques maybe of little or no use in an emergency. They are skills which require considerable practice to master; they will generally work only on siliceous minerals which frequently are not available; and they require flaking tools of antler, bone, or hardwood (which may also be unavailable).

I'll grant that a skilled flintknapper can create tools which are not only aesthetically pleasing but also preeminently functional (it is possible, for example, to make obsidian knives with edges sharper than the finest surgical steel), but for the average primitive technologist, the odds are against being able to make serviceable pressure or percussion-flaked tools in an emergency without previous training or experience.

I would thus like to introduce a few techniques of stone tool manufacture that have none of the disadvantages discussed above. The techniques are: the **Oldowan bashee**; **bipolar percussion**; and **discoidal knife**. These methods of stoneworking require no previous practice, need no tools to aid manufacture, and can be done with a wide variety of stone. Most important, they are functional. Using these techniques, a totally unskilled person can make serviceable tools in a matter of minutes.

Oldowan Bashee Technology

Two and a half million years ago, hominids that are considered by some to be man's predecessors, were making pebble choppers in the Olduvai region (Oldoway in German) of East Africa. But for countless millennia before the development of chopper tools, stone tool technology must have been pathetically crude. It probably involved picking up any old rock, heaving it mightily against another rock or boulder, and dimly hoping that this bashing would produce useful pieces. Any archaeologist worth his safari hat would scoff at me, but I cannot resist the urge to name this, earliest possible tool-making culture. Thus, we have the "Oldowan Bashee" technology.

When this is applied to the manufacture of stone tools for survival, the Oldowan Bashee falls in the same category as covering your head when it's cold - the idea is so obvious that

(more)

This article is reprinted by permission of the author and is adapted from "Easy To Make Stone Tools," first published in Woodsmoke Journal #7, (pp. 30-35, 1979) and again in Primitive Outdoor Skills, Richard Jamison, Editor (Horizon Press, 1992). Paul Hellweg is the author of Flintknapping: The Art Of Making Stone Tools. He may be contacted at Star Rt. 190, Lake of the Woods, CA 93225.

If a stream cobble is struck forcefully while resting on an anvil rock, the cobble will shear neatly in half. Ideally, your selected cobble should be about fist-size. Be sure not to mash your fingers in the process.

Wrap a small sapling around the rock you intend to split. This allows you to exert additional force without fear of hitting your fingers. Note the lipped edge on the piece flying out. This edge is sharp enough to do a variety of jobs.

it is frequently overlooked. But now that the bashee has been named and written about, we have no excuse for overlooking this type of tool-making.

Bashee tools are not very imposing, and they are not likely to be displayed to friends. But they are functional, and they can be extremely useful in emergencies. Almost any rock - fist-sized or smaller - will suffice. Ideally, it should be hard (quartzite is perfect) and it should have thin crack-lines visible. You can easily pick out the harder rocks; their surfaces are smoother and less grainy. Also, they will feel comparatively heavy for their size. If the rocks are already cracked, they will shatter much more readily. Be sure to duck your head when you throw, lest you be hit in the face or eye by bashee fragments. If the original rock was hard enough, the resulting pieces, or bashee tools, will have sharp edges. These pieces will cut leather, dress small game, and so forth.

A bi-polar flake being used to cut leather.

Bi-polar Percussion

Bi-polar percussion is a uniquely satisfying technique for working stone. It requires no more skill than does the Oldowan Bashee, but it leaves one with the proud feeling of actually making a tool. The technique is used to split cobble Without any previous practice, the primitive technologist should be able to shear a cobble cleanly in half. The separate halves make superb scrapers and they often provide good cutting edges.

To accomplish the bi-polar technique, select a hard, roundish stream cobble of about fist-size, or slightly larger. Set the cobble upright on an anvil rock, then strike the cobble sharply on its top. The blow must be forceful, and it must be directed straight down upon the cobble. The force generated by the blow travels through the cobble, hits the anvil rock, and then rebounds upon itself. Since the force thus comes from both ends (or poles) of the cobble, the technique is known as bi-polar percussion. If properly executed, the result is a neatly sheared rock.

The skill involved is not in the execution of the technique, but in the selection of the proper cobble. The most common mistake is to select a rock too large to split handily. The cobble must be only about fist-size, and it should be free of cracks. A properly selected cobble will split with surprising ease, and the fracture will be slightly lipped at both ends. The lipped portions will, typically, be sharp enough to cut leather or dress small game (see photographs). These split cobbles are not only functional, they are also

A simple discoidal knife is sharp enough to slice, skin, and scrape.

aesthetic. Unlike bashee tools, cleanly split cobbles are sometimes displayed proudly to friends and fellow primitive technologists.

Discoidal Knives

Discoidal refers to an object that is disk-shaped; that is, roundish and flatish. Discoidal knives are difficult to manufacture, sometimes frustratingly so. However, the technique is

Freehand hard-hammer percussion is much easier to teach once a student understands the process of obtaining a discoidal knife. It simply reverses a process that has already been mastered.

not complicated, and it does not really need to be practiced in advance. As in bi-polar percussion, the key to making discoidal knives lies in the selection of a suitable rock.

To get started, select several small pebbles about two or three inches across. They should be round, flat, hard, and of smooth texture. Unfortunately, the range of stones that will work is much more restricted than is the case for bashee or bi-polar technology - basalt, chalcedony, chert, and flint would be the best choices, if they are available. If a pebble seems promising, the only real test is to give it a try. Hold the pebble securely in one hand and strike its edge sharply against another rock. The intent is to strike small flakes off the pebble's edge. But, in order to do this, it is imperative that the pebble be struck with as much force as can be mustered (keeping fingers carefully out of the way, of course).

Expect quite a few failures at first, but you should even-

tually be striking off flakes which are round, flat, and have sharp edges; i.e., discoidal knives. These knives will be small, averaging about an inch in diameter. But their edges are extremely sharp; these little knives will cut meat, leather, or almost anything you would want a knife to cut.

Admittedly, manufacturing discoidal knives will take some practice, but the practice does not have to be in the form of a previously learned skill. It can be accomplished on the spot, in an emergency situation. Besides, if your selected pebble refuses to yield up a discoidal knife, you can always resort to the Oldowan Bashee technique. This not only sends the offending pebble to its just reward, but also assuages one's damaged ego by clearly establishing who's boss. All that, plus you'll have some bashee tools.

And tools, if you'll remember, are what we were after in the first place.

The anvil method of detaching a discoidal knife is perhaps the easiest way to teach the basic principles of Hertzian Cone, margins, and platforms. By alternating faces or removing additional discs, a simple chopper can be produced.

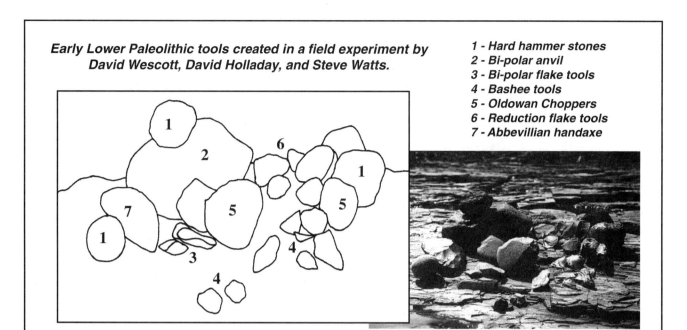

Early Lower Paleolithic tools created in a field experiment by David Wescott, David Holladay, and Steve Watts.

1 - Hard hammer stones
2 - Bi-polar anvil
3 - Bi-polar flake tools
4 - Bashee tools
5 - Oldowan Choppers
6 - Reduction flake tools
7 - Abbevillian handaxe

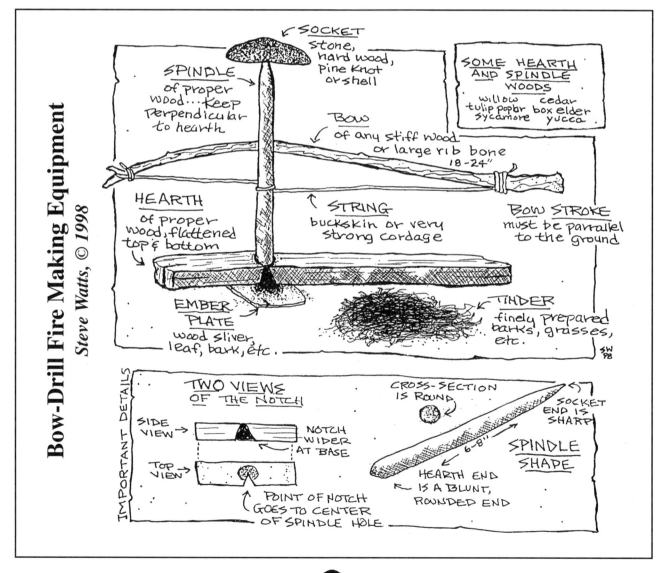

Bow-Drill Fire Making Equipment
Steve Watts, © 1998

SOCKET
stone, hard wood, pine knot or shell

SPINDLE of proper wood... Keep perpendicular to hearth

SOME HEARTH AND SPINDLE WOODS
willow   cedar
tulip poplar   box elder
sycamore   yucca

BOW of any stiff wood or large rib bone 18-24"

HEARTH of proper wood, flattened top & bottom

STRING buckskin or very strong cordage

BOW STROKE must be parrallel to the ground

EMBER PLATE wood sliver, leaf, bark, etc.

TINDER finely prepared barks, grasses, etc.

SW 98

IMPORTANT DETAILS

TWO VIEWS OF THE NOTCH

SIDE VIEW →

NOTCH WIDER AT BASE

TOP VIEW →

POINT OF NOTCH GOES TO CENTER OF SPINDLE HOLE

CROSS-SECTION IS ROUND

SOCKET END IS SHARP

6-8"

SPINDLE SHAPE

HEARTH END IS A BLUNT, ROUNDED END

Simple Comparative Tests Between Oldowan, Abbevillian and Acheulean Technology
taken from <u>Experimental Archaeology Papers #1 (APE #1)</u>, 1972
Errett Callahan, Editor

EXPLANATION OF THE ASSIGNMENTS for Experimental Archaeology, 1972

One assignment concerned the comparative efficiency of Oldowan choppers to Abbevillian or Acheulean handaxes (three random sample papers are excerpted) considering a comparison of:

1. Total time to do a job,
2. Rate (inches, ounces, pounds per minute),
3. Ease of handling.

The choppers and Abbevillian handaxes were fairly good replicas, being sufficiently crude, not surprisingly. Abbevillian and Acheulean handaxes were separated on the basis of fabrication rather than morphology, the former being executed with hammerstone, the later with hammerstone followed by baton. Interesting comparisons came about when the weight of the tools was reversed over the expected ratio. There was considerable variation in the weights of each. The Oldowan choppers varied from 4 to 16 ounces, the usual being near 12 ounces. The Abbevillian handaxes varied from 6 to 12 ounces, the usual also being near 12 ounces. The Acheaulean handaxes varied between 6 ounces and 16 ounces, the usual being near 16 ounces. Lack of sufficient raw material to practice on has been a constant source of frustration.

from **Fixin' A Hole** - comparisons of an Oldowan Chopper and Abbevillian Handaxes - by Donald Ruecroft
Experience - To test the digging capabilities of the Oldowan Chopper and Abbevillian Handaxe, and compare the performance of each.
Insights Gained - Abbevillian Handaxe - felt like a part of the hand; very comfortable; lighter, but sharp tip increased penetration; struck at 20 degree angle to earth; too narrow for hoeing motion; axe turned sideways removed additional dirt; could switch ends to expand utility; too small to chop roots adequately; knapped edges could be used as a saw; good for working in a narrow area; **Oldowan Chopper -** was much heavier, but size and shape restricted penetration; struck at 90 degree angle to earth; removed large amounts of dirt like a hoe; easstriking hard objects; massive butt worked well as a hammer; two handed power for striking.
Conclusion - not enough difference in time to really matter; significant difference in the way the tools were used and performed; handaxe acts as modern spade, chopper acts like a dull hoe; each had its own efficient use.

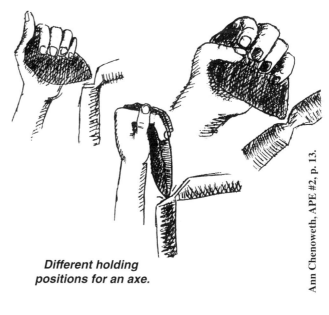

Different holding positions for an axe.

Ann Chenoweth, APE #2, p. 13.

(more)

Tool Used	Tool Size	Hole Size	Time	Inches/min.
Oldowan Chopper	5 3/8" X 5 1/4" 1 3/4" tip 2 1/4" thick 2.5 #	1' 1.5" X 1' 6" X 7" 1701 cubic "	25 min.	68
Abbevillian Handaxe	5" X 2 1/2" 1/4" tip 1" thick 5 1/4 ounces (?)	1' 1.5" X 1'6" X 7"	30 min.	56.7

from **A Comparison of an Oldowan Chopper and an Acheulean Handaxe** by Jay Mangan

Experience - An Oldowan Chopper and Acheulean Handaxe were used to cut down several small softwood trees (3/4" to 1 1/2") for a shelter

Insights Gained - Oldowan Chopper - slightly less than 1#; not very sharp; 3 minutes to make; too small to use comfortably in one hand. **Acheulean Handaxe -** weighed about 1 1/2#; fit well in the hand; increased control; very sharp.

Conclusion - conventional cutting technique (for a modern steel axe) did not work at all; inadequate cuts and mashed thumbs were the result; a cut/slice motion was used with arms around the tree, cutting from the back side towards the body - downward cuts were made completely around the trunk and tree snapped off. Trees over 4" would be prohibitive with this method.

Whole process difficult and time consuming. Took all day to get wood for "temporary" shelter. In efficient use of time; none left for gathering or cooking. Trees used for spears seem to be good assumption.

A chop/slice technique is used in a motion that is toward the body. Chopping trees requires either very durable hands, or a set of heavy leather pads.

---

from **Comparison of the Effectiveness of the Abbevillian and Acheulean Handaxes** by Jeff Raskin

Experience - An Abbevillian and Acheulean Handaxe were used to dig a hole, and chop and saw branches.

Digging	Method	Time	Rate	Efficiency	
Abbevillian	chopping	3 min.	1#/min.	hard to hold	poor control
Acheulean	chopping	2 min.	1.5#/min.	easy to hold	good control

Digging	Method	Time	Rate	Efficiency	
Abbevillian	plowing	1 min.	3#/min.	plowed well	good control
Acheulean	plowing	30 sec.	6#/min.		excellent control

Insights Gained - Abbevillian - shape reduced cutting ability; plowed better than chopped. **Acheulean** - size made it easier to handle; cut the ground with more ease; more effective and efficient tool in both methods.

Cutting	Method	Time	Rate	Efficiency	
Abbevillian	chop/saw	1 min.	1" / 1.25min.	poor handling	poor cutting
Acheulean	chop/saw	1 min.	1" / 1.75min. 12 sec.	good handling	good cutting

Insights Gained - Both cut poorly through green wood due to poor cutting edge. **Abbevillian** - chopped and sawed more quickly due to its mass. **Acheulean** - refined edge, thickness and shape was more effective as a saw.

On an exam question, students were asked to consider and try out all the possible uses they could come up with for a pebble chopper, being imaginative but realistic."
42 of these are presented below.

OLDOWAN CHOPPER

To throw at predators & scavengers (3 by 10 men at hyena = 30 blows)

Communication- reaching for tool means danger (or food , etc.) ahead

Dig trenches & walls for windbreak

Cut grass, etc. for bedding

Remove edible bark or fruit rind

Dig root vegetables

Butcher & skin animals

"Butcher" plants

Smash nuts

Mash roots

Dig insects

Debranching sticks

Smash skulls for brains

Dividing meat portions

Digging in rotten logs

Leveling ground for shelter

Dispatching medium and small game

Chop thru fibrous materials which will not snap

Cut roofing material - sharp grasses, weeds, reeds, brush

Rough work on tools of bone or wood

Make sharp edges (and points) on sticks for jabbing spears

Tenderizing food materials for infants

Soften hides slightly by beating

Clearing living area of brush, etc.

Smash bone for marrow.

Scaling fish

Defense

Open termite mounds

To kill hard (ticks) insects

Pounding holes in hide

To open bee nests

Crack shellfish and turtles

Digging roots for lashing

Cut vines for tying branches for shelter (to 3/4" or 1" only)

Bluffing opponents (increasing stature/status, like showing fangs)

Scraping hides for protection and stiff roofing sheets

from Newsletter of Experimental Archaeology #2, 1973

A Quick Guide To Classic Old World Paleolithic Chopper and Handaxe Forms

By Steve Watts, 1996

The classification of the oldest or Paleolithic cultures is mainly based on the succession of stone industries found in north-west Europe, notably in France, where the early researches were carried out. Now that detailed studies have also been made in other parts of the Old World, it is possible to present a general picture of the evolution of culture in Paleolithic times.

Kenneth P. Oakley, Man The Tool Maker

Oldowan Choppers *(not actual size)*

These choppers (with their associated flakes) are among humankind's oldest tools. Close to 2 million years ago, African *Homo habili* created unifacial (flakes on one side) and bifacial (flakes on both sides) edged cutting/hacking/chopping tools from large pebbles and small cobbles (stones average about 3" around) of lava, quartz and quartzite.

Both bipolar and hard hammer direct percussion techniques were used. Sometimes as few as 3 or 4 flakes were struck to create the cutting edge, with most of the tool's surface remaining unaltered.

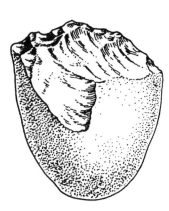

YEARS	PERIOD	GROUP	INDUSTRY
	Neolithic		
10,000			
	Mesolithic		Magdalenian,
12,000			Solutrean,
	Upper		Aurignacian,
40,000	Paleolithic	*Homo sapiens*	Perigordian, and others
	Middle		
125,000	Paleolithic	*Homo sapiens (Neanderthals)*	Mousterian
			Acheulean
2,000,000	Lower Paleolithic	*Homo erectus*	Abbevillian
		Homo habilis	Oldowan
3,000,000		*Australopithecus*	No Tools
4,000,000			

Abbevillian Handaxes

Our early *Homo erectus* ancestors created larger bifacial handaxes (averaging 6-7" long and 4-5 "wide) called "Abbevillian" in Europe and "Early Acheulean" or "Chellan" in Africa. "These tools represent the dawn of the hand-axe culture".

Most often knapped on all edges, from nodules or cobbles—these tools exhibit deep, relatively short flake scars. The resulting cutting edges are sinuous. Cortex bearing surfaces may remain on one or both faces.

Acheulean Handaxes

Acheulean handaxes were the tools of choice for *Homo erectus* and continued to be used to some extent into the Middle Paleolithic.

Prepared platforms and soft hammer percussion techniques become more evident as we examine later Acheulean examples. Made from nodules, cobbles or large spalls—these tools, are typically almond-shaped in plan view, exhibiting straight cutting edges with relatively smooth and symmetrical lenticular cross-sections. Mid-Acheulean axes may retain cortex surfaces on the butt end, while later forms often exhibit fully-flaked margins and faces.

Acheulean handaxes are found throughout the Old World—Africa, Europe and Asia.

For an introduction to classic treatments of handaxe forms see **Tools Of The Old And New Stone Age,** *Jacques Bordaz, 1970,* **The Old Stone Age,** *Francois Bordes, 1968., and* **Man The Tool Maker,** *Kenneth P. Oakley, 1957. For a more recent treatment see* **Making Silent Stones Speak** *Kathy Schick and Nicholas Toth, 1994*

All illustrations are from Bordes, 1968.

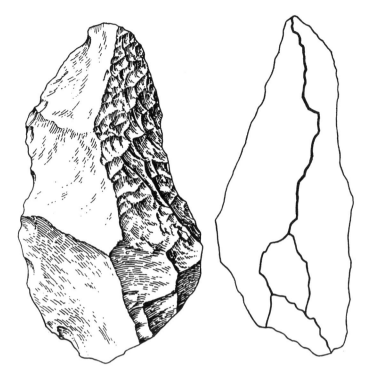

Abbevillian Handaxes
(not actual size)

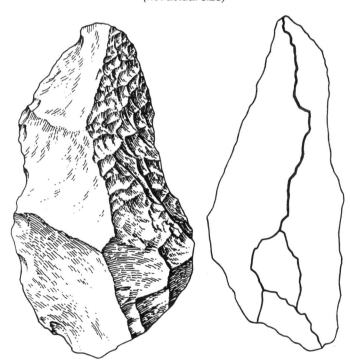

Acheulean Handaxes
(not actual size)

Handaxemanship

Text and Illustrations By Steve Watts,© 1995

*"...the advantage of the hand axe lies
not in its suitability for any one particular
task, but in its usefulness for any number
of tasks... "*
L.H.Keeley,
**Experimental Determinations
of Stone Tool Uses, 1980**

"Old World Handaxes: The Birth of the Biface" was the theme of the sixth annual Knap-In at the Schiele Museum in Gastonia, North Carolina (August 4-6,1995). Using both cast and original Old World African and European handaxes for inspiration, forty-six knappers from seven eastern states (plus a stray Californian) explored their Lower Paleolithic tool heritage. Working mostly in tough North Carolina metarhyolites and Virginia quartzites, participants produced a variety of replica and near-replica Acheulean handaxes.

Adding information to the inspiration, Scott Jones of

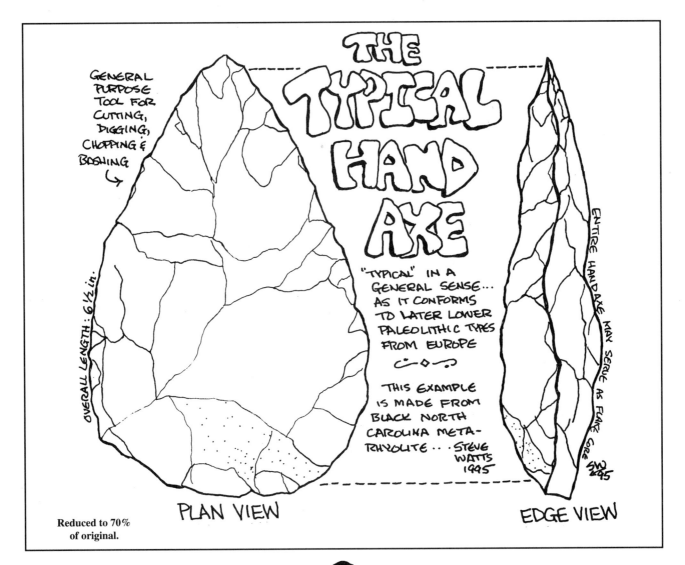

Hofunee Programs and the University of Georgia-Athens presented "The Handaxe-Maker's Tale: Confessions of a Reluctant Handaxe Knapper". Errett Callahan also presented some of the latest information (including a cast) on the magnificent handaxes from the Late Acheulean site of Kalambo Falls, Africa. He also reviewed some of the most up-to-date writing being done on the subject - a soon to be published paper, "Defending Acheulean Technology: An African Perspective" by Stephen Edwards".

Sunday was set aside as an experiential/applied session. Twenty of the handaxes produced during the weekend were used to accomplish a variety of tasks. Though referred to as handaxes (or the more quaint, "fist hatchets"), it has long been suggested that these tools served a variety of functions. In the bush, the handaxe might have been the perfect tool for *Homo erectus*—as is suggested by over 1,000,000 years of use. It was certainly portable enough for a people without pockets, and with the addition of a percusser (found or carried) it could serve as the core for a multitude of flake tools. We tried it out as a knife (skinning and butchering), pick (digging a hole), anvil/hammerstone (bone breaking and brain extraction), axe (manufacturing a digging stick), a ritual object and a weapon (hunting hay bales at twenty yards). Refer to photos on page 40-41.

In all tasks, our replicas performed admirably—being best suited to knife and digging functions. Most of the edge-wear analysis that has been done on prehistoric handaxes suggest soft tissue use—though some are beaten and battered, suggesting digging and chopping functions as well. In fact, though viewed (correctly, I believe) as a multifunctional tool, some handaxes may have evolved toward some specialization—with big thick diggers and smaller thin, knife-like cutters appearing in the archaeological record. Some thoughts on both the general and specialized forms are presented here (see illustrations).

(more)

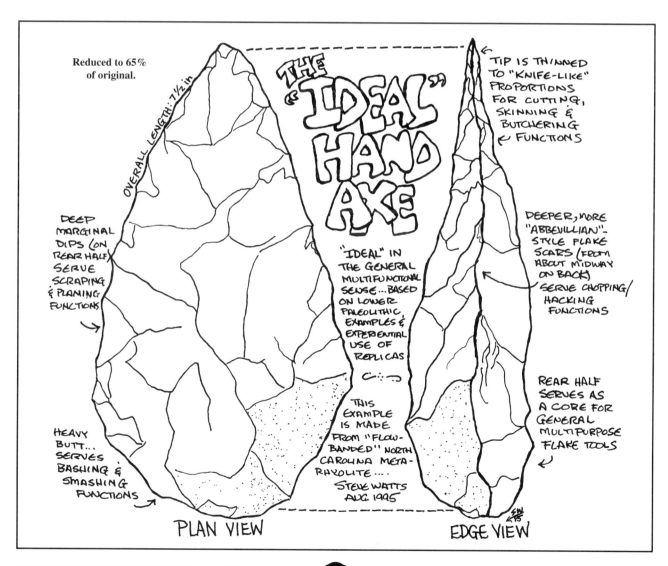

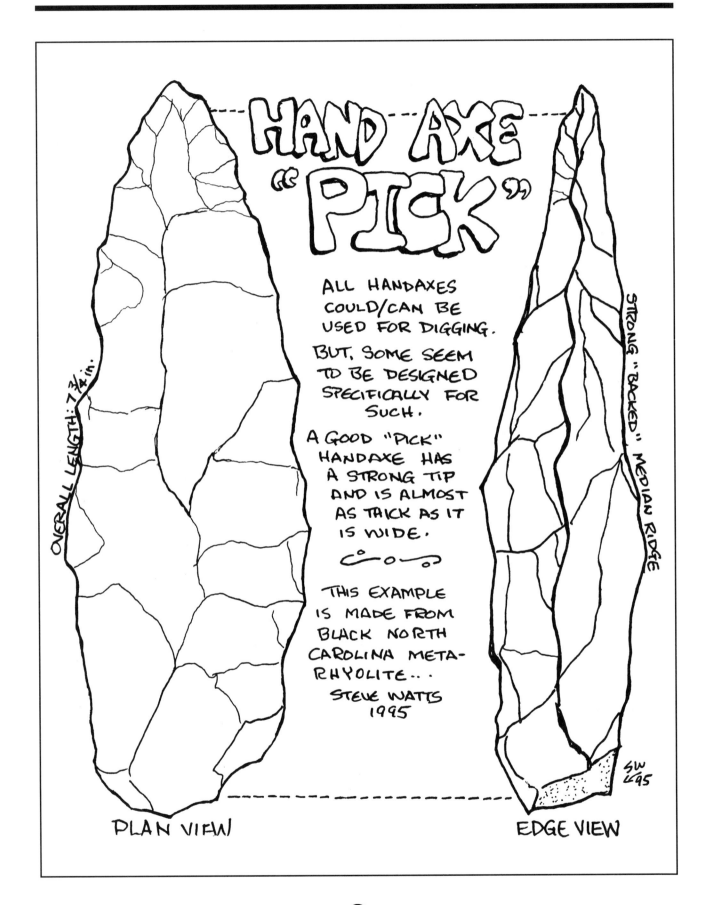

HAND AXE "PICK"

ALL HANDAXES COULD/CAN BE USED FOR DIGGING.

BUT, SOME SEEM TO BE DESIGNED SPECIFICALLY FOR SUCH.

A GOOD "PICK" HANDAXE HAS A STRONG TIP AND IS ALMOST AS THICK AS IT IS WIDE.

THIS EXAMPLE IS MADE FROM BLACK NORTH CAROLINA META-RHYOLITE...

STEVE WATTS
1995

OVERALL LENGTH: 7¾ in.

STRONG "BACKED" MEDIAN RIDGE

PLAN VIEW

EDGE VIEW

SW '95

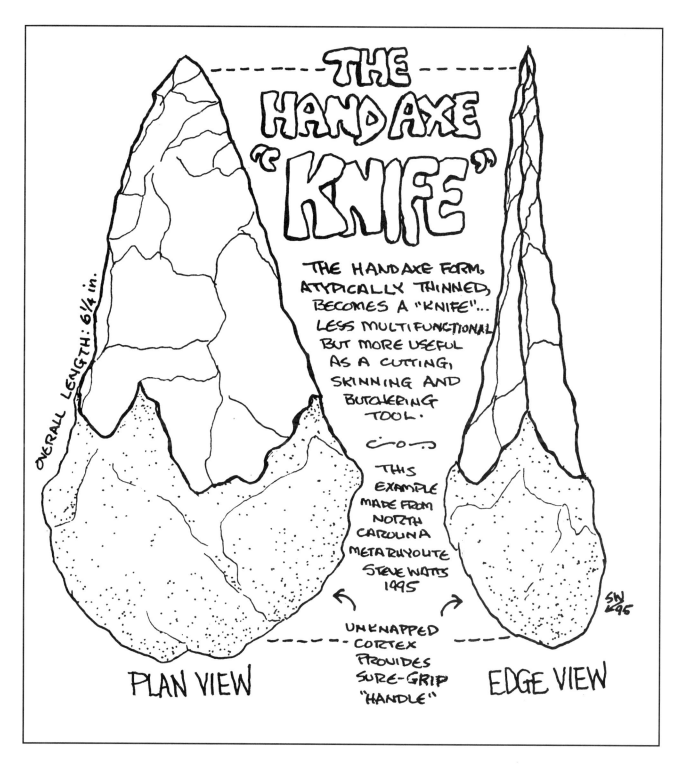

THE HAND AXE "KNIFE"

THE HAND AXE FORM, ATYPICALLY THINNED, BECOMES A "KNIFE"... LESS MULTIFUNCTIONAL BUT MORE USEFUL AS A CUTTING, SKINNING AND BUTCHERING TOOL.

THIS EXAMPLE MADE FROM NORTH CAROLINA METARHYOLITE STEVE WATTS 1995

OVERALL LENGTH: 6¼ in.

PLAN VIEW

UNKNAPPED CORTEX PROVIDES SURE-GRIP "HANDLE"

EDGE VIEW

The technological shift toward these highly stylized, large cutting tools for heavy-duty butchery is, in our view, probably an adaptive response to the dietary shift among early hominid populations in some parts of the Old World toward more habitual and systematic butchery, especially the dismembering of large animal carcasses obtained by scavenging or hunting. Picks, on the other hand, appear to emphasize the pointed tip rather than sharp edges. Such forms make excellent digging tools in hard earth and woodworking tools for shaping and hollowing wood, and also would have been lethal weapons for dispatching game with a handwielded blow to the cranium.

from _Making Silent Stones Speak_, Kathy Shick and Nick Toth

The handaxe as knife: Butchering and skinning.

The handaxe as hammerstone and anvil: Bone breaking and marrow extraction.

Rocky Culbertson working on a large metarhyolite handaxe.

Old World Handaxes

From *the Sixth Annual Knap-In at the Schiele Museum in Gastonia, North Carolina August 4-6,1995*

The handaxe as axe: Manufacturing a digging stick (oak).

The handaxe as pick/shovel: Jack Cresson
heads the hole digging. (Note:
No fingers were lost in the application.)

The handaxe as bashing/prying tool:
Opening the skull and removing the brains.

This photo essay is from the applied session of the Sixth Annual Knap-In at the Schiele Museum in Gastonia, North Carolina (August 4-6,1995). Each year the knap-in follows a central theme so that everyone is investigating a common project with a variety of facets. The theme for '95 was "Old World Handaxes: The Birth of the Biface"

Photos by Tom Hall

Replica handaxes used in the
various applications.

235

HAND-DRILL FIRE MAKING

By Steven Edholm, © 1992, revised 1994

Hand-drill fire making was practiced by variously primitive people world-wide. While it may not be quite as reliable as the bow and drill method, with which more people are familiar, it is still quite effective in the hands of a proficient individual. It is also lighter in weight, easier to construct, and does not require the use of a string or cord as does the bow and drill. However, like the bow and drill, a hand-drill kit will usually provide many fires once a good combination is found. People who relied on this technology undoubtedly prized good kits and under everyday circumstances did not count on being able to construct one on the spot when a fire was needed.

In this method of fire making, a smooth shaft, the drill, is twirled between the palms in a hole which is burned into another piece of wood, the hearth, by the twirling or drilling action. This drilling action, a combination of speed and downward pressure, creates great friction at the interface of the two woods and causes the drill and/or hearth materials to burn and slowly crumble into a charred powder. A notch is provided in the side of the hearth as an exit for this powder. Constantly exuding through the notch, fresh from intimate contact with the source of heat, the powder eventually reaches a peak temperature and ideal conditions for the formation of an ember. The ember is then transferred to tinder which is manipulated and blown into flame.

Materials

The following suggestions on materials are based on research and experience, both mine and others'. You can use them as a guideline, but remember that many of them were discovered through experimentation and that there are many more materials/combinations which await discovery,

Also remember that while a given species, in a certain condition and sometimes in a specific combination with another species, may very often be successful, it will sometimes just not work.

Drills

Drills from weed stalks and yucca are harvested dead. Drills from woody plants, trees, and shrubs are usually harvested "green". Dead drills can be used right away, and if a good one is found and weather conditions are favorable a fire can often be made on the spot,

The best hand-drills from trees and shrubs often seem to be what is called nascent growth. Nascent growth is straight, tall and slender with few or no side branches. It also tends to have a large pith to wood ratio (more on the pith side) which seems to be a valuable quality in a hand-drill. Nascent growth usually results from the plants being burned, pruned or damaged in some way the previous year or two. Road crews frequently whack down entire trees and shrubs which can grow back as a profusion of arrow shafts, hand-drills, and atlatl darts. Look in a fire area a year or two after the fact, or if you know it is the type of plant which will sprout back easily you could cut it down and wait a year or two.

- **Peel green drills while fresh.** They can be tied in a tight bundle and allowed to season. This will do away with some of the job of straightening later. They will, however, dry faster if left singly. I've gotten fires from green drills seasoned two days in hot sun and wouldn't be surprised if one long hot day would do it. You could, of course, bake drills dry over a fire if you've got one.

- **The ideal drill is smooth and straight.** Try to smooth off any major bumps and sharp spots or they'll shred your hands. This is especially important with weed stalks like mullein. Variously zig-zaggy and crooked drills will often work OK as long as the working tip spins in one spot as you drill. Most drills will need some straightening by heat.

- **Sight down the drill to spot major bends and crooks.** Heat one of these (without scorching the wood) until it's thoroughly hot. Bend it straight while still hot, allow it to cool a minute and then repeat on other bends until it's at least fairly straight.

For drills try: maple, elderberry, willow, mock orange, mullein stalks, buckeye, teasel stalks, oceanspray, box elder, seep willow, cattail (dead leaf stalks inside old leaf clumps), currant, sotol, yucca, and anything else that seems like it might work.

-Drill should be 1 1/2" to 2" long and between 1/4" and 1/2" in diameter.

-Thinner drills will cause more blisters while thicker ones feel awkward to use.

-Thicker end at the tip, thinner end at the top.

Hearth 1/2" to 1/4" thick.

Hearths

Hearths can be split out of stumps or logs. I prefer this to branches which often seem too hard. Smaller vines, roots, and branches can be flattened on the bottom to prevent wobbling during drilling.

- Somewhat weathered but not rotten wood such as an old stump, exposed dead roots, or driftwood seems to work well,
- I've heard of using very hard hearths but don't know anyone who uses one regularly. Generally, a fairly soft wood is preferred,
- Hearths should be well seasoned. Reasonable dimensions are given in Figure 1.

For hearths try: boxelder, redwood, incense cedar, clematis, yucca stalks, maple, buckeye, elderberry, cottonwood, saguaro, seep willow, red cedar, roots of cottonwood, fir, pine, maple and others. Experiment and diversify.

Tinder

- Some tinders catch and spread the coal well but won't actually burst into flame easily or at all. Cattail down, the fluff from milkweed seed pods and dogbane fibers fall into this category,
- Other tinders make good bulk material for the outer layers of the nest, flame well, but won't always spread and catch the coal. Certain grasses, as well as lichens, moss, and coarsely shredded bark fall into this category,
- Some tinders accomplish both. Examples of this are dead mugwort leaves rubbed between the palms, soaproot fibers, and finely shredded barks of willow, maple, cottonwood, and sagebrush. Old bird and rodent nests are often ideal as they are. In fact, use them as a model to construct the nest of tinder which will receive your hand-drill coal.

    - make a nest of coarser material.
    - line the inside with somewhat finer stuff.
    - put a small amount of really fine tinder in the
      center to catch and spread the coal.

Have a nest like this ready and a good supply of kindling prepared before you begin drilling. Keep your tinder dry.

FACTORS IN HAND-DRILL FIRE MAKING
-inspiration
-composition of materials
-condition of materials (damp, cold, greasy)
-speed (twirling)
-downward pressure
-efficiency

Composition and condition of materials have been dealt with above.

Speed and downward pressure are self explanatory but trying to do both at once can be difficult for beginners to accomplish efficiently, It is necessary to achieve a smooth transfer of power to the tip of the drill, spinning the drill at a fairly high speed while maintaining a <u>consistent</u> downward pressure. In trying to achieve this transfer much energy is expended; however, expending a minimum amount to reach the desired end, or being able to deliver a massive amount to the appropriate spot when necessary, requires an efficient use of energy. The combination of these details is "technique".

It is often difficult to spot efficiency problems but here are a few hints and some concepts to keep in mind:

- Make a few passes down the drill until your muscles feel barely fatigued. Then take a minute or two to rest. Resting helps to tone the muscles, allowing them to work more efficiently.
- You can expend a lot of energy by holding tension in your body. Try to relax the parts of your body which are not working, and breathe. Don't hold your breath through the whole thing.
- Make sure you are using/moving both hands, not holding one still while moving the other.
- Try using different parts of the hand. I get my best power from the meaty part of the palm just below the pinky finger, but in warming up the set I often use the full palm and fingers which makes for a longer stroke.
- If the drill slips across your hand, lick your palm lightly. The moisture will increase your grip.
- If the board isn't sitting solid and moves while you are drilling, do something to make it stationary. Otherwise another waste of energy is incurred.
- Try to keep the drill fairly straight up and down while you're working. If it's moving from side to side a lot, the consistency of the downward pressure is compromised and energy is wasted. If you tip the drill towards or away from you, it may bind against the side of the hole, causing unnecessary drag.
- When you've drilled halfway through the board, the drill will probably begin to bind in the hole. Open the edges of the hole out with a knife. DO NOT whittle the tip of the drill down or the problem will be compounded.
- If the drill jumps out of the board while you are drilling, it wastes heat and sets you back somewhat. It's also a symptom of drastic inconsistency in downward pressure.

Try this exercise:
- Get into drilling position with your hands at the top of the drill.
- Instead of drilling, just push the drill into the board and hold it there. This force is the downward pressure that you want to maintain while drilling.
- Maintaining that pressure, slowly move your hand back and forth. This action is hand-drilling in slow motion. It may give you a better idea of what needs to be happening.
- Now, speed up!

(more)

Strength _is_ a factor in hand-drilling, but not as much as most people think. Success is mostly in technique. Some very young, old, or handicapped people may have a prohibitive lack of strength and/or coordination, but don't limit yourself, or others, prematurely, There's only one way to find out,

However, don't expect to succeed too easily. Some people don't get fires or coals in our full day classes even with a lot of coaching. Just keep practicing and try tandem drilling with a friend. Two or more people taking turns can often get a fire where one cannot.

If you're one of the naturals and succeed easily, don't think you've got it made, especially if you want to be able to rely on this skill for your survival someday. Practice, diversify in materials, and observe others' techniques.

Before you actually try hand-drilling, remember to give your hands a break. I don't know of anything that will give you blisters faster than hand-drilling except sliding down a rope. Practice a little 2 to 3 times a week until you build up some calluses. It won't take long. Conversely, when calluses become too deep they may have to be shaved down a few layers or they can hurt your hands even worse than blisters.

MAKING FIRE

Seating the drill

The first step is to burn a slight depression in the hearth, thereby determining exactly where the drill will ride, and allowing you to cut the notch accurately. Start by carving a slight depression in the top of the hearth about the same diameter as the drill tip. Make it about 1/8" in from the edge of the hearth.

When drilling, you can sit on your butt and hold the board steady with the out side of one foot or you can kneel on one knee while the other foot holds the board. I prefer the former. Try both.

The business end of the drill, the thicker end, should be flattened off so that it will spin well in the depression you carved. Start drilling, moving your hands from the top to the bottom of the drill. Carefully but quickly shift your hands back to the top of the drill one at a time. The drill should not come off the board while you move your hands or heat will be lost.

If the drill begins to squeak against the hearth, put in a few grains of sand or dust to break up the polish and create friction.

If the drill doesn't burn into the hearth very well, reread the previous tips on technique and just keep practicing.

When the drill has burned into the hearth somewhat and is spinning in one place, it is well seated. You can now cut the notch.

Notching

The notch should be placed about 1/2 way to the center of the seating. The inside of the notch should be smooth and not too wide (see Fig. 1). (For future reference, if the powder piles up around the hole on top of the board while you are drilling, the notch is probably not deep enough.)

Before you begin drilling, place a dry leaf or small chip of bark under the notch to catch the coal.

Making the coal

Now everything is set and you can begin drilling in earnest. It will be necessary to work hard but don't expend yourself too quickly. It's safer to increase your input gradually and save some energy for later than to use it all right away just to get there quicker,

You can't always tell whether or not the powder has ignited. If a copious amount of smoke is coming up from the powder itself, you've usually got a coal. Always make a few more strong passes down the drill to be sure.

If the powder continues to smoke strongly even after you stop drilling, you've got a coal. But don't panic. You have probably worked very hard to get your coal and are most likely shaky from exertion. The next step is to rest awhile. You can blow gently on the coal but let it get established a little before you move your foot. At this stage the coal is spreading through the loose powder, and being jolted could break it apart and snuff it out. We've timed these coals burning for over 3 minutes on their own with no manipulation. I usually allow 15 to 30 seconds for the coal to form a nice cohesive lump.

Creating Flame

Take your foot off the board carefully so as not to damage the coal. If need be, you can gently "pry" the coal out of the notch with a knife tip as you move the board away. Again the object is to not shatter and scatter the coal. Keep it lumpiform. Pick up the piece of bark you put under the notch to catch the coal on and gently dump the ember onto the finest material in the center of your tinder bundle. From here you will be manipulating the bundle constantly as you blow until it bursts into flame.

1-Start immediately by folding the bundle in, snuggling it around the coal slightly, and blowing gently. If you blow too hard at first you could scatter the coal and possibly put it out,

2-The coal should start to spread and burn a cavity in the center of the bundle. Always try to keep that cavity small by folding and pushing the bundle inwards. If you pack it too tightly it will go out from lack of oxygen but if you don't pack it enough it could go out because of lack of fuel,

3-Don't stop blowing for too long, and too long is not very long at all. When you cease to blow things start going out fast.

4-You should only be blowing through a small hole in the front of the tinder bundle. (No gaping open fronts.) Keeping things closed up minimizes heat loss and maximizes the burning nucleus.

5-Hold the bundle up and downwind so that at least most of the smoke doesn't go right in your face.

The idea is to have the bundle burst into flame before your fingertips get burned trying to hold and manipulate your crumbling tinder. If it gets too hot to hold, put it on the ground (preferably in a fire pit) and use two sticks to manipulate and pack it together, blowing extra hard and long.

At this point it would also be advisable to have reasonable fire building skills so that you can expand on your fire once you get a flame and so you don't have to stand in front of a smoking fire of variously misplaced chunks of green, rotten, large, pressure treated, or otherwise unsuitable fuel units. But that's another story. Good luck!

More On Fire By Friction
By Evard H. Gibby

I would like to comment on statements made by Dick Baugh in two articles about friction fire. He indicates that he has wasted countless hours trying to light a fire by friction with willow, and that his experience with it has been a total failure. (**BPT** #5 page 70 and **BPT** #8 page 80)

Least others reading this think that willow is not suitable for fire by friction, I would like to say that in my experience willow is a very fine material for fire by friction. In fact it is my material of choice for bow drill spindles. I have also used it successfully as a hand drill spindle.

In my area (southern Idaho) willow is abundant and it is easy to find a strait piece at the right diameter and length to make a spindle. I have tried several varieties from small willows by streams to large willow trees. They have all worked well for me. I don't recall having tried weeping willow however. (Maybe that's what Dick has been using!) And a willow drill on a willow hearth has not worked for me either. But there are several other combinations that have worked well using materials from my locality.

Listed below are some of those combinations, also listed are combinations of other materials from my local that work good for bow drill fire making.

Drill	Hearth
willow	cottonwood
	cottonwood root (very soft)
	sagebrush
	clematis
	yucca
sagebrush	sagebrush
	cottonwood
rabbit brush	sagebrush
	cottonwood
cottonwood	cottonwood
	sagebrush
yucca	cottonwood
	cottonwood root
	sagebrush
	clematis

Note: Yucca is not native to southern Idaho but is cultivated as an ornamental.

Ready to Use Stone Containers
By Jeff Gottlieb

I have come across a few types of naturally hollowed stone containers. Some are just the perfect size and shape to use for specific jobs such as cooking small amounts of food, mortars for grinding herbs or pigments, places to keep small parts of craft projects or quantities of liquids. They are great for hide glue or pitch because, being stone, they take up heat slowly and evenly, and hold it well.

One type is red ocher. Soft, powdered ocher pigment is often contained in hollow concretions. Once the stone "shell" is cracked, the softer materials inside are worn away by water. I often find these "Indian paint pots" on the shore of the Long Island Sound. They vary from thumbnail size to over a cup in capacity.

My favorite naturally made stone bowl was released from a large piece of hard sandstone/shale. Apparently, in the bottom of some ancient sea, a lump of some material sank and was included in the formation of sedimentary rock. When this material, millions of years later, was uplifted and eroded until it was on the surface again, the lump was included in a 50 lb. stone. Sometime in the last decade, someone set it near a fire (or vice versa) and cracked it. The piece that fell away was a nice cast of this oval lump. It holds about a cup. I looked for the cast that came off the other side of the lump and found it. It was also recognizable, but broken.

One day while looking at rocks in northern New Jersey with my friend and fellow technologist Anthony Follari, we came upon a large, rounded cobble that "looked like something". It had a hairline crack in it, so we smashed it with a larger cobble. Evidently, the rock was formed in concentric layers, because the curved surface broke away, forming a shallow bowl. This material is quite hard. I began pecking it, and it wears away about as fast as greenstone.

I really love these found objects. I like them as much as the things I make, I guess because of the fun of serendipity. I like that feeling of good fortune. They save labor, being ready to use. I can assure myself, when using found objects, that I am really using a tool exactly like those the ancients used, and not a best-guess replica surrounded by conjecture. These tools are free for anyone to find and use, and always have been.

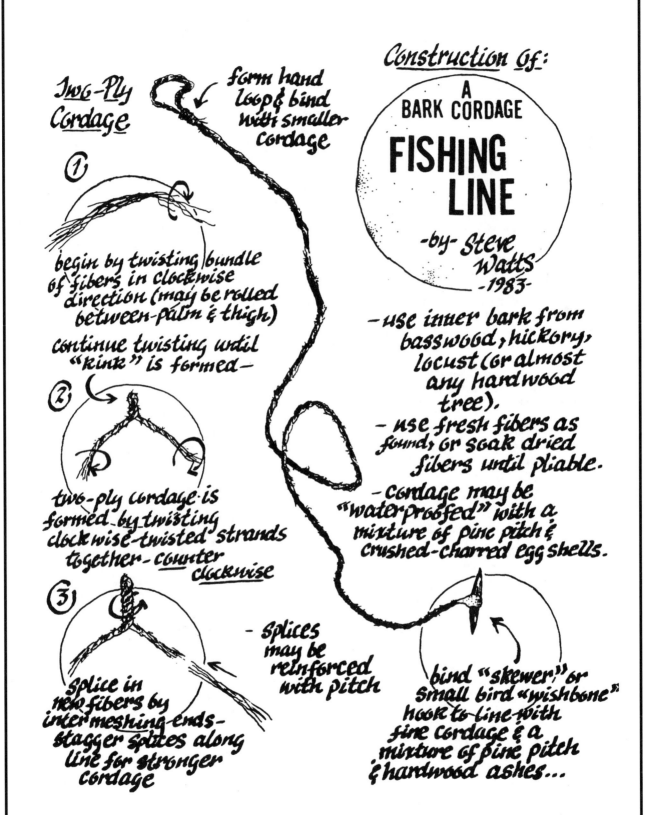

Two-Ply Cordage

form hand loop & bind with smaller cordage

① begin by twisting bundle of fibers in clockwise direction (may be rolled between palm & thigh)

continue twisting until "kink" is formed —

② two-ply cordage is formed by twisting clockwise-twisted strands together – counter clockwise

③ Splice in new fibers by intermeshing ends – stagger splices along line for stronger cordage

– splices may be reinforced with pitch

Construction Of: A BARK CORDAGE FISHING LINE

-by- Steve Watts -1983-

– use inner bark from basswood, hickory, locust (or almost any hardwood tree).

– use fresh fibers as found, or soak dried fibers until pliable.

– cordage may be "waterproofed" with a mixture of pine pitch & crushed-charred egg shells.

bind "skewer" or small bird "wishbone" hook to line with fine cordage & a mixture of pine pitch & hardwood ashes...

By Steve Watts, © 1983

MAKING CORDAGE BY HAND

Text and Illustrations By Norm Kidder

Cordage (rope and string) can be made from many different fibers including (Bast) Dogbane, Milkweed, Nettles, Hemp, Flax; (Leaves) Cattail, Yucca, Agave, Douglas Iris; (Bark) Willow, Maple, Basswood, Cedar; (Root) Leather Root, Beach Lupine; (Whole stem) Tule, straw, Juncus. Each material has specific requirements for extracting and preparing the fibers, but there are only two basic ways for using the fibers to make a cord: braiding (or plaiting) and twining. Braiding was usually done with flat, split materials such as cattail or flattened straw. The instructions in this article will deal only with twining, specifically with two ply (S-twist, Z-ply, also called right handed) cordage.

After preparing a bundle of fiber half the thickness of the finished cord, place your hands six to twelve inches apart and about one third of the way from one end. Twisting the fibers clockwise with both hands, wind the bundle tight (making single-ply cordage).

Figure 1a & b - Keep twisting until a kink forms.

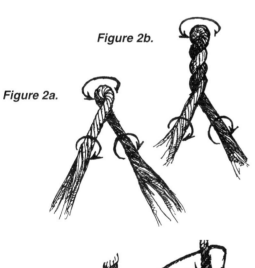

Figure 2b.

Figure 2a.

Figure 3a.

Figure 3b.

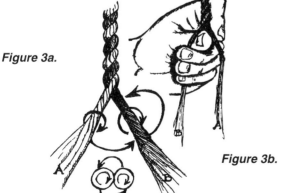

Bring your hands closer together and keep twisting. The kink should rotate on its own in a counter-clockwise direction (Fig. 1a & b). Twist until two or three rotations occur (Fig. 2a & b). This is the start of a two-ply cord. At this time you can attach the end to something (or someone) which can rotate (free-end) and keep twisting with both hands turning clockwise OR you can attach the end to something solid (fixed-end) and begin twisting and counter-rotating (see below).

Counter-rotating, one form of finger-twisting, involves each hand applying a clockwise (S) twist into a ply, while passing the right ply over, and the left ply under (counter-clockwise or Z-plying). In Figure 3a, your left hand twists ply A clockwise, while your right hand does the same with ply B'. At the same time, you pass ply B over and behind your left thumb and lock it in place with your remaining fingers, as in Figure 3b. You then take A in your right hand and B in your left and repeat, over and over and over again! These two methods are particularly handy with larger and coarser materials such as cattail and tule ropes.

Finger-twisting finer material is usually done completely in the hand, with the finished string being wound on a bobbin or netting needle as you go. Your left hand acts to control tension while your right hand does the twisting. Begin as in Figure 1, then place the Y (the point where the two plys come together) between your left thumb and fore finger. Take the lower of the

(more)

from CORDAGE
by Steven Edholm & Tamara Wilder, ©1995
MATERIALS & PREPARATION

The following is a partial listing of natural materials which yield good fiber for making cordage. It is far from complete and other cordage materials may await rediscovery.

Information given on when to harvest plants is intended only as a guideline. Species, climate, environment, genetics and intended use may all effect when plants can or should be harvested.

Fibers may be cleaned and separated by many methods. Here are some which will be mentioned later or which you may want to try:

RUBBING BETWEEN THE PALMS - This is efficiently accomplished by holding one end of the fiber in the teeth as the hands move down the length of the fiber. This allows one to keep the fibers taut and prevents them becoming tangled, Alternatively the fiber may be rolled back and forth on the thigh with one hand while being pulled taut with the other.

SCRAPING - Aside from the pre-scraping of dogbane, which may be applicable to other species, this refers to scraping with a duller tool after the fiber is removed from the stalk. We usually use our thumbnails but semi-sharp bone, shell or metal tools can also be used. If you do use the thumbnail beware of getting splinters of material under your nails. Scraping removes non-fiber chaff and makes the fibers more flexible and workable.

HACKLING - This consists of using a pointed spike-like tool to comb, clean and separate the fibers. We haven't used it much but plan to try it more in the future. Ethnographies from California mention running a bone awl repeatedly through a bundle of fiber.

POUNDING & WASHING - Pulpy things like yucca and agave can be pounded and washed to good advantage. Select younger leaves as they clean much easier. Some tree barks and fiber yielding roots can also be pounded and washed, Use a smooth peeled branch to pound with and a smoothed peeled log as an anvil.

POUNDING DRY - Twist the hank of fiber into a loose rope twist and pound it lightly with a smooth mallet on a smooth surface, We've had this work well on milkweed and nettle.

RETTING - This is the rotting of the fiber-yielding plant to weaken all materials except the fiber itself. This allows for easy cleaning by washing or other methods. The plants are usually soaked in plain water. If the retting is carried on too far the fiber begins to weaken and eventually becomes worthless. Plants will ret faster in warm weather. After five days check progress every couple of days. Retting plant fibers can smell absolutely putrid so don't do this in your house. After retting use the above methods to clean your fiber.

(more)

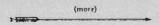

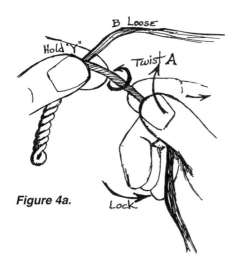

Figure 4a.

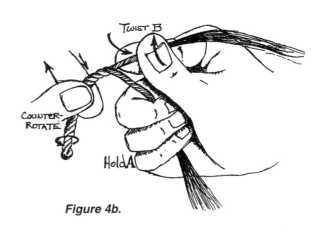

Figure 4b.

Dogbane, Indian Hemp - *Apocynum cannabinum*

An excellent native perennial fiber plant, Widespread throughout U.S. but uncommon. Prefers wet areas.

Harvest dry stalks autumn/early winter after plant dies back completely. There are usually several years worth of old stalks in a dogbane patch. Try to collect the previous season's growth. They are usually the reddest. In arid areas, stalks from even several years ago may be found to have sound fiber. Crack or snip the small stems and thin tips from each stalk. Store in a dry place. The outer layer of each stem is a thin bark. It has no tensile strength and should be removed. Given a set diameter, cordage made from well cleaned fiber will, theoretically, be stronger than that made from fiber which contains non-fiber materials. We prefer to remove most of the outer bark by gently scraping with a sharp knife or stone flake at a ninety degree angle. Only the very outer layer should be removed. If fibers are seen under the knife you have scraped far enough or maybe even too far. Be especially careful around the leaf and stem nodes, Scrape less rather than more until you learn some boundaries. Most of what's left can be removed later by rubbing or scraping with the thumbnail.

Crack the stem into 4 equal parts by squeezing it up and down its length. Crack the woody part into many small pieces and remove carefully leaving as much fiber in tact as possible. There is a much more specific way to remove the woody portion which retains the maximum amount of fibers but it is too complex for inclusion in this article. If possible ask someone who uses dogbane how they remove the fiber from the stalks. Rub between hands and scrape with fingernails to clean further.

Milkweeds - *Asclepias species*

Excellent white fiber,

Harvest late summer through winter. Remove fiber from stalks as with dogbane. Clean by rubbing between hands scraping, and dry pounding.

Nettles - *Urtica species*

Some species are very good, others are nearly worthless. It tends to rot quickly. Used in wartime as a linen (flax) substitute.

Harvest at peak height or dead but not rotten. If harvested green, it may need to be retted. Remove fiber from stalks as with dogbane. Clean by rubbing, scraping, and dry pounding.

Yucca - Yucca species, esp. *mohavensis* (best); *bacatta*

Widely used in desert areas for nets, ropes, sandals, and fiber skirts.

Harvest green. Pound and wash or ret and wash.

Sinew - (preferably from large animals)

Achilles tendons from deer, elk, moose etc... and also sinew which overlays the sirloin muscle on either side of the backbone.

Very strong but gets slimy when wet. Sinew is an excellent material for bowstrings. Also glued to backs of bows for strength and power. Fine threads moistened in mouth and used for attaching arrowheads and feathers to arrowshafts. Dry and shred. Leg tendons may be easier to shred if pounded lightly first.

Other materials are: agave (sisal), coconut fibers, *Iris macrosiphon/tenax*, basswood bark, fireweed, New Zealand flax, flax, hemp (*Cannibus sativa*), mulberry bark, willow bark, primrose, sagebrush, ribbonwood, mountain mahogany, cottonwood, *Fremontia californica,* mesquite bark, western red cedar, redwood, beach lupine root, elm bark, leatherroot, cattail, tule, maple bark, and many more. Experiment.

two ply strands and twist it tightly clockwise until it begins to kink. Lock the twist in by closing your remaining three fingers over the strand (see Fig. 4a.). Then, while holding the twisted ply A securely, twist ply B with your right thumb and forefinger. As you twist, you should feel the completed string begin to twist counter-clockwise (step Fig. 4b.). Follow this motion with your left thumb and forefinger while maintaining even tension and a symmetrical Y . Next move your left thumb up to the fork in the Y as before and repeat steps 1 and 2 until you need to add more fiber.

(more)

Splicing

If you began your cord off-center, then one side will run out of fiber first. As you get to within about 3 inches of the end of this short ply, prepare another bundle of fibers the same size as you began with, but taper the end of the bundle for about 4 inches. Lay this bundle parallel to the bundle being replaced, and sticking out about an inch beyond the Y (Fig. 5). Continue twisting as before. You should also add in if one ply becomes thinner than the other, or if both plies become thinner than they started. In these cases add just enough fiber to bring them back to correct size. Ideally, your cord should stay the same size throughout, although aboriginal cordage did vary about fifty percent in nets. Bow strings and fish lines under heavy pull should be very even. It is also possible to add to both sides at the same time by bending a bundle of fiber in half and placing the Y of the bundle into the V of the Y, but it is harder to keep from making a lump at this point. After your string is finished, you can cut or burn (carefully) off the overlap ends to make your string less fuzzy.

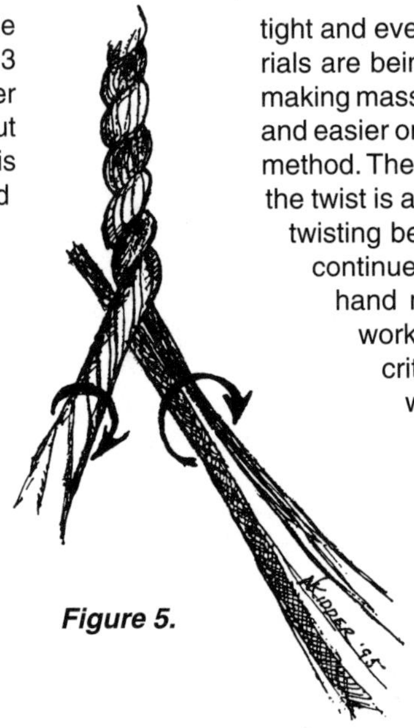

NOTE: dry surfaces tend to slip, so you should keep your hands and the fiber damp while you are working. Squeeze out excess water though or your string will be loose when it dries.

Finger-twisting methods are best used when a relatively small amount of string is being made and/or has to be very

Figure 5.

tight and even, and when very stiff or coarse materials are being used, such as cattail or tule. When making mass quantities of cordage, it is much faster and easier on the hands to use the leg (thigh) rolling method. The principle is the same, S-twist, Z-ply, but the twist is applied by rolling on the leg, rather than twisting between the thumb and finger. You can continue to work without getting cramps in your hand muscles, and you can (with practice) work faster (about ten feet per hour). The critical element in making this method work is having the right surface on which to roll. Traditionally the bare left thigh is used. If you do not want to expose your skin, or if your legs are hairy, you can use pants, but these should be tight around your leg, so they won't bunch up as you roll, and they should have a rough enough surface to give traction. Keeping them damp is also critical. I keep a bucket of water next to me while I work. This method is illustrated in Figure 6a-c.).

Before you begin, prepare as much fiber as you will be using during that session. Once you get into the rhythm of the work, you won't want to stop and clean material.

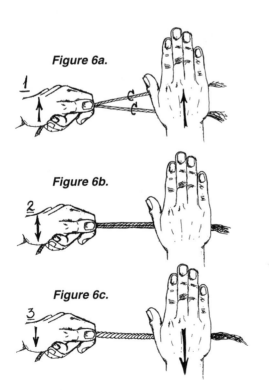

Figure 6a.

1

Figure 6b.

2

Figure 6c.

3

Roll both plies away from you with the palm of your right hand (pre-roll each separately). Your left hand holds the Y and follows the movement.

Bring the two plies together by moving the left hand forward and back. If the two plies did not get tightly rolled the first time, carefully pick up both plies and repeat step one first.

When the plies are tight and touching, bring the right palm back towards you, counter-rotating the two plies into two-ply cordage.

Before repeating step one, it necessary to untangle the loose ends of fiber, separate into two plies, and move the left hand up to the new Y.

GOOD LUCK!

SOME SHELTER CONCEPTS

By Mors Kochanski

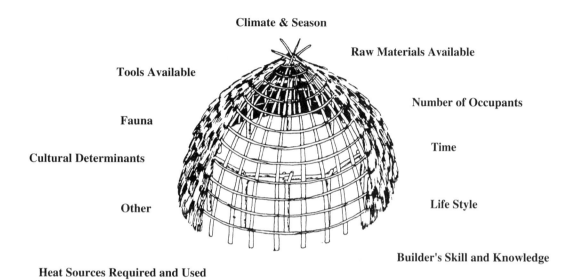

Climate & Season

Raw Materials Available

Tools Available

Number of Occupants

Fauna

Time

Cultural Determinants

Life Style

Other

Builder's Skill and Knowledge

Heat Sources Required and Used

Psychological & Social Factors

FIG 1. SOME SHELTER DETERMINANTS

There are many different types of natural shelters available for survival. The following diagram shows the different factors that might have a bearing on how shelter is selected. Some of the determinants might be a little far-fetched but have been included to round out the picture from an ethnographic point of view.

The determinants shown are not necessarily in their proper order of importance.

1. **Climate & Season**
2. **Raw Materials Available**
3. **Tools Available**
4. **Number of Occupants**
5. **Heat Sources Required and Used**
6. **Builder's Skill and Knowledge**
7. **Time**
8. **Psychological & Social Factors**
9. **Fauna**
10. **Life Style**
11 **Cultural Determinants**
12. **Other**

Determinants chosen concern a shelter built with natural raw materials and with tools normally used in the bush. The following are not included in this scheme:
a) animal shelter products such as hides, hair, or wool, felt, etc.
b) woven fabrics such as cloth, nylon, etc.
c) Technological materials such as polyethylene film, reflective mylar, etc.

(more)

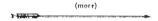

Mors Kochanski is the author of __Northern Bushcraft__ and __Bush Arts__ and is a master of the skills used to live in the Boreal North. His research into the basics of technology related to outdoor living, has provided a number of important insights. Mors is currently working on a sequel to __Northern Bushcraft__ and a new survival training manual. He can be contacted at RR 1, Peers, Alb, Canada, T0E 1W0, (780) 693-2428.

1. Climate & Season: The shelter may have to protect the user from one or more of the following: cold, snow, wet, rain, sand, and sun.
Seasonal availability of materials.

2. Raw Materials Available: Log- in the form of rounds, half-round, and split into boards; poles, boughs, snow, grass, leaves, bark, earth, clay, sod, dried mud, flexible wands, moss, etc. Consideration must be given to the degree of disturbance to the natural environment.

3. Tools Available: Axe/celt, knife, flakes/blades, shovel, wedge, awls, snowshoes, skis, etc. Tools play a very important role in the amount of energy expended, the speed with which a shelter is built, and the quality of the finished product.

4. Number of Occupants To Be Accommodated: Usually the more people that can fit into a shelter, the less effort each individual has to contribute to the construction of the shelter. Eventually, the raw materials used limit the size of the shelter. To accommodate an even larger number under one roof may require a change in shelter form.

5. Heat Sources Required and Used: The most common heat source is (a) fire and its concomitant demands: open fire, stove, fire places, types of fuel, utilization of radiant energy, warmed air, smoke problems, carbon monoxide, stored heat, etc. (b) animal and body heat- critical volume of living/storage space, low ceiling, efficient seal of roof, sleeping bench, etc. (c) the earth as a heat source or sink, depth of shelter in the ground. Availability and locality of fuel sources.

6. Builder's Skill and Knowledge: With little practice or experience one may have to use simpler shelters and be confined to a smaller selection of types.

7. Time: Some shelters have the virtue of being easily and quickly put up in extreme weather conditions. Time Factors: affordable time to build, duration of occupancy, desired degree of performance.

8. Psychological & Social Factors: Some people may build a shelter mostly for the psychological security it provides against a real or imagined danger. In some cases, shelters are built to take into account unexpected visitors, or entertaining friends.

9. Fauna: Effective protection against such animals as bears, mice, and insects.

10. Life Style: Temporary survival, sedentary, semi-nomadic, nomadic, permanent, etc.

11. Cultural Determinants: Anthropological, geographical and religious determinants, customs and habit.

12. Other: The most important (technological) item for quick, efficient and effective shelter building is a fabric in sufficient quantity, cut to the proper shape, with suitable properties. The fabric should be:

    a. waterproof
    b. windproof
    c. portable
    d. light
    e. durable
    f. insulative
    g. highly reflective on the inside
    h. highly visable on the outside

Excerpted and reprinted by permission of the author from Wilderness Arts and Recreation Vol. 2, No. 4.

Framing a wickiup with dead pine poles, the construction of a wickiup for a Jim Riggs Aboriginal Life Skills course, begins with a simple tripod and progresses with the addition of more poles.

The open front of the wickiup allows for a long trench fire to be built in front. The finished wickiup, thickly covered with slabs of dead pine bark, is "moved into" immediately. People are roasting fish on sticks and mixing ashcakes.

Though intended to be a short-term seasonal shelter, the wickiups below have stood at an elevation of 8500', through snow and summer storms, for over 15 years and are still very serviceable. The floor covering is removed after each BOSS course and added to the covering.

Latter-day wickiups found in national forest in Utah

BOULDER,UTAH - Someone in this area is borrowing a page from the book of Indian life by building wickiups, primitive shelters used by Western Indians before the coming of the whiteman.

At least three wickiups-aspen pole structures covered by bark and pine needles-were found recently in an open meadow of the Boulder Mountain in Dixie National Forest. Deer hunters who discovered the abandon wickiups said each had a stone-lined fire pit inside that had carefully been cleaned of old ashes.

An opening in the apex of the lodges allowed the smoke to leave. The earth floor was covered with a layer of soft leaves for sleeping. Eight to 12 people could sleep inside each wickiup. Faint paths led from one lodge to the other and the largest had a square made of fallen logs with an outdoor campfire site in the middle.

There was no litter about to indicate who the builders were.Wickiups, which resemble teepees, were used by Indians in Utah and Arizona because of the abundance of wood and because they had few buffalo robes to make skin lodges like those built by the Plains Indians.

ARIZONA REPUBLIC NEWSPAPER December 12, 1986

For The Future.

ABOUT OUR LOGO: *Our logo was designed by David Callahan, using his and Jack Cresson's sketches, with suggestions from the board. The skull of our common ancestor, Neanderthal, becomes a cavern into which we peer to see a campfire swirling about, symbolizing the spirit of our movement. The ancient technologies, long forgotten, await our rediscovery, to unite us all.*

ABOUT OUR AUTHORS: *The Bulletin is produced by the Society of Primitive Technology. The opinions expressed herein are those solely of the authors. Authors have dedicated their talents and skill to create each issue of the Bulletin of Primitive Technology. Although the SPT is allowed to use contributions in a variety of formats, authors maintain ownership and copyrights of their own works.*

JOIN THE SPT: HERE'S HOW

We need you to make this effort come to life. Membership in the society costs $25 ($35 US for Canada and $40 US for international members). Subscriptions include the **Bulletin of Primitive Technology** which comes out twice a year (May 1 & November 1). Each issue conyains a main theme, newsworthy notes, timely articles, society business, and the *Bulletin Board*. Membership shows that you support one of the most unique movements in the field. Make checks payable in U.S. funds to the **Society of Primitive Technology (SPT)**. New members please complete the membership information on the application form. Current members are sent a subscription renewal card automatically with your last issue. Renew your membership immediately! Remember, a subscription year is two issues of the Bulletin.

The **Society of Primitive Technology** networks with others working towards the preservation of our prehistoric and world culture. **This is your organization. If you are interested in what the Bulletin and Society stand for, don't just sit back, get active!**

Letters, articles, questions, announcements, news, etc, should be sent "Attention Editor". Memberships should be sent to the SPT Subscription Secretary at the Idaho office. Current members, please forward address change information immediately. Specific questions or articles will be directed to the editorial board members. We look forward to your active membership.

The Bulletin is a vehicle to support networking, problem solving and education in the primitive/ prehistoric arts and technologies. Do you have a specialty that you want help perfecting, a discovery you want to share, or a question you wish to explore? Get those communications flying and join us.

Society of Primitive Technology
P.O. Box 905, Rexburg, ID 83440
or call/FAX (208) 359-2400

All membership fees must be paid in U.S. funds and/or have a U.S. Banking Institution backing. All countries outside of the U.S. and Canada must register at the International rate.

The SPT Membership Directory is published annually. If you wish your name to remain off this list, please indicate. _____

Please print clearly

NAME _____
ADDRESS _____
CITY_____ STATE _____ ZIP_____
COUNTRY_____ PHONE_____
MAIN INTEREST AREA _____

FREE NOTICE IN BULLETIN BOARD (20 words or less)   1 ISSUE PER YEAR.
PLEASE INDICATE ISSUE NOTICE WILL APPEAR: SPRING _____ FALL _____

_____
_____
_____
_____
_____

$25 per year - U.S
$35 per year - Canada
$40 per year - International

Mail application and membership fee to : S.P.T., P.O. Box 905, Rexburg, ID 83440
or phone/FAX and apply via Mastercard or VISA - (208) 359-2400.